MAKING SENSE OF HUMAN BIOLOGY

Jackie Hardie

Head of Science, Clapton School, London

Chris Avery

Head of Mathematics and Science Faculty, Sir Frank Markham School, Milton Keynes

Graham Wells

Head of Science, Kingswood School, Corby

This book is in the series *Making Sense of Science*

Longman Group UK Limited,
*Longman House, Burnt Mill, Harlow,
Essex CM20 2JE, England
and Associated Companies throughout the world.*

© Addison-Wesley Publishers Limited, 1981

© Longman Group Limited 1985

All rights reserved. No part of this publication may be reproduced, stored in a retrieval system, or transmitted in any form or by any means, electronic, mechanical, photocopying, recording, or otherwise without either the prior written permission of the Publishers or a licence permitting restricted copying issued by the Copyright Licensing Agency Ltd, 33-34 Alfred Place, London, WC1E 7DP

ISBN 0 582 00528 0

First published by Addision-Wesley Publishers Limited 1981
First published by Longman Group UK Limited 1985
Sixth impression 1989

Phototypesetting by Parkway Group,
London and Abingdon
Colour separation by Positive Colour Limited,
Maldon, Essex
Produced by Longman Group (FE) Ltd
Printed in Hong Kong

Preface

We have tried to produce a Human Biology book that you will want to look at and enjoy reading.

The book is written so that each new idea is explained on a single page or on two facing pages. The explanations are straightforward and the number of technical words used has been kept low. Whenever a technical word is used for the first time, it is shown in **bold**. We hope you will read through the book from the beginning, so the ideas move on from one to another through the book. Page references are given to help you check back. A collection of ideas related to a topic is grouped as a section. At the end of each is a **summary** of the main facts covered by that section.

Diagrams, charts, graphs and photographs illustrate the book. They are in colour and black and white. The illustrations are placed so that they are next to the written explanation. You do not have to search around the page or book for the diagram that goes with the text.

There is a collection of questions at the end of the book. The questions are arranged in section order and include word tests and questions of the type used in examinations at 16+. Revision hints are also given.

The book will provide a good foundation for all work done in Human Biology examination courses at 16+. We hope that when you have read the book, you will understand how your body is built, how it works and how to keep it healthy. You should get some idea of the part everyone plays in the life of the community and the future of the world. We hope you enjoy your studies.

Jackie Hardie

Chris Avery

Graham Wells

Contents

Preface	ii
1 The human body	1
Living things	1
How the body is built	2
Cells	4
Tissues and organs	6
2 Nutrition	8
Food	8
Nutrients in food	9
Balanced diet	14
3 Food and the future	16
Green plants	16
Food chains	18
Plant and animal farming	19
Farming and food supply	20
Improving food production	21
Solving the food problem	22
4 Energy release	24
Breathing	24
Breathing – How is it done?	26
Using oxygen and food	28
Getting enough energy	30
5 Digestion	32
Food must dissolve	32
Teeth	33
Enzymes	36
The gut at work	38
Absorption	41
Where the food goes	42
6 Transport in the body	44
Blood	44
The heart	46
The heart at work	48
Blood vessels	50
Transport systems	52
Diseases of the transport system	54
7 Keeping the steady state	56
The liver	56
Keeping warm	58
The skin	60
Adapting to cold surroundings	62
Cells and water	64
Water balance	66
How kidneys work	68
Kidney machines	70
8 Coordination	72
Reacting to changes	72
Nervous system	74
The brain	76
Learning	78
Eyes	80
Eye faults	82
Ears	84
Ear damage	86
Other senses	87
Glands	89
Hormones at work	90
Sex hormones	92
9 Reproduction	94
Making gametes	94
Conceiving	96
Growth of the baby	98
Birth	100
Post-natal care	101
Multiple births	102
Population change	103
Contraception	104
10 Inheritance	106
Variation	106
Cell division	108
The work of Mendel	110
Inheritance in families	112
Male and female	114
Faulty inheritance	116
11 Support and movement	118
The skeleton	118
Skull and backbone	120
Growth of bones	121
Bones and joints	122
Muscles	124
Muscles bones and levers	126
Broken bones	128
Exercise and fitness	130
Lifting and posture	132
Sleep	133
Growing up and growing old	134

12 Disease and its causes — 136
Disease — 136
The cause of disease — 138
Viruses — 140
Bacteria — 142
Protozoa — 144
Fungi — 145
Worms — 146
Sexually transmitted diseases — 148
Vectors of disease — 150

13 Using and fighting microbes — 152
Controlling microbes — 154
Keeping clean — 156
Protecting the body — 158
Blood and immunity — 160
Blood transfusions — 163

14 Clean food and water — 166
Kitchens and cooking — 166
Preserving food — 167
Processing food — 169
Supplying clean water — 170
Treating sewage — 172
Getting rid of rubbish — 174

15 Homes — 176
House construction — 176
Building and health — 178

16 Using drugs — 182
Drugs — 182
Smoking and drinking — 184

17 Pollution — 186
Air pollution — 186
Cars and air pollution — 188
Noise — 189
Water pollution — 190
Pest control — 192
Radiation — 193

18 First aid — 194
Accidents — 194
Helping others to breathe — 196
Bleeding — 198
Burns — 199

19 Health in the community — 200
The health service — 200
Healthy adults — 202
Healthy children — 204
Community services — 205
International health — 206

Questions — 207
Index — 216
Acknowledgements — 220

1 The human body

1 Living things

Being alive

Living things include all the plants and animals of the world. Humans are alive for about 70 years. Other living things have different **life spans**. A fly lives only for a few weeks; an oak tree may have a life span of over 200 years. To stay alive living things *release energy* inside their bodies. They must also *feed, get rid of waste, grow and repair their bodies, move* and *be sensitive to changes in their surroundings*. Plants and animals can also *produce offspring*. This makes sure that there will be living things in the future.

Humans are mammals

Humans belong to a group of animals called **mammals**. All mammals have a body covered with hair or fur and produce living offspring that they feed with milk. They have a steady body temperature (Fig. 1.1). Other groups of animals, such as birds and fish, do not have *all* these features.

Unlike all other animals, we have a complicated language. We use this to **communicate** or pass on our ideas to others. Speaking, reading and writing are all ways of communicating. We can work out the answers to questions and difficult problems. Humans can also make and use many tools and machines.

Fig. 1.1 An orang-utan and a human – both are mammals.

1 The human body

2 How the body is built

Building blocks

The way the human body is put together can be compared to the design of a house (Figs. 2.1 and Figs. 2.2). A house is made up from small 'building blocks'. Bricks and floorboards are two types of building blocks.

Parts of a room

The different parts of a room are built from different building blocks. Bricks are grouped together to form walls. Floorboards make the floor.

Rooms and groups of rooms

Walls, a floor, ceiling and door make up a room. Each room is used for a certain activity. The living room is for relaxation and the bathroom is used for washing the body. Some rooms can be grouped together as they are used for the same sort of activity. For instance the kitchen and the dining room are both used for feeding ourselves.

A house

The groups of rooms are all linked together as one house. Living rooms, bedrooms, a bathroom and kitchen are all needed to form one house.

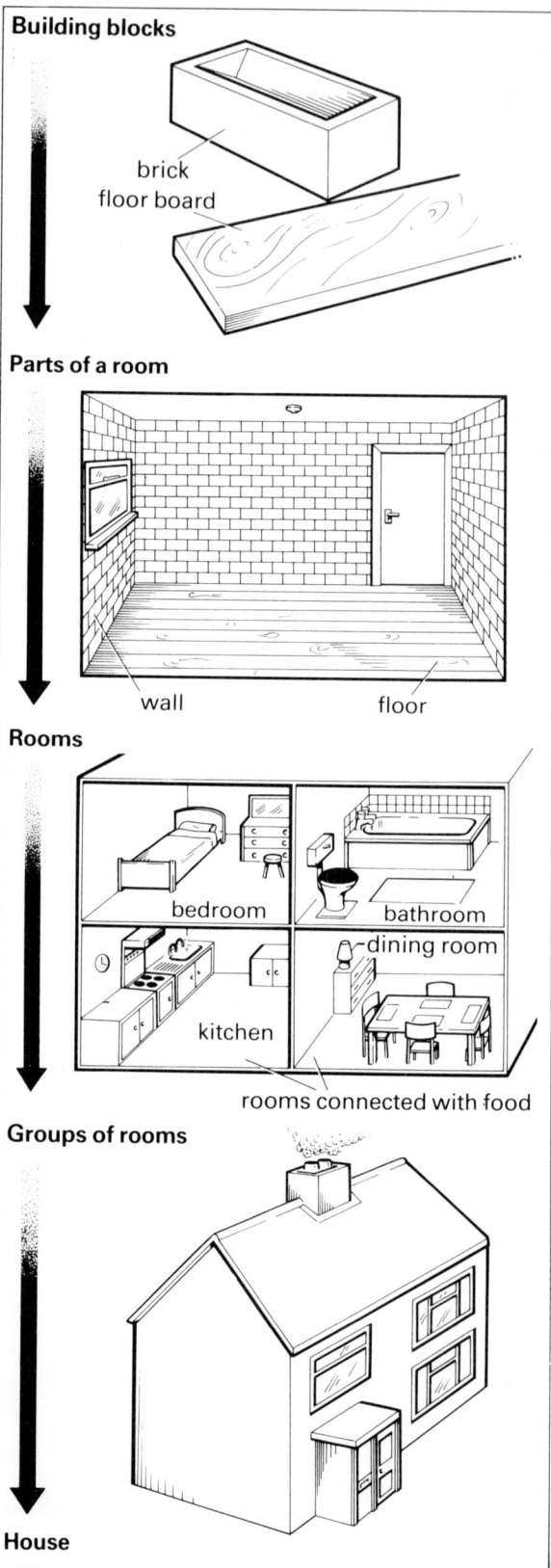

Fig. 2.1 A house is built from many parts.

1 The human body

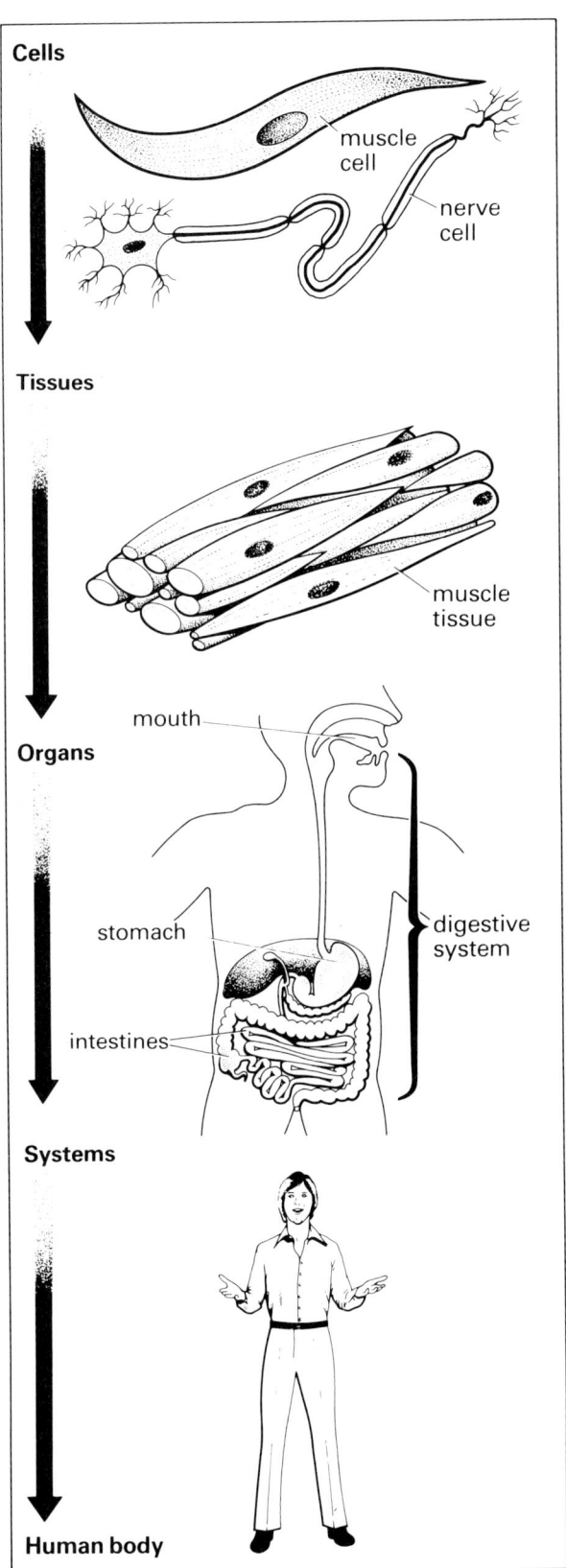

Cells

A human body is also built up from small building blocks called **cells**. Muscle cells and nerve cells are two of the many types of cells found in the body.

Tissues

Cells can be grouped together. A group of cells of the same type is called a **tissue**. A group of muscle cells is called muscle tissue. A collection of nerve cells is nerve tissue.

Organs and systems

An **organ** is a part of the body with a particular job to do. For instance the heart pumps blood and the stomach helps digest food. Each organ is made from a few different tissues. The stomach contains muscle and nerve tissue.

More than one organ is needed to digest food. The stomach does some of the work but the mouth and intestines are other organs that help. The mouth, stomach and intestines form the digestive **system**. The heart and blood vessels are organs of the circulatory system. They work together to move blood around the body.

A human body

All these systems are grouped together to make a human body. The systems are needed to keep a human alive.

Fig. 2.2 The human body.

1 The human body

3 Cells

Preparing cells for viewing

Cells can only be examined when they are removed from the body. Liquids from the body which may contain cells can be smeared across a microscope slide. This is how a **blood smear** is made (Fig. 3.1). Another way is to take a thin slice or **section** from a part of the body. The section can then be examined under a microscope (Fig. 3.2).

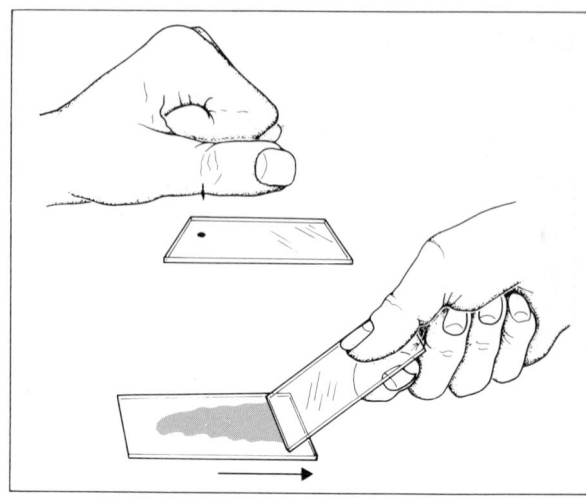

Fig. 3.1 Making a blood smear.

The light microscope

Cells are extremely small. To see them clearly, the cells must be **magnified**. A **light microscope** can be used to make things look bigger. A light microscope has several magnifying **lenses** fixed into a tube. To find out how many times a microscope magnifies, the number on the eyepiece and the number on the objective lens are multiplied together. The result is the **magnification**. The microscope in Fig. 3.3 is magnifying 40 times ($\times$ 40). It can also magnify by 100 times or 400 times if different objective lenses are moved into position. If you were magnified 100 times, you would look as tall as the Post Office Tower, now called the London Telecom Tower.

1. A tube from the body. The wall is one-cell thick. A sharp blade is used to cut a very thin slice.

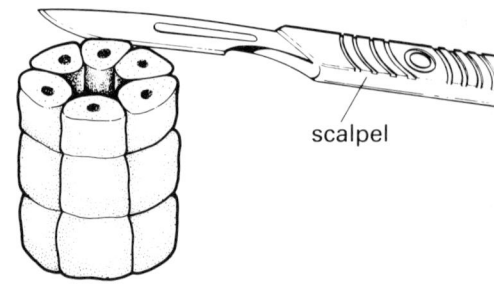

2. The slice or **Section** is put on a slide. A dye or **Stain** may be added to show up details inside.

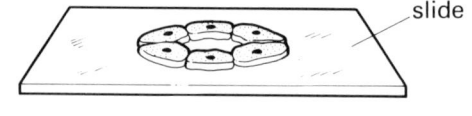

3. Looking down on the section using a microscope.

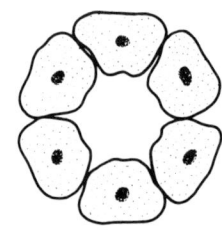

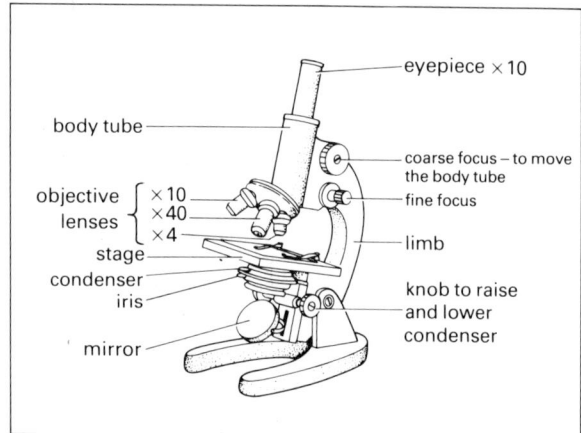

Fig. 3.3 A light microscope.

Fig. 3.2 Cutting a section from a tube of cells.

1 The human body

The electron microscope

The best light microscope will magnify objects 1500 times. It is possible to magnify objects 200 000 times using an **electron microscope** (Fig. 3.4). This passes electrons through the object instead of light. The electrons produce a picture on a screen in a similar way to a television.

The sizes of cells

A few cells are about one millimetre across but most are much smaller. Cells are measured in units that are smaller than a millimetre. The units used are **micrometres** (μm). One micrometre is one thousandth of a millimetre.

$$1 \,\mu m = \frac{1}{1000} \text{ mm or } 0.001 \text{ mm}$$

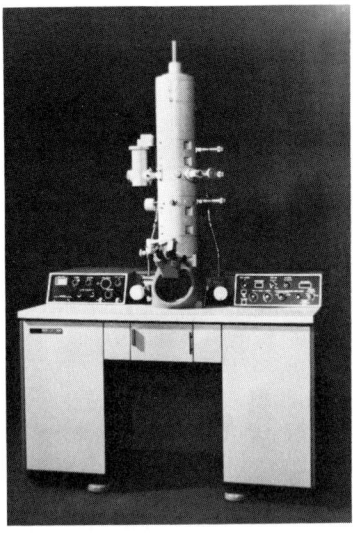

Fig. 3.4 An electron microscope.

A cell from inside the human cheek is a fairly typical size. It is about 10 μm across (Fig. 3.5).

The parts of a cell

A cell is made up of many smaller parts. All of these together make the **structure** of the cell (Figs. 3.6 and 3.7). Cells are mainly made up from a jelly-like material called **cytoplasm**. Around the cytoplasm is a thin 'skin' or **membrane**. Near the centre of the cytoplasm is the **nucleus**. The tiny parts scattered in the cytoplasm are **organelles**. One type of organelle is a **mitochondrion**.

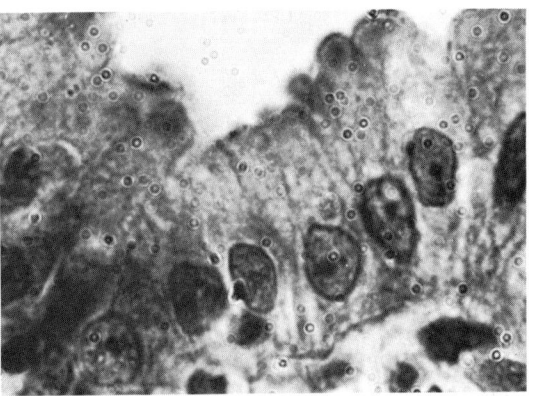

Fig. 3.6 A photograph of cells lining the stomach taken on a light microscope ($\times$ 1500).

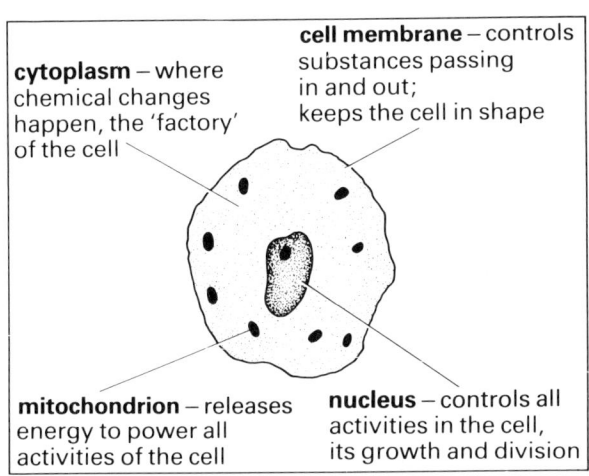

Fig. 3.5 The structure of a human cheek cell showing the work of each part.

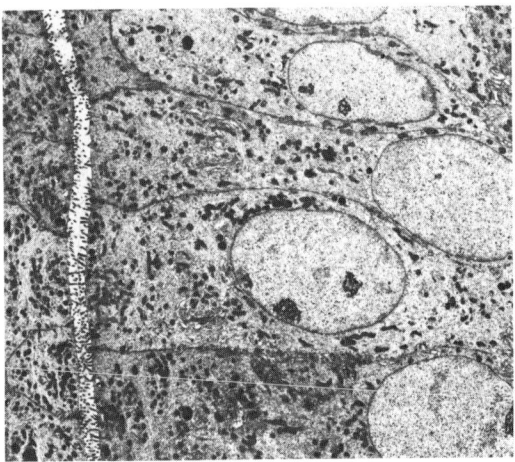

Fig. 3.7 A photograph of cells lining the stomach taken on an electron microscope ($\times$ 4000).

1 The human body

4 Tissues and organs

Types of tissues

Groups of cells that are similar to each other are **tissues**. There are several kinds. Each type of tissue is designed to suit the job it has to do.

Covering tissues

Thin layers of cells cover or line the surfaces of the body (Fig. 4.1). A covering tissue is called an **epithelium**. For example the inside of a blood vessel is lined with this type of cell. The skin on the outside of your body is layers of epithelial cells.

Connective tissues

Connective tissues bind together different parts of the body. They also support some parts. **Tendons** connect muscles to bones (Fig. 4.2). Tendons are made from very tough connective tissues. Bone is another connective tissue.

Muscle tissue

Muscle tissue is made from groups of muscle cells bound together (Fig. 4.3). Muscle tissue makes movement possible because it can shorten or **contract** and pull on the bones.

Nerve tissue

Nerve tissue is made up of nerve cells that can send 'electrical messages' (Fig. 4.4). Most nerve cells have a long fibre. A message can be passed along the fibre from one part of the body to another. Most of the brain is made up from nerve tissue.

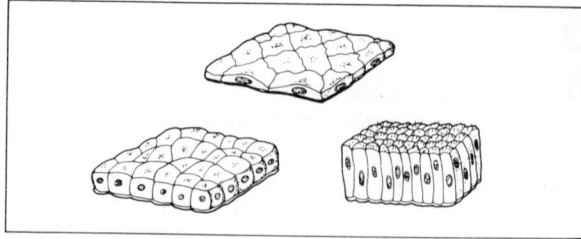

Fig. 4.1 Epithelial tissue. Three types are shown.

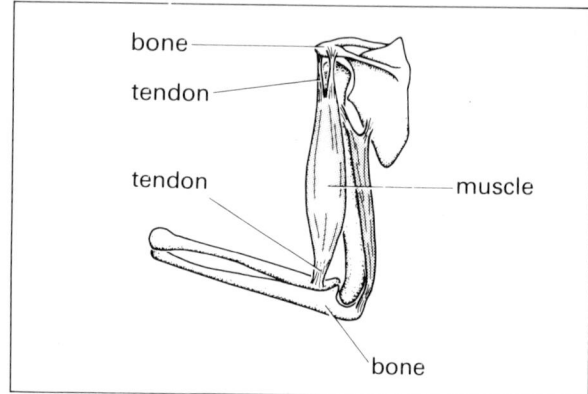

Fig. 4.2 Bone and tendon are two types of connective tissue.

Fig. 4.3 Muscle tissue. This type of muscle moves the bones of the skeleton.

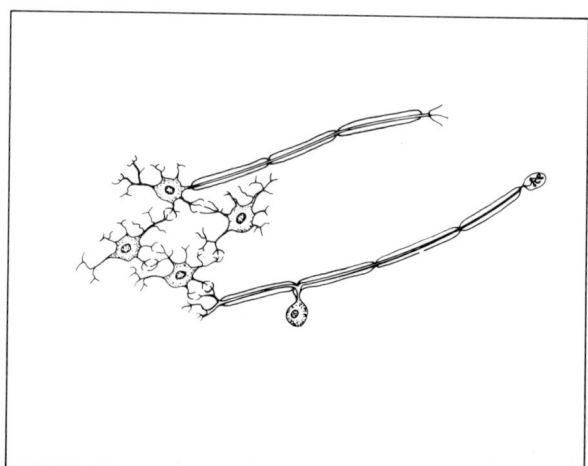

Fig. 4.4 Nerve tissue.

1 The human body

Organ systems

Cells and tissues may be grouped together to form **organs** like the stomach and the eye. Groups of organs are linked together to carry out important **functions** or jobs. A group of organs that work together is an **organ system**. For instance the **excretory system** is made up from the kidneys, ureters, bladder and urethra (Fig. 4.5). These parts work together to keep the right amount of water in the body and get rid of waste chemicals. Three other systems are shown below.

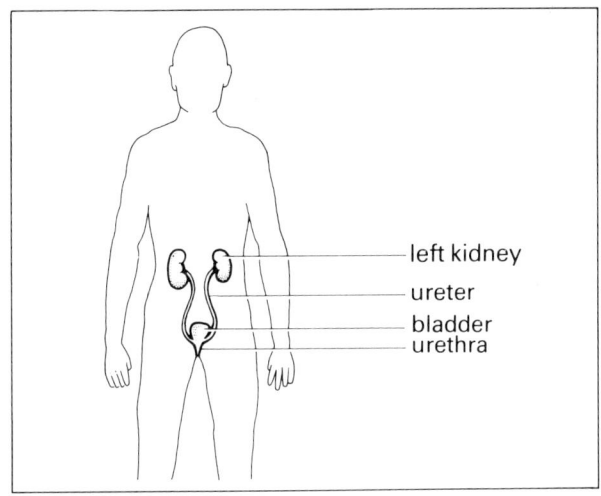

Fig. 4.5 The excretory system removes waste chemicals from the body.

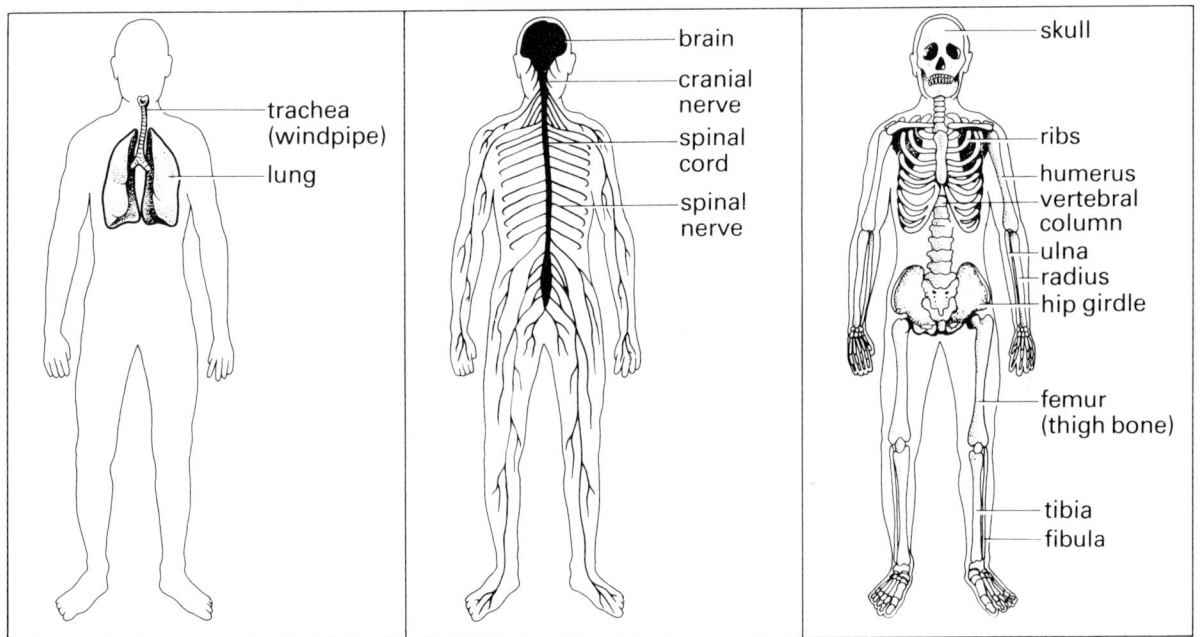

Fig. 4.6 The breathing system gets oxygen into the blood.

Fig. 4.7 The nervous system controls many of the body's activities.

Fig. 4.8 The skeletal system supports the body and protects some organs.

Summary: The human body

* All plants and animals must carry out certain activities to keep them alive.
* Humans belong to a group of animals called mammals.
* The human body is made up of cells.
* Cells can be grouped in tissues and organs.
* Cells are tiny. They must be specially treated and magnified if they are to be seen.
* The units used to measure cells are micrometres.
* Cells are made up of parts called organelles.
* Tissues are grouped by the jobs they do.
* Organs work together in systems to carry out the functions of the body.

2 Nutrition

5 Food

Nutrition and food

Nutrition means eating the right sorts of food to keep us healthy and to keep our cells growing. All animals eat food to keep them alive. Humans eat food that comes from other animals (meat and fish) and from plants (vegetables, cereals and fruits). Humans have a wide-ranging diet so they have been able to settle all over the world. The Japanese enjoy raw fish; Aborigines eat insect grubs; some Arabs like sheep's eyes. Some people in England eat tripe which is specially treated cow's stomach. Others find this unpleasant!

What is a food?

A food is something which does one or more of the following jobs:
1 gives the body energy,
2 supplies materials that can be used in growth and repair of the body,
3 supplies certain chemicals that help control important process in the body.

Flavourings, like pepper are not foods because the body does not use them. In a cup of tea the water and milk are foods. The flavourings from the tea leaves affect the nervous system so they are **drugs**. The alcohol in beer is a drug. But the body can use alcohol as a source of energy, so it is a food as well!

Fig. 5.1 Would you enjoy seaweed and raw egg for breakfast? They do in Japan!

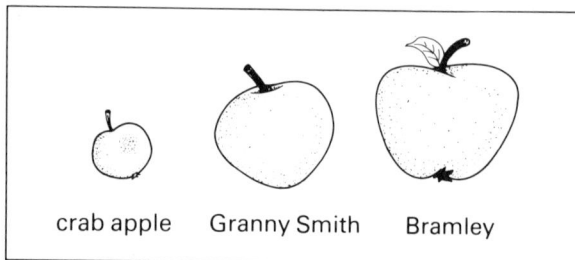

Fig. 5.2 Apples come in different sizes but are used in the same way by the body.

Food groups

Scientists need to study foods to find out how they are used in the body. They need to sort the foods into groups. They could group the foods by colour but some foods change colour. Bananas are green at first but change to yellow as they ripen. Similar kinds of food come in different sizes, so size is not a good way to group foods (Fig. 5.2).

6 Nutrients in food

Six food types

The best way to group foods is by the chemicals they have in them. These chemicals are called **nutrients**. Scientists have found that at least 45 nutrients are needed by the body. These nutrients can be divided into six groups. The six are **protein, carbohydrates, fats, water, minerals** and **vitamins**. No matter how much food is eaten a human will only stay alive if the right amounts of these nutrients are eaten regularly.

Protein

Protein is a very important nutrient group. A lot of the living tissues of animals and plants are made from protein. So for growth and repair of the body, protein is necessary. Without protein in the diet you will die. This is because protein cannot be made from any of the other nutrient groups.

How proteins are made

Proteins are made of units called **amino acids**. These amino acids contain **nitrogen**. There are 23 different amino acids. They can be joined up in many different ways to form many different proteins (Fig. 6.1). Most proteins do not contain all the 23 amino acids.

Protein-rich foods

Some of the amino acids are more important to us than others. Humans will not be able to grow and repair their bodies if they do not get these amino acids. Growing children need 10 out of the 23, adults need 8. Meat, eggs, fish and milk have all the 10 amino acids. The proteins from plants do not always contain the necessary ones. But some plants are better than others. The **pulses** (peas and beans), nuts and cereals (wheat and rice), are rich in the amino acids that humans need (Fig. 6.2).

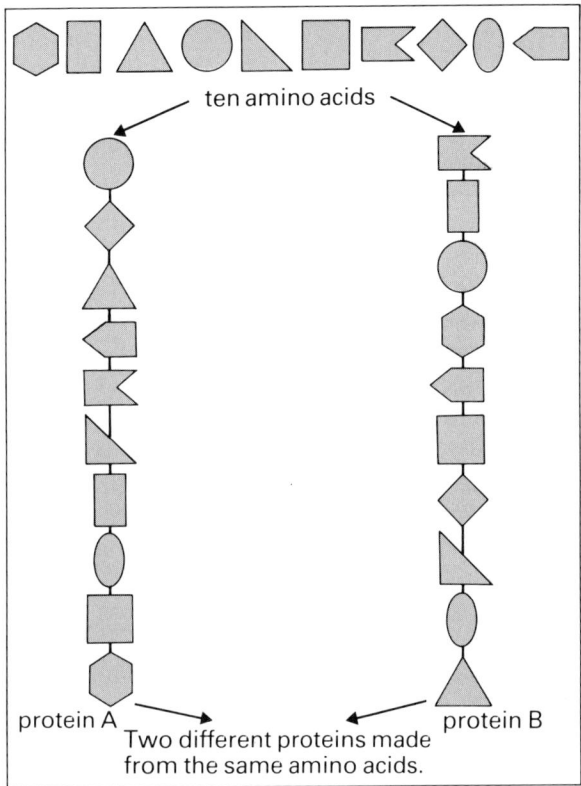

Fig. 6.1 *How proteins are made.*

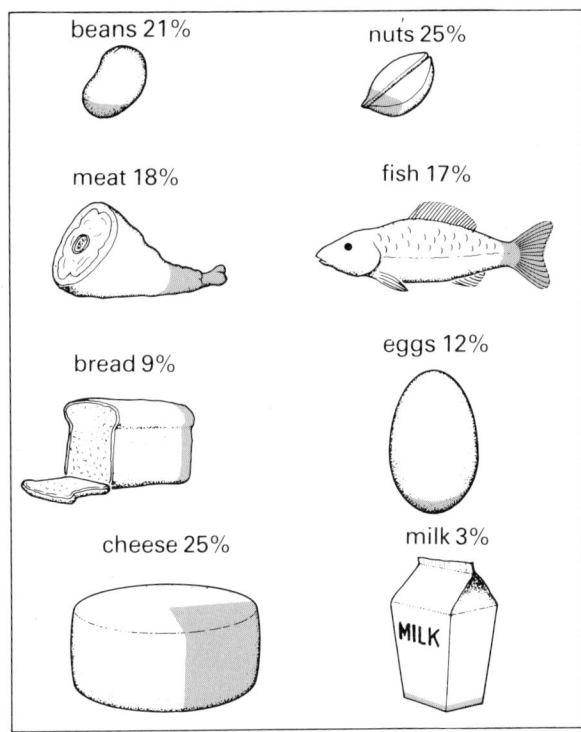

Fig. 6.2 *The amount of protein in some foods.*

2 Nutrition

Carbohydrates

Much of the food eaten by most people contains a lot of **carbohydrate**. These foods are ones that are 'sugary' and 'starchy'.

Sugars

There are several different **sugars**. One of them is **glucose**. It is found in animals' blood and in parts of most plants, such as the juices in fruit. **Fructose** is another sugar found in fruits and honey. **Sucrose** is found in the sugar-beet and sugar-cane plants. Household sugar is sucrose (Fig. 6.3). Sugar units can be joined together to form long, complex chains. A sugar unit is a sugar **molecule**. Molecules of different substances, like starch, can be made from sugar molecules (Fig. 6.4).

Starch

Starch is found in potatoes, rice and flour (Fig. 6.5). It is just one of the complex substances found in the carbohydrate group. Some of the others are **glycogen** (found in liver) and **cellulose** (in all plants). Sometimes cellulose is given other names; it can be called **fibre** or **roughage**. This helps the gut muscles work.

The energy trapped in starch and sugar molecules is released in the body. So starchy and sugary foods are good 'fuels' for the body.

Fats

Fats tend to be greasy chemicals. Fats can be liquids, like olive oil, or solids, like bacon fat and butter (Fig. 6.6). Fats do not dissolve in water. Fats, like starch and sugar, are used by the body to supply energy. They have about twice as much energy as the same weight of carbohydrate. We can store fat beneath our skin and around our organs. Fat under the skin is an **insulating** layer which helps to keep the body warm. Fat around delicate organs like the kidneys protects them from damage.

Fig. 6.3 The amount of sugar in some foods.

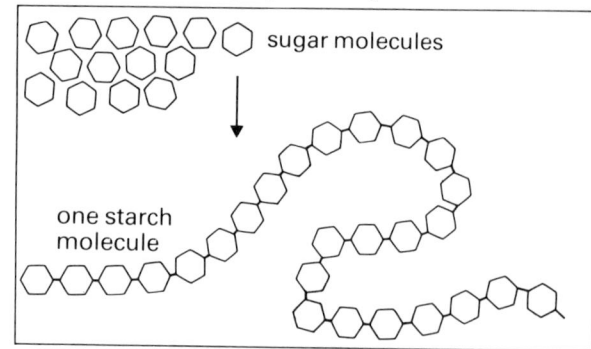

Fig. 6.4 Sugar molecules can be joined to make starch.

Fig. 6.5 The amount of starch in some foods.

Fig. 6.6 The amount of fat in some foods.

2 Nutrition

Water

Most foods contain **water**. About three quarters of your body is water. Imagine if all the water was removed from a man who weighs 76 kg (about 12 stone). His dried body would weigh 19 kg (4 stone). This is because most of every cell is water. Humans drink water, but it is also found in solid food. Even a peanut is one tenth water (Fig. 6.7). Water (in the blood) is also used to carry dissolved chemicals round the body.

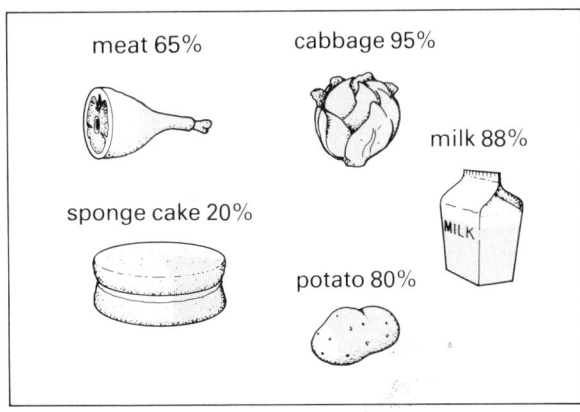

Fig. 6.7 *The amount of water in some foods.*

Minerals

If any food is burned an ash is left. Scientists have found many **elements** in this ash. Some of the elements are metals and some are non-metals. The elements in our diet are called **minerals**. They are used to help build up parts of the body and to keep some processes under control. They are not used to supply energy. Minerals are needed in much smaller amounts than water, protein, carbohydrates and fats. Some minerals, like **iron**, **iodine**, and **fluorine** are needed in extremely small amounts. Others like **calcium**, **sodium**, **potassium** and **sulphur** are needed in larger amounts. For instance, a 12-year old boy needs 700 mg of calcium and 13 mg of iron each day for healthy growth.

How different minerals are used

The minerals are used in different ways. Calcium and **phosphorus** (as the chemical calcium phosphate) are used in the building of the skeleton. Sodium and potassium are needed to send 'messages' along nerve cells, and to help muscles work. Sulphur is used in a chemical that keeps the amount of glucose in your blood steady. Sulphur is also used in the making of hair, nails and skin. If you do not get enough of any mineral, the body will not be healthy. You may suffer from a **deficiency disease** (Figs. 6.8 and 6.9).

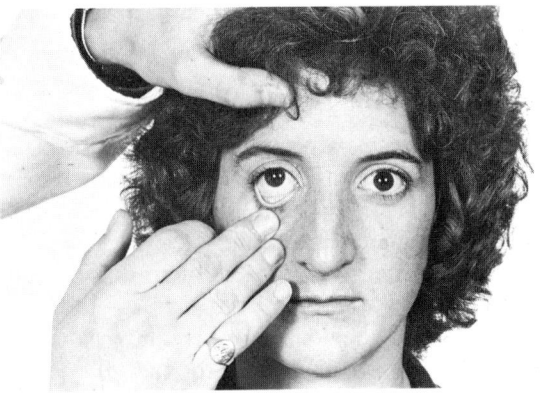

Fig. 6.8 *The doctor is looking inside the patient's eyelids to check for* **anaemia**. *This is caused by a lack of iron in the blood. A patient with anaemia feels tired and weak.*

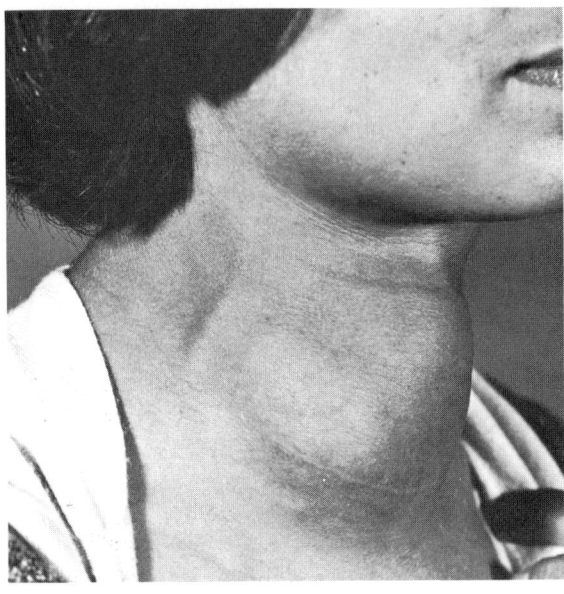

Fig. 6.9 *This person is suffering from* **goitre**, *a swelling of the* **thyroid gland**. *This is caused by a lack of iodine.*

2 Nutrition

Vitamins

Vitamins were discovered this century. Long before this scientists were trying to find out how to cure diseases. One of these was **scurvy**. Anyone suffering from scurvy is very weak, will bleed inside their body, at the gums or hair roots. A wound will take a long time to heal (Fig. 6.11). If scurvy is not treated, the sufferer will die.

James Lind's experiment

In the eighteenth century, James Lind found a cure for scurvy. He was a captain in the Royal Navy who did an experiment (Fig. 6.10). He found 12 sailors suffering from the disease. He divided them into six pairs. They were all given meals of 'gruel', mutton broth, boiled biscuit and one other food. Each pair was given a different food. The first pair of scurvy sufferers were given cider; the second pair had vinegar; the third pair were given dilute sulphuric acid! The fourth pair had to drink sea-water and the fifth pair were give a paste made of garlic and mustard. None of these men recovered. The sixth pair of men had to eat oranges and lemons. After six days these two sailors were better. James Lind had found that fresh fruit was needed in the diet to stop scurvy.

Naming vitamins

The reason why the fruit cured the disease was not found until the early 1900s. Scientists found that fruit and other foods contained 'accessory food factors' needed for the healthy growth of the body. These factors were called vitamins, a name which comes from the Latin word for life. Citrus fruits like oranges and lemons contain a substance called vitamin C. Without this vitamin in the diet, scurvy will begin. At first, the vitamins were named after the letters of the alphabet. But it was soon found that vitamin B was more than one substance. So today each vitamin has a special name. The names are very long so most people still use the alphabet name.

James Lind

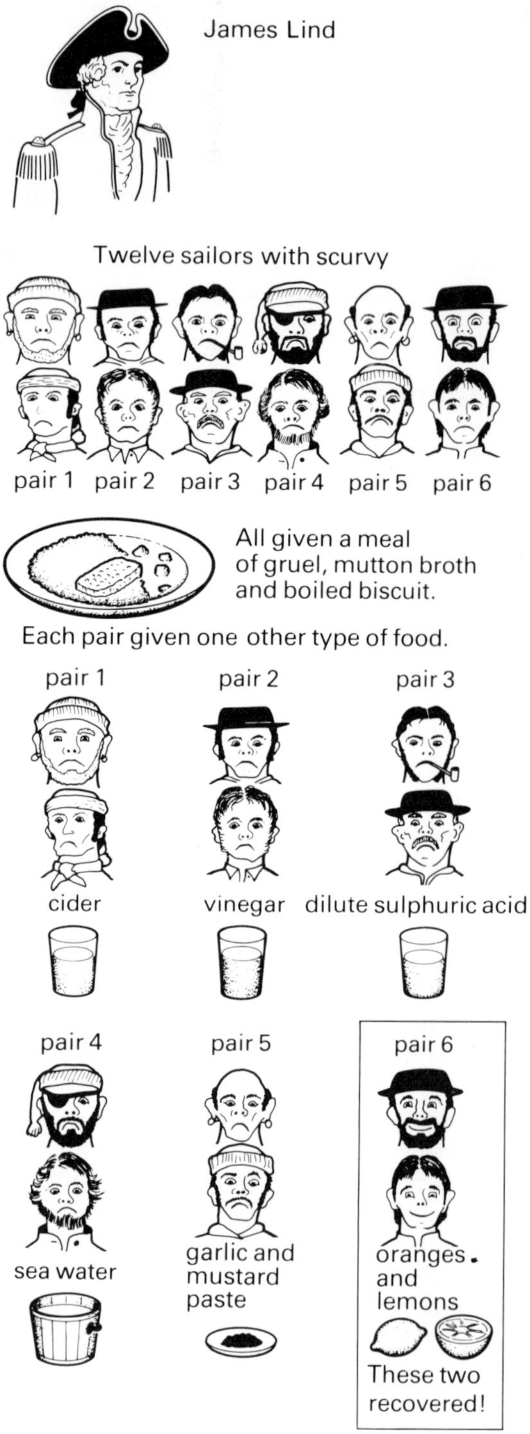

Twelve sailors with scurvy
pair 1　pair 2　pair 3　pair 4　pair 5　pair 6

All given a meal of gruel, mutton broth and boiled biscuit.

Each pair given one other type of food.

pair 1　　　pair 2　　　pair 3
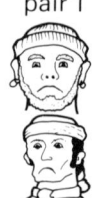  
cider　　　vinegar　　dilute sulphuric acid

pair 4　　　pair 5　　　pair 6

sea water　garlic and mustard paste　oranges and lemons

These two recovered!

Fig. 6.10 James Lind gave special diets to pairs of sailors suffering from scurvy. Only the diet with fresh fruit cured the disease.

2 Nutrition

The work of vitamins

Vitamins, like minerals are needed regularly but in small amounts. A 12-year old boy needs about 25 mg of vitamin C and about 1·0 mg of vitamin B_1 each day.

Vitamin A is needed for healthy growth. It keeps the lining of the gut, nose, eyes and the skin in order. It also helps you see as it is used to make a chemical found in the eye.

Vitamin B_1 (or thiamine) helps the body make good use of the carbohydrate we eat.

Vitamin B_2 (or riboflavin) is necessary for the proper growth of the skin, hair and nails.

Vitamin C (or ascorbic acid) prevents us getting some diseases. It also helps to make up some types of protein.

Vitamin D helps the body to use calcium when the bones of the skeleton are growing.

If you do not have enough of any vitamin, you may suffer from a deficiency disease. Some of these are shown in the photos on this page. The body can make one vitamin. If the skin is in sunlight, some of the cells in it make vitamin D. All the other vitamins must be obtained from the food we eat. The amount of vitamins in some foods we eat is shown in Fig. 7.4 on page 15.

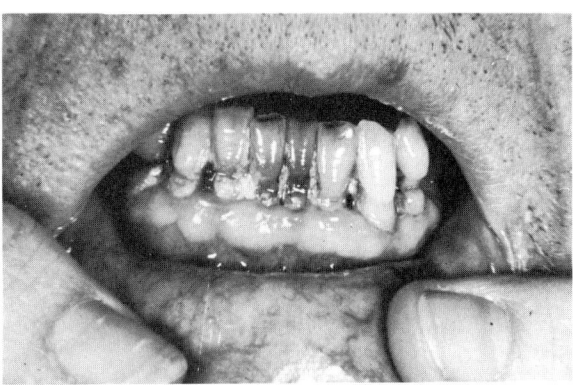

Fig. 6.11 *Scurvy is caused by a lack of vitamin C. The gums bleed easily and the teeth fall out.*

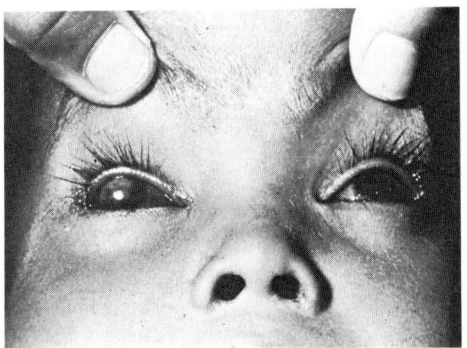

Fig. 6.12 *This child is suffering from* **xerophthalmia** *which can lead to blindness. The disease is caused by a lack of vitamin A.*

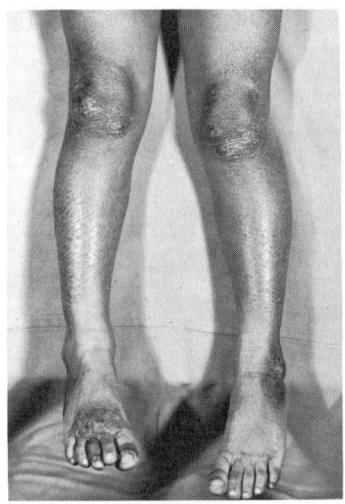

Fig. 6.13 *A shortage of one of the B-group vitamins causes* **pellagra**. *This disease leads to rough, scaly patches on the skin (as shown above), diarrhoea and sometimes, mental disorders.*

Fig. 6.14 **Rickets** *is caused by a lack of vitamin D. The bones are softer than normal and may not grow straight.*

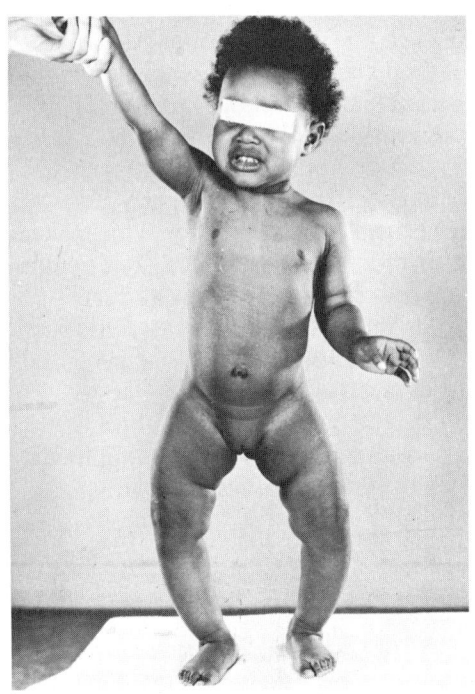

2 Nutrition

7 Balanced diet

Malnourishment

To work properly the human body needs the right amount of the right sort of foods. The body needs protein for growth and repair, carbohydrates and fats for energy, vitamins and minerals for some processes, and water. If a person gets enough of these nutrients the diet is **balanced**. Some people do not get a balanced diet – they are **malnourished**.

Too much food

Many people eat too many energy foods but do not make their bodies work enough. The extra food is stored as fat under the skin. These people become overweight or **obese** (Fig. 7.1). Obese people tend not to live as long as slimmer people (see page 54).

Too little food

Many people in the world do not get enough food to eat. They become **under-nourished**. If the shortage of food goes on, they use up all their bodies' stores of fat and become very thin. This is known as **starvation** (Fig. 7.2).

Children that do not receive enough protein and energy foods will not grow properly. Also too much water is held inside the body. This makes the joints and abdomen swell (Fig. 7.3). The skin may develop sore patches and the child will be very weak. This condition is called **kwashiorkor**. It can be cured by giving a proper balanced diet to the child.

The table on the next page shows the amounts of each type of nutrient in some common foods. It also shows the energy values of the foods measured in **kilojoules (kJ)**.

Fig. 7.1 These two men are seriously overweight! They both weigh over 240 kg (38 stone).

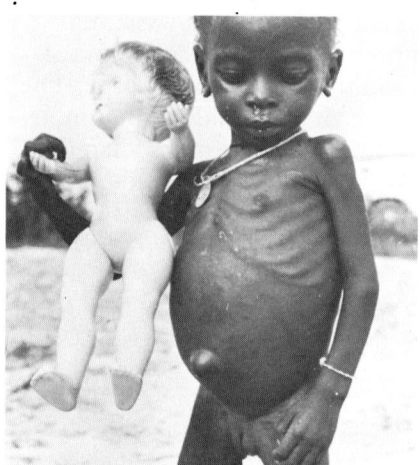
Fig. 7.2 This girl is suffering from starvation because of a famine in her country.

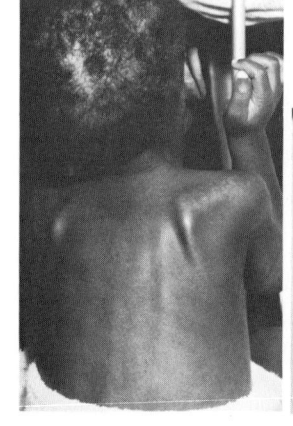 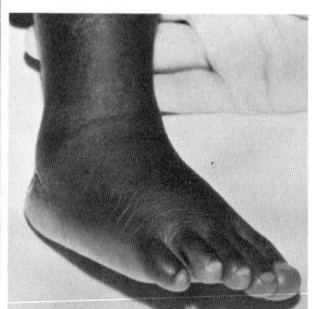

Fig. 7.3 This child is suffering from kwashiorkor. The photos show sore patches on the skin and a swollen ankle joint.

2 Nutrition

Food	Amount in 100 g of each food			Minerals and vitamins in foods (x – very little or none; ✓ – a little; ✓✓ – a lot)						
	energy (kJ)	protein (g)	carbohydrate (g)	fat (g)	calcium	iron	Vit A	Vit B_1	Vit B_2	Vit C	Vit D
apples	197	0·3	40·4	14·4	x	x	x	x	x	✓	x
bacon, cooked	1852	24·5	0·5	38·8	✓	✓	x	✓✓	✓	x	x
beef, raw	940	18·1	0·0	17·1	✓	✓	x	✓	✓	x	x
biscuits, chocolate	2087	7·1	65·3	24·9	✓✓	✓	x	✓	x	x	x
bread, white	1068	8·0	54·3	1·7	✓✓	✓	x	✓	x	x	x
butter	3006	0·5	0·0	81·0	✓	x	✓✓	x	x	x	✓✓
cabbage	92	2·8	2·3	0·0	✓✓	x	✓	x	x	✓✓	x
cheese, Cheddar	1708	25·4	0·0	34·5	✓✓	x	✓✓	x	✓	x	✓
cod, raw	321	17·4	0·0	0·7	✓	x	x	x	x	x	x
eggs	612	12·3	0·0	10·9	✓✓	✓	✓✓	x	✓✓	x	✓✓
flour	1483	10·0	80·0	0·9	✓✓	✓	x	✓✓	x	x	x
ice-cream	805	4·1	19·8	11·3	✓✓	x	✓✓	x	✓	x	x
liver, fried	1020	24·9	5·6	13·7	✓	✓✓	✓✓	✓	✓✓	✓✓	✓
milk	274	3·3	4·8	3·8	✓✓	x	✓	✓	✓	x	x
oranges	150	0·8	8·5	0·0	✓✓	x	x	x	x	✓✓	x
peas	208	5·0	7·7	0·0	✓	✓	✓	✓	x	✓	x
potatoes boiled	339	1·4	19·7	0·0	x	x	x	x	x	✓	x
potatoes, chips	1028	3·8	37·3	9·0	✓	✓	x	x	x	✓	x
sugar	1680	0·0	100·0	0·0	x	x	x	x	x	x	x

Fig. 7.4 The nutritional value of some foods.

Summary: Nutrition

* Foods give the body energy; supply the materials needed for growth and repair; help to control the activities of the body.
* Foods are grouped by the nutrients they contain.
* Protein is used to build and repair the body.
* The carbohydrate and fat nutrients provide the body with energy.
* Water is used to transport substances.
* Minerals and vitamins are needed in small amounts.
* A shortage of any mineral or vitamin causes a deficiency disease.
* A person is malnourished if they have too much or too little food.

3 Food and the future

8 Green plants

The food problem

People living in all parts of the world are suffering from malnutrition. It is a problem to get food to the people who need it. Scientists think that the problem is going to get worse in the future. Places where food is in short supply often have populations that are getting larger. Our food comes from plants and animals. It is important to know how to get as much food as possible from them.

The importance of green plants

Green plants are alive and, like us, need energy to make their cells work and grow. Unlike all other living things, green plants can make their own food. The materials they use are **carbon dioxide** from the air and **water** from the soil. **Chlorophyll** is the green substance in plants and it can trap light energy. This energy is used to make carbohydrates (e.g. sugar and starch) from carbon dioxide and water. The process of food-making by green plants in light is called **photosynthesis** (Fig. 8.1). When a leaf is photosynthesising, oxygen is given off and may pass out of the leaf (Fig. 8.2).

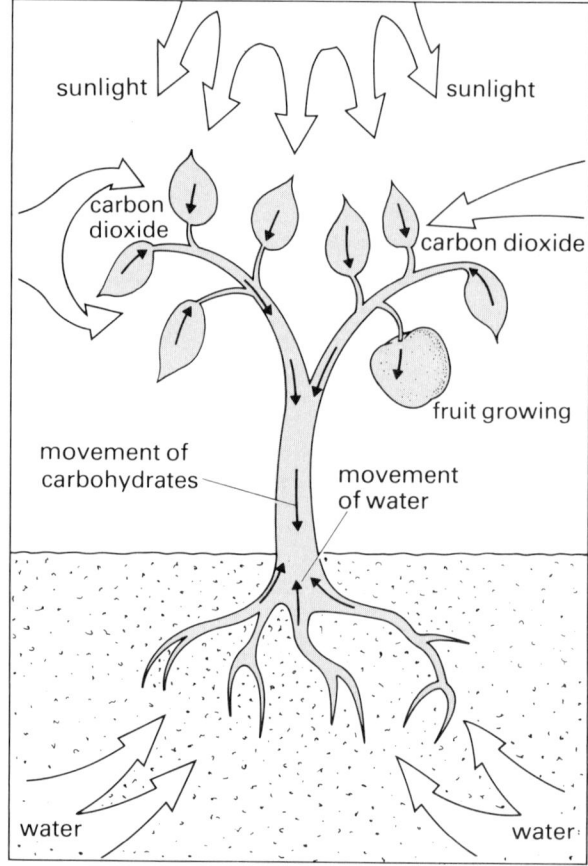

Fig. 8.1 *A plant making carbohydrates.*

Plants build up fats and proteins from the carbohydrates. **Nitrogen** is needed to make protein. **Nitrates**, which contain nitrogen, are taken up from the soil to help make plant proteins.

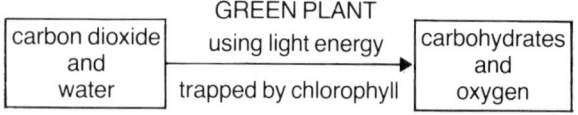

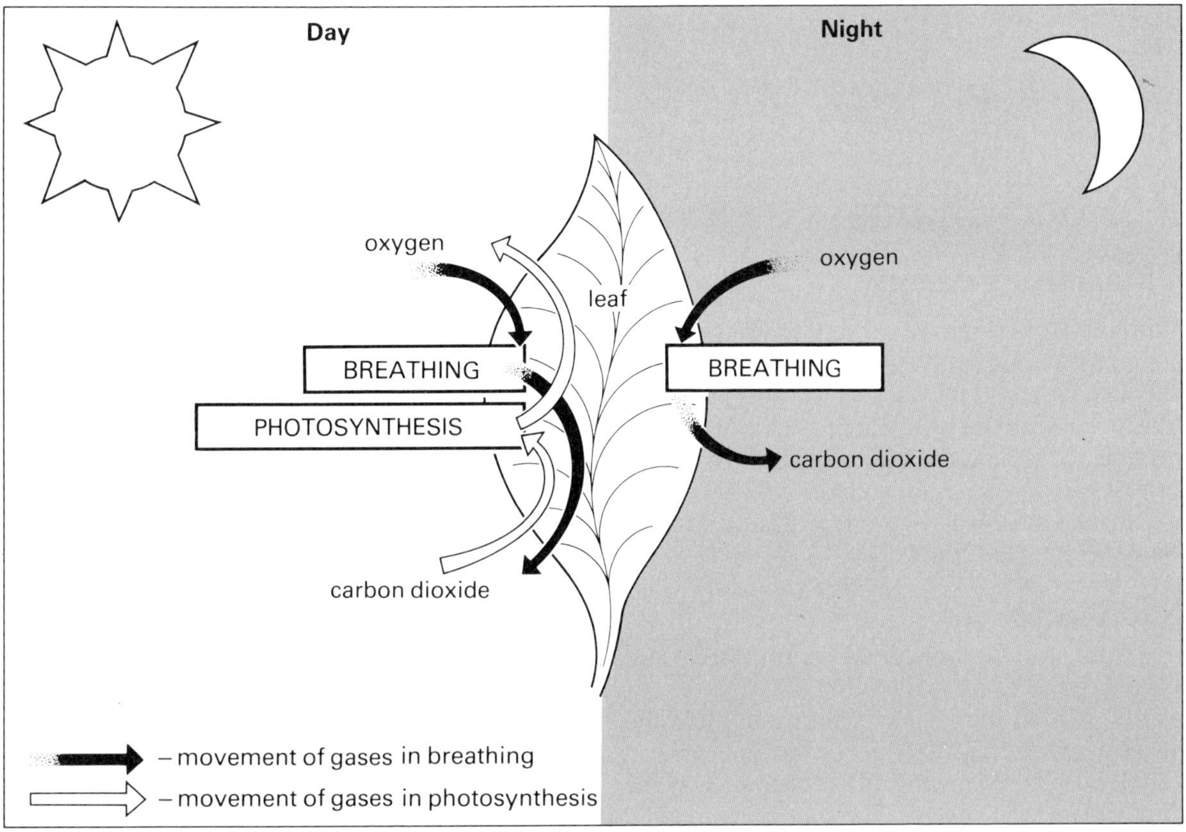

3 Food and the future

Fig. 8.2 The oxygen and carbon dioxide cycle.

Plants store food

Photosynthesis takes place in the green parts of plants – mainly the leaves. The food in the leaves can be moved to other parts of the plant, where it can be stored (Figs. 8.1 and 8.3). This stored food can be eaten by us or other animals. We eat food stores in leaves when we eat plants such Brussels sprouts or lettuce. Plant leaf-stalks are eaten as rhubarb, celery and leeks. Plant stems are eaten as asparagus. Underground food stores of plants are eaten as carrots, cassava, yams and potatoes. Even flowers are eaten, as globe artichokes or cauliflower. Plants produce fruits, nuts and seeds. These are sources of human food as well.

Fig. 8.3 Some parts of plants that we eat.

3 Food and the future

9 Food chains

Transferring energy

Humans cannot survive without food so we eat plant and animal products. Even if we ate only animals, we could not survive without plants. This is because the plants are food for our animals. Grass is eaten by a lamb and the killed lamb is eaten by us. A **food chain** shows how the energy and chemicals in food are passed on from plants to animals (Fig. 9.1).

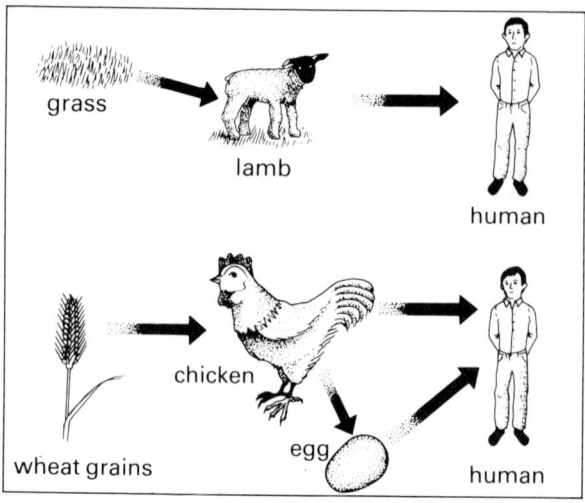

Fig. 9.1 *Two simple food chains.*

Food webs

In nature most food chains are complicated. One animal may feed on many different types of plants. Also an animal may eat other animals. For instance an owl may eat mice, voles and even young rabbits. By having different animals in the diet, the owl can survive when one of its food animals is not available. The complicated feeding pattern can be drawn as a **food web**. In the sea there are many food chains linked to form food webs. One food web is shown in Fig. 9.2.

Needing the sun and green plants

Food chains and food webs show that humans and all other animals rely on plants for chemicals and energy. Green plants are the only living things that can trap light energy. They store the energy in carbohydrates, made from carbon dioxide and water. They do this by photosynthesis. The stored energy is made available to animals when they eat the plants. So all animals, including humans, rely on the sun for energy.

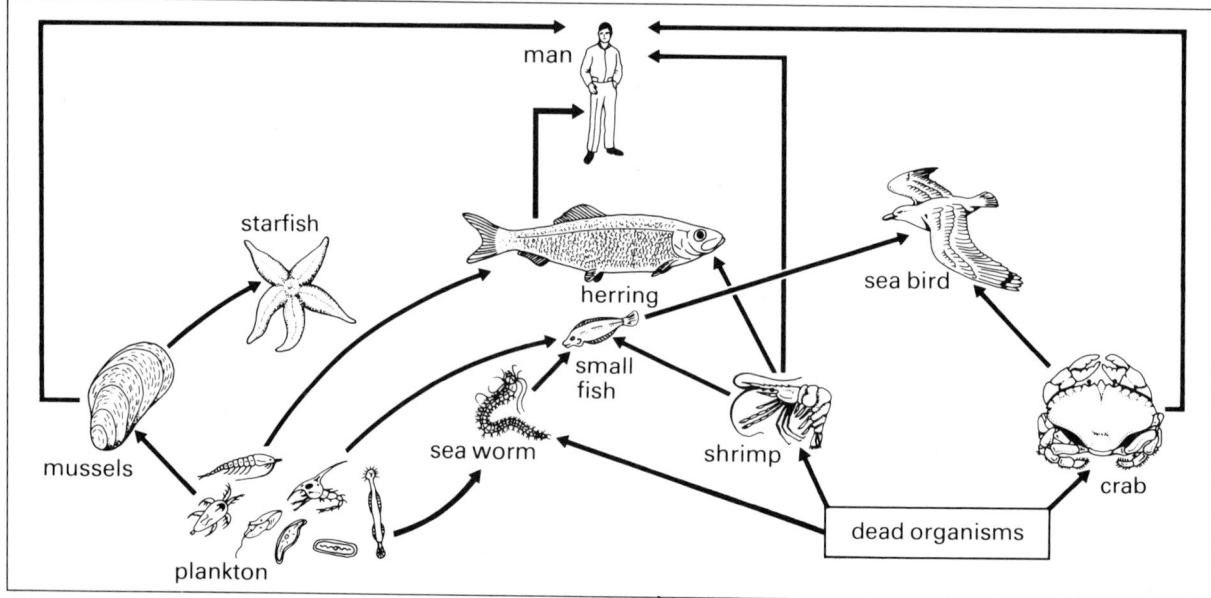

Fig. 9.2 *A food web in the sea.*

3 Food and the future

10 Plant and animal farming

Cultivating plants

As plants are a source of food, humans grow or **cultivate** them. Wild grasses were the first plants to be cultivated as **crops**. Today these crops are mainly **cereals** (Fig. 10.1). Cereals are grain-bearing plants and the most important ones are **wheat** and **rice**. The grains (seeds) are specially treated before we eat them. Wheat grains are ground into flour. Wheat flour can be made into bread, cakes, semolina, spaghetti and breakfast cereal (Fig. 10.2).

Other ways of using plants

Humans use plants in many ways. Chemicals from plants can be used to make drugs, dyes and other products like soap. Fibres, from cotton and flax plants, can be woven into cloth. Wood from trees can be made into paper, furniture and buildings. Rubber is made from **latex** tapped from rubber trees.

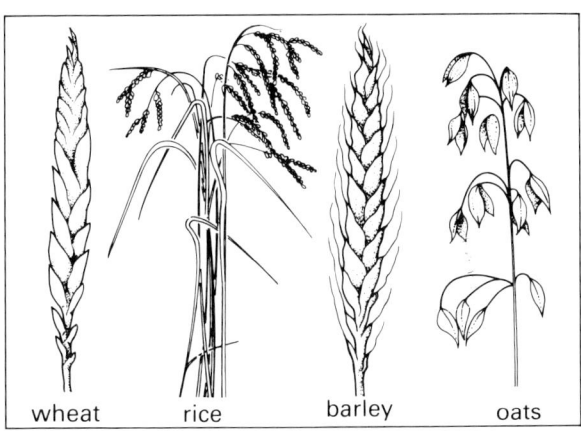

Fig. 10.1 Some of the cereals we use to make food.

Keeping animals

Humans also keep animals. The animals are used for food and also to provide us with other materials we need. Animals that are kept include cows and goats (for milk, cheese and meat), sheep (for meat and wool), and poultry (for meat and eggs). All of them need food. For many animals, grass is the chief food. If there is plenty of grass in summer, farmers cut and dry it, and store it as **hay**. Rotting grass or other crops is made into **silage**, another animal food. Some specially made animal foods are mixed from soya beans, cotton seeds and linseed oil.

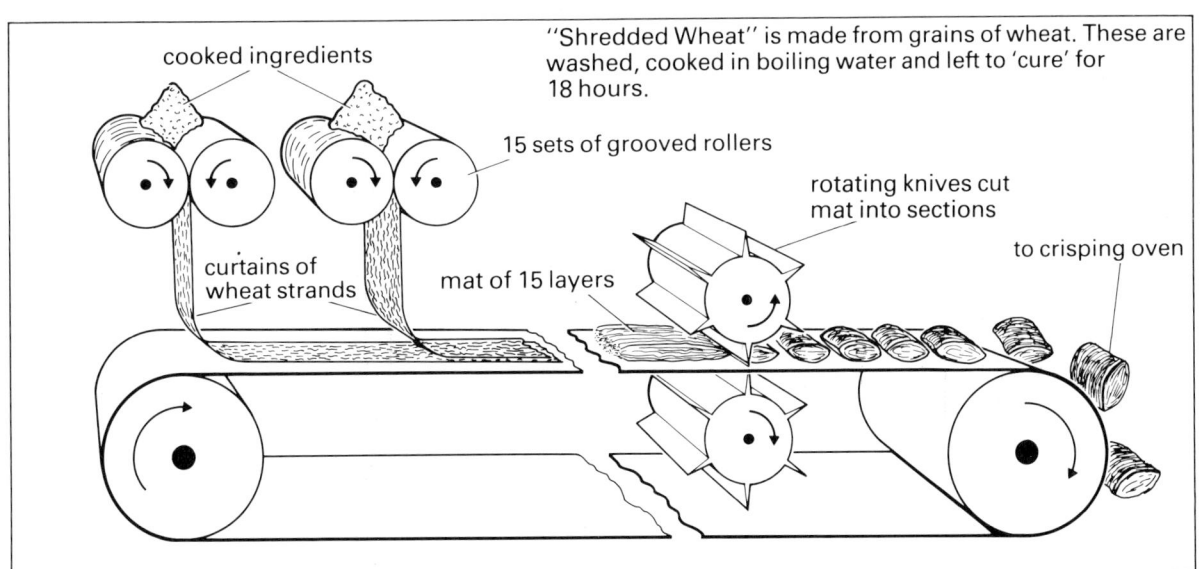

Fig. 10.2 Processing wheat to make breakfast cereal.

3 Food and the future

11 Farming and food supply

More mouths and less space

The population of the world is increasing very rapidly (see page 103). The population is increasing most quickly in countries where there is already a food shortage. It is a problem to get food to these people.

Crops are grown and animals are kept on farmland. Nearly all the good land is already being farmed. A lot of valuable farmland is being used up for building (Fig. 11.1). Towns, cities, motorways and airports are spreading.

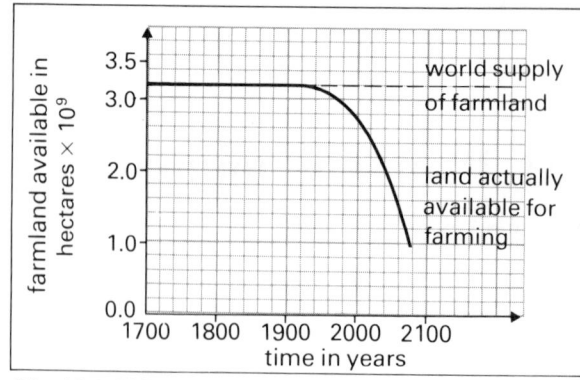

Fig. 11.1 *This graph shows that the amount of land available for farming is getting less.*

Using farmland economically

When plants grow, they need space, light, water and carbon dioxide. To make a loaf of bread, wheat from about one square metre of land is needed. You might want to get the same amount of energy from chicken meat instead. To do this ten square metres of land are needed! This is because much more land is needed to grow the food to feed the chickens (Fig. 11.2).

Producing meat from grazing cattle needs a lot of space (Fig. 11.3). This is because although a bullock will eat 2000 kg of plant food, its carcass in the butchers will weigh about 250 kg. Each carcass will provide 125 kg of meat that humans eat.

Photosynthesis traps energy in the plants that the bullock eats. The animal uses some of this energy for its own activities. Only a little is stored in the muscles or meat of its body.

So to feed a lot of people it is better to cultivate plants than keep cattle. Plant food and its energy will go straight to the human. It will not be 'wasted' by going to an animal first. However, some animal protein should be eaten so that humans get the amino acids they need (see page 9).

Fig. 11.2 *Plant crops need less space to provide the same amount of 'food energy' as animals.*

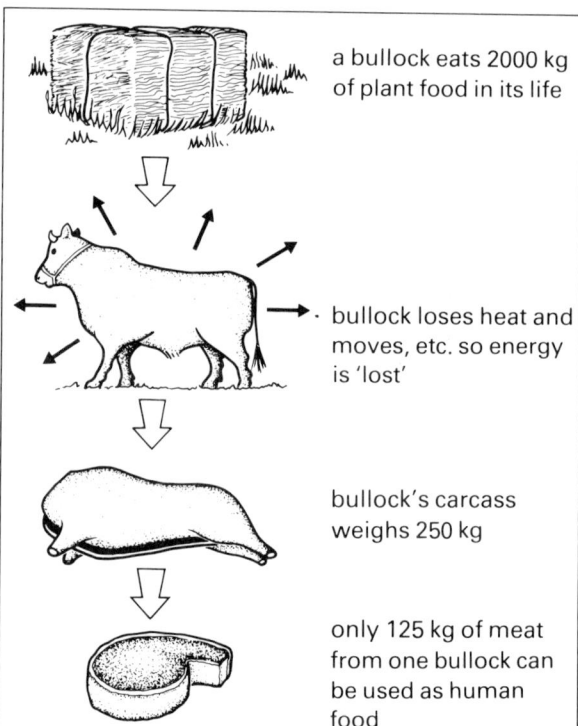

Fig. 11.3 *Energy is 'lost' when animals are kept for food.*

3 Food and the future

12 Improving food production

One way of helping to solve the food problem is by improving our ways of producing food.

Fig. 12.1 Wheat grown with and without fertiliser.

Improving soil

We can increase the growth of crops by adding things to the soil. Dung or **manure** from farm animals was used in the past. It improved the **fertility** of the soil. Now chemicals, like ammonium sulphate are added to the soil. These chemicals are called **fertilisers**. They improve the **yield** of a crop. The yield is the amount of food produced by a crop. On some soils, fertilisers can increase the yield of a crop by about four times (Fig. 12.1).

Saving crops from pest damage

Fig. 12.2 Leaves from a diseased potato plant.

Many crops are ruined as they are attacked by pests or plant diseases (Fig. 12.2). These crops may be saved if they are sprayed with chemicals known as **pesticides**. However, there are disadvantages. Many chemicals can be washed from the land into rivers and lakes. They may damage animals and plants living there.

Improved machinery

Better farm machinery is being invented. Modern ploughs help break up the soil to make sure air and water can enter. Combine harvesters gather in large amounts of crops when they are ripe (Fig. 12.3).

Fig. 12.3 A combine harvester with one side cut away. The rotating drum in the centre separates the wheat grains from the stalks.

Teaching farmers

Farmers must learn new methods if they are to produce as much food as possible from their land. In countries with old-fashioned farming methods, like India, this is very important.

3 Food and the future

13 Solving the food problem

Birth control

There are ways of helping to overcome the problem of food supply. Improving food production is one way (see page 21). Another way is to persuade people to have fewer children. Using **contraceptives** will mean smaller families. The population will then increase more slowly. Persuading people to use contraceptives is most important in countries where the population is increasing very rapidly (Fig. 13.1).

Fig. 13.1 Teaching people about contraceptives.

Making more land available

Some land cannot be used for farming. It may be too wet, too dry or has poor soil. Modern machinery can be used to drain wet areas. In hot, dry areas canals can be built. These can bring water to places of low rainfall. This is known as **irrigation** (Fig. 13.2). Special plants can be put in sandy areas. When they die they rot. The rotting plants hold the sand grains together. Chemicals from the plants blend with the sand to make a better soil. Deserts or sand dunes can become places for growing crops.

Fig. 13.2 An irrigation system. Water is pumped up into the reservoir. When the land is dry, the water is allowed to flow out into drainage channels.

Breeding better plants and animals

It is not known when humans began to control cattle-breeding. We do know that today's beef and milk cattle look very different from the cattle of the past. By controlling breeding, we can produce cattle that are meatier, or chickens that lay more eggs. Animals have been bred that are less likely to catch diseases and die.

Scientists have bred varieties of cereal crops that have more cereal grains, are easier to harvest, or do not catch diseases (Fig. 13.3).

Fig. 13.3 Scientists are breeding maize or sweet corn plants which are more resistant to disease. The upper cob has been damaged by disease; the lower one is healthy.

3 Food and the future

New sources of food

Many other different ways of easing the food problem are being tried. Some people are farming animals that have never been farmed before. These include trout and deer (Fig. 13.4). Scientists have made new kinds of food. One example is **kesp**. This is made of fibres of protein. The protein is obtained from soya beans. The fibres can be built up into chunks and flavoured to taste like meat. Some scientists are trying to make food from oil. They use harmless microbes to change **paraffin**, which is made from oil, into protein. This is then turned into a food (Fig. 13.5).

Fig. 13.4 Part of a trout farm.

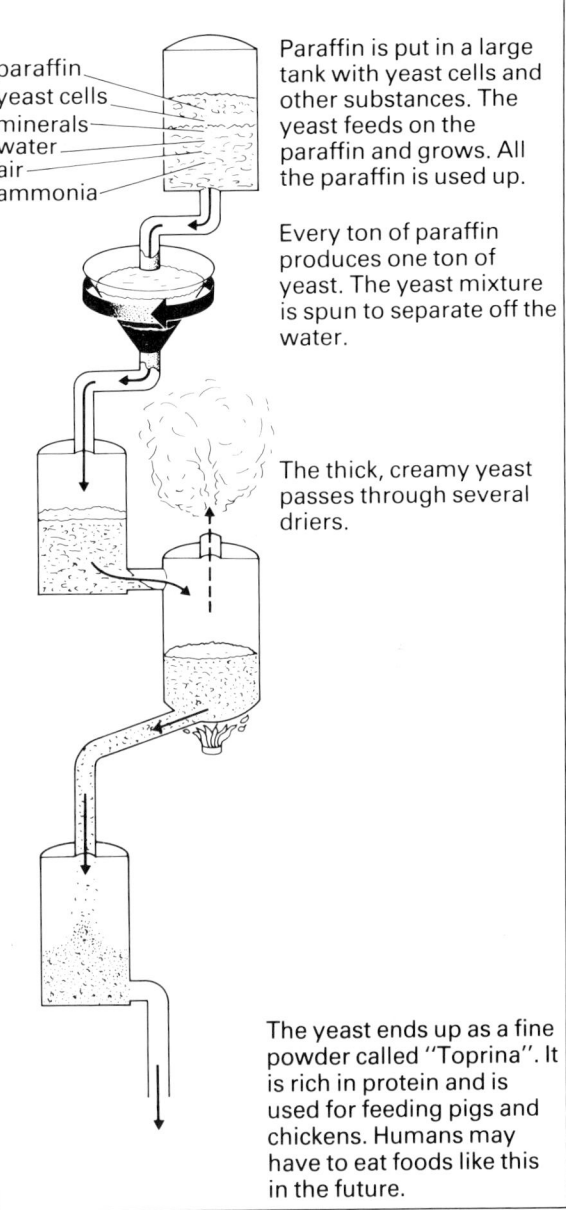

Paraffin is put in a large tank with yeast cells and other substances. The yeast feeds on the paraffin and grows. All the paraffin is used up.

Every ton of paraffin produces one ton of yeast. The yeast mixture is spun to separate off the water.

The thick, creamy yeast passes through several driers.

The yeast ends up as a fine powder called "Toprina". It is rich in protein and is used for feeding pigs and chickens. Humans may have to eat foods like this in the future.

Fig. 13.5 Converting paraffin into food.

Summary: Food and the future

* Chlorophyll is green.
* Plants trap light energy to make sugars and starch. This is photosynthesis.
* Plants make proteins and fats.
* Plants store food.
* Food and energy is passed from plants to animals along food chains and webs.
* Some plants are cultivated for food.
* Others are used to supply drugs, chemicals and other materials.
* Animals are kept to supply humans with food and other products.
* The world population is increasing so food supplies must improve.
* Energy is 'wasted' as food is passed along a food chain.
* Crop production is increased by using fertilisers, pesticides, better machinery and by teaching farmers to use new methods.
* Scientists are improving breeds of plants and animals.
* Industry is developing food from oil.

4 Energy release

14 Breathing

Why you must breathe

You start to breathe the moment you are born. A human can live for at least five weeks without food, and for five days without water. A human can only live five minutes without the **oxygen** in air. To stay alive, plants and animals need to release energy in every cell of their bodies. The energy release from food is known as **respiration**. Oxygen is needed to release this energy from food. We obtain oxygen from the air around us when we **breathe**.

How often do you breathe?

You breathe in air through your nose and mouth. You breathe out through the same openings. When resting you breathe in and out about 15–18 times a minute. Each breath is about 500 cm^3 of air (about as much as in a milk bottle). In one day you breathe a very large amount of air (Fig. 14.1). If you start to walk or run, you take deeper breaths. You may also breathe more quickly. When you are active you take in more air. This gets more oxygen into the body for energy release.

A person can be made to breathe in special smoke. An **X-ray** of the chest will show up the smoke. The air you breathe in goes through many tubes inside your chest (Fig. 14.2).

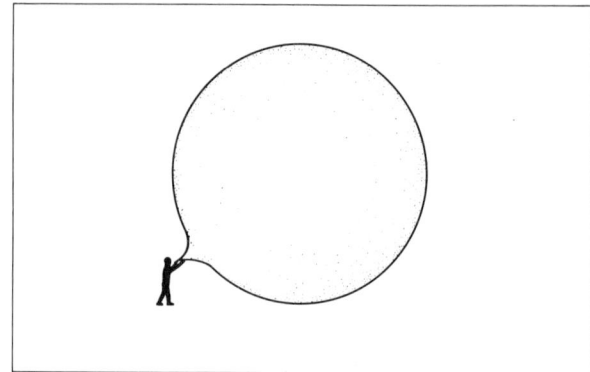

Fig. 14.1 *In a day, the air breathed out by a man would blow up an enormous balloon.*

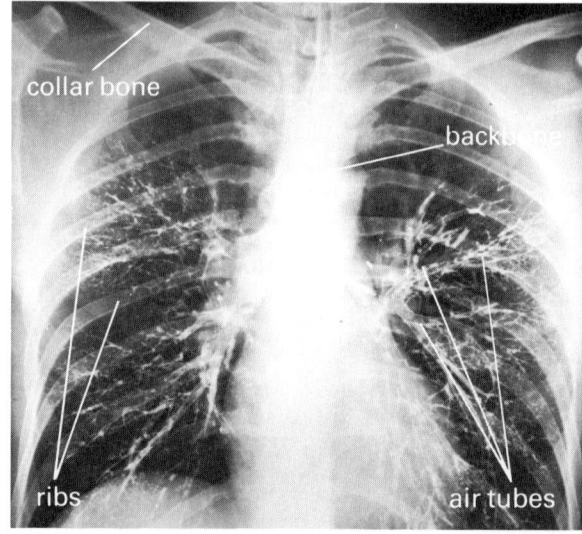

Fig. 14.2 *Some of the air tubes inside the chest.*

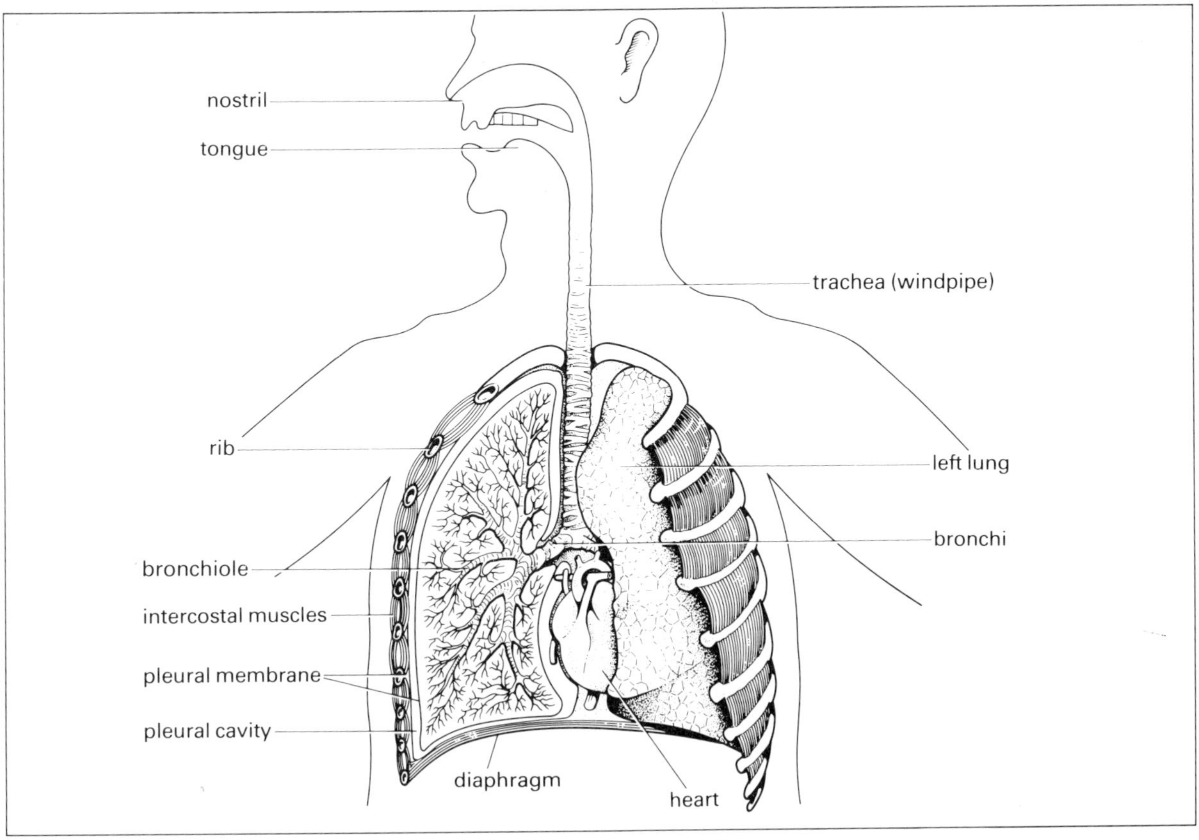

4 Energy release

Fig. 14.3 The human breathing or respiratory system.

Air tubes

When you breathe in, air goes down the **windpipe** or **trachea**. This tube divides into two. Each of these tubes is called a **bronchus**. One bronchus goes into each of your elastic **lungs**. Each bronchus branches many times forming tubes that get finer and finer (**bronchioles**). At the tips of the finest tubes are **air sacs** or **alveoli** (Fig. 14.3). An air sac is like a cluster of tiny 'balloons'. It has very narrow blood vessels around it (Fig. 14.4). An air sac has very thin, moist walls. So a gas can pass easily from inside the air sac across into the blood. Also a gas can easily pass out of the blood into the air sac spaces. Each lung is a complicated collection of fine tubes (bronchioles), air sacs (alveoli) and narrow blood vessels.

The lung is not a smooth balloon. The tiny air sacs have lots of folds. This means there is a *large surface*. A large surface area means lots of gas can pass through at the same time. If unfolded the surface of one lung could cover one tennis court.

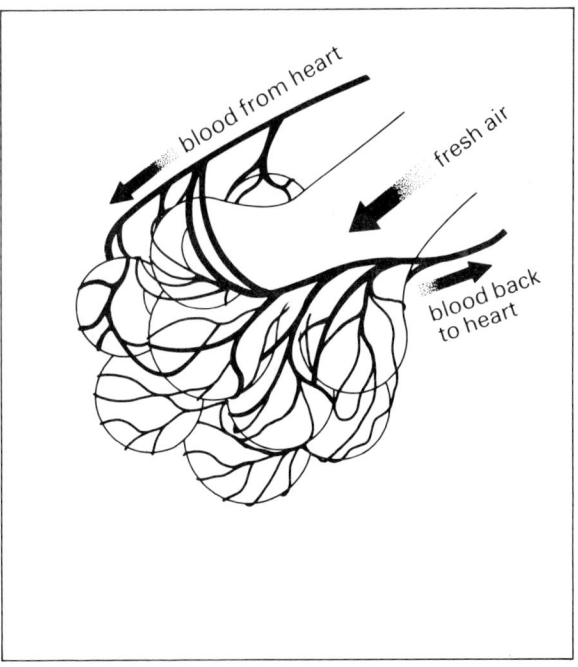

Fig. 14.4 An air sac or alveolus.

4 Energy release

15 Breathing – How is it done?

The movements of breathing

Breathing is different from many of the body's other movements. We can alter how quickly or how deeply we breathe for a short time. As soon as we stop thinking about it, our breathing goes back to normal.

When we breathe the chest changes shape. These changes are brought about by movements of the **ribs** and **diaphragm**. Muscles work to move these. The **intercostal muscles** raise the rib cage. The diaphragm is a tough, dome-shaped sheet. It is made up of tendon in the middle. Around this there is a band of diaphragm muscles. These pull the diaphragm down (Fig. 15.1).

Breathing in (inhaling or inspiring)	Breathing out (exhaling or expiring)
rib cage raised	rib cage lowered
diaphragm lowered	diaphragm raised
chest gets bigger	chest gets smaller
lungs inflate	lungs deflate

Fig. 15.2 Comparing breathing in and breathing out.

Inhaling or breathing in, happens in the following way. The diaphragm is pulled down and the rib cage is pulled upwards. The space inside the chest gets bigger. Air rushes in to fill up the extra space.

Exhaling or breathing out happens when the muscles relax. The diaphragm moves upwards and the rib cage is lowered. The space in the chest gets smaller. Air is forced out of the lungs (Fig. 15.2).

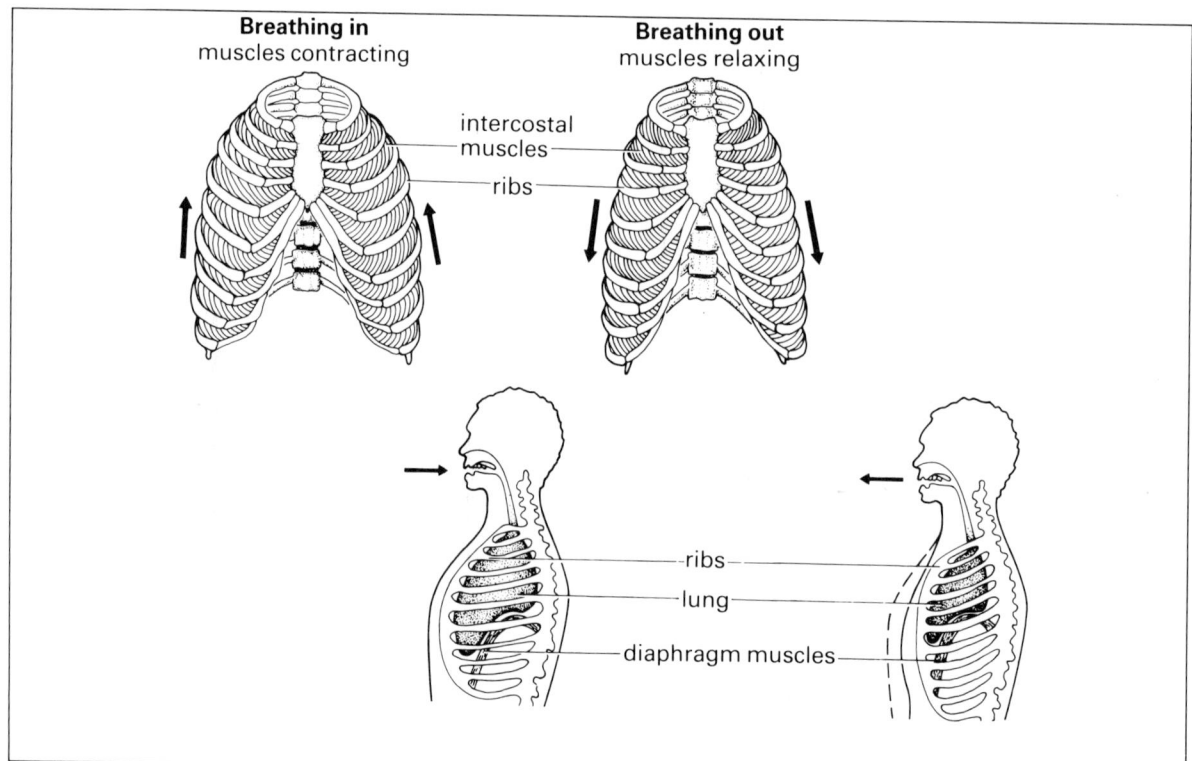

Fig. 15.1 The muscles used in breathing.

4 Energy release

Pleural layers

The lungs are surrounded by two very thin layers – the **pleural membranes**. These have liquid between them and are slippery. The outer membrane lines the rib cage and the diaphragm. The inner membrane forms a lining around the lungs. These slippery 'skins' make a good contact between the lungs and the ribs and diaphragm. The membranes help make smooth breathing movements. They also stop the ribs damaging the lungs (Fig. 15.3).

Making the air moist and warm

The breathing passages (trachea, bronchi and bronchioles) are lined with cells. Some of these lining cells make a slippery liquid called **mucus** (Fig. 15.4). This moistens the air as it is breathed in. The blood vessels around the tubes carry warm blood. This heats up the air. Oxygen in the warm, moist air can then pass through the air sac more easily.

Keeping the lungs clean

Inhaled air may contain dust and 'germs' that could damage the lungs. As the lungs are important organs they must be kept clean. Some of the cells lining the air tubes have small hairs sticking out into the tube (Fig. 15.4). These hairs or **cilia** are always moving. They move in waves and work like a brush. The movement of the hairs sweeps mucus and trapped dirt and germs towards the mouth. The dirty mucus can be blown out of the nose into a handkerchief. Any mucus that gets into the throat is swallowed and goes to the stomach. Germs in the mucus will be killed by the acid in the stomach.

Speech

When air is breathed out it passes between the **vocal cords**. These are in the **larynx** or voice box (Fig. 15.5). The air makes the cords **vibrate** (like the movement of a drum skin when hit). These vibrations produce sounds. The mouth and tongue shape the sounds into words.

Fig. 15.5 *The larynx or voice box and the vocal cords.*

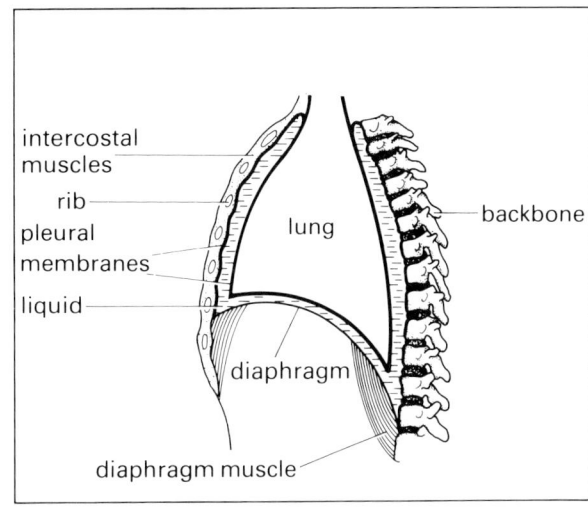

Fig. 15.3 *The position of the pleural membranes.*

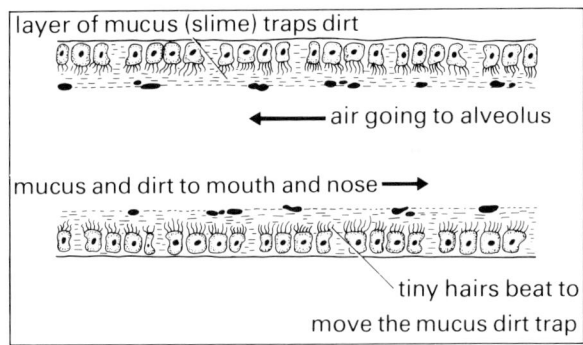

Fig. 15.4 *The lining of the air tubes makes the air warmer and moist. The moving hairs 'sweep out' the dust.*

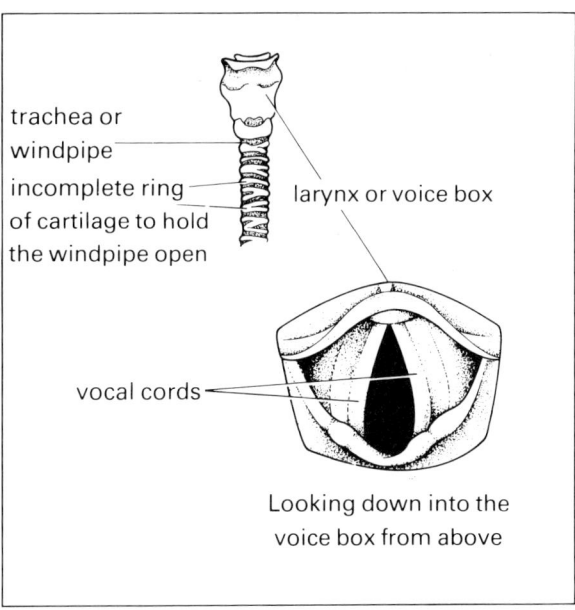

4 Energy release

16 Using oxygen and food

Breathing changes air

Scientists have found that air is a mixture of gases. Air is 20 parts **oxygen** and 79 parts **nitrogen**. The remaining one part is gases such as **water vapour** and **carbon dioxide**. Breathed in and breathed out air contain different amounts of the gases. Breathing changes the air (Fig. 16.1). The changes happen because breathing removes some oxygen from the air. Breathing also puts more carbon dioxide and water vapour into the air.

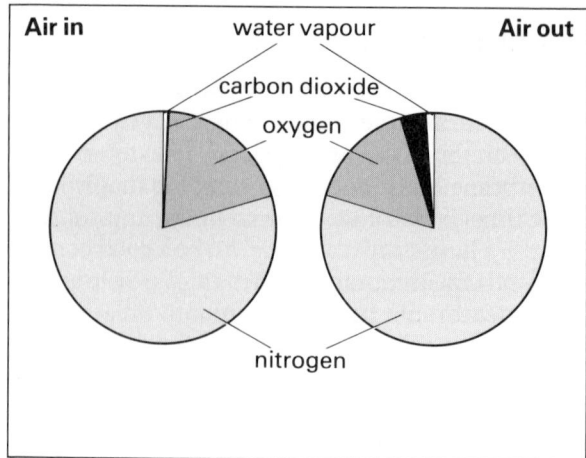

Fig. 16.1 The air is changed inside the lungs.

Energy and engines

Energy is needed if living cells are to stay alive. Humans use energy for many activities. The human body is like an engine and all engines need fuels. Coal is a fuel that can be used to make an engine work (Fig. 16.2). The stored energy in coal is released when it is burnt. As the coal burns, it uses up oxygen from the air. Burning produces carbon dioxide and water vapour (steam). The more work the engine does, the more fuel and air it will need. If there is not enough oxygen near the fire the fuel will stop burning or will not be fully burnt.

Fig. 16.2 An engine that uses coal for fuel.

Food is our fuel

All food contains stored energy. Food is the fuel of plants and animals. If a peanut is held in a flame for a while, it starts to burn. The peanut keeps burning even when the flame is taken away (Fig. 16.3). Burning releases the stored energy in the chemicals of the peanut as heat and light energy. In the body, stored energy in food can be released and used in many different ways.

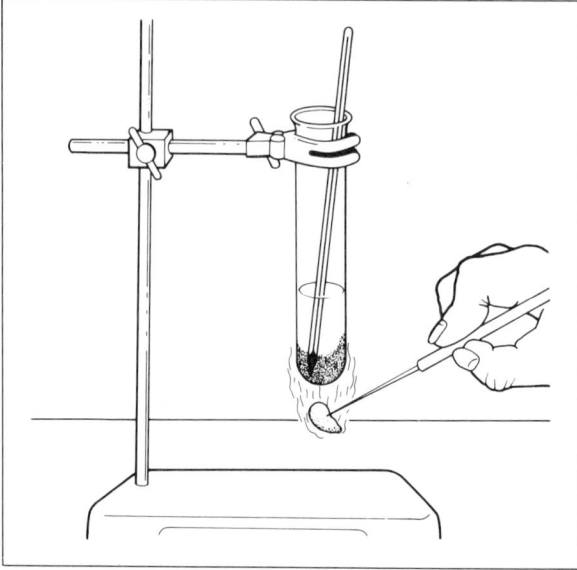

Fig. 16.3 A burning peanut releases heat energy.

4 Energy release

Respiration is releasing energy

Respiration is a process that goes on all the time in every cell of the body. Sugar from the food we eat is 'burnt up' slowly using oxygen from air. This releases the energy to keep our bodies working (Fig. 16.4). The sugar and oxygen are used up inside the cells. Two chemicals are made – carbon dioxide and water. The carbon dioxide is breathed out. Some of the water may be used by the cells of the body.

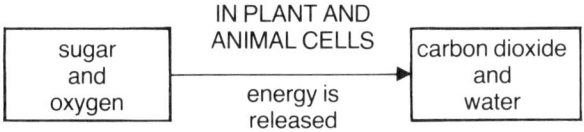

Because oxygen is used in this process it can be called **aerobic respiration**. ('Aero' comes from the Greek word meaning air.) The chemical changes that happen in respiration show why exhaled air is different from inhaled air. There are tiny organelles inside every cell called **mitochondria**. These are needed for respiration.

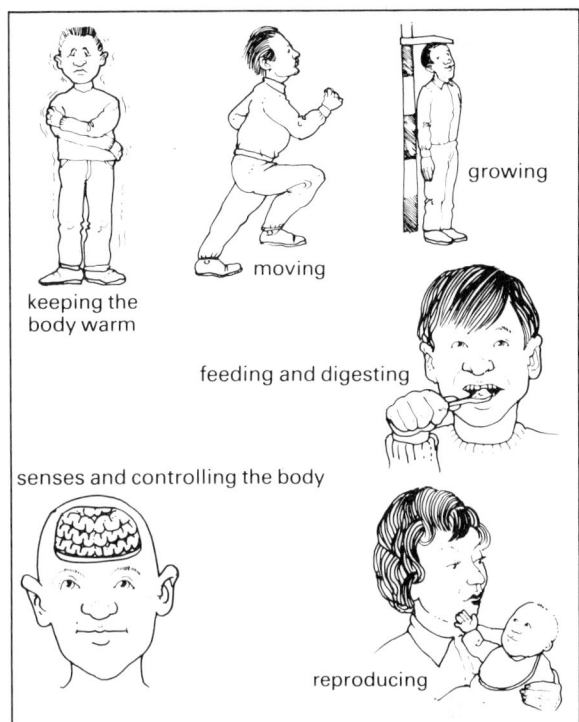

Fig. 16.4 *How the energy from respiration is used.*

Transporting and exchanging gases

Respiration uses oxygen and makes carbon dioxide. These gases must be moved round the body by the blood (Fig. 16.5). The oxygen must be taken from the lungs to all the cells of the body. Oxygen gets into the blood in the lungs. It passes through the air sac walls into the narrow blood vessels. **Red blood cells** carry the oxygen. When these come near to tissue cells needing oxygen, the oxygen leaves the red blood cells. Oxygen moves across into the tissue cells. Respiration uses up the oxygen. Carbon dioxide and water are produced when energy is released from food. The carbon dioxide passes out of the cells and enters the blood **plasma**. It is carried back to the lungs. The carbon dioxide passes across into the air sac spaces and is breathed out.

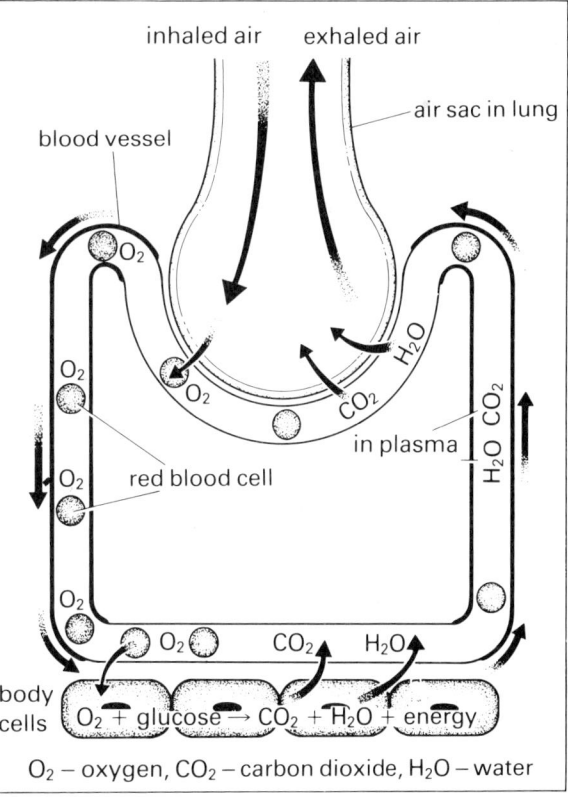

Fig. 16.5 *Gases move round the body.*

4 Energy release

17 Getting enough energy

The amount of energy in foods

The stored energy in food can only be used by the body cells when it has been released by respiration. Energy is measured in **kilojoules** (**kJ**). It has been found that 1 g of pure carbohydrate has 16 kJ of stored energy, 1 g of fat has 39 kJ of stored energy and 1 g of protein has 23 kJ. Sugar is the main fuel of respiration. Starch and fats can be changed into sugar. So starch and fat can also be used as fuels.

Carbohydrates and fats are the foods used to supply energy. The energy values of some foods are given in Fig. 7.4 on page 15. Proteins supply the chemicals needed for growth. The more a human works and grows, the more energy is needed. The amount of energy needed by the body changes during a lifetime. It also depends on the person's sex and job (Fig. 17.1). If anyone eats a lot of food much of it will not be used in respiration. This extra food is built up into fat and stored. A person may become seriously overweight or obese (see page 14).

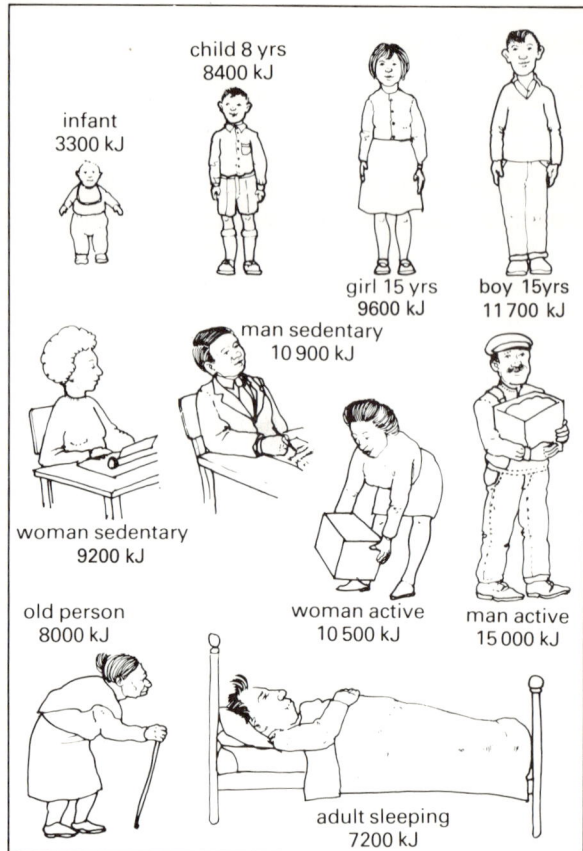

Fig. 17.1 *Different people use up different amounts of energy in a day. The numbers are kilojoules (kJ).*

Energy and exercise

When you have been very active you can become 'puffed out' or 'winded'. Two things cause this. You have used all the oxygen that gets to your cells from your lungs. Also you are releasing energy from food without using oxygen. Food has not been fully burnt by this process of **anaerobic respiration**. This leads to a build up of a chemical called **lactic acid**. Lactic acid makes muscles become tired. If there is a lot of lactic acid in the cells, the muscles will ache and stop working. The body will not move properly. This is why a runner who is not in condition may have to stagger across the finishing line (Fig. 17.2). It takes time for lactic acid to be broken down in the body. When it is, energy is released and carbon dioxide and water are formed. A hot bath or massaging the muscles speeds up the breakdown of lactic acid.

Fig. 17.2 *The athlete in second place is struggling to keep up. He may be suffering from a greater build up of lactic acid than the man in front.*

4 Energy release

Breathing in high places

At the tops of mountains, the amount of oxygen in the air is less than at sea level (Fig. 17.3). When people visit cities in high places, they find it harder to breathe. They may get out of breath even when sleeping. However if they live in such places for a week or two, they get used to the air. They get **acclimatised**. Their bodies have made more red blood cells. Their blood can carry more oxygen, enough to supply all the cells of the body.

Breathing underwater and in space

Astronauts and deep sea divers work where there is no air. They must be given air from cylinders (Fig. 17.4).

When a diver works at a great depth, the water presses heavily on the chest. This makes it harder to breathe. To help the diver, air is supplied at high pressure. At these high pressures, the nitrogen in the air dissolves in the diver's blood. This does not matter as long as the diver is deep down. But, if he comes up too quickly, nitrogen will come out of the blood as bubbles. This makes it painful to move or bend the limbs. The diver has the **bends**. The diver will die if bubbles form in the fine blood vessels of the brain and heart.

Fig. 17.3 A mountaineer may have to use breathing apparatus.

Fig. 17.4 Astronauts may take air with them for breathing. The 'umbilical cord' carries the air supply. The astronaut also has an emergency oxygen supply pack in case the cord is damaged.

Summary: Energy release

* Respiration releases energy from food.
* Oxygen needed for this process is obtained when we breathe in air.
* Breathed in air goes to the lungs.
* Air is inhaled when the diaphragm is lowered and the rib cage is raised.
* Air is exhaled when the diaphragm rises and the rib cage drops.
* Breathed in air is warmed and moistened.
* Breathed in air contains dust so the air passages must be kept clean.
* Sounds for speech are made when we breathe out.
* Air is a mixture of nitrogen, oxygen, carbon dioxide and water vapour.
* When oxygen is used to release energy from food, it is aerobic respiration. This process also makes carbon dioxide and water.
* Oxygen is carried from the lungs to the body cells in the blood.
* Carbon dioxide is carried from the body cells to the lungs in the blood.
* Oxygen and carbon dioxide are exchanged in the lungs.
* Different foods release different amounts of energy.
* If not enough oxygen is present, foods do not release all their energy. This happens in anaerobic respiration.

5 Digestion

18 Food must dissolve

Making food dissolve

Humans use food for energy and to build up and repair the body. Food must be changed inside the body so that it can be used in these different ways. The nutrients in the food must be able to **dissolve**. They can then move through the gut wall and be carried all round the body by the blood. Many of the nutrients are inside the cells of the plants and animals that make up our food. Our bodies must break open the cells to get at the nutrients. Vitamins and minerals dissolve in water. The very large molecules of protein, fats and some carbohydrates do not dissolve. To make these nutrients dissolve the body has to break these molecules into smaller ones. The breakdown of large molecules into smaller ones that dissolve is called **digestion**.

The alimentary canal

Food is digested inside the gut or **alimentary canal** (Fig. 18.1). The gut is a tube about 8 metres long. It is coiled to fit inside the body. Most of the coils are in the **abdomen**. Each part of the alimentary canal has a different job to do. The journey of the food from the mouth to the **anus** is slow and may take 1½ days.

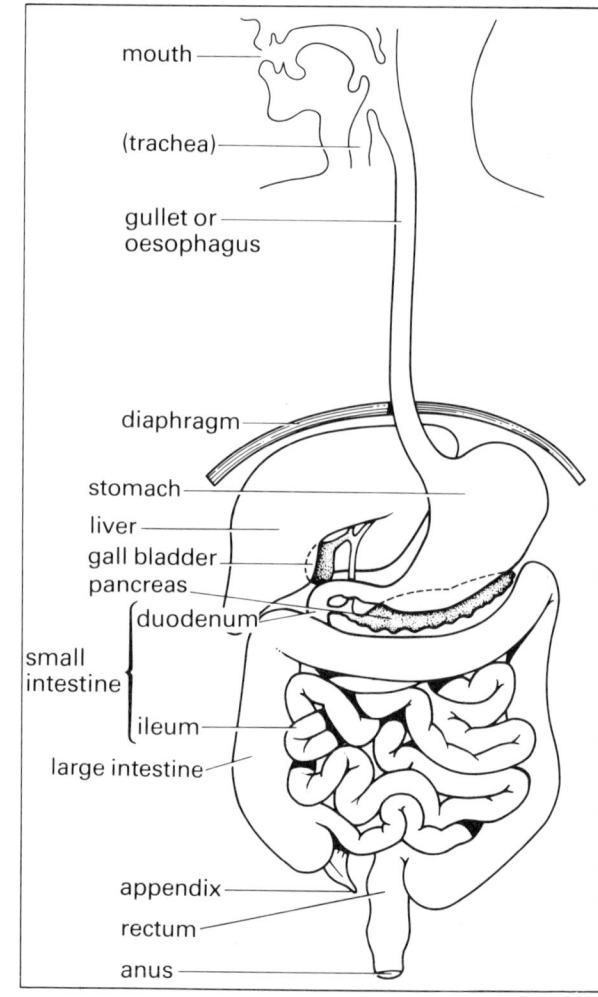

Fig. 18.1 *The human digestive system or alimentary canal.*

5 Digestion

19 Teeth

We need our teeth

Without teeth we could not talk properly and we could eat only liquids or very soft baby foods (Fig. 19.1).

Parts of our teeth are alive. They are not all the same shape. They are grouped in the mouth so they can do their different jobs well. Their main job is to get the food into smaller pieces. Then digestion can begin and the food is easier to swallow.

Fig. 19.1 Life without teeth!

Structure of teeth

All the teeth are built in the same way (Fig. 19.2). The **crown** is the part of the tooth you see. On the outside is a layer of hard **enamel**. This protects the softer parts inside and makes a strong surface for biting.

Underneath the enamel is a layer of **dentine**, which is similar to bone. In the middle there is a space – the **pulp cavity**. The space contains blood vessels and nerves. The blood vessels bring food and oxygen to the cells of the dentine layer. The nerve endings are sensitive to changes in temperature and some chemicals. When the nerve endings are touched, the pain of toothache occurs.

The **root** of the tooth is fitted into a hole or **socket** in the jaw bone. **Cement** and **elastic fibres** help to hold the tooth in place. They also absorb shock – they 'bounce' when teeth bite against something hard. This helps to stop teeth breaking.

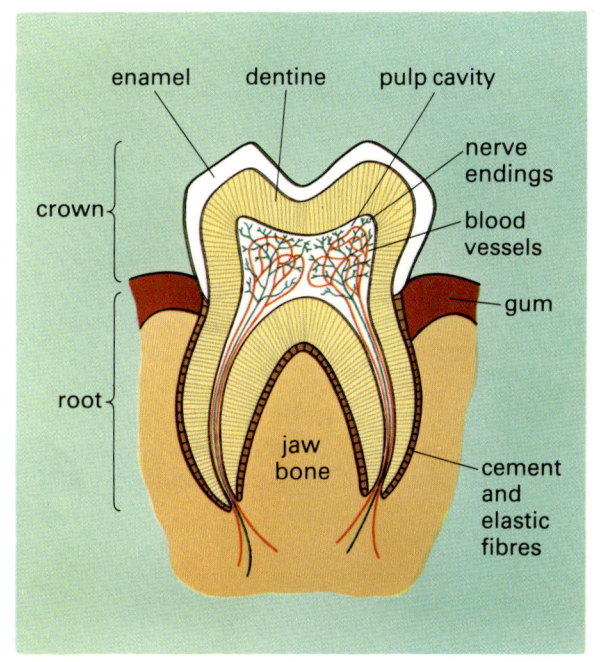

Fig. 19.2 The structure of a tooth.

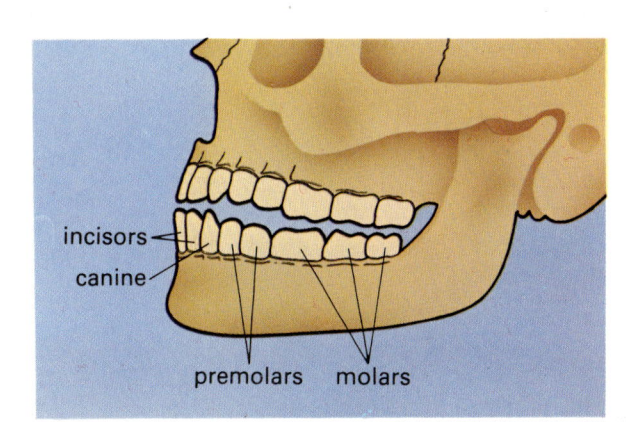

Fig. 19.3 The teeth of an adult.

5 Digestion

The four types of teeth

Incisors are chisel-shaped. They are used for biting off small pieces from a large lump of food. **Canines** are a bit longer and more pointed. They are used for biting and tearing off pieces of food. The cheek teeth have broad, bumpy surfaces for grinding food into a paste. **Premolars** have two blunt points or **cusps**. The large **molars** at the back have four cusps. When we eat, the teeth meet to form a good biting, grinding or chewing machine (Figs. 19.3 and 19.4).

Two sets of teeth

Babies have no teeth when they are born. After a few months they start 'teething'. This is their first set of teeth growing up through the gums. Incisors usually grow or **erupt** first. As the teeth grow so do the jaws. Eventually the child gets 20 teeth. This first set is the 'milk' or **deciduous** teeth.

The milk teeth fall out as they are pushed by the second set growing below (Fig. 19.5). These are the **permanent** teeth and they have to last about 60 years. If we lose a permanent tooth it cannot be replaced – except by a false one! An adult should have 32 teeth. Teenagers and some adults may have only 28 teeth. This is because their 'final' molars or **wisdom teeth** have not grown.

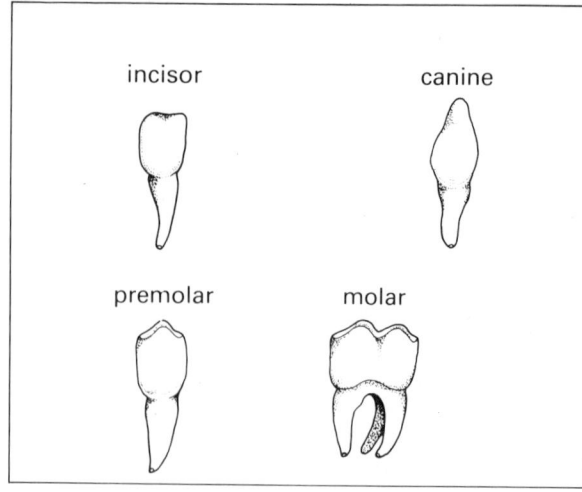

Fig. 19.4 The four types of teeth.

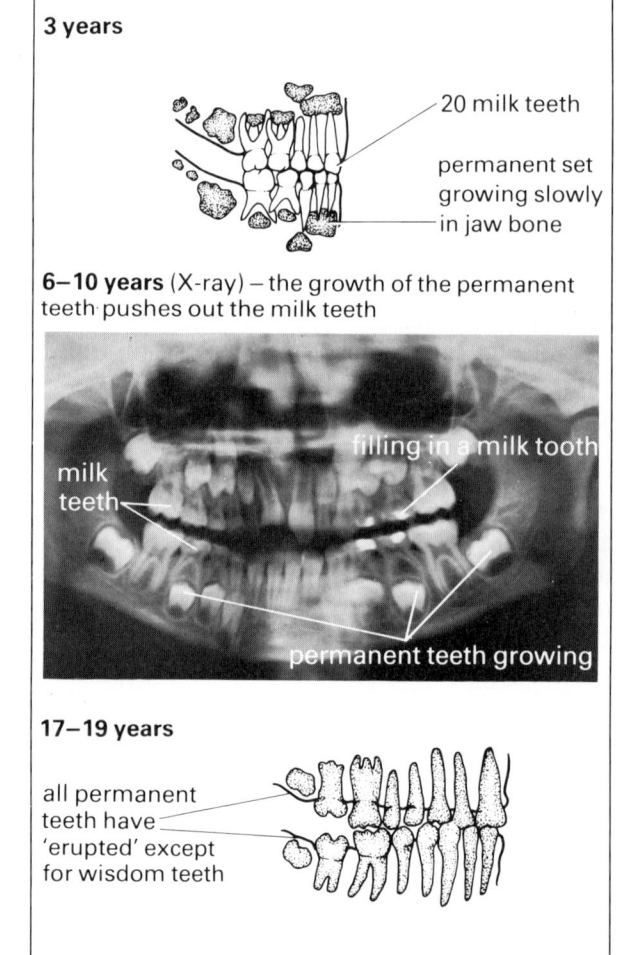

Fig. 19.5 The growth of the two sets of teeth.

5 Digestion

Tooth decay

Sadly only two people in a hundred have perfect teeth. Most of us have some bad or missing teeth. **Tooth decay** happens when the bacteria that live in the mouth feed on food trapped between the teeth. This mixture of bacteria and trapped food is called **plaque**. The bacteria make acids which dissolve the enamel (Fig. 19.6). If the teeth are not cleaned properly the acids may dissolve a hole through the enamel to the dentine. Enamel, unlike many parts of the body, cannot repair itself. A dentist can drill out the decay and fill the hole with metal or acrylic plastic. If the tooth is not filled, the decay will reach the pulp cavity. When it reaches the nerve ending toothache will start. If the decay carries on, an **abscess** may form. This is a collection of bacteria and **pus**. An abscess often forms at the root and bacteria may enter the bloodstream.

Plaque can also cause **gingivitis**. This is a gum disease. If it is not treated, the gums bleed and the teeth become loose in their sockets.

Keeping teeth healthy

You can do the following to keep your teeth healthy (Fig. 19.7).
1 Have fewer sugary foods and drinks, especially sweets.
2 Eat more foods like milk and cheese. These contain the **calcium** and **phosphate** needed to build strong teeth.
3 Use toothpaste with **fluoride**. This makes the enamel stronger and more likely to stand up to decay.
4 Clean teeth regularly – if possible after every meal. The bristles of the toothbrush must not be too sharp as this might damage the gums. Brushing should massage or rub the gums as well as teeth.
5 Visit the dentist regularly. Six-monthly visits will mean the dentist can make sure the decay gets no further than the enamel layer.

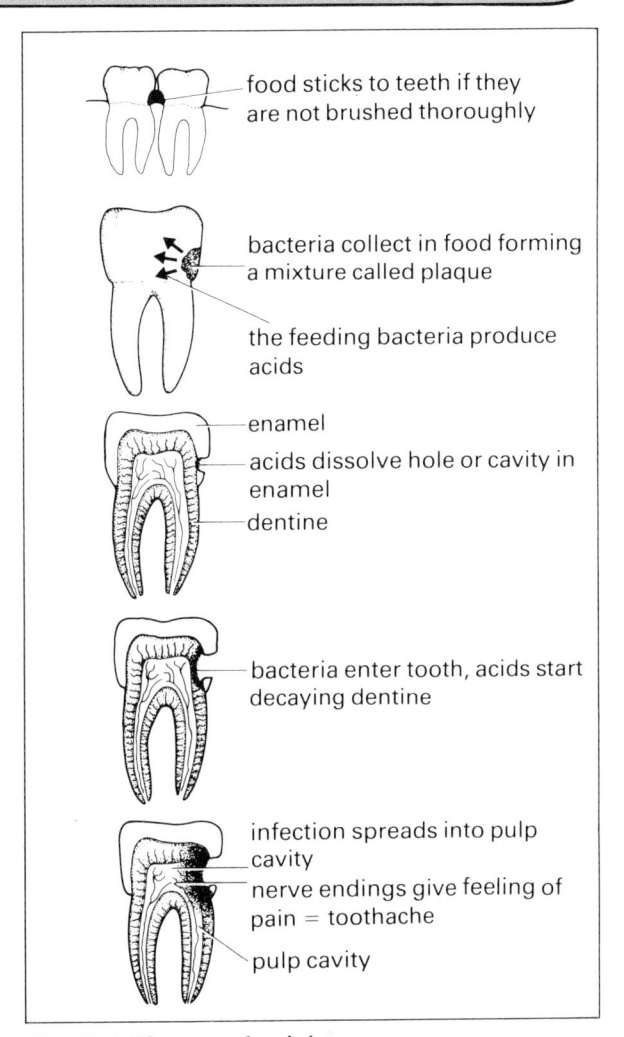

Fig. 19.6 The stages of tooth decay.

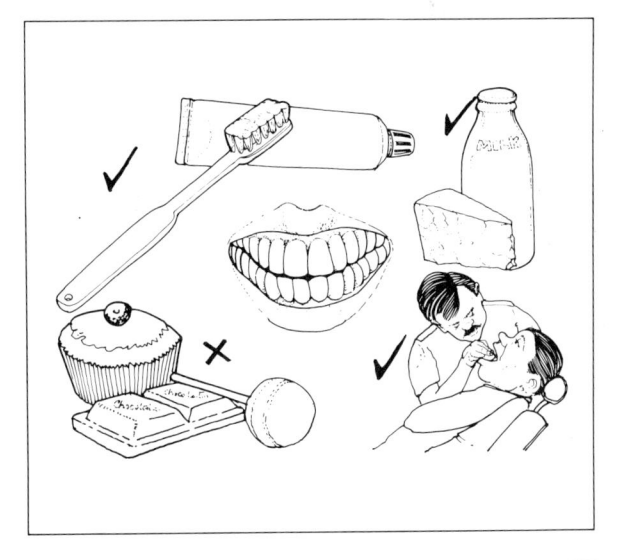

Fig. 19.7 How to keep your teeth.

5 Digestion

20 Enzymes

Speeding up digestion

The breakdown of large molecules into smaller ones happens very slowly in nature. In the gut it is speeded up by chemicals known as **enzymes**. Enzymes are found in **digestive juices**. These liquids are made by cells that are grouped together in **glands**. The juices pass along tubes or **ducts** into the space inside the gut (Fig. 20.1).

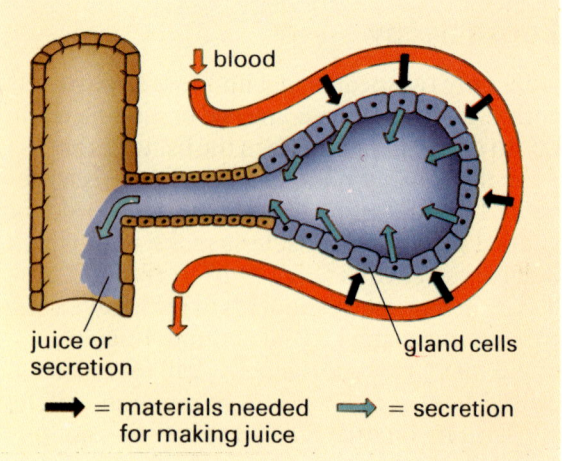

Fig. 20.1 Cells in glands make digestive juices containing enzymes.

Different types of enzymes

Enzymes are grouped according to the type of nutrient they help digest. The nutrient that an enzyme works on is the **substrate**. The smaller, soluble, food molecules that are made are the **products**. There are three main groups of digestive enzymes. Their substrates and products are shown in Fig. 20.2. (The names of most enzymes end in 'ase'.)

How enzymes work

Enzymes come in many shapes. They work in a very complicated way. A simple model should make it clearer (Fig. 20.3). Imagine that a large nutrient molecule is like a lock that can be broken into two parts. The enzyme is the key that fits this lock and breaks it apart. Each lock needs its own key. It is the same for enzymes. A protease will only work on protein molecules. It will not break up a starch molecule.

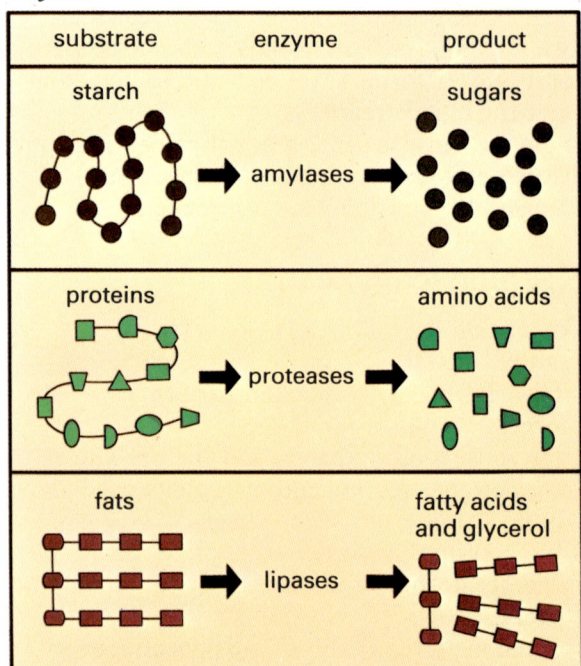

Fig. 20.2 The digestive enzymes.

Fig. 20.3 An enzyme works like a key in a lock.

5 Digestion

Enzymes at work

When you eat a slice of bread you put a lot of starch into your gut. **Amylases** start breaking up the starch into sugar. At first there is a lot of starch present. After a short time all the starch is gone as it has been broken down into sugar. At first there was no sugar in the gut. At the end of the reaction there is a lot of sugar. The two graphs in Fig. 20.4 show these changes.

Enzymes can be damaged

All enzymes are made from proteins and proteins can be damaged easily. If an enzyme is damaged it will not work; a twisted key will not fit its lock. Enzymes are affected by heat. They work most quickly at 37 °C (body temperature). This is the **optimum** or best temperature. At warmer or cooler temperatures they work more slowly (Fig. 20.5). If enzymes are heated to 60 °C they are destroyed or **denatured**. Then they do not work at all.

Enzymes are all damaged by **acids** and **alkalis**. Each enzyme is designed to work at a certain level of acidity. If the acidity changes, an enzyme will work more slowly.

Heat and acids affect enzymes because they change the shape of an enzyme.

Main points about enzymes

All enzymes:
1 are made by living cells,
2 are made from protein,
3 speed up reactions but are not changed themselves,
4 work on one type of substrate,
5 are affected by changes in temperature and acidity.

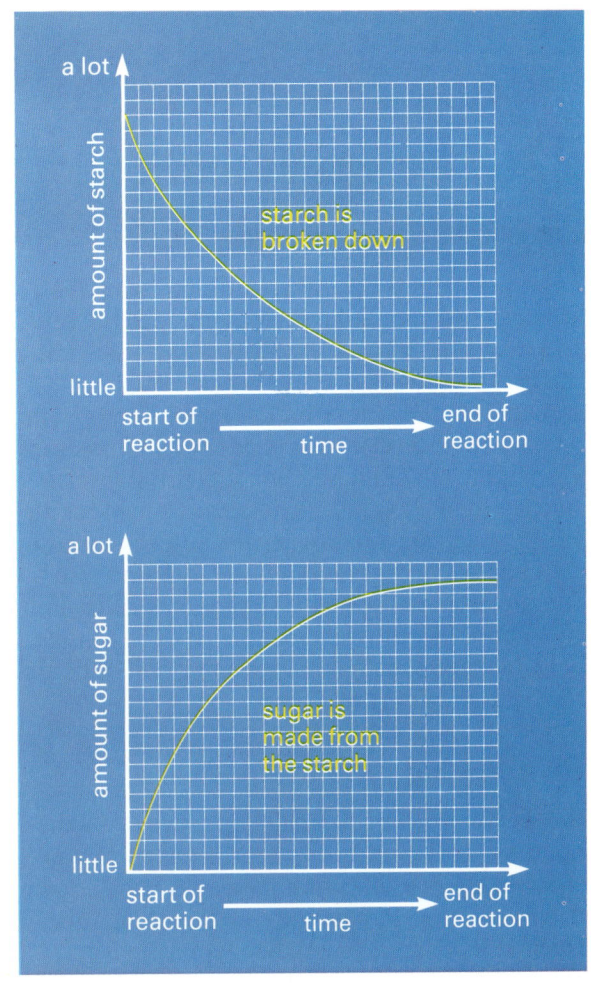

Fig. 20.4 Graphs showing what happens when starch is mixed with an amylase.

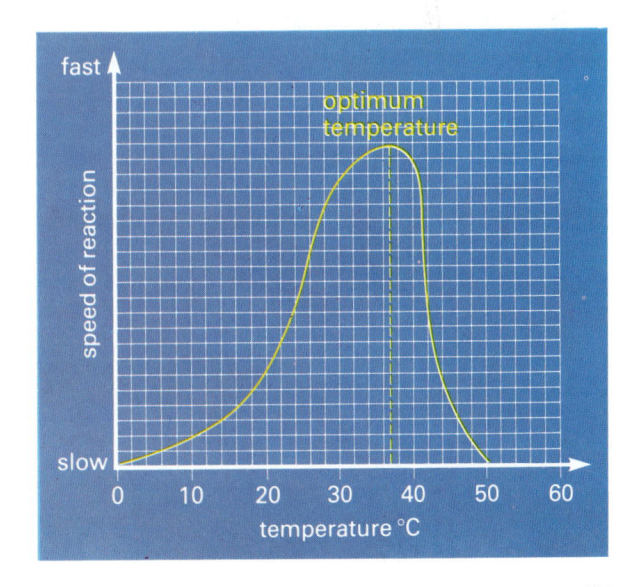

Fig. 20.5 A graph showing that human digestive enzymes work best at 37 °C.

5 Digestion

21 The gut at work

Digestion in the mouth

Digestion begins in your mouth. Chewing food shreds it into smaller pieces, tears open the cells and mixes the food with **saliva** or spit. Saliva is the first digestive juice and is made by the **salivary glands** (Fig. 21.1). (One of these can be felt as a lump inside your cheek.) Saliva contains an enzyme (an amylase), which helps digest starchy food. If you suck a lump of bread for a while, it will start to taste sweet. This is because starch is being digested into sugar. Saliva also contains **mucus**, which is slimy. This helps food slip along the gut when swallowed. The **tongue** helps to shape the food into a small ball or **bolus** that is easy to swallow.

Swallowing

When you swallow, a small flap moves over the opening to the windpipe. This is the **epiglottis** (Fig. 21.2). It makes sure food does not go down the wrong way and get into the breathing tubes. If some food lands on the flap, you cough and splutter to jerk the food away.

Moving food through the gut

Food does not fall down through the gut. It is pushed by the muscles in the gut wall. Muscles behind the food ball work and make the gut narrower. The food is squeezed along to the next part where the muscles are relaxed. This process is **peristalsis** (Fig. 21.3). You cannot control this movement. The bolus of food is pushed down the **gullet** (or **oesophagus**) until it reaches the **stomach**.

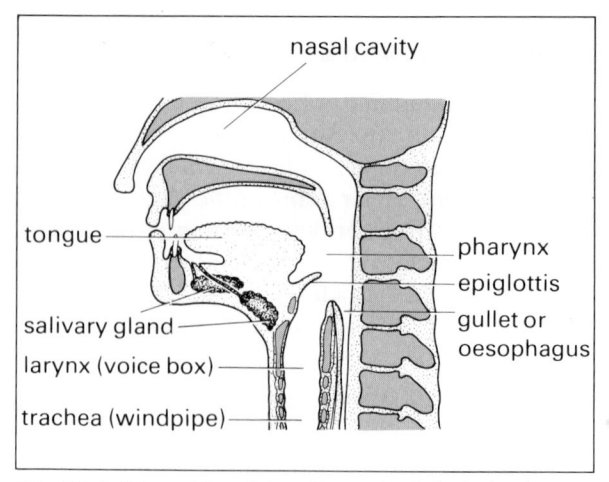

Fig. 21.1 *The position of the salivary glands in the head.*

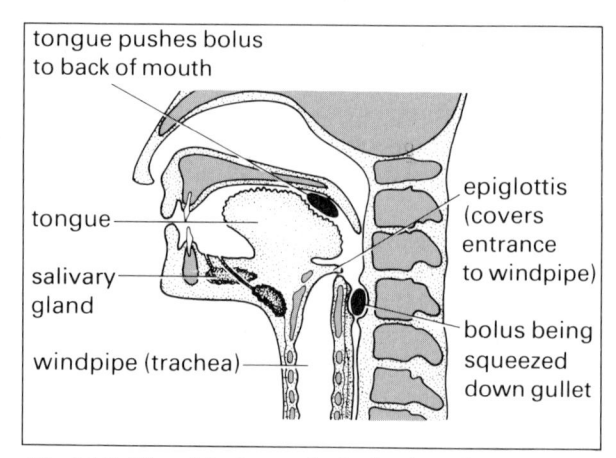

Fig. 21.2 *The epiglottis stops food going down the wrong way.*

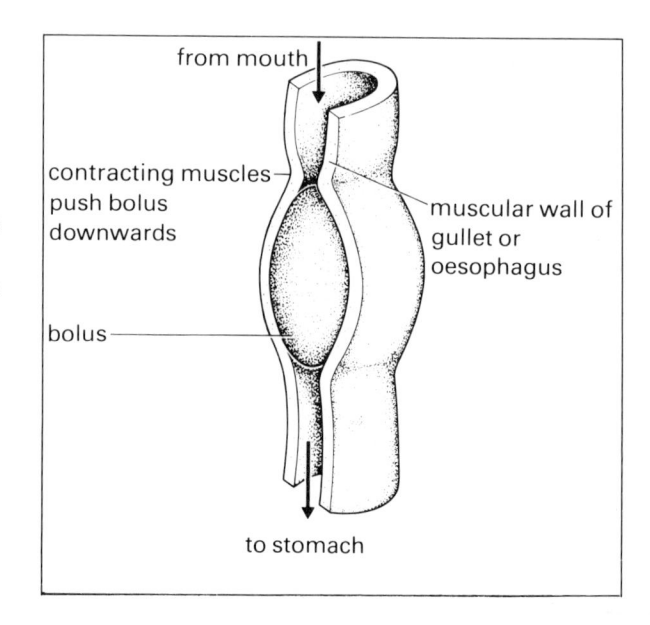

Fig. 21.3 *Peristalsis moves food through the gut.*

5 Digestion

The work of the stomach

The stomach is a bag with thick muscular walls (Fig. 21.4). It can expand to hold all the food eaten at one meal. It has rings of muscle at both ends called **sphincter muscles**. These work like elastic bands round the neck of a bag. They trap the food in the stomach for several hours. During this time the muscles of the stomach wall **churn** the food around. The churning can sometimes be heard – when your stomach 'rumbles'!

The churning helps to mix the food with **gastric juice**. This contains **pepsin**. This enzyme is a **protease** which helps digest proteins. In children there is another enzyme, called **rennin**, in gastric juice. This helps to solidify milk. This is important as babies are only fed on milk for several months.

Gastric juice contains **hydrochloric acid**. This kills nearly all the bacteria that may be swallowed with the food. The stomach enzymes work best in very acid conditions.

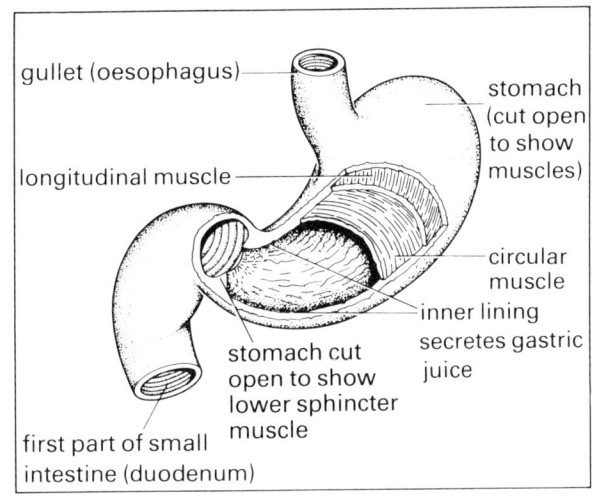

Fig. 21.4 The structure of the stomach.

Into the small intestine

After several hours, most of the food will have been changed into a liquid called **chyme**. The sphincter muscle at the lower end of the stomach opens. Some chyme is squirted into the next part of the gut – the narrow **small intestine**. The first part of the small intestine is called the **duodenum**. In here, the chyme is mixed with **bile** and **pancreatic juice** (Fig. 21.5).

Bile

Bile juice is made by the liver and stored in the **gall bladder**. Bile is like a detergent. It breaks up fat into many tiny droplets. (This is **emulsification**.) It is then easier for **lipases** to digest the fat. Bile also **neutralises** the stomach acid. This makes the conditions less acidic and right for the duodenal enzymes.

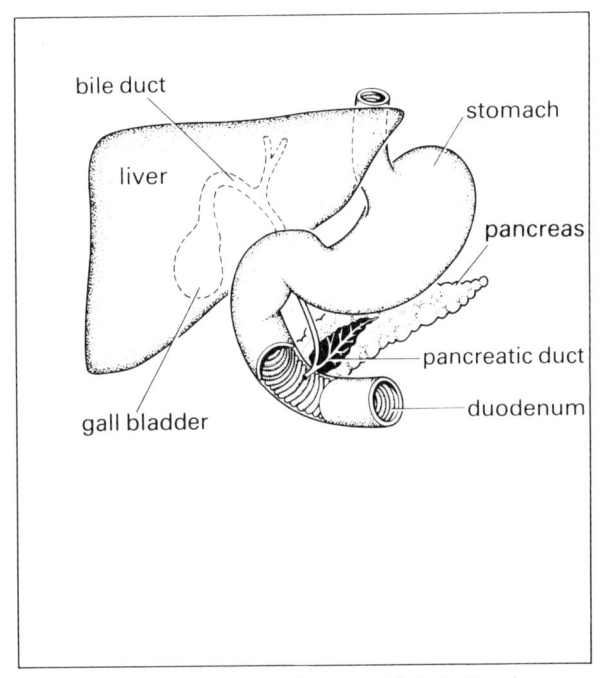

Fig. 21.5 Many organs near the stomach help in digestion.

Pancreatic juice

More enzymes come from the **pancreas** in the pancreatic juice. This contains three types of enzyme – an amylase, a protease and a lipase. These continue the digestion of starch, protein and fat molecules. By the time food leaves the duodenum, the digestion of nutrients is almost finished.

5 Digestion

Intestinal juice

Food is pushed on to the next part of the small intestine, the **ileum**. Glands in the ileum wall make **intestinal juice**. This juice contains more enzymes which will finish the digestion of a meal. All the large nutrient molecules have been broken down into small ones – **sugars**, **amino acids**, **fatty acids** and **glycerol**. These pass across the wall of the ileum. It **absorbs** these chemicals and also some of the water. Absorption is done by the **villi** (Fig. 21.6). These tiny finger-like projections line the inside of the ileum. (Absorption is explained fully on the next page.) Anything left is material that cannot be digested and water. This is pushed by peristalsis into the **large intestine**.

The large intestine

Many foods contain substances which we cannot digest. The cell walls of cabbages, carrots and other plants are made of **cellulose**. Humans cannot digest this. Food that contains a lot of cellulose (**roughage** or **fibre**) makes the intestines work well. The fibre is bulky material which gives the gut muscles something to squeeze against.

The first part of the wide large intestine is the **colon**. The colon absorbs as much water as it can from this remaining material. If it did not do this, valuable water would be lost and the body might **dehydrate** (dry up).

The last part of the large intestine is the **rectum** (bowel). Here cellulose and other undigested materials are turned into solid waste (**faeces**). They are stored before being passed out of the anus or back passage. This is **defaecation**. If you stop defaecating, this condition is called **constipation**. If you defaecate too often and the waste is very liquid, you are suffering from **diarrhoea**.

Fig. 21.7 shows what happens to food on its journey from one end of the alimentary canal to the other.

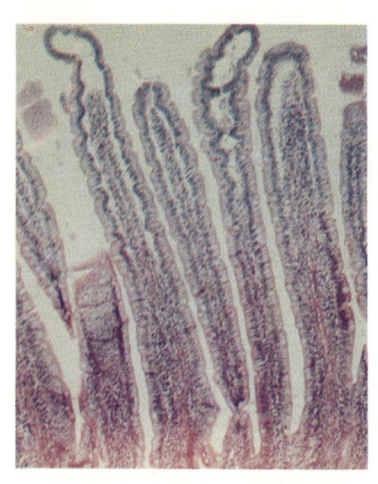

Fig. 21.6 The villi inside the ileum ($\times 80$).

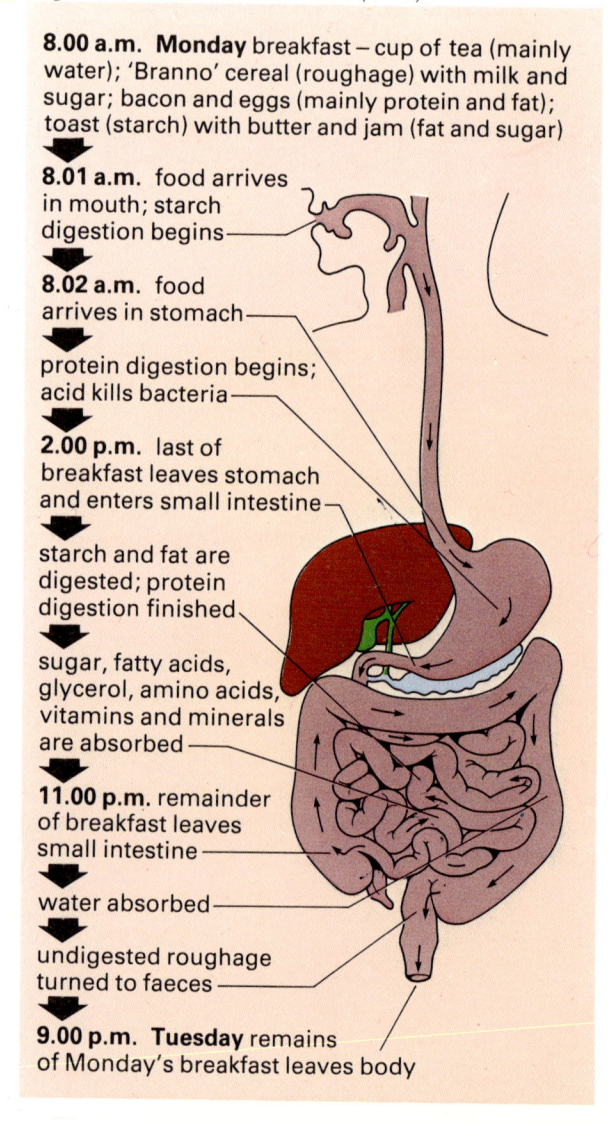

8.00 a.m. Monday breakfast – cup of tea (mainly water); 'Branno' cereal (roughage) with milk and sugar; bacon and eggs (mainly protein and fat); toast (starch) with butter and jam (fat and sugar)

8.01 a.m. food arrives in mouth; starch digestion begins

8.02 a.m. food arrives in stomach

protein digestion begins; acid kills bacteria

2.00 p.m. last of breakfast leaves stomach and enters small intestine

starch and fat are digested; protein digestion finished

sugar, fatty acids, glycerol, amino acids, vitamins and minerals are absorbed

11.00 p.m. remainder of breakfast leaves small intestine

water absorbed

undigested roughage turned to faeces

9.00 p.m. Tuesday remains of Monday's breakfast leaves body

Fig. 21.7 A timetable of events in the gut. The times taken for each stage depend on the size and type of meal eaten.

5 Digestion

22 Absorption

Moving the food chemicals

After digestion, the nutrient molecules are small and **soluble** (able to dissolve). The walls of the alimentary canal are like a barrier through which these chemicals must pass. Some of the molecules move through automatically by **diffusion** (see page 65). Energy is needed to pull other molecules across the gut barrier. This is **active transport**. The movement of food molecules through parts of the gut wall is called **absorption**.

The wall of the ileum

Digested nutrients are absorbed through the walls of the gut – mainly in the ileum. The inside surface of this is covered with tiny finger-like projections (Fig. 21.6). Each one is a **villus**. There are abut five million villi and each is about one millimetre long. They move up and down. The villi increase the amount of lining surface in contact with the digested food.

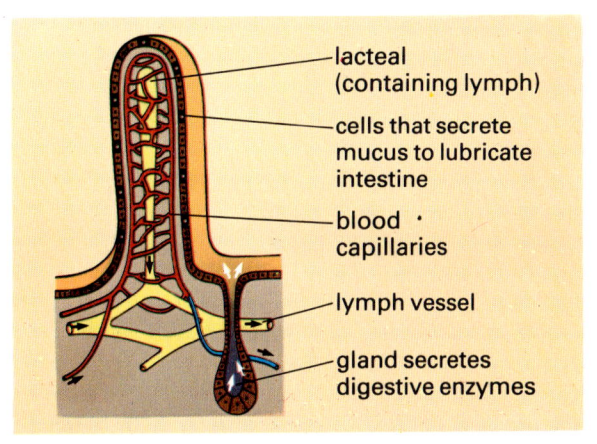

Fig. 22.1 The parts of a villus.

Inside a villus

A villus has a thin outer surface. Below there is a net of fine blood vessels or **capillaries**. Inside the network of capillaries there is a single dead-end tube. This is a **lacteal**. The lacteal is filled with a liquid called **lymph** (Fig. 22.1).

Sugars and amino acids move through into the blood capillaries of each villus. The absorbed nutrients dissolve in the blood **plasma**. They are carried to the **liver** in the **hepatic portal vein**. Fatty acids and glycerol pass into the lacteal and are carried away in the lymph along **lymph vessels** (Fig. 22.2).

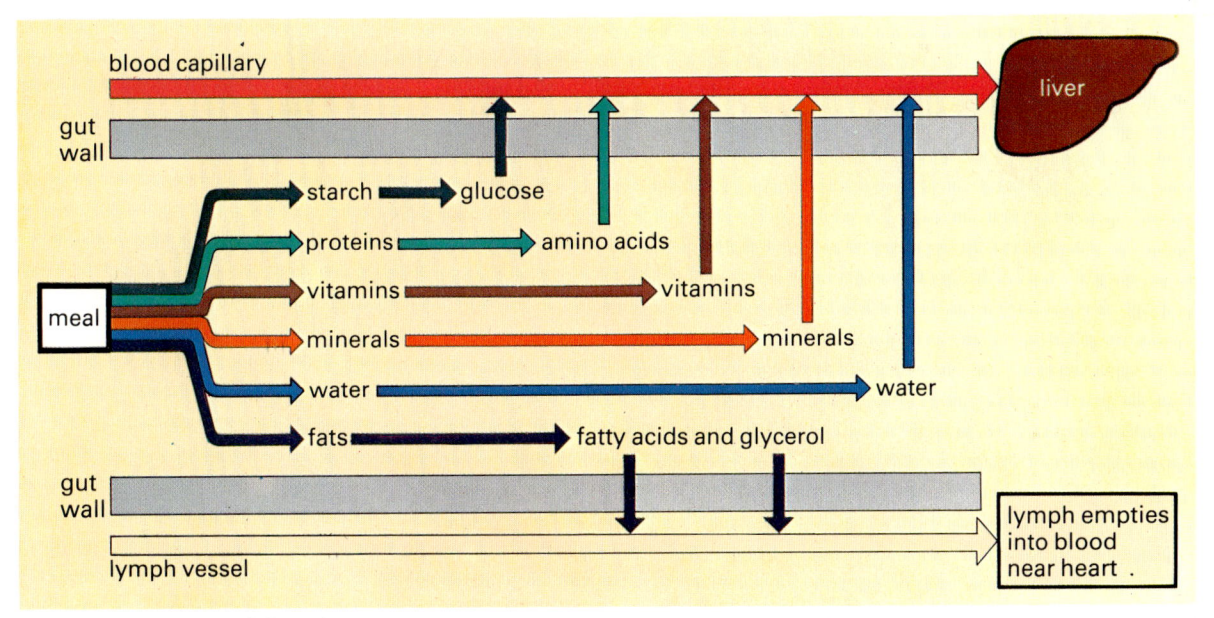

Fig. 22.2 A summary of absorption.

5 Digestion

23 Where the food goes

The liver and food

The liver stores sugars particularly **glucose**, by changing them into **glycogen**. Amino acids which are not needed by the body are broken down in the liver or **de-aminated**. The 'amino' part which contains nitrogen, is made into **urea**. This substance is harmful to the body in large amounts. So, it is sent to the **kidneys** to be passed out of the body (Fig. 23.1) in the urine.

Movement of the lymph

Fatty acids and glycerol are carried away from the ileum in the lymph. Eventually lymph is poured slowly into the large blood vessels going into the heart (Fig. 23.2). In this way, the fatty acids and glycerol 'by-pass' the liver, which could not deal with them in sudden large amounts.

Using the nutrient chemicals

The digested, absorbed nutrients soon reach the living cells that need them. Glucose is used in respiration to give energy. Amino acids are used to build cells and make substances like enzymes. Fatty acids and glycerol are used to give energy or stored in fat cells. Vitamins and minerals help to control some of the body's processes.

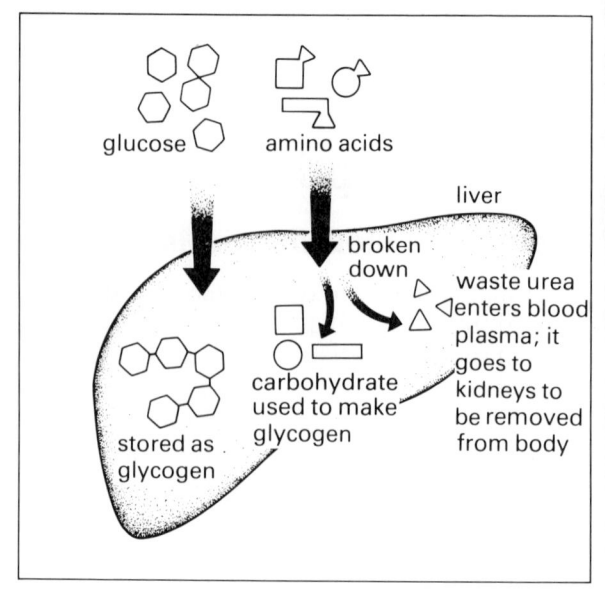

Fig. 23.1 The liver can store glucose as glycogen and break down unwanted amino acids.

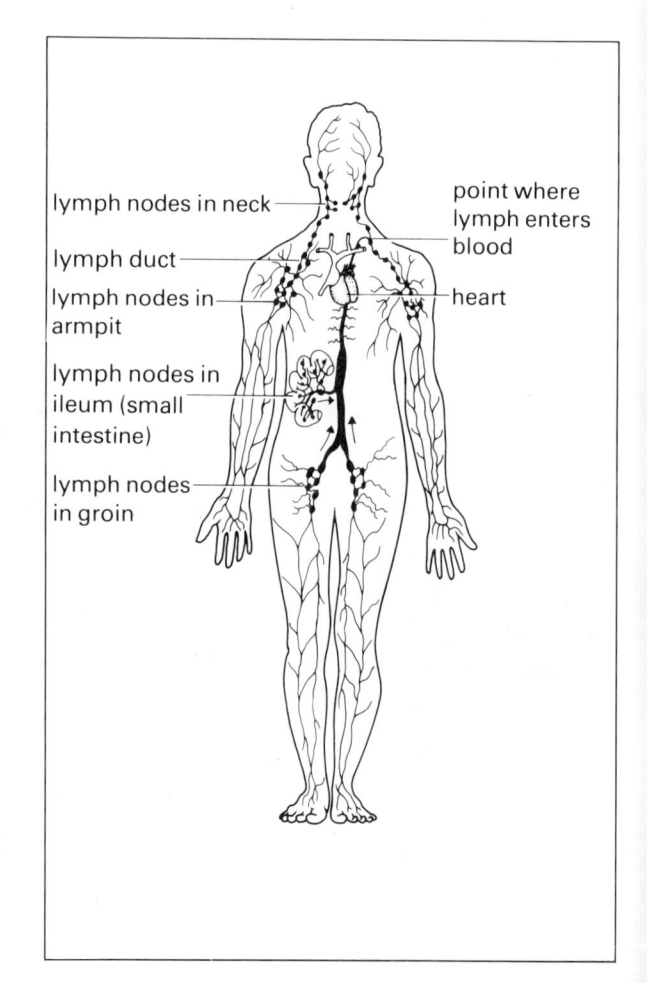

Fig. 23.2 The human lymph system. Lymph vessels take fatty acids and glycerol to the blood stream.

5 Digestion

Name of part	Glands present	Juice made	Substances in juice	Effect of substances on gut contents	Other events in this part of gut
mouth	salivary	saliva	amylase mucus water	starch → sugars	food chewed and shaped into ball (bolus)
gullet	gland cells in wall	mucus	mucus	lubricates wall of gullet	bolus pushed down to stomach
stomach	gastric	gastric	pepsin acid mucus water (rennin)	protein digestion begins	swallowed bacteria killed by acid
duodenum	liver	bile	bile salts	changes fat to tiny droplets	acid from stomach is neutralised
	pancreas	pancreatic juice	amylase protease lipase	starch → sugars protein → amino acids fat → fatty acids and glycerol	liquid food moved on through gut by peristalsis
ileum	intestinal	intestinal	amylase protease lipase	digestion is finished	glucose, amino acids, fatty acids and glycerol are absorbed
large intestine	gland cells in wall	mucus	mucus	lubricates wall of intestine	water is absorbed; solid waste is stored in last part

Fig. 23.3 An outline of digestion in humans.

Summary: Digestion

* Food is broken down into small molecules to cross the gut barrier.
* The breakdown is digestion.
* Each part of the alimentary canal has a different job.
* Enzymes made by gland cells pass into the gut.
* Enzymes speed up the breakdown of nutrient molecules in food.
* Each nutrient is broken down by a different enzyme.
* The mouth contains teeth which help to open up the cells in food.
* Teeth are grouped to do different jobs.
* All humans grow two sets of teeth.
* The surface of teeth cannot be repaired.
* Acid dissolves enamel causing tooth decay.
* Carbohydrate digestion starts in the mouth.
* When food is swallowed, it goes down the gullet.
* In the gullet and all along the gut, food is pushed along by peristalsis.
* Protein digestion starts in the stomach.
* Fat digestion is started in the duodenum.
* Most digestion is finished off in the duodenum.
* Glucose, amino acids, fatty acids and glycerol are the products of digestion.
* The products pass across the gut barrier in the ileum. This is absorption.
* The liver is the first place most absorbed nutrients go.

6 Transport in the body

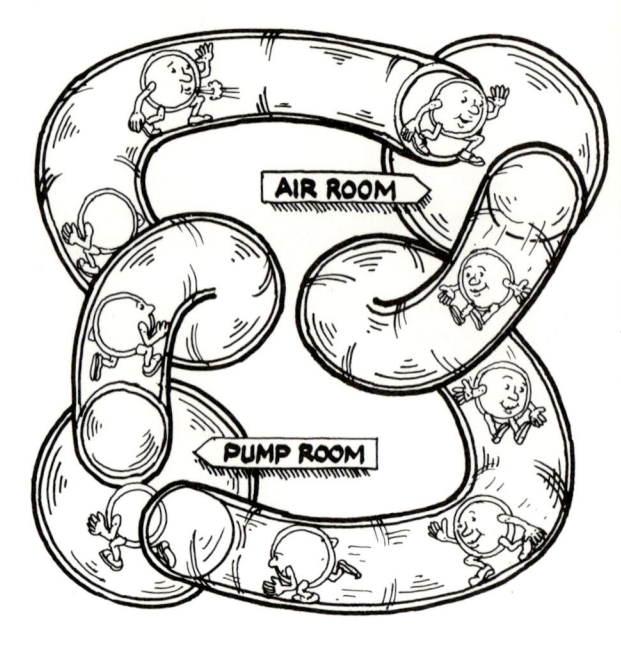

24 Blood

Blood transports chemicals

Food is digested in the gut. The digested food is needed by cells in parts of the body far away from the gut. Digested food must be **transported** (carried) around the body. Oxygen, in breathed in air, passes across an air sac's wall into the blood. Oxygen and digested food are just two things that must be transported. The blood transports these and many other chemicals from one part of the body to another.

Blood is a mixture

Blood can be taken out of the body, treated and left to stand in a glass bottle (Fig. 24.1). The blood settles into two parts. The pale yellow liquid on top is **plasma**. It is made up of water, dissolved chemicals and some **blood proteins**. The deep red layer at the bottom is a mixture of **blood cells**.

If a drop of blood is put on a slide, and smeared into a thin layer, it can be looked at with a microscope. When blood is magnified the blood cells can be seen (Fig. 24.2).

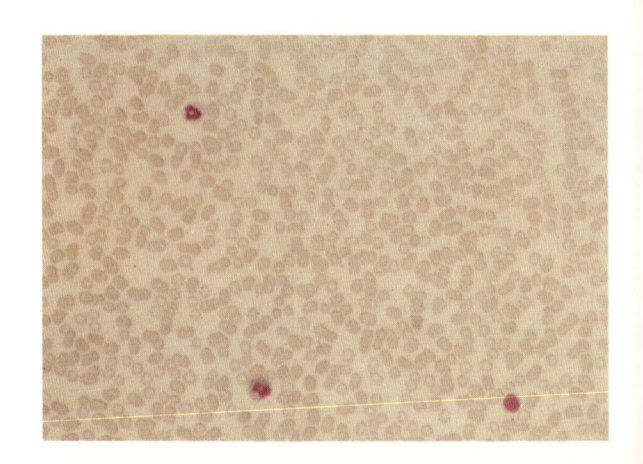

Fig. 24.1 Two bags of blood: the one on the right is fresh and mixed up; the one on the left has been left to stand for a few hours.

Fig. 24.2 A smear of human blood as seen under a microscope (× 200). A purple stain has been used to show up the white blood cells.

6 Transport in the body

Red blood cells

Most of the cells are **red blood cells**. Each one is round and **bi-concave** (meaning both surfaces are hollowed out, Fig. 24.3). The red colour is caused by the pigment **haemoglobin** which is inside the cell. There is no nucleus in the cell, so red blood cells have a short life. A red blood cell lives for about one hundred days. The dead cells are broken up in the liver. New cells are made in the **red bone marrow** of the main body bones. The membrane of the red blood cell is elastic. The cell can change its shape as it moves through narrow tubes (Fig. 24.4). In a drop of blood of 1 mm^3 there are 5 000 000 red blood cells!

The main job of red blood cells is to transport oxygen from the lungs to every cell in the body.

White blood cells

There are several types of **white blood cell**. Each type has a different shaped nucleus (Fig. 24.5). As they have a nucleus, these cells can live for a long time. White blood cells are also made in bone marrow. In 1 mm^3 of blood there are about 6000 white cells.

White blood cells help defend the body against disease. They eat or **engulf** bacteria and produce chemicals to make you **immune** to some diseases (see pages 160 and 161).

Platelets

Platelets are very small cell fragments made in the bone marrow. There are about 250 000 in 1 mm^3 of blood. Each one has a sticky membrane and does not have a nucleus. Platelets help to seal wounds by **clotting** the blood. Clotting is when the blood goes solid near the wound.

Plasma

This watery liquid transports many dissolved food chemicals – glucose, amino acids, vitamins and minerals. It also carries **hormones** and waste chemicals. Plasma transports dissolved carbon dioxide from the body cells back to the lungs. Plasma contains some blood proteins. One is called **fibrinogen**. The proteins in plasma help blood to clot. **Serum** is plasma from which the fibrinogen has been removed.

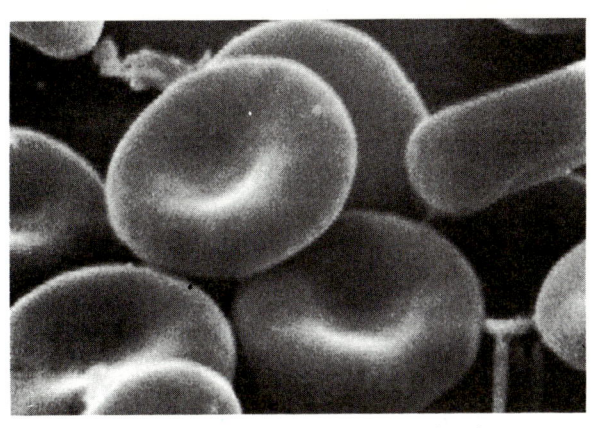

Fig. 24.3 Red blood cells as seen with a scanning electron microscope (× 20 000).

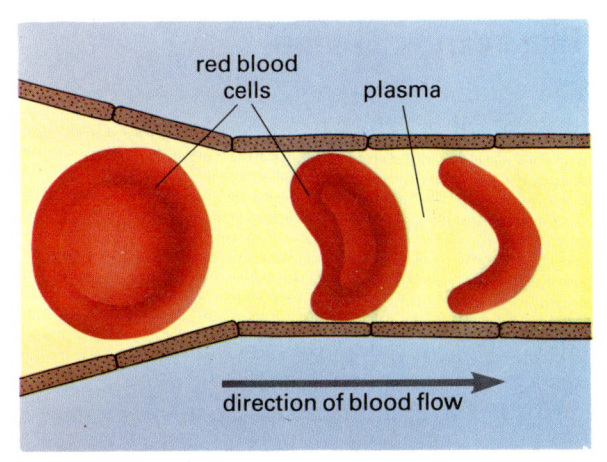

Fig. 24.4 Red blood cells squeezing through narrow blood vessels.

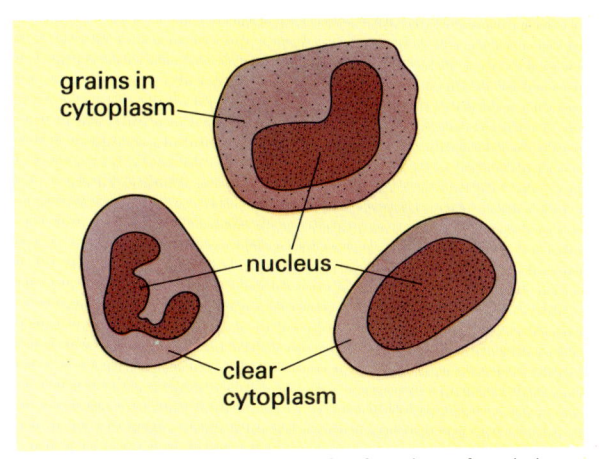

Fig. 24.5 White blood cells are colourless. A purple stain is sometimes used to make them show up (see Fig. 24.2).

6 Transport in the body

25 The heart

Size and position of the heart

The heart of an adult weighs about 300 g and is the size of a clenched fist. The heart is inside the **thorax** or chest, between the lungs. Around the heart there is a tough bag – the **pericardium**. The bag is fixed to the breast bone by strong threads or **ligaments**. These help anchor the heart inside the rib cage (Fig. 25.1).

The heart is a pump

Throughout your life, blood must be pushed through tubes that go to all parts of your body. These tubes are **blood vessels**. The heart is the pump which pushes blood into these tubes. The blood vessels which take blood away from the heart are **arteries**. (The two largest arteries are shown in Fig. 25.2.) The walls of the heart are made of muscle. When the hollow heart is full of blood, these muscles **contract** (shorten). This squeezes the blood out, pushing it into the arteries. The pumping heart can be heard and felt as the **heart beat**. Blood comes back to the heart along **veins**. (Some are shown in Fig. 25.3.)

Cardiac muscle

Heart muscle is known as **cardiac muscle**. When you are at rest, this muscle contracts about 70 times a minute. When exercising the number of beats in a minute goes up. This is because during exercise your body needs more oxygen. Blood carries oxygen, so the heart must pump faster to move the blood more quickly. This gives your arm and leg muscles more oxygen each minute. Cardiac muscle works day and night throughout your life and never get tired! It needs much more food and oxygen than most other parts of the body. The muscle does not take food and oxygen from the blood in the heart. It has its own blood supply – the **coronary arteries**. Waste is taken away from the heart muscle by the **coronary veins** (Figs. 25.2 and 25.3).

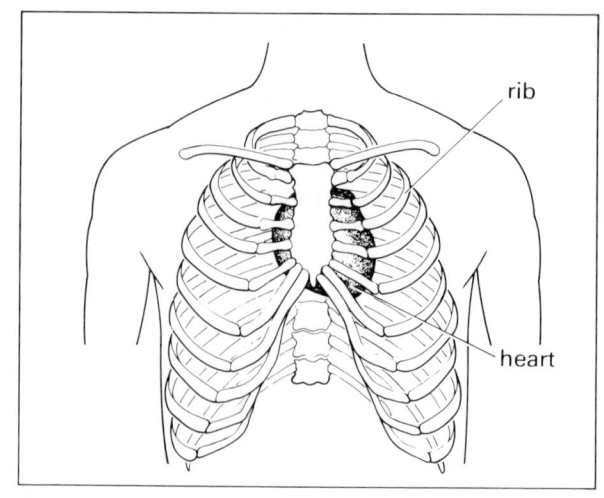

Fig. 25.1 The position of the heart.

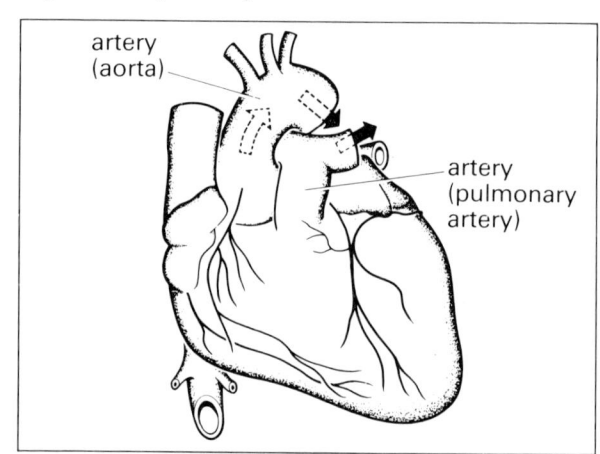

Fig. 25.2 The heart seen from the front.

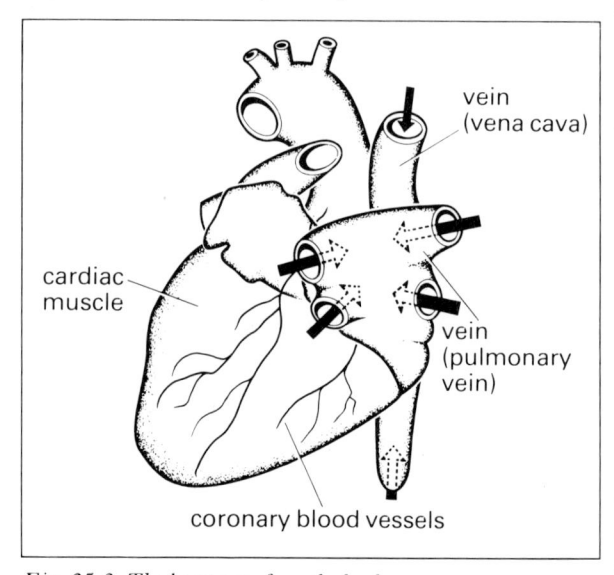

Fig. 25.3 The heart seen from the back.

6 Transport in the body

Chambers in the heart

The heart is divided in half down the middle by a thick wall (Fig. 25.4). The right side pumps blood to the lungs. The left side pumps blood to all other parts of the body. The heart is really two pumps working side by side. Each pump has a top space or **chamber**. This receives blood from veins and is called an **atrium**. The lower chamber on each side is a **ventricle**. This pumps blood out of the heart through arteries. So there are four chambers in the heart.

Each day your heart pumps blood through 100 000 miles of blood vessels. That is the same distance as a journey round the world four times!

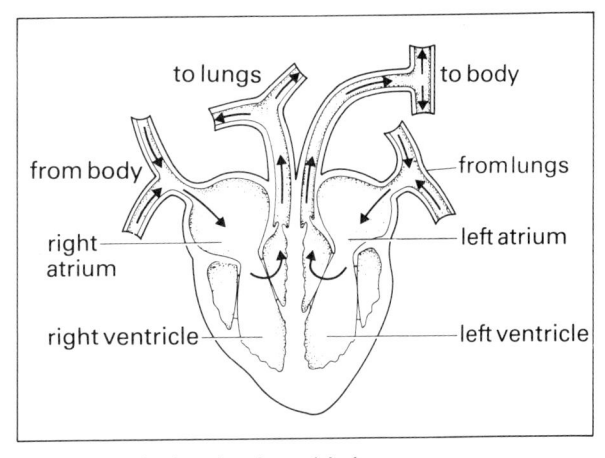

Fig. 25.4 The four chambers of the heart.

Valves in the heart

Between the atrium and ventricle on each side, there are **valves**. These are tough flaps. The edges of the flaps are joined to the ventricle wall by **cords** (Fig. 25.5). The valves can open and close. When open, they let blood go through in one direction only (from atrium to ventricle). When closed, they stop blood flowing backwards. The work of these valves is shown on the next two pages.

There are other valves at the places where arteries leave ventricles. These valves look like half-moons, so they are called **semi-lunar valves**. Like heart valves, the semi-lunar valves let the blood move in one direction only (from ventricle to artery).

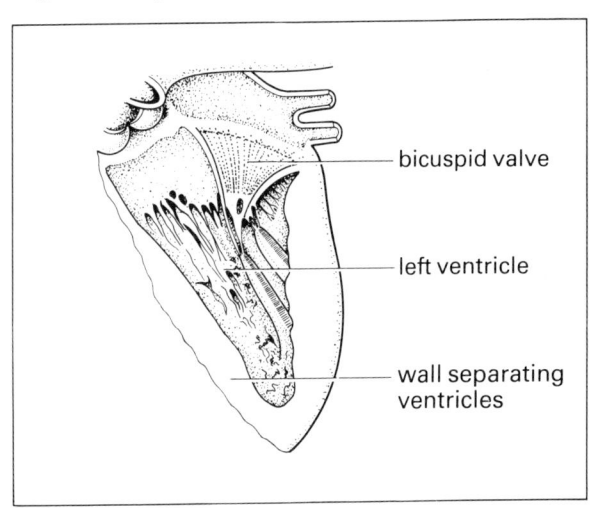

Fig. 25.5 A heart valve.

Listening to the heart

A doctor or nurse listens to the human heart with a **stethoscope** (Fig. 25.6). Two sounds can be heard with this instrument – 'lub-dup' . . . 'lub-dup' . . . 'lub-dup'. The 'lub' sound is heard when the main heart valves slam shut. The 'dup' sound is the sound of the semi-lunar valves closing.

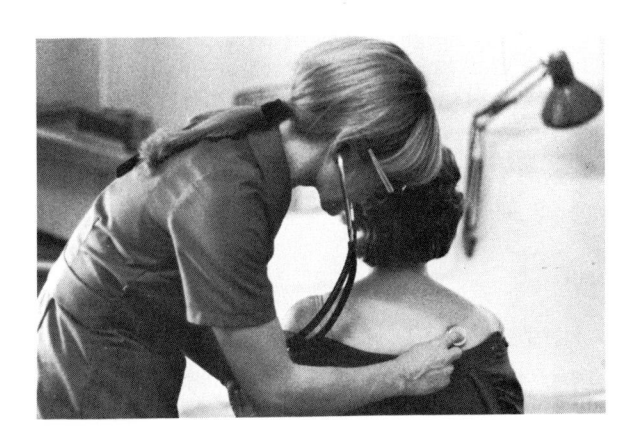

Fig. 25.6 A nurse using a stethoscope.

6 Transport in the body

26 The heart at work

The right side of the heart

The heart is two pumps working together. The right side pumps blood to the lungs to get oxygen (Fig. 26.1).

Deoxygenated blood

Deoxygenated blood carries very little oxygen and a lot of waste carbon dioxide. This blood comes from all parts of the body to the heart. Two large veins, the **venae cavae** bring blood to the right side of the heart. The blood pours into the **right atrium**. It is then sucked down through the open valve into the **right ventricle**. During this time, the muscle of the ventricle is relaxed. This period is called **diastole**.

Contraction

The heart muscle of the ventricle **contracts** or shortens suddenly. This period is called **systole**. The contraction makes the ventricle walls press inwards on the blood inside. The **tricuspid valve** is slammed shut so no blood goes back into the right atrium. The walls of the right ventricle force the blood out up the **pulmonary artery**.

To the lungs

The pulmonary artery divides into two. One branch goes to each lung. As the blood flows through the lungs it picks up a supply of oxygen. At the same time the waste carbon dioxide leaves the blood. It goes into the air sacs and is breathed out.

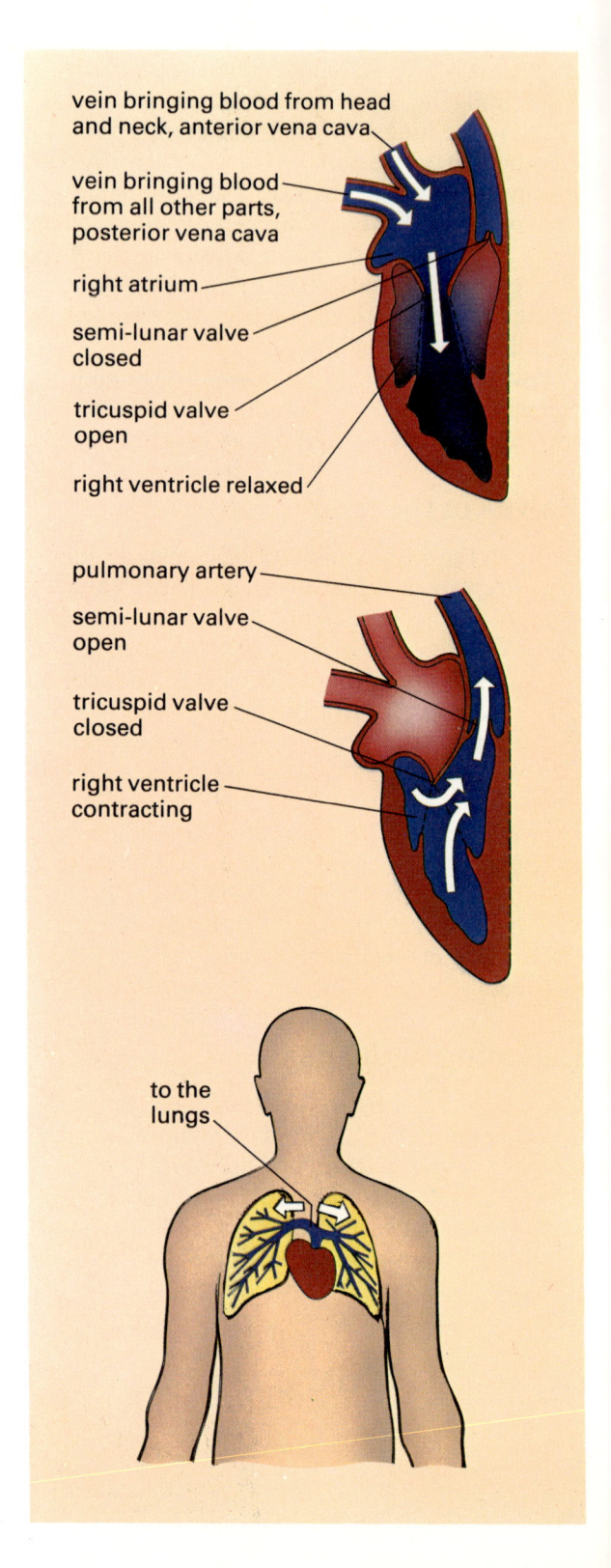

Fig. 26.1 *The work of the right side of the heart.*

6 Transport in the body

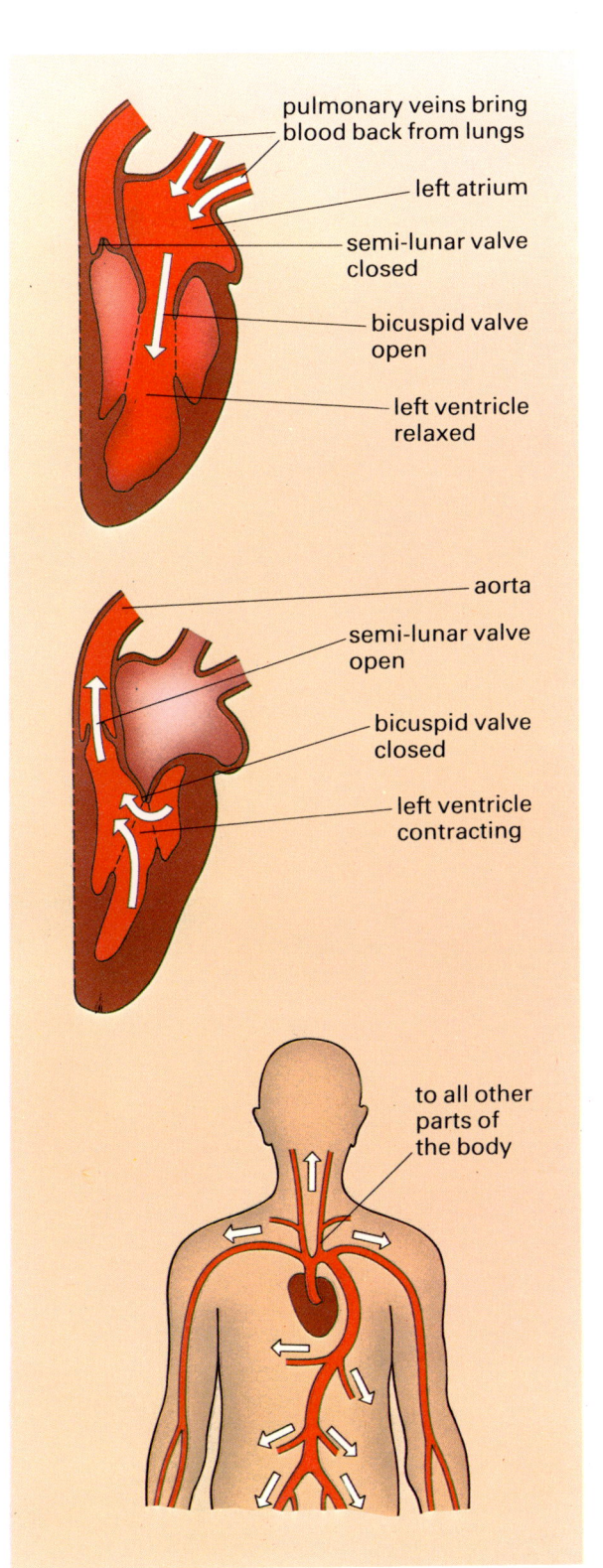

The left side of the heart

The left side of the heart works in a similar way to the right side. The left side pumps blood containing a lot of oxygen. The central wall in the heart keeps the two types of blood apart. The left side pumps blood to all parts of the body *except* the lungs (Fig. 26.2).

Oxygenated blood

Oxygenated blood carries a lot of oxygen and very little carbon dioxide. Oxygenated blood comes to the heart from the lungs. The **pulmonary veins** bring the blood to the left side of the heart. The blood pours into the **left atrium**. It is sucked down through the open **bicuspid valve** into the **left ventricle**. All this is happening when the muscle of the ventricle is relaxed (diastole).

Contraction

During contraction (systole), the left side of the heart works in the same way as the right. The walls of the left ventricle contract, pressing hard on the blood inside. This slams the bicuspid valve shut, so no blood goes back into the left atrium. The blood is forced up the giant artery known as the **aorta**. As the left ventricle has to pump blood further, its walls are thicker than those of the right ventricle.

To all other parts of the body

The aorta branches many times to form important arteries. Each of these arteries goes to a different part of the body. So oxygenated blood is sent to all body cells very quickly. Oxygen leaves the blood and is used by the cells in respiration. The blood is deoxygenated. The cells make carbon dioxide. This waste gas passes from the cells into the blood. The blood then returns to the right side of the heart.

Fig. 26.2 The work of the left side of the heart.

6 Transport in the body

27 Blood vessels

Three types of blood vessels

The ventricles of the heart pump blood into **arteries** that take blood to the lungs or to the body. **Veins** bring blood back to the atria of the heart. The walls of arteries and veins are thick. Chemicals cannot travel through their walls. Blood **circulates** or goes round and round the body. There must be a link between the arteries and the veins. This is the network of **capillaries**. These are very narrow blood vessels. The wall of a capillary is made of just one layer of thin cells. Substances can only get into and leave blood as it flows through capillaries.

Arteries have strong walls of elastic fibres and muscle. They swell and contract as blood surges through them every time the heart beats. Blood is at a high pressure as it surges through an artery. In the capillary, the flow becomes steady. In the veins the pressure is lower. There are valves in the veins (Fig. 27.1). These keep blood flowing one way. Fig. 27.2 gives a summary of the main points about the three types of blood vessels.

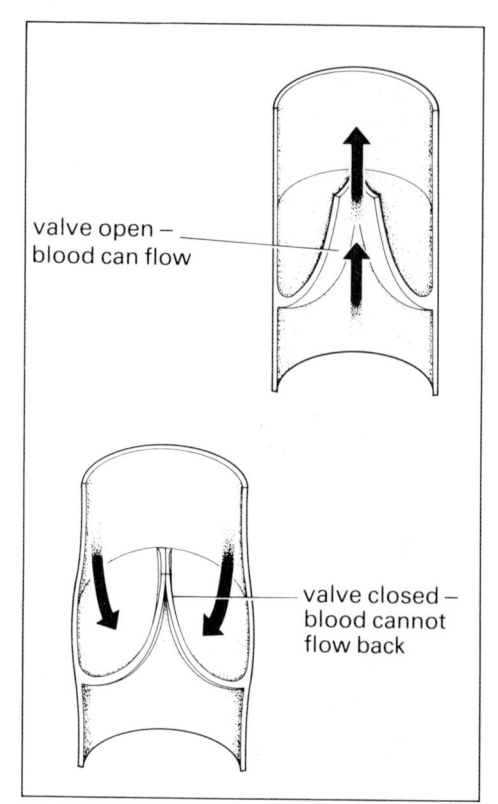

Fig. 27.1 Valves in veins.

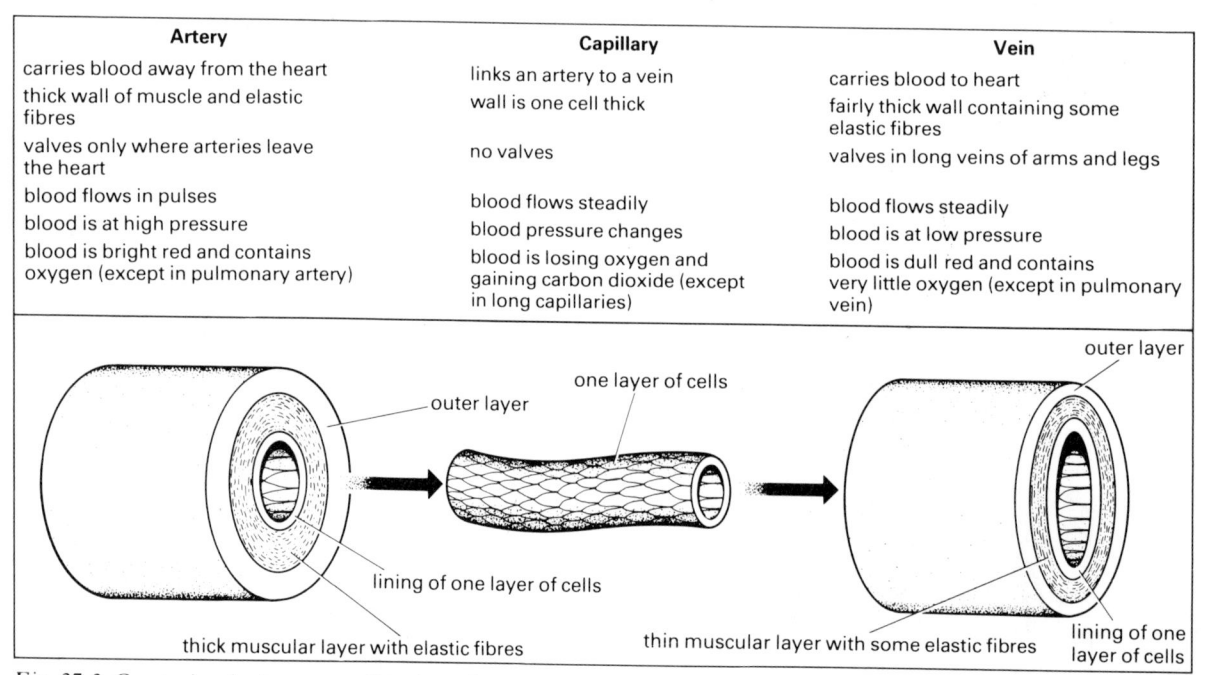

Artery	Capillary	Vein
carries blood away from the heart	links an artery to a vein	carries blood to heart
thick wall of muscle and elastic fibres	wall is one cell thick	fairly thick wall containing some elastic fibres
valves only where arteries leave the heart	no valves	valves in long veins of arms and legs
blood flows in pulses	blood flows steadily	blood flows steadily
blood is at high pressure	blood pressure changes	blood is at low pressure
blood is bright red and contains oxygen (except in pulmonary artery)	blood is losing oxygen and gaining carbon dioxide (except in long capillaries)	blood is dull red and contains very little oxygen (except in pulmonary vein)

Fig. 27.2 Comparing the three types of blood vessels.

6 Transport in the body

The pulse

The heart pumps blood round the body. The surge of blood in an artery can be felt as a **pulse** at a **pressure point** (Fig. 27.3). This is where an artery lies near to the skin and can be pressed against a bone. If an artery is cut, bright red blood gushes out in spurts.

Measuring blood pressure

The pressure at which blood is being pushed through the arteries can be measured. A **sphygmomanometer** is used (Fig. 27.4). A cuff is fastened round the arm and blown up with air. The cuff becomes tight. This stops blood surging through the artery in the arm. The doctor or nurse then puts a stethoscope over the pressure point in the elbow. While listening, air is slowly let out of the cuff. Blood starts to come through the artery and pushes against the tight cuff. Tapping sounds can be heard as the blood starts to flow. The sound is made as the blood is forced through the artery after being pumped by the heart's ventricle. The pressure at which blood starts to come along the artery can be measured on the tube of mercury (pressure gauge or manometer). A healthy person has a reading of about 120 on the pressure gauge.

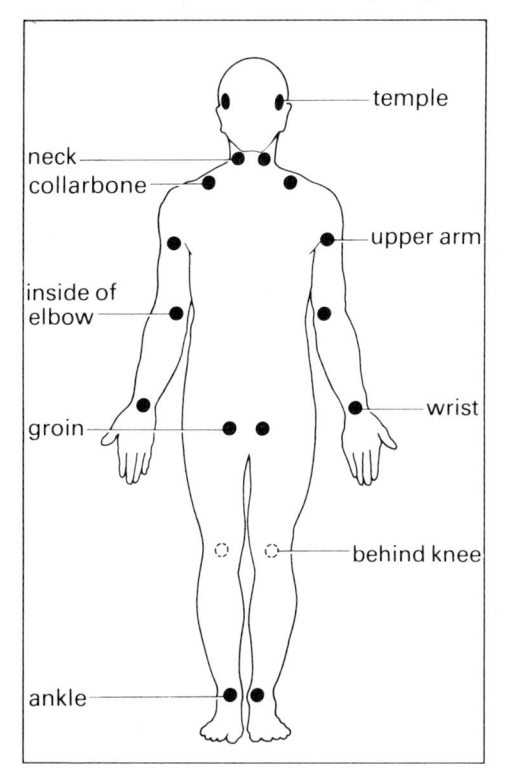

Fig. 27.3 Pressure points.

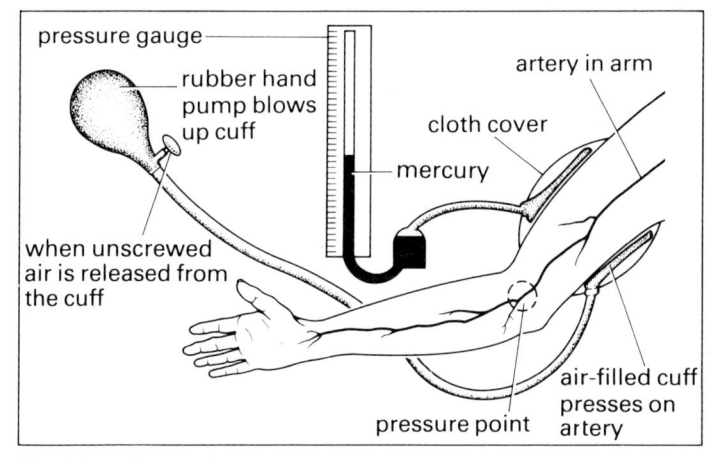

Fig. 27.4 How a sphygmomanometer works.

Helping blood flow in veins

Blood is pumped through arteries by the heart. Blood in veins is helped back to the heart by the muscles of the body. The veins in the arms and legs lie between muscles and the bones. As the muscles contract they squeeze the veins against the bone. Because the veins contain valves, the blood is squeezed one way – back to the heart (Fig. 27.5).

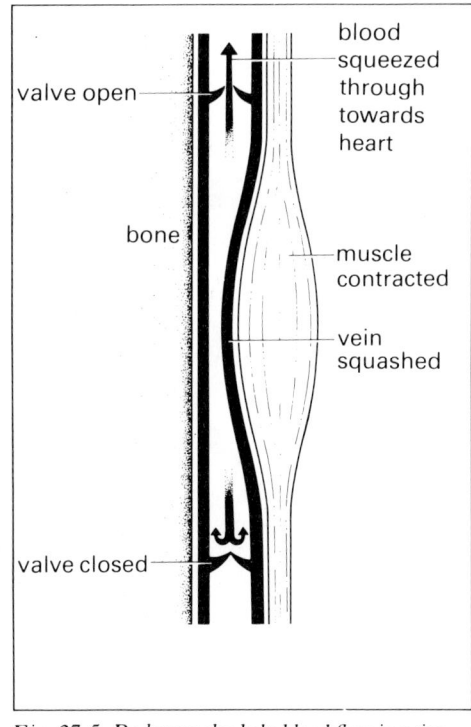

Fig. 27.5 Body muscles help blood flow in veins.

6 Transport in the body

28 Transport systems

The route of the blood through the body

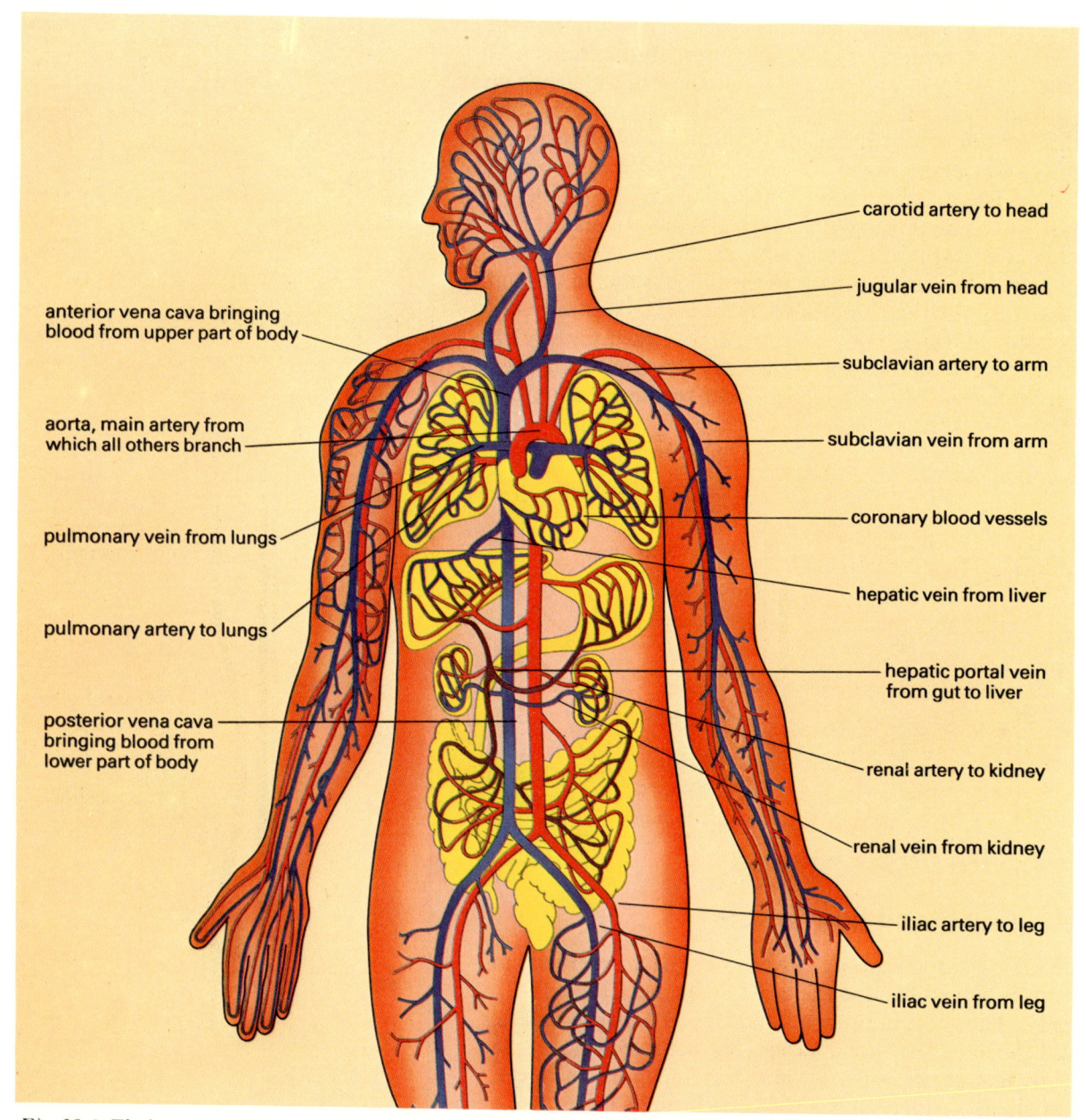

Fig. 28.1 *The human circulatory system.*

6 Transport in the body

Blood circulates

The heart, blood vessels and blood can be called the **circulatory system** (Fig. 28.1). The job of this system is to move blood around the body along *one way routes*. In this way substances can be taken from one part to another. For instance some waste chemicals are turned into **urea** by the liver. The urea dissolves in plasma and travels in the blood to the kidneys. The kidneys get rid of it. Food chemicals must be taken from the intestines to all parts of the body. Many substances like these travel dissolved in the plasma.

Oxygen is carried in the red blood cells. They contain haemoglobin. This protein 'picks up' oxygen when there is a lot nearby, as in the lungs. It is then **oxy-haemoglobin** (bright red, oxygenated blood). Haemoglobin lets the oxygen go when the surroundings are short of this gas, as in respiring cells. (The blood then becomes dull red, deoxygenated blood.)

Tissue fluid

Substances in the blood must cross a barrier to get to the body cells. Blood is pushed to the finest capillaries at high pressure. The capillary walls are thin and plasma can pass through. The plasma that leaks out is called **tissue fluid**. It surrounds the body cells (Fig. 28.2). Chemicals needed in the cells must travel through the capillary wall, through the tissue fluid and into the cells. Waste chemicals made in the cells must move in the opposite direction.

The lymph system

If tissue fluid built up, the amount of plasma in the blood would get less and less. Some tissue fluid drains back into the capillaries. The rest drains into blunt-ended tubes known as **lymphatic vessels**. The tissue fluid in these is called **lymph**. The fine lymphatic vessels link up to form wider tubes (see Fig. 23.2 on page 42). At some places several tubes go into an oval ball. This is a **lymph node**. Lymph nodes have many white blood cells inside them. These help fight disease by eating any passing bacteria. The largest lymph node is the **spleen**.

Only one large lymphatic or **lymph vessel** leaves a lymph node. These large lymph vessels lead back to the chest. They join the large blood vessels that go to the heart. The lymph pours into these. As in veins, movement of the body muscles helps to move lymph. The vessels contain valves. If the body muscles are not working or if the lymph vessels are blocked, the tissue fluid collects in the part of the body below the block.

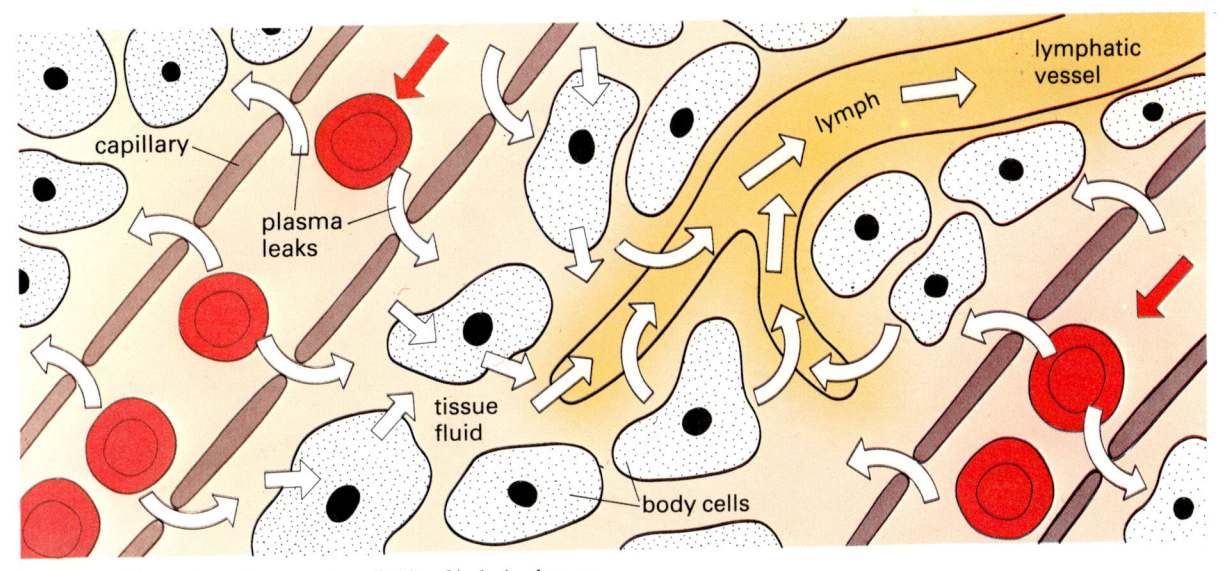

Fig. 28.2 How plasma becomes tissue fluid and is drained away as lymph.

6 Transport in the body

29 Diseases of the transport system

Blood diseases

There are many diseases of the blood. **Anaemia** is common and happens when there is not enough iron in a person's diet (see page 11).
Haemophilia is a disease that can be passed on by parents to their children. A haemophiliac cannot make the chemicals needed to heal wounds (see page 116).

Thrombosis

A **thrombosis** is a lump of blood protein (**fibrin**) and blood cells inside a blood vessel. If a thrombosis gets stuck in a vessel it will stop the flow of blood. A thrombosis in the brain cuts down the blood supply to that part. This lowers the amount of oxygen reaching the brain cells. This happens in a **stroke** which can kill or cause brain damage.

The coronary arteries of the heart may be blocked or made narrower when fat collects in the wall (Fig. 29.1). A thrombosis in these vessels stops oxygen getting to the heart muscle. The

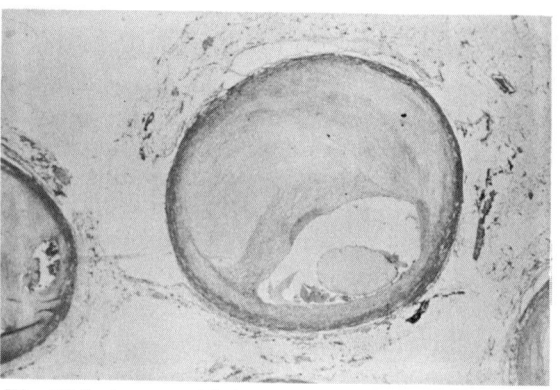

Fig. 29.1 An artery blocked by fat (× 16).

heart stops working properly. The person suffers great pain in the chest and the heart may stop beating. This is a heart attack or **coronary thrombosis**. Obese or overweight people with high blood pressure are more likely to have heart attacks than people of average weight. Some causes of high blood pressure and obesity are shown in Fig. 29.2.

Varicose veins

The valves in the veins of the legs may not work properly. The veins will swell and become **varicose veins**. In bad cases a vein may have to be taken out of the leg. Other healthy veins are joined up by the surgeon to carry blood up the leg.

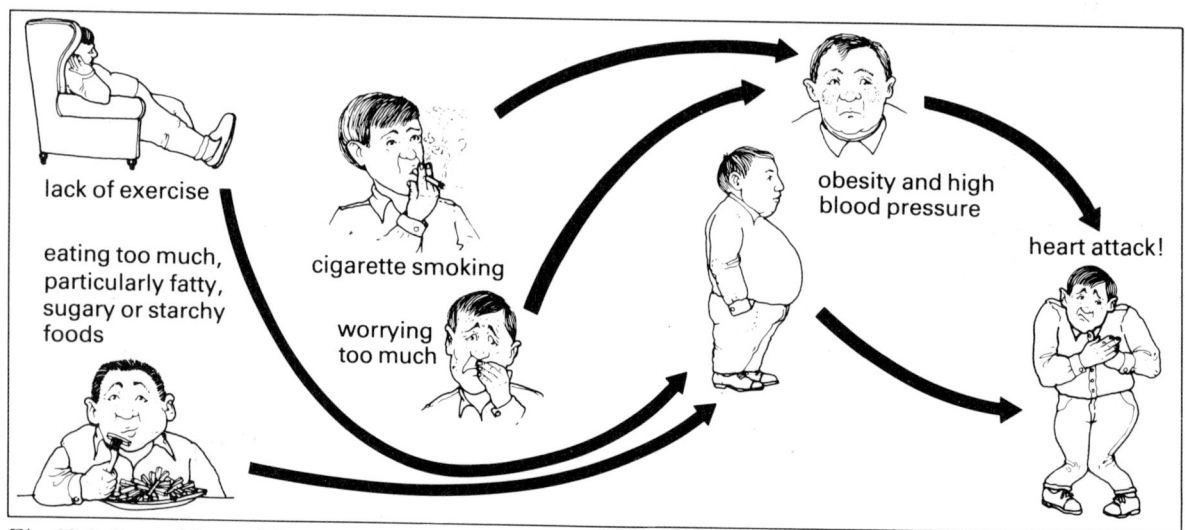

Fig. 29.2 Some of the possible causes of heart attack.

6 Transport in the body

Heart disease
Leaking valves

If the valves in the heart do not shut properly, the heart cannot pump efficiently. Sometimes a faulty valve can be replaced. One type of replacement valve works like the ping-pong ball in a snorkel tube (Fig. 29.3).

To fix an artificial valve in the heart, it must be opened. Operations cannot be done while blood is passing through the heart. The blood can by-pass the heart when a **heart-lung machine** is used. This machine does the work of both heart and lungs during the operation.

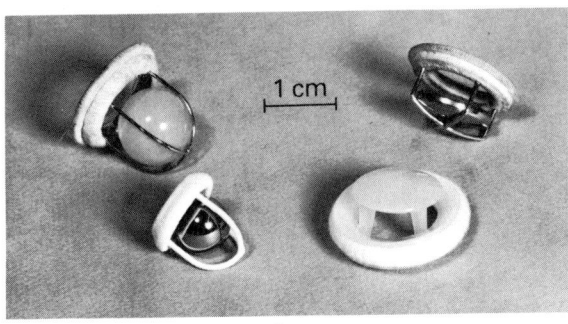

Fig. 29.3 Artificial heart valves.

Faulty pace-maker

The **pace-maker** of the heart keeps the heart beating steadily. The pace-maker is a group of cells in the right atrium. These produce a very small amount of electricity (about 70 times a minute). This spreads through the heart muscle making it contract. The amount of electricity can be measured by a machine. The record made is an **electro-cardiogram** (ECG). Today, a human who has a faulty pace-maker can have a small battery fitted inside the chest near the heart. The battery produces electricity and makes the heart beat in rhythm (Fig. 29.4).

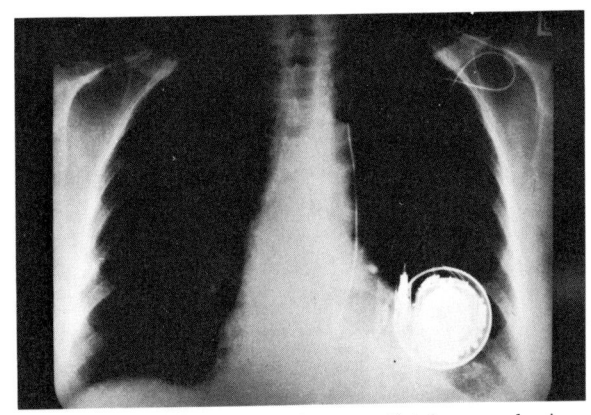

Fig. 29.4 A chest X-ray showing an artificial pace-maker in position.

Summary: Transport in the body

* Blood transports materials around the body.
* Blood is made of liquid plasma, red and white blood cells and platelets.
* Blood travels round the body in arteries, veins and capillaries.
* The heart pumps blood into the arteries; veins return blood to the heart.
* The heart is a double pump; each side has a top chamber (atrium) that receives blood, and a lower chamber (ventricle) that pumps blood.
* The right side of the heart receives and pumps deoxygenated blood; the left receives and pumps oxygenated blood.
* The pumping action of the heart is felt as the heart beat.
* The closing of heart valves can be heard.
* The pumping of blood into an artery can be felt as a pulse.
* Movement of blood in veins is helped by valves and body muscles.
* Capillaries are thin-walled and allow materials to enter and leave the blood.
* Plasma leaks from capillaries and forms tissue fluid.
* Tissue fluid is drained into lymphatic vessels and forms lymph.
* Blood vessels and the heart can be damaged.

7 Keeping the steady state

30 The liver

The liver is the largest organ in the body. It weighs about 1·5 kg. The liver has a double blood supply. Blood comes from the aorta along the **hepatic artery** and from the gut along the **hepatic portal vein**. Blood leaves the liver through the **hepatic vein** which joins the vena cava (Fig. 30.1).

The jobs of the liver

The liver is the chemical factory of the body. Its cells break down or store chemicals. In this way it helps remove waste and poisons. It also keeps the amount of many chemicals in the blood steady (Fig. 30.2).

Fig. 30.1 The blood supply of the liver.

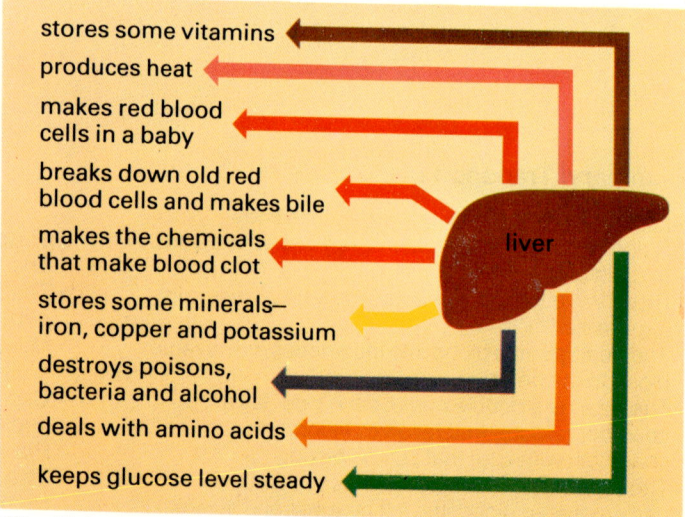

Fig. 30.2 The jobs of the liver.

7 Keeping the steady state

Keeping the glucose supply steady

We eat at definite times during the day. Digesting a meal will make a lot of glucose and amino acids. These will go into the blood leaving the intestines in the hepatic portal vein. Body cells work properly only if they have a steady supply of these nutrients. The portal vein takes the nutrients to the liver. The liver controls the supply of these materials to the body. When there is a lot of glucose in the blood, the liver will store some as **glycogen**. When the level of glucose in the blood drops, glycogen is turned back into glucose. It is then released into the blood. The supply of glucose to the cells is kept steady (Fig. 30.3).

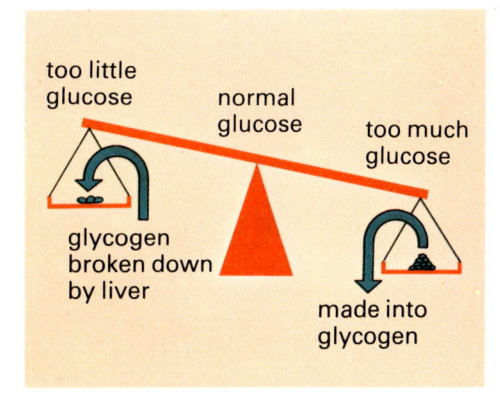

Fig. 30.3 Keeping the glucose level balanced.

Dealing with amino acids

Amino acids are made when protein is digested. They are used to make the human protein needed for growth and repair of body cells. Amino acids cannot be stored in the body. If the blood contains too many amino acids, they are broken down. The liver changes amino acids into **urea** and glycogen. This process is called **de-amination** (Fig. 30.4). The glycogen is stored in the liver. The urea is a waste which is carried away from the liver in the hepatic vein. It travels in the blood to the kidneys. These remove urea from the blood.

Breaking down red blood cells

Red blood cells die after about 100 days. The liver cells deal with these dead cells. The red pigment, **haemoglobin**, is changed into other substances. As it is broken down, its colour changes from red to blue. It ends up as two chemicals, one green and one yellow. These colour changes can be seen in a bruise. Here the blood cells have been damaged and haemoglobin is being broken down in the skin, in the same way as the liver (Fig. 30.5).

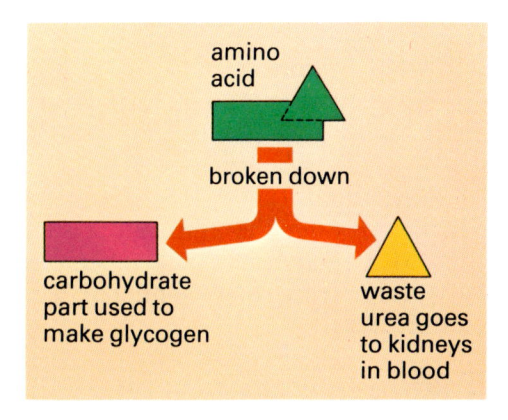

Fig. 30.4 De-amination.

Making bile

The green and yellow chemicals are used to make **bile** (Fig. 30.6). The bile is stored in the **gall bladder**, near the liver. If the liver or gall bladder are not working properly the green and yellow chemicals build up in the blood. This makes fair-skinned people look yellow, and they have **jaundice**.

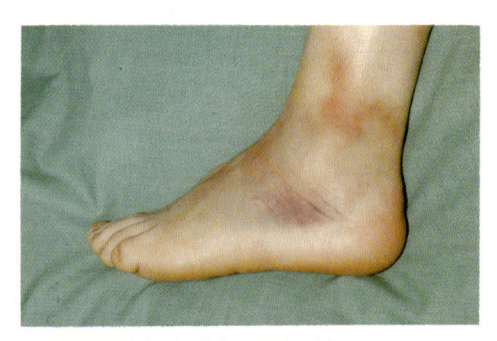

Fig. 30.5 A bruised foot and ankle.

Making heat

All this chemical activity produces heat. Heat from the liver warms the blood and helps keep the body at 37 °C.

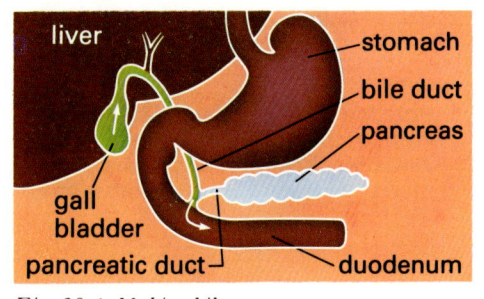

Fig. 30.6 Making bile.

7 Keeping the steady state

31 Keeping warm

The human body is a machine. Even at rest, it still needs energy. Some of the energy is used to keep the body warm and some is lost as heat from the body's surface. If the body is to work properly, the temperature must be kept between 36 and 37·5 °C.

The clinical thermometer

Body temperature is taken with a **clinical thermometer** (Fig. 31.1). Usually this is put under the tongue. This is not reliable if the person has had a hot or cold drink in the previous half hour (Fig. 31.2). A special procedure must be followed when the temperature is taken (Fig. 31.3). Sometimes the temperature is taken by putting the thermometer in the person's armpit or rectum.

Taking your temperature

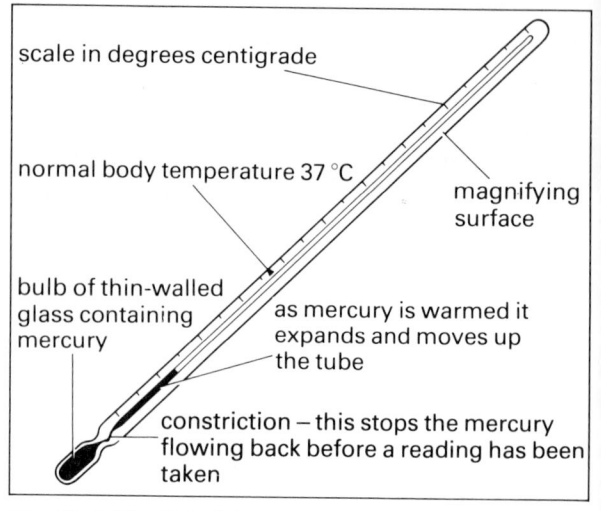

Fig. 31.1 The clinical thermometer.

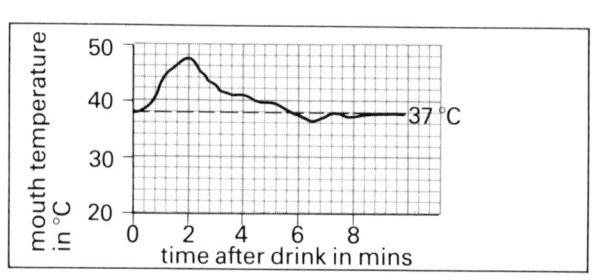

Fig. 31.2 Graph to show how the temperature in the mouth changes after drinking hot tea.

1 Hold the thermometer away from the bulb. Shake down the thread of mercury.

2 Dip the bulb end of the thermometer in disinfectant. Wipe the bulb with cotton wool.

3 Put under the tongue and leave for three minutes.

4 Read the thermometer. Put the thermometer back in the disinfectant.

Fig. 31.3 The correct way to take your temperature.

7 Keeping the steady state

Changes in body temperature

A healthy person's temperature goes up and down slightly through the day (Fig. 31.4). It is at its lowest during sleep. If the body is trying to fight off a disease, lots of heat may be released. This is a **fever** and body temperature may rise to 40 °C.

The body produces enough heat to raise the temperature 0·5 °C every half hour. For the body to work properly, the temperature must be kept steady. Enzymes work best at 37 °C (see page 37). So, in warm weather the body must lose some of the heat it makes (Fig. 31.5). In cold weather the body needs to make more heat to keep it at 37 °C. This is done by taking in more fuel (food), and keeping active. Humans also use clothes to control their body temperature.

Body temperature and body shape

The bigger the area of skin in contact with the air, the more heat is lost from the body. A tall, thin person has a large skin surface and will lose heat quickly. A short, fat person has a smaller skin surface for the same body weight (Fig. 31.6). The short, fat person will lose heat more slowly. Tall, thin people are well suited to living in hot climates; shorter, fatter people to living in cold places.

Some people live in deserts where food and water may be in short supply. They must be able to store energy supplies. People in the Hottentot tribe in Africa store more fat than most people. This emergency food supply makes them look rather overweight. When this fuel is respired, water and energy become available.

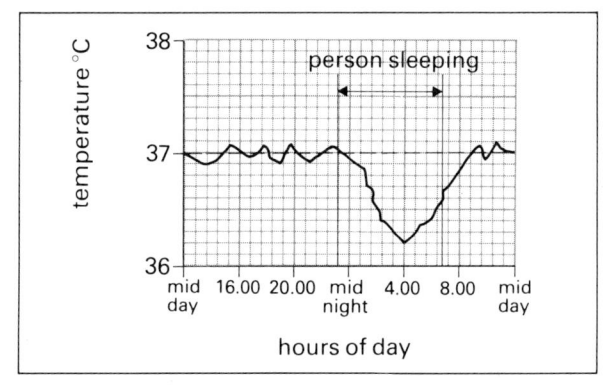

Fig. 31.4 Body temperature varies slightly through the day.

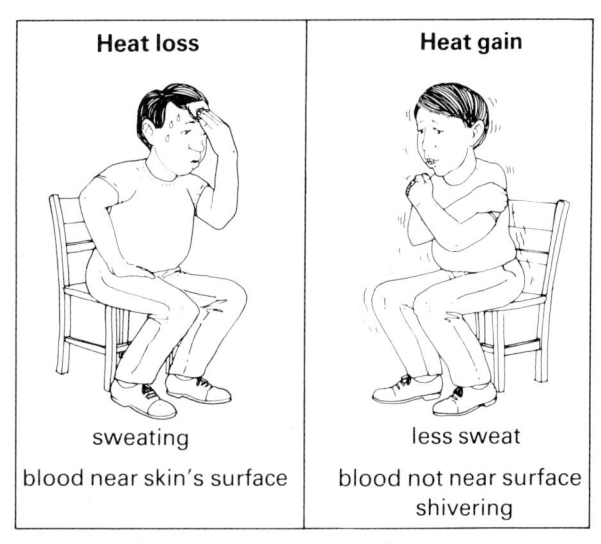

Fig. 31.5 The body loses and gains heat in many ways (see page 63).

Fig. 31.6 A tall, thin body loses heat more quickly than a short fat body.

7 Keeping the steady state

32 The skin

Skin covers the surface of the body. If removed, the skin of an average man would cover a single bed. Most skin is between 1 and 2 mm thick. On the eyelid it is very thin (0·5 mm) and on the soles of the feet it is about 6 mm thick. Here it gets a lot of wear. The skin on the palms and soles is ridged. The ridges help the skin to grip (Fig. 32.1).

The skin we see

Skin is made up of many layers of cells. The top or outside layer is called the **epidermis**. It is made up of dead, flattened cells held together to make a tough, water-proof surface (Fig. 32.2). Throughout life the dead cells are rubbed off. New cells take their place from the living layers beneath. About 20 kg of dead skin is shed by an average adult in a lifetime. Much of this dead skin ends up as dust in homes.

Lower layers

The lower layers of the skin are called the **dermis** (Fig. 32.3). It contains glands (sweat and oil), blood vessels and fat. There are lots of nerve endings. The skin is sensitive to pain, touch and temperature. (See page 88 for the skin as a sense organ.)

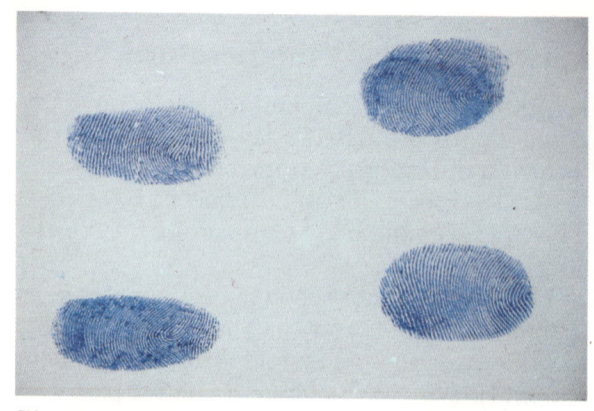

Fig. 32.1 Fingerprints show up the ridges on the skin.

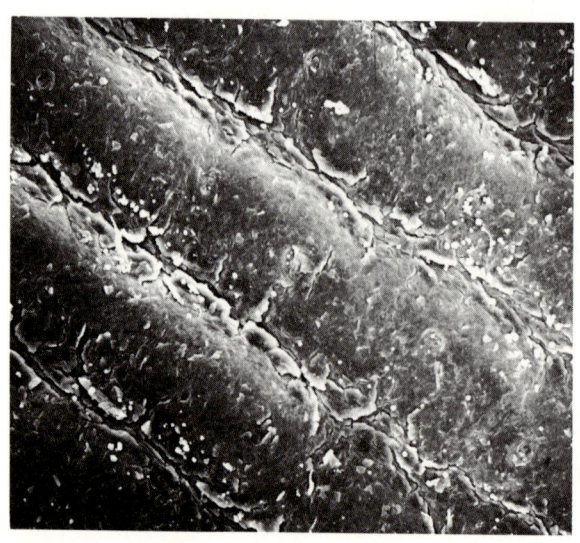

Fig. 32.2 The surface of the skin on the finger magnified 10 000 times. Flakes of dead skin cells and the ridges can be seen.

The skin at work

The skin is a complicated organ that protects the inside of our bodies from damage.

The **sebaceous glands** make an oil called **sebum**. This forms a water-proof, antiseptic layer on the surface of the skin and hairs. It helps to stop germs entering the body and prevents a lot of water leaving the body surface. In teenagers these glands may make so much oil that the hair is greasy. The sebum may clog up the pores on the skin and cause spots and blackheads.

The arm-pits have special **sweat glands**. They make a milky fluid that contains fat and proteins. When the fats come into contact with the air, they break down. If allowed to build up, they can smell. This is **body odour**.

Under the dermis there is a layer of cells filled with oil and fat. This is an important energy store for the body. The layer cuts down heat loss from the body. It is an **insulator**.

The skin contains cells that can make vitamin D in sunlight. Another of its important jobs is controlling body temperature (see page 62).

7 Keeping the steady state

Structure of the skin

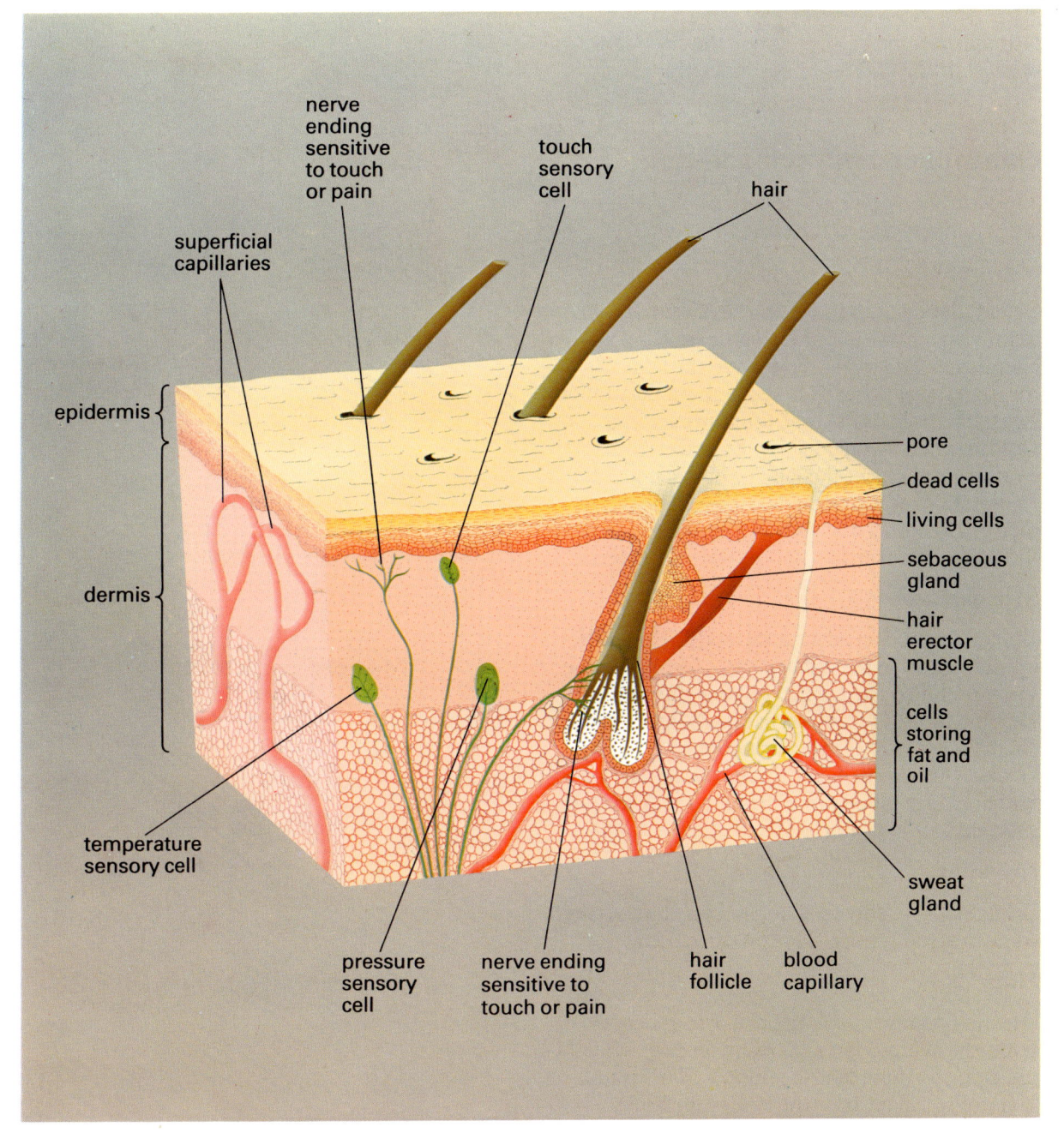

Fig. 32.3 The skin is a complicated organ made up of many parts.

7 Keeping the steady state

33 Adapting to hot and cold surroundings

Humans can live in cold or hot climates. Our skin, clothing and buildings make this possible (see Homes, pages 176 to 181).

Controlling body temperature

The skin, body hair and muscles help keep our body temperature at the steady level of 37 °C.

Making sweat

Sweat glands in the skin secrete **sweat**. This is mainly water but it contains some salts and waste chemicals. The sweat flows on to the skin through sweat **pores**. There are about 2½ million sweat glands in our skin! Liquid sweat changes to **vapour** when it is heated by the body. This **evaporation** of sweat cools the body (Fig. 33.1). In certain conditions the body loses about half a litre of sweat in a day. When a person is active or the weather is warmer, more sweat is made.

Skin capillaries

Blood carries heat around the body. Under the epidermis there are many capillaries. When the body is chilled the capillaries near the surface become narrow. Less warm blood flows through them so less heat is lost through the skin's surface. When the body is hot, the capillaries widen. More blood flows through them and so more heat is lost (Fig. 33.2).

Shivering

When cold we **shiver**. The muscles contract and relax in rapid bursts. This produces heat.

Hair

The hair on the head stops a lot of heat being lost from the **scalp**. Hair can 'stand on end' when we are cold, forming 'goose pimples'. This traps a layer of warm air near the skin (Fig. 33.3). Humans have very little body hair. Instead we use clothing to keep heat in.

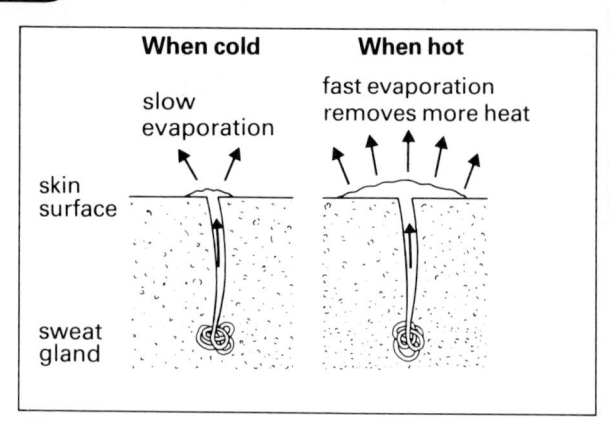

Fig. 33.1 Sweating cools the body.

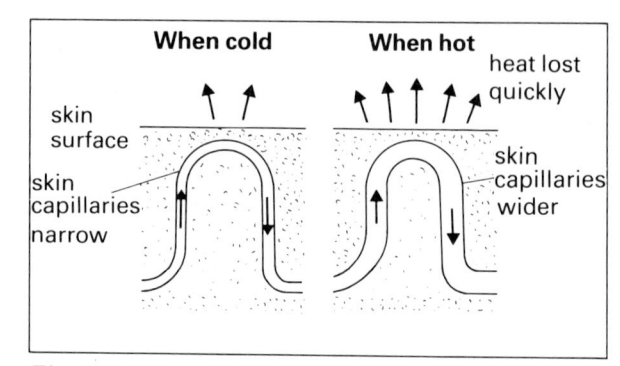

Fig. 33.2 Skin capillaries help control heat loss.

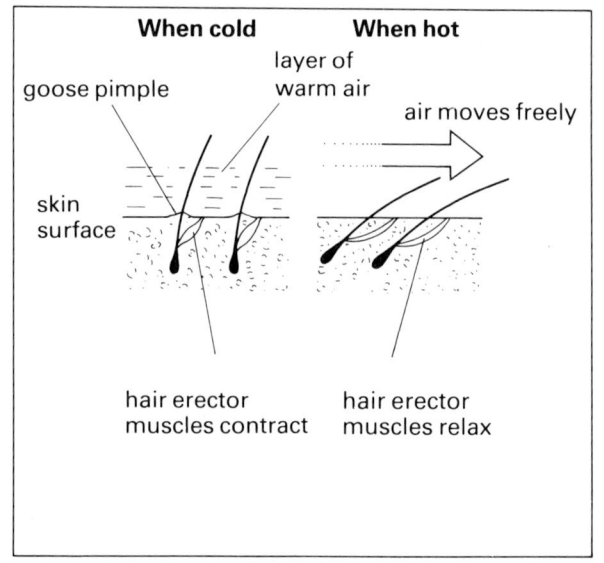

Fig. 33.3 Hair or fluffy clothing traps a layer of air near the skin.

7 Keeping the steady state

Clothes

The clothes we wear help to control our temperature. In cold surroundings we wear more clothes. Fur or wool clothes trap a lot of air amongst their fibres. Air helps to keep things warm as it is an **insulator**. Thin, light materials like cotton, trap less air. These are worn in hot places. White clothes **reflect** heat. Black clothes take in or **absorb** heat.

Skin pigments

Melanin is a dark pigment made in the skin. Fair-skinned people have less melanin than dark-skinned people. Melanin protects the body from damage by the harmful ultra-violet rays from the sun. If fair-skinned people get too much sunlight, their skin may burn. Pigments also protect the eyes from too much light. Dark brown eyes give more protection than paler colours.

Hair and face types

The people of China and Mongolia have folded eyelids to protect their eyes from the bright sun (Fig. 33.4). Dark-skinned people have tight, curly hair to protect the scalp from the hot rays of the sun. It does allow heat loss by sweating from the neck. Long, straight hair of paler-skinned races covers the neck and ears, protecting them against the cold. Nose shape can vary. In very dry countries long, narrow noses are useful! This makes breathed in air moister. The flat face of Mongolian people is a protection – the nose is not too exposed to the cold.

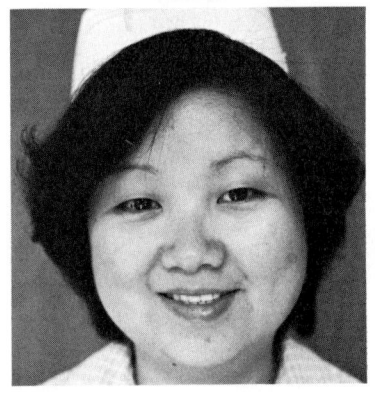

Fig. 33.4 Three different types of human faces.

Overcooling

Tired climbers on a cold mountain, or old people sitting still in chilly rooms can die from cold. Their bodies cannot make enough heat to keep the body temperature steady. Their temperature drops and they become tired, weak and unconscious. This condition is called **hypothermia**. If they are to recover, people must be warmed up slowly or they will die from shock.

Overheating

In very hot, humid conditions, sweat does not evaporate quickly enough to cool the body. The body overheats and a person will feel weak, sick and dizzy. This condition is **heatstroke**, sometimes called sunstroke. Eventually sweat production may stop. Then the overheating may make a person collapse and possibly die.

7 Keeping the steady state

34 Cells and water

All the living cells of the body are surrounded by liquid. The cells of tissues and organs have **tissue fluid** around them. Tissue fluid contains dissolved substances, but over $9/10$ of tissue fluid is water. Blood cells are carried in a liquid called plasma. It also contains dissolved chemicals, but $9/10$ of plasma is water. If the amount of water in the plasma, or tissue fluid, changes, it can affect the way cells look and work (Fig. 34.1).

The cell membrane

Water can enter or leave cells by passing through the **membrane** around each one (Fig. 34.2). The membrane is **selectively permeable**. This means it will allow some things through but not others. Small molecules like water pass through more easily than larger molecules like sugar (Fig. 34.3). The membrane has tiny holes or **pores** in it which help molecules move in and out of a cell (Fig. 34.4).

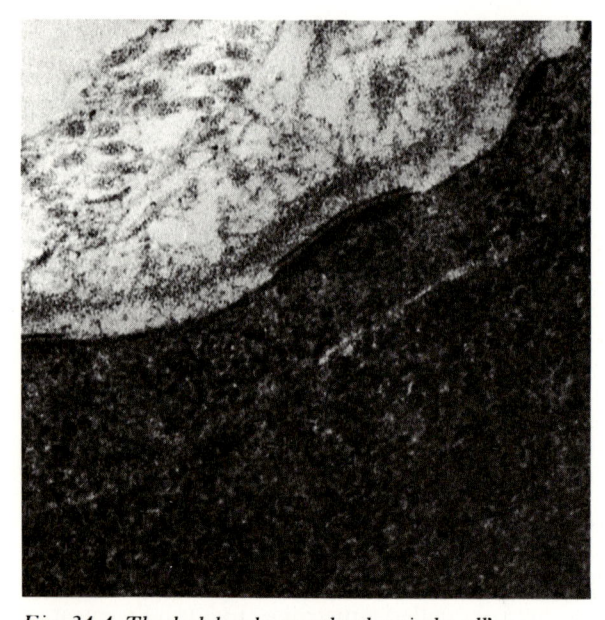

Fig. 34.4 The dark band across the photo is the cell's membrane. The 'gaps' in the band are pores where substances can pass in and out of the cell ($\times 60\,000$).

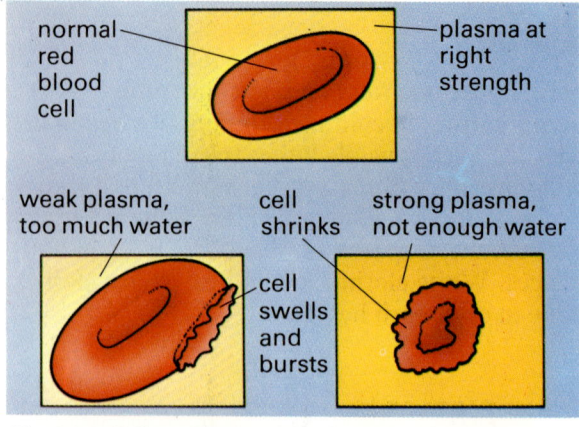

Fig. 34.1 Cells are surrounded by liquids. If the liquids are at the wrong strength, the cells are damaged.

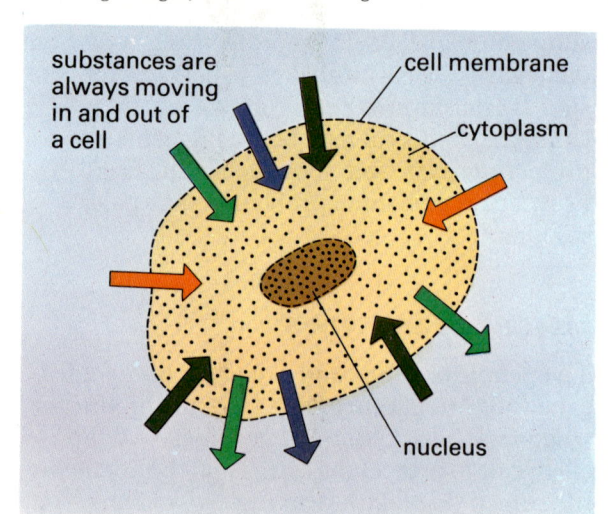

Fig. 34.2 Cell membranes are selectively permeable.

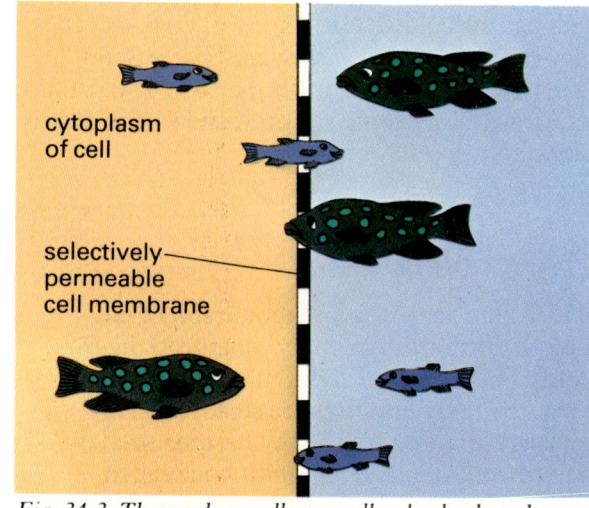

Fig. 34.3 The membrane allows small molecules through more easily than large molecules.

7 Keeping the steady state

Diffusion

When a sugar lump is put into water, the solid sugar seems to disappear. The sugar has dissolved in the water. The molecules that make up the sugar have spread through the water. The sugar dissolves in the water (**solvent**) to make **sugar solution**. The sugar and water molecules move around in the solution until the sugar is evenly spread through the water (Fig. 34.5). The movement of molecules from where there is a lot to where there is a few is called **diffusion**.

Solutions and cells

A weak sugar solution contains a little sugar and a lot of water. This is a **dilute** solution. A strong or **concentrated** solution contains a lot of sugar and a little water (Fig. 34.6).

Movement through membranes

Imagine that a weak sugar solution is separated from a strong one by a **permeable** membrane. This membrane allows sugar and water to pass through very easily (Fig. 34.7). Sugar and water molecules diffuse through the membrane until both are evenly spread through the liquid.

Osmosis

Now imagine that the weak sugar solution is separated from the strong one by a *selectively permeable* membrane. A special kind of diffusion takes place (Fig. 34.8). Water molecules can pass through the membrane quickly. Sugar molecules are bigger; they can only get through slowly. Diffusion of water molecules through a selectively permeable membrane is called **osmosis**. Water can enter or leave cells by osmosis. It caused the changes shown in Fig. 34.1.

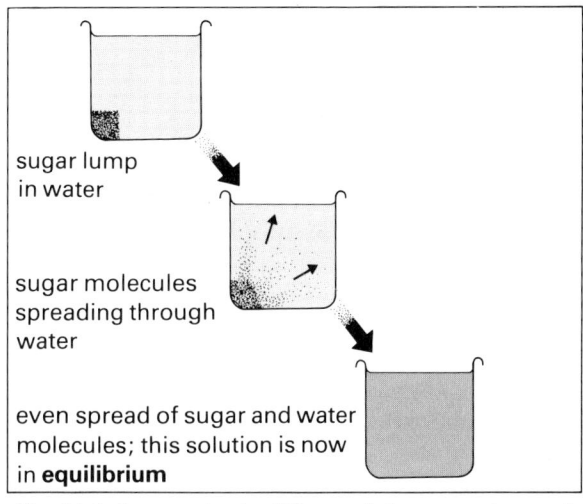

Fig. 34.5 Sugar molecules diffuse until they are evenly spread through water.

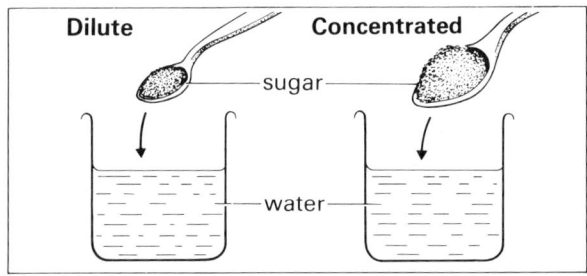

Fig. 34.6 Making dilute and concentrated solutions of sugar in water.

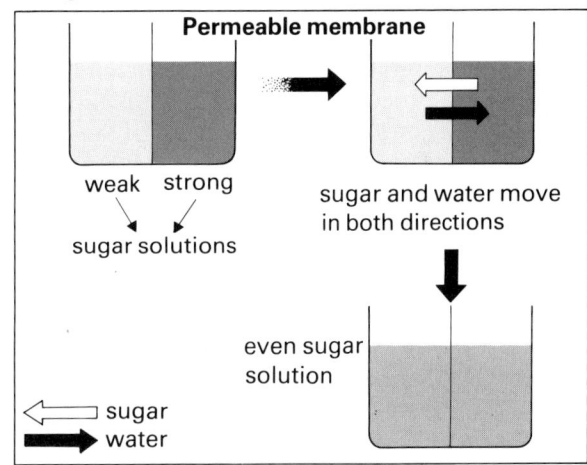

Fig. 34.7 Diffusion through a permeable membrane.

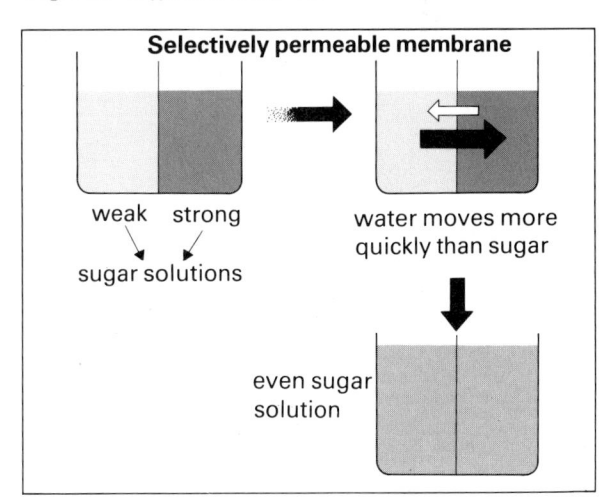

Fig. 34.8 Diffusion through a selectively permeable membrane = osmosis.

7 Keeping the steady state

35 Water balance

If body cells are to work properly, the amount of water in the body fluids must be kept steady. The amount we lose must be equal to the amount we take in. This is **water balance**. We keep many things steady inside our bodies. Examples are body temperature and the level of glucose in the blood. Keeping things inside the body steady is called **homeostasis**.

Fig. 35.1 These men are losing water by sweating.

Taking in and losing water

We take in water when we drink liquids. Even the solid food we eat contains water – a cabbage is $9/10$ water. In one day, a person in this country will take in about three litres of water in food and drinks. The process of respiration happening in all cells makes water inside the body. If there is not enough water available for the body's needs, you feel thirsty (Fig. 35.2).

We also lose water. It is lost through the mouth and nose when we breathe out. It is lost through the skin surface as sweat, from the eyes as tears, and it is in our faeces. We also lose water from our bladder when we get rid of **urine**.

Input

- food and drink 2650 cm³ (can be much more)
- water made in respiration 350 cm³

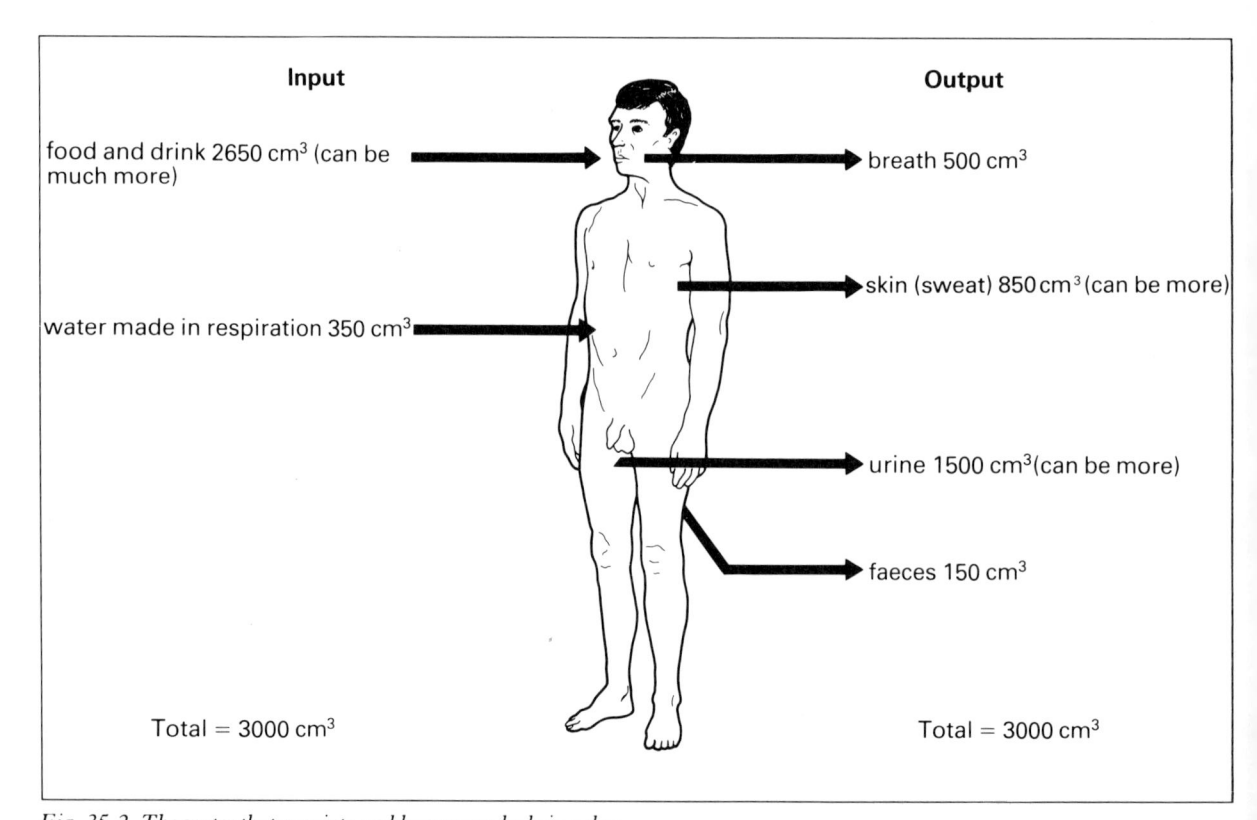

Total = 3000 cm³

Output

- breath 500 cm³
- skin (sweat) 850 cm³ (can be more)
- urine 1500 cm³ (can be more)
- faeces 150 cm³

Total = 3000 cm³

Fig. 35.2 The water that goes into and leaves your body in a day.

7 Keeping the steady state

Urine and the kidneys

Urine is a yellow liquid. It contains **water**, **urea** and a very small amount of **ammonia**. Urine is made in the **kidneys**. A tube, the **ureter**, leads from each kidney. Urine is carried down these tubes to the **bladder** where it is stored (Fig. 35.3). The kidneys are inside the body, just below the rib cage. They are not protected by any part of the bony skeleton. So kidneys can be bruised or damaged if you are knocked in the back. 'Kidney punches' are dangerous because the cells of the kidney cannot be replaced or repaired.

Making urine

Each kidney is supplied with blood and makes urine from the blood. Urea and ammonia are waste materials and would poison the body unless removed. They are made in the liver and are carried to the kidneys in the plasma. Blood goes to the kidneys along the renal artery (Fig. 35.4). Blood leaving the kidneys along the renal vein has no waste in it. The kidney has separated the waste from the blood. The urea and ammonia are carried away from the kidney in water. This solution is urine.

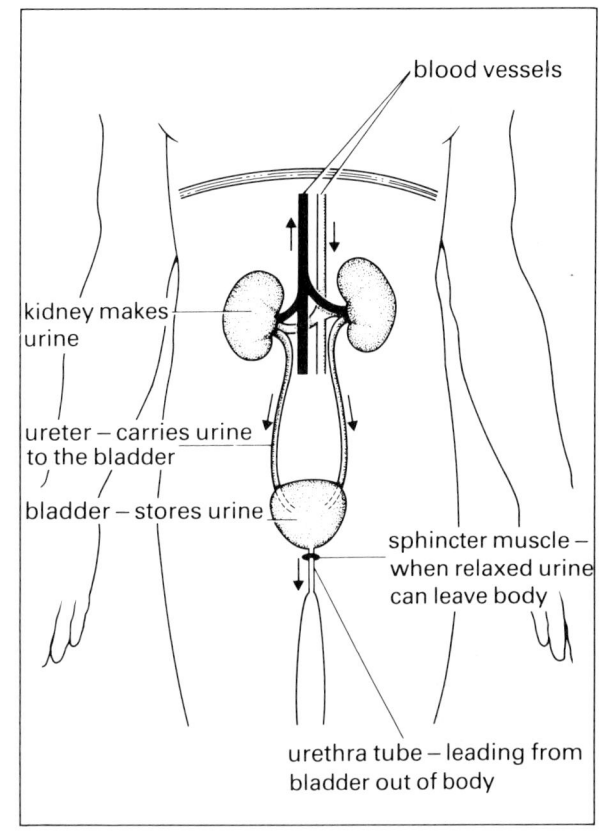

Fig. 35.3 The human excretory system.

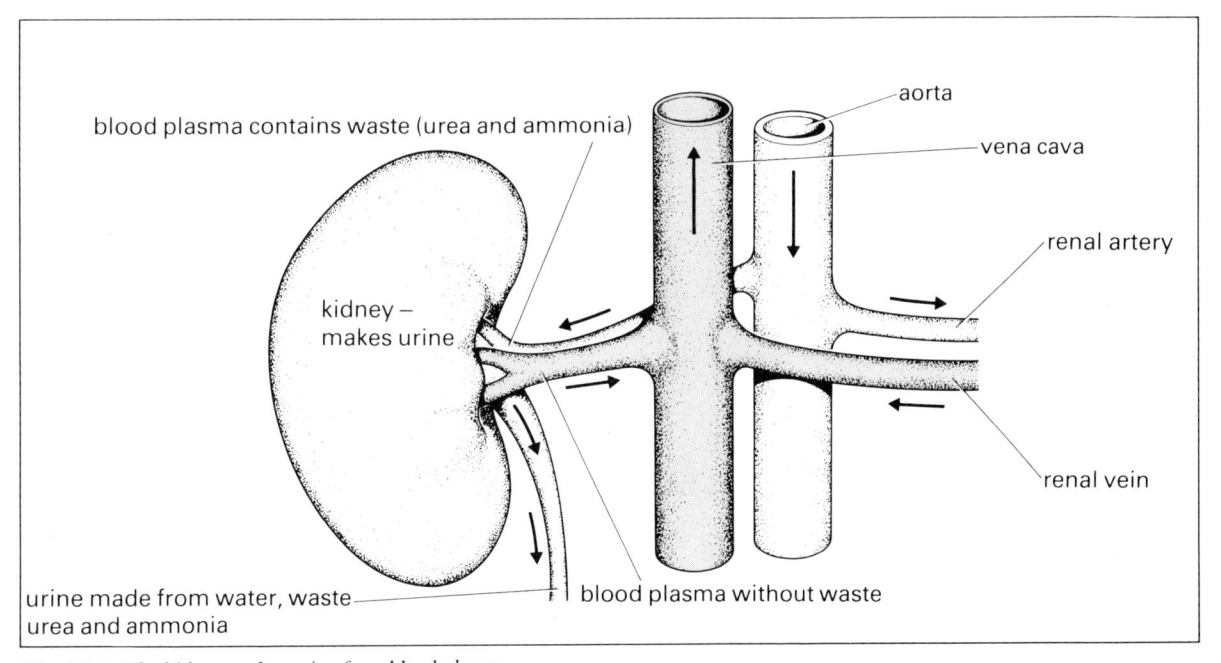

Fig. 35.4 The kidney makes urine from blood plasma.

7 Keeping the steady state

36 How kidneys work

Inside the kidneys

If a kidney is sliced in half, blood vessels can be seen branching through the kidney tissue. A kidney has three main parts (Fig. 36.1).

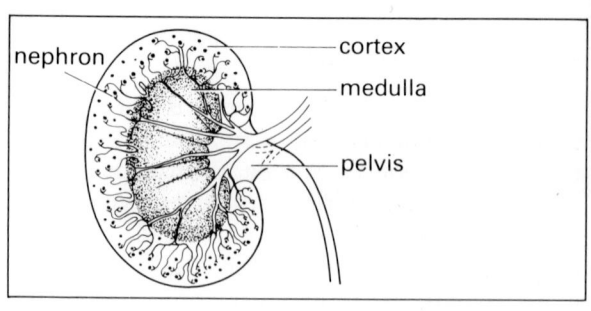

Fig. 36.1 The parts inside a kidney.

Nephrons

A very thin slice of kidney can be examined under a microscope. Kidney tissue is made up of thousands of tiny **tubules**. Each is surrounded by a mesh of blood vessels. Each part of the tube or **nephron** has a special name (Fig. 36.2).

Nephrons make urine

Urine is made in each of the nephrons. The drawing of a nephron below is simplified. It explains how urine is made (Fig. 36.3).

Both kidneys **filter** out about 170 litres of liquid in a day. The amount of urine going out of the body is only about 1·5 litres a day. Most of the water is **reabsorbed** or taken back into the blood. All other substances needed by the blood are also reabsorbed. **Glucose** is one of these substances.

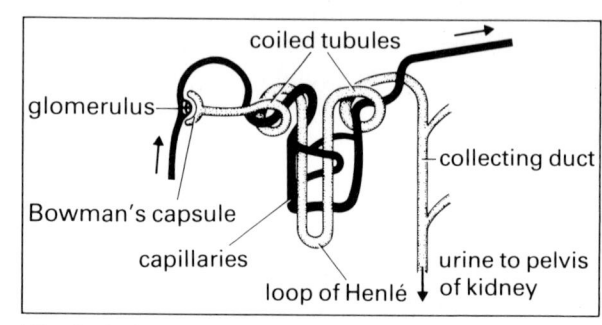

Fig. 36.2 A nephron.

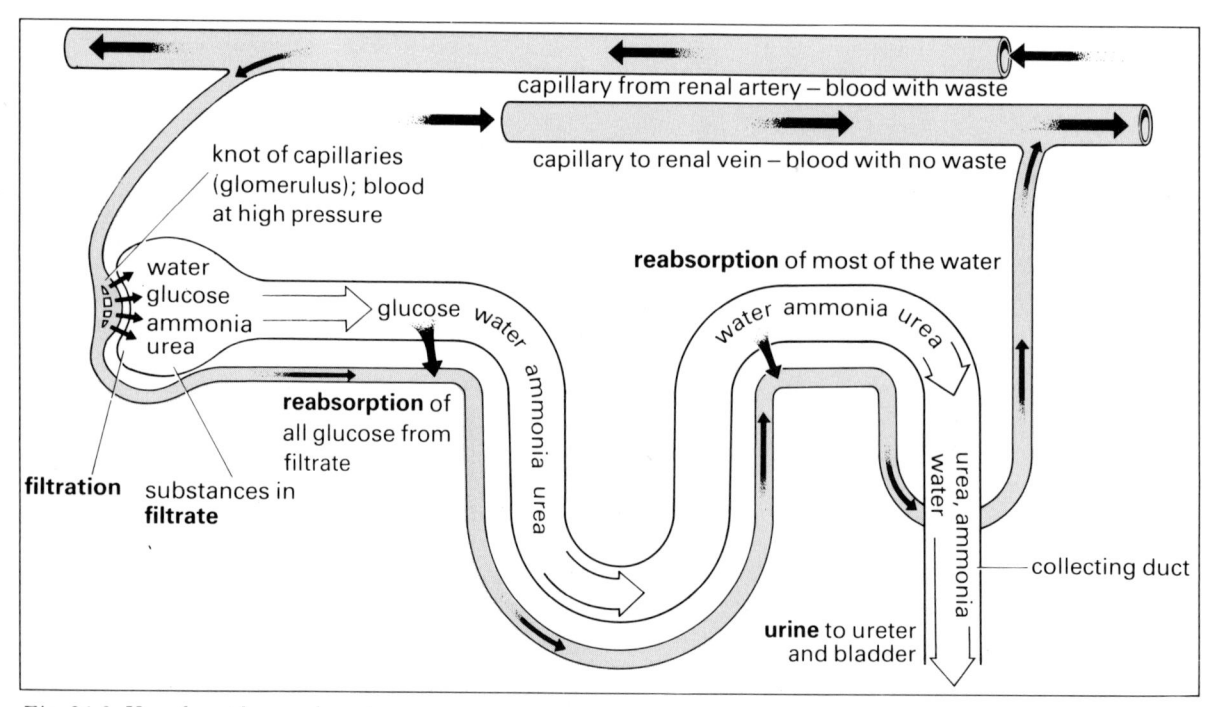

Fig. 36.3 How the nephron makes urine.

7 Keeping the steady state

Urine goes to the bladder

All the nephrons open into tubes which carry urine to the **pelvis** of the kidney. Drops of urine are carried down the ureters to the bladder by **peristalsis** (see page 38).

Urine leaves the body

The liquid waste is released from the bladder. The outlet from the bladder is the **urethra**. This tube is guarded by muscles. Babies cannot control the opening and closing of this ring of muscle. After about two years, most people can control the emptying of their bladder (Fig. 36.4).

Keeping the water balance

If you have drunk a lot of liquid, you will produce a lot of weak urine. If your body is short of water, you get rid of a small amount of strong, dark yellow urine. This shows that one job of the kidneys is keeping the water balance inside the body.

Excretion

If you have been eating a lot of protein, the amount of urea in your urine increases. Amino acids are made when protein is digested. They are used to repair cells and make new ones. If we eat too much protein, the amino acids cannot be stored anywhere in the body. They are broken down in the liver and urea is made (see page 57).

This shows that the kidney has a second job (Fig. 36.5). This is to get rid of waste substances made by chemical processes in the body. This is **excretion**. Without excretion the body would be poisoned. Carbon dioxide is another waste chemical. It is excreted from the lungs.

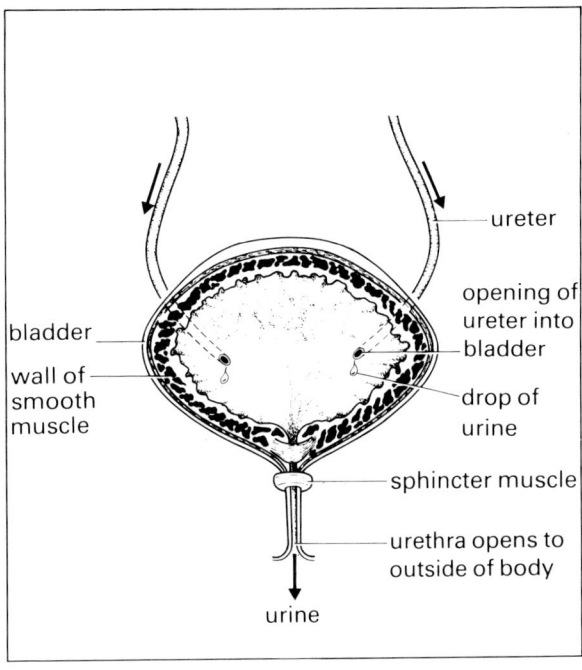

Fig. 36.4 The opening of the bladder is controlled by muscles.

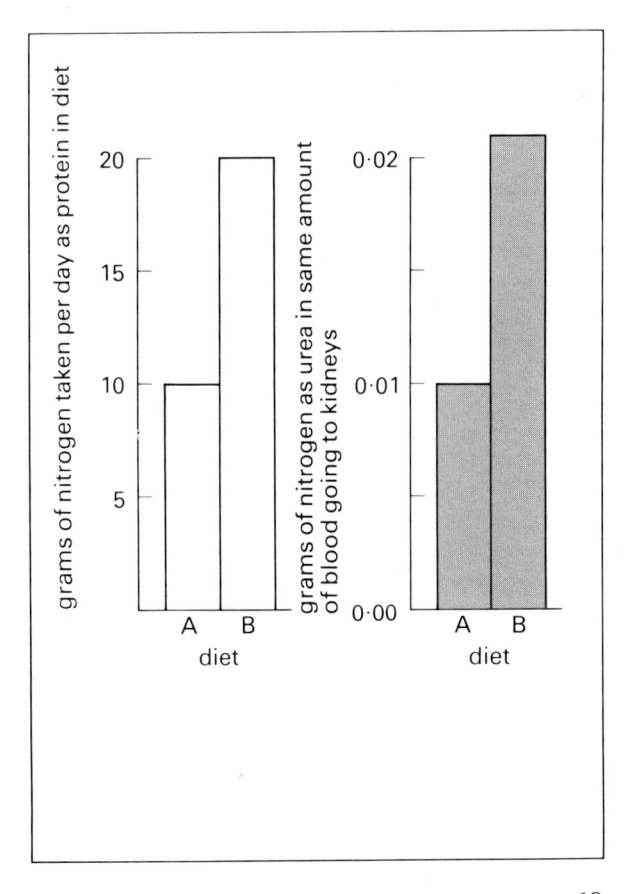

Fig. 36.5 The more protein you eat, the more urea is made.

7 Keeping the steady state

37 Kidney machines

Kidney failure

Your kidneys contain more nephrons than you need. If some nephrons go wrong, there are spare ones to take over the work. So you can live with one kidney, but if both kidneys fail you will die. Today, people suffering from kidney failure may be attached to a **kidney machine** for short periods (Fig. 37.1). The kidney is a special kind of filter. This process of **filtration** is fairly straightforward. So it has been possible to make a machine do the job. If the kidney did as many chemical processes as the liver, it would be very hard to invent a machine to do its job.

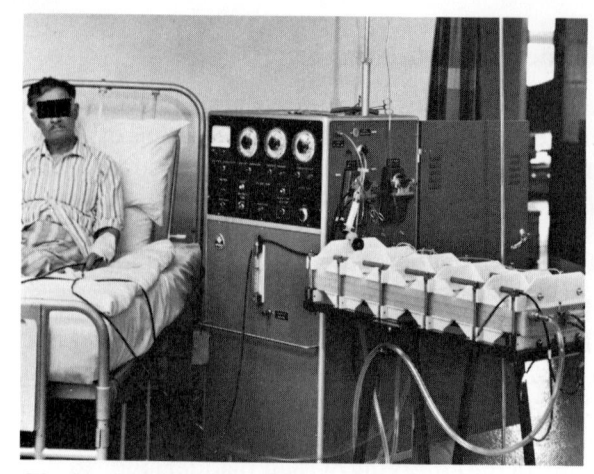

Fig. 37.1 A patient attached to a kidney machine.

The main part of a kidney machine is circular. Blood from the artery passes through a tube made from two membranes. The tube is arranged in a spiral.
Kidney machine liquid flows the opposite way on the outside of the membrane.

Looking down on the grooves in the machine

kidney machine liquid goes out

plastic case

blood from artery goes to machine

blood goes back to vein from machine

kidney machine liquid goes in

⟶ = direction of blood flow

---▶ = direction of flow of kidney machine liquid

Kidney machine cut open to show how the blood and liquid move.

double sheet of selective membrane, acts as a filter

plastic case

blood from artery goes to machine

blood goes back to vein from machine

------▶ = movement of waste from blood to machine liquid

kidney machine liquid goes out

kidney machine liquid goes in

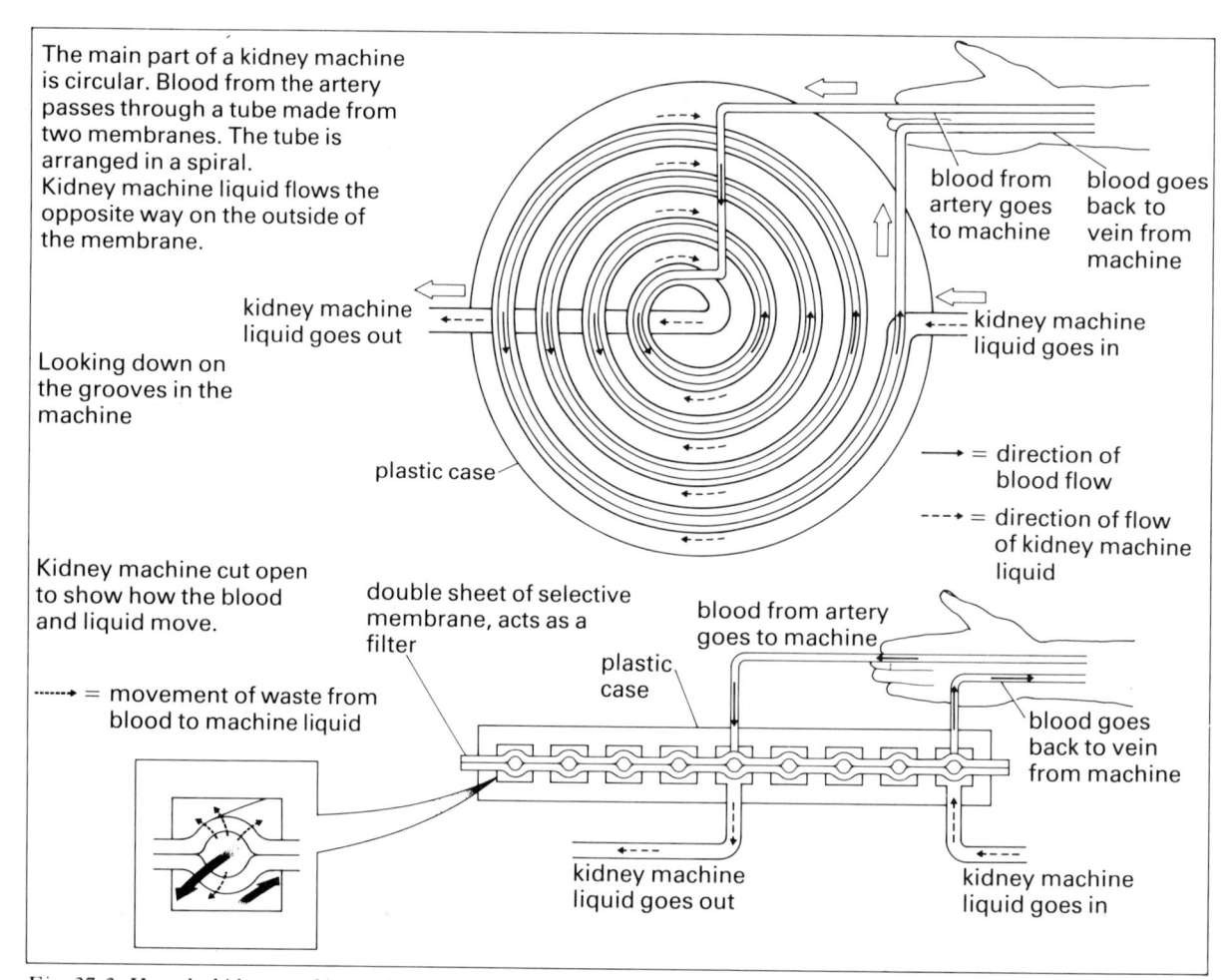

Fig. 37.2 How the kidney machine works.

7 Keeping the steady state

The kidney machine at work

All kidney machines have a filter or membrane. Blood from the patient passes along one side of the membrane. On the other side there is a liquid. This contains the same amount of water, sugar and salts as blood plasma. Unwanted waste materials pass from the patient's blood into the liquid of the machine. Blood cells and proteins cannot pass through the membrane. Sugars and salts are needed by the body. They are present in plasma and the machine liquid and pass equally in both directions (Fig. 37.2).

The patient and the machine

A patient suffering from kidney failure is usually attached to the machine at least twice a week. By doing this, the amount of waste in the blood is kept under control (Fig. 37.3). The patient must be careful about the food eaten. The diet must not contain too much protein.

The patient is attached to the machine by **cannulae**. These are tubes fixed into the blood vessels of an arm or leg (Fig. 37.4). When kidney machines were first used, these tubes lasted in one place for about three years. As a patient has two arms and two legs, the longest time a patient could continue to use a machine was 12 years. Now it is longer. Kidney machines are in short supply. The machines are expensive and they need costly membranes and liquid. They need skilled people to operate them. Instead of a machine, a patient may be able to get a kidney from another person. This is a kidney **transplant**.

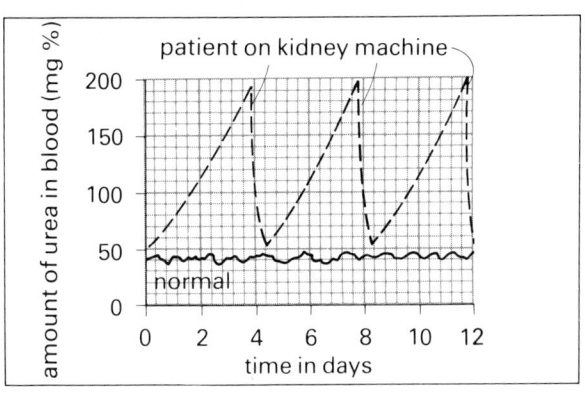

Fig. 37.3 This graph shows the amount of urea in the blood of two people. One person (∼∼∼) has normal kidneys. The other (– – – –) has kidneys that have failed. This patient is attached to a kidney machine every four days.

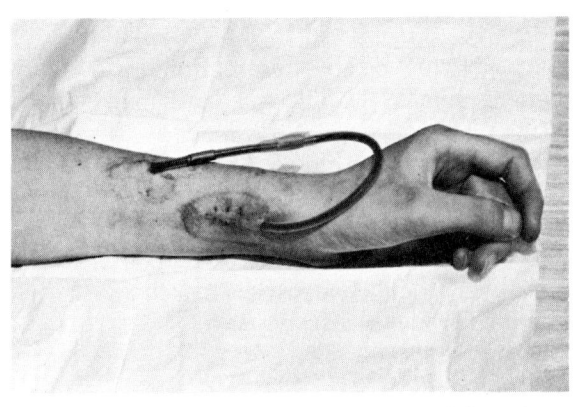

Fig. 37.4 Two tubes (cannulae) are used to attach the patient to the kidney machine.

Summary: Keeping the steady state

* The liver has a double blood supply.
* The liver is the chemical factory of the body.
* It keeps the supply of chemicals to body cells steady.
* The liver produces heat that helps keep body temperature steady at 37 °C.
* The body carries out different activities that help to produce or lose heat, or keep heat in.
* Skin is a water-proof, protective cover. It also helps regulate body temperature.
* All body cells are surrounded by liquid. The amount of water in this liquid must be kept steady if cells are to work properly.
* Water enters and leaves cells by osmosis.
* The amount of water in the body is kept steady by the kidney.
* The kidney also gets rid of, or excretes, some waste chemicals.
* The kidney is made up of tiny tubes called nephrons. These filter the blood to remove waste.
* The waste liquid passed out of the kidney is urine.
* Body activities that help keep steady levels are known as homeostatic processes.

8 Coordination

38 Reacting to changes

The body must be able to react quickly to changes (Fig. 38.1). These changes may be taking place *outside* or *inside* the body. If your hand touches something red hot, you immediately pull your hand away. When food arrives in your stomach, it reacts by making digestive juice. The change you react to is a **stimulus**. When a body reacts to a change it responds or makes a **response**.

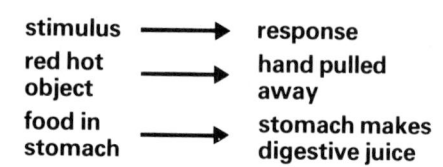

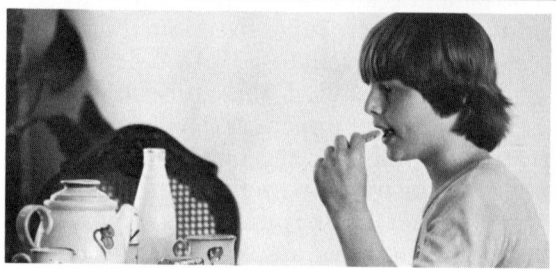

Fig. 38.1 The body must be able to react to changes.

stimulus	→	response
red hot object	→	hand pulled away
food in stomach	→	stomach makes digestive juice

Sensing changes

The body must be able to **sense** or detect these changes. Stimuli are sensed by groups of special cells. These are called **sensory cells**. These cells are often grouped in **sense organs** (Fig. 38.2). Each sense organ detects a particular type of stimulus. Temperature receptors in the skin sense a hot object. They cannot detect light. Sensory cells in the eye detect light.

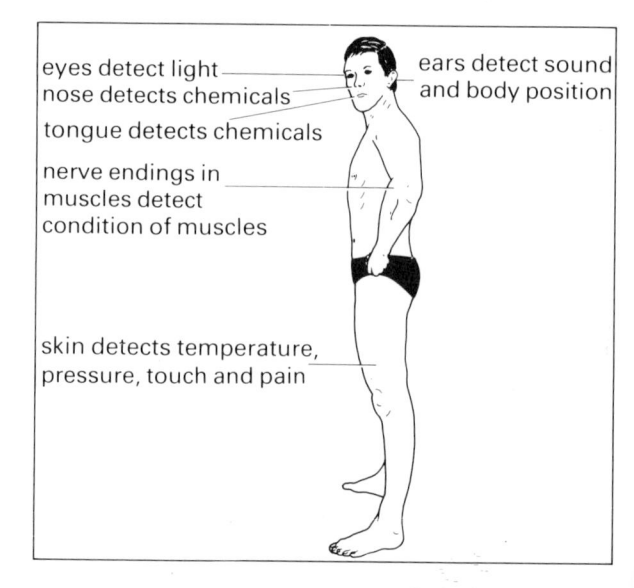

Fig. 38.2 The sense organs.

8 Coordination

Making a response

The part of the body that reacts or produces an effect is called an **effector**. Effectors can be **muscles** or **glands**. Your arm and shoulder muscles pull your hand away from a hot object. Glands in the stomach wall make digestive juices.

Linking sense organs and effectors

The stimulus may be sensed by a part of the body some way off from the part which reacts. There must be a link between the sense organ and the effector. The link is the **central nervous system** (**CNS**) and the **nerves**. The CNS has two parts, the **brain** and the **spinal cord** (Fig. 38.3). The nerves link the CNS to the sense organs and effectors. The CNS is important in **coordinating** the body's actions. This means it brings about the responses at the right time (Fig. 38.4). The **nervous system** is made up of the sense organs, nerves and the central nervous system.

The brain and spinal cord are protected by bone. The sense organs are not shown.

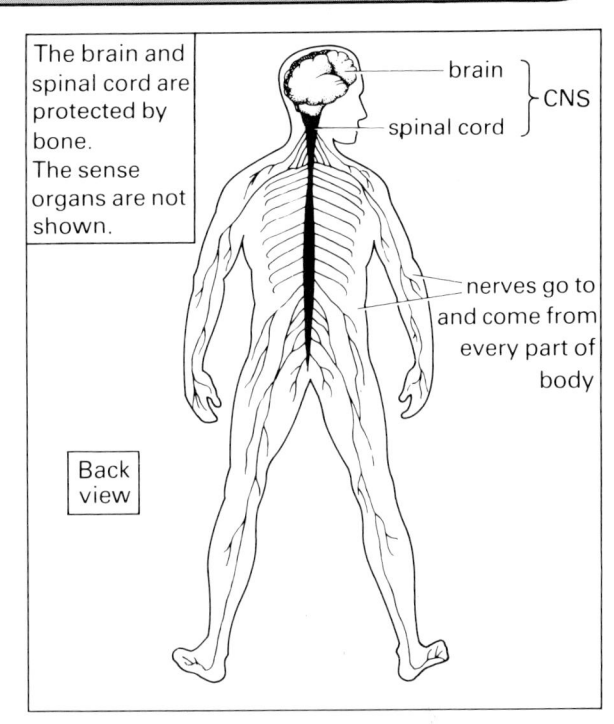

Fig. 38.3 The human nervous system.

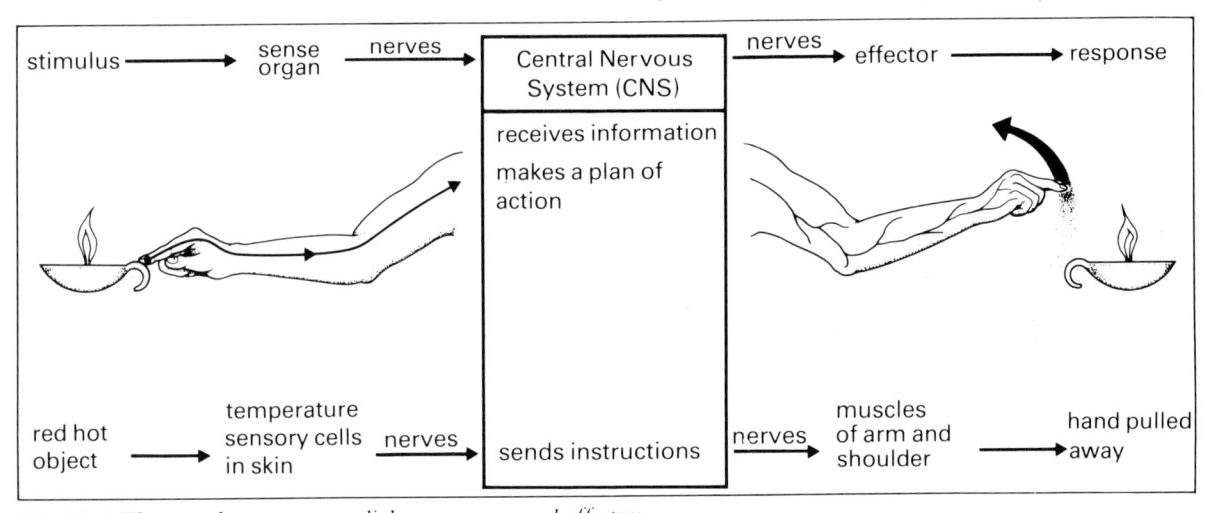

Fig. 38.4 The central nervous system links sense organs and effectors.

Muscles and glands

Muscles and glands can be effectors. There are three types of muscles (see page 124). **Voluntary** or **skeletal muscles** move the body's limbs, back, neck and parts of the face. You can decide how and when they are moved. They can be controlled by the will **consciously**. **Involuntary** or **smooth muscles** control the movements of the gut and blood vessel walls. These muscles work automatically. They have a nerve supply but it is different from that going to voluntary muscles. **Cardiac muscle** in the heart does not need a nerve supply. Nerves to the heart only speed up or slow down the heart beat.

There are many different glands in the body (see page 89). Cells in glands make juices or **secretions**. For instance the **salivary gland** makes **saliva** (spit). This happens when the food is smelt, seen or tasted.

8 Coordination

39 Nervous system

Nerves carry information

Nerves carry 'information' to the brain and spinal cord and carry 'instructions' out (Fig. 39.1). Electrical and chemical changes take place in the nerve as the message is carried. These changes are the **nerve impulse**.

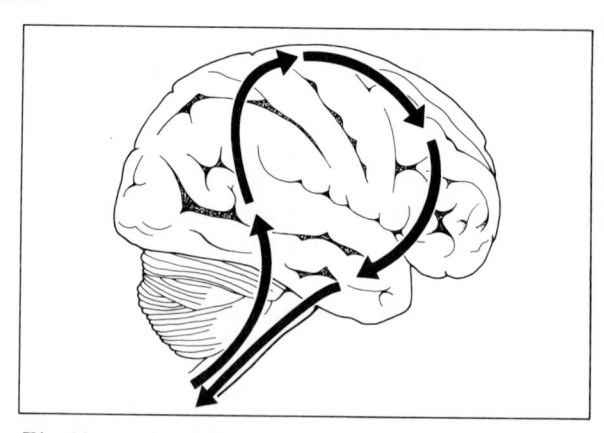

Fig. 39.1 Information in – instructions out

Nerve cells

A nerve can be examined under a microscope. A nerve is really a bundle of fine threads or **nerve fibres**. (Fig. 39.2). Each fibre comes from a **nerve cell** or **neuron**.

There are three types of neurons (Fig. 39.3). **Sensory neurons** carry information from a sense organ into the brain or spinal cord. **Motor neurons** take instructions out from the brain or spinal cord to make the body work. Motor neurons take the instructions to muscles or glands. In the brain or spinal cord there is a third kind of nerve cell – the **connector neuron**.

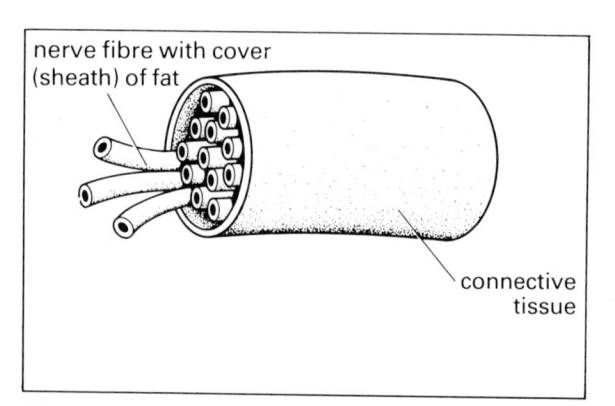

Fig. 39.2 A nerve is a bundle of nerve fibres

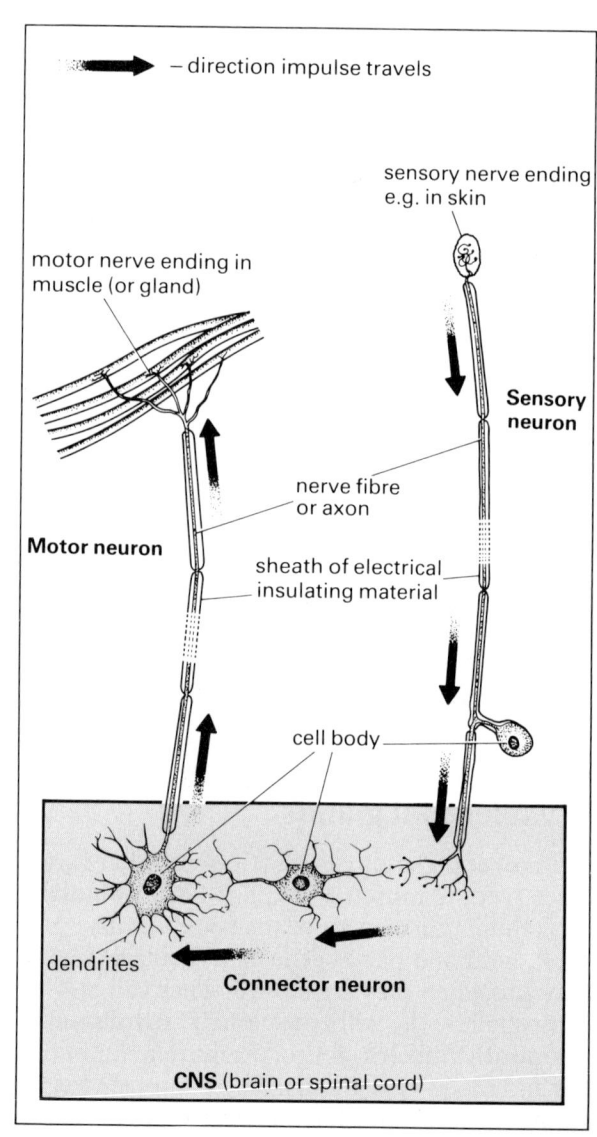

Fig. 39.3 The three types of nerve cells.

8 Coordination

Reflex actions

Some of the body's responses cannot be controlled by the will. For instance, you cannot stop yourself pulling your hand away from a red hot object. You always sneeze when pepper gets up your nose. These responses are called **reflex actions**. Reflex actions are automatic and fast. In a reflex action, any one stimulus always leads to the same response. A few reflexes need only three neurons to make the response (as in Fig. 39.3). The position of these neurons in the spinal cord is shown in Fig. 39.4. Two examples of reflex actions are shown in Fig. 39.5.

Gaps between neurons

There is always a gap between neurons. The impulse has to 'jump' across this gap or **synapse**. Some drugs work at these gaps. They can affect the way the nerve impulse is passed from neuron to neuron. This can change our behaviour.

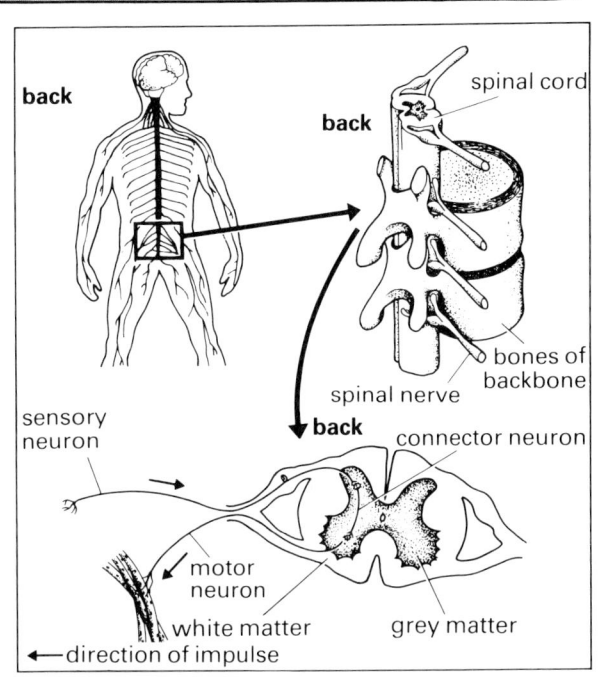

Fig. 39.4 Nerve cells and the spinal cord.

Stimulus	Sense organ detects stimulus	Sensory neuron carries information to brain or spinal cord	Brain or spinal cord receive information	Motor neuron carries information to effector	Effector is made to work	Response is a reflex action
dirt in eye	touch sensory cell in skin of eye lid	impulse passes along sensory neuron	impulse passes through connector neurons in brain	impulse passes along motor neuron	tears made by tear glands	eyes water
sharp blow below knee-cap	stretch sensory cell in leg muscle	impulse passes along sensory neuron	impulse passes through connector neurons in spinal cord	impulse passes along motor neuron	thigh muscle contracts	leg straightens

Fig. 39.5 How two reflexes are brought about.

8 Coordination

40 The brain

Protecting the brain

The **brain** is a large, delicate organ. It is surrounded by the skull for protection (Fig. 40.1). The brain is held inside a fluid cushion so it is not knocked against the bone of the skull when the head is moved quickly.

The work of the brain

You can control many of the body's actions, learn skills, remember things that have happened in the past and solve problems. These are all brought about by the brain. The brain has many parts. Each part has different jobs to do (Fig. 40.2). There are about 10 000 million neurons in the brain. Each neuron makes many connections (synapses) with other neurons.

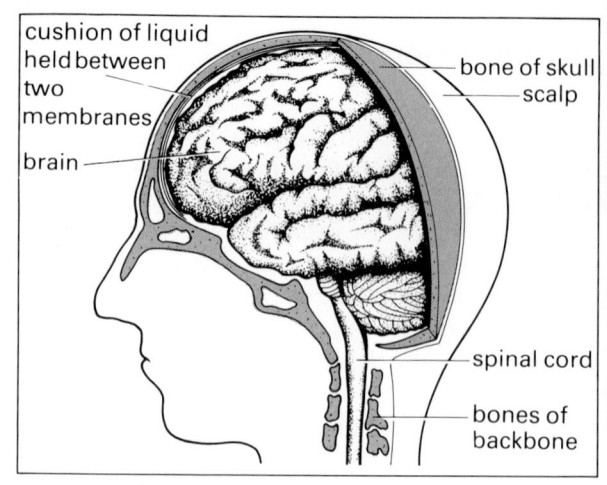

Fig. 40.1 The parts that protect the brain.

Millions and millions of complicated pathways are possible in the brain. The brain receives thousands of impulses (bits of information) every second. These come up through the spinal cord and in from the sense organs in the head. At the same time the brain is sending out thousands of impulses each second!

cerebrum or cerebral cortex – receives information from all sense organs in head; the part of the brain used for thinking, problem-solving, memory, personality and control of conscious actions

cerebellum – helps coordinate movements of the body's skeletal muscles

thalamus – containing the 'pain centre'

pituitary gland – the 'master endocrine gland' that controls other endocrine glands

medulla – controls heart and breathing rate

hypothalamus – controls sleeping and waking, feeding, drinking, body temperature and amount of water in the blood

spinal cord

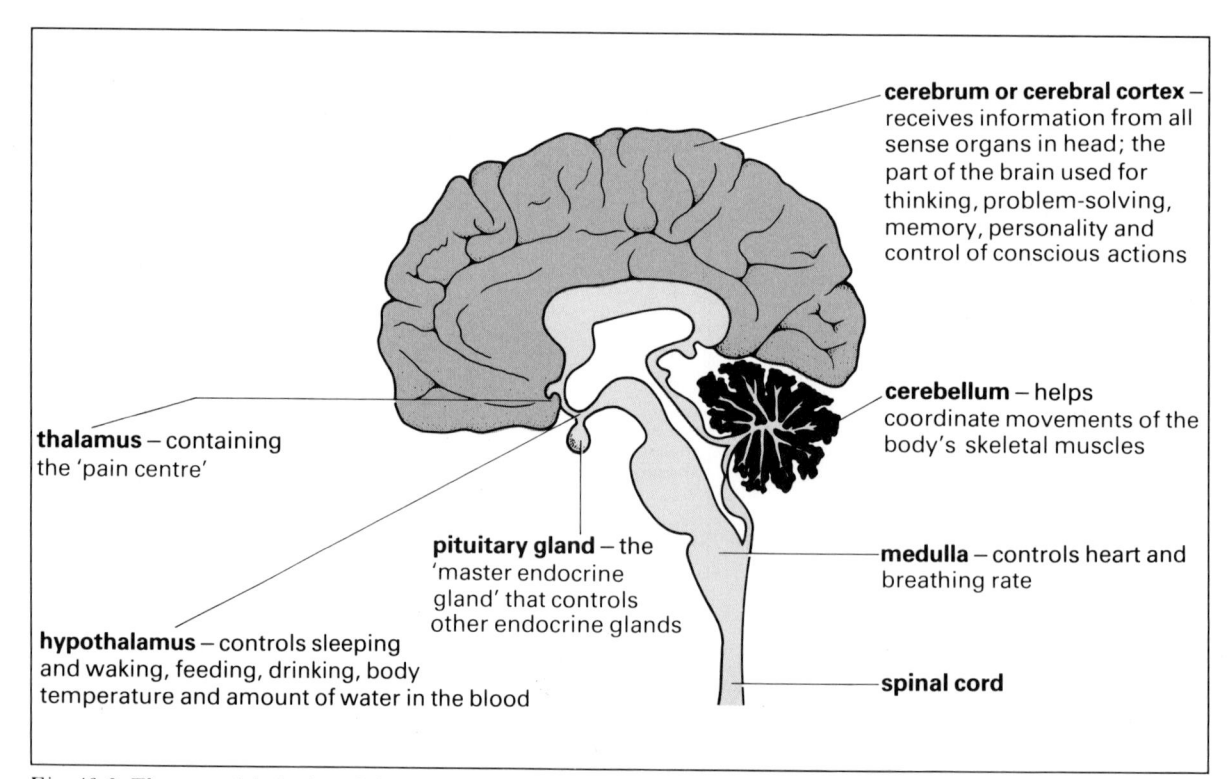

Fig. 40.2 The parts of the brain and their work.

8 Coordination

The brain's map of the body

The brain contains a 'map' of your body. So the location of each sensation (feeling) or action is known (Fig. 40.3). This map is not to scale (Fig. 40.4). The hands are very sensitive. They need more brain space than the thighs because the hands are used for feeling objects and for delicate tasks.

Conscious actions

A speck of dirt in the eye makes your eye 'water'. This reflex action is automatic. But you look in a mirror to find out what has made you cry. This is a **conscious** action or one that you think about. A conscious action is far more complicated than a reflex action (Fig. 40.5). Many neurons are needed for a conscious action. Also many impulses are passed along these neurons at the same time. So lots of information goes into the brain, where decisions are made, and many detailed instructions are sent out. (Fig. 40.5 and 40.6).

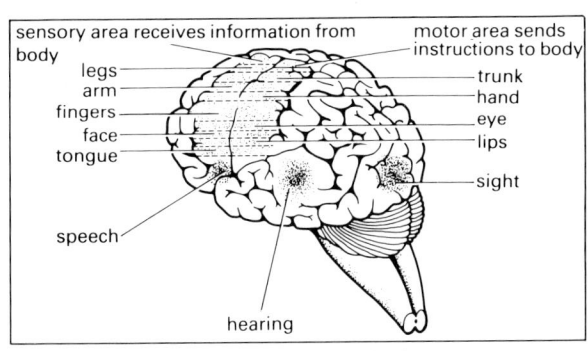

Fig. 40.3 The 'map' of the body in the brain

Fig. 40.4 The 'body' in the brain: the bigger the part in the drawing, the more 'space' it has in the brain.

Reflex action	Conscious action
very fast	may take a few seconds
may use just 3 neurons	involves many neurons
neuron pathways are in brain or spinal cord	neuron pathways are always in brain
the response to the stimulus is always the same	the response may vary depending on the circumstances

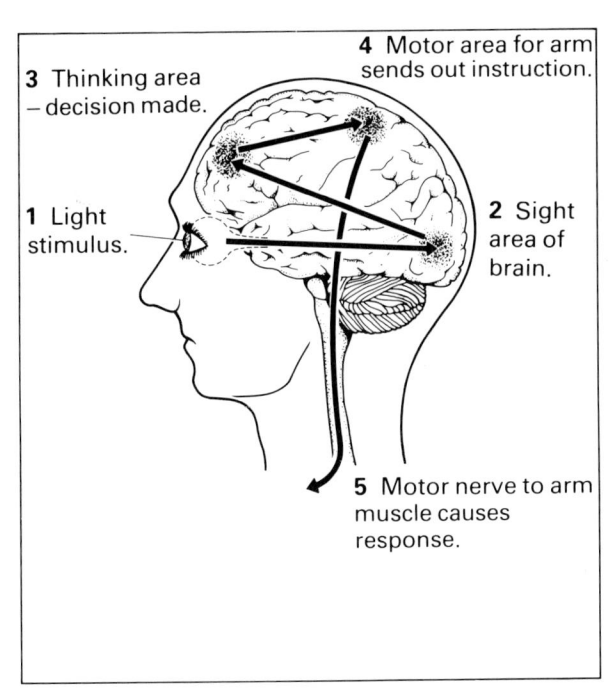

Fig. 40.5 A conscious action. This person sees something and decides to touch it.

1 Light stimulus.
2 Sight area of brain.
3 Thinking area – decision made.
4 Motor area for arm sends out instruction.
5 Motor nerve to arm muscle causes response.

Fig. 40.6 Comparing reflex and conscious actions.

8 Coordination

41 Learning

You are born with many of the reflexes that build up the way you behave. Your mouth waters when food is in it; you blink if dirt enters the eye. These reflexes that are with you at birth are **innate**. Some types of behaviour are **learned** after birth. In humans a great deal of learning happens during childhood. This is the time when we learn to speak, read and write. Learning makes us able to respond or behave in complicated ways.

Fig. 41.1 Ivan Pavlov (the older man) with one of his dogs and some helpers.

Pavlov's experiment

One simple type of learning was worked out by a Russian scientist called Pavlov (Fig. 41.1). He did experiments on dogs. He noticed two innate reflexes in dogs; when hungry, they make saliva if food is nearby and they react to the sound of a bell by becoming alert. Pavlov's experiment is shown below (Fig. 41.2).

Two stimuli given separately

Making saliva is a reflex action that helps the dog eat food. Paying attention to an unusual sound is another reflex. It has nothing to do with food.

Both stimuli given at the same time on many occasions

The dog always hears the bell as the food arrives. It begins to 'link' the two stimuli (food and bell) in its brain.

Sound stimulus given alone

The dog expects the sound of the bell to mean that food is coming. So it makes saliva.

The dog had learnt that the sound of the bell and food were always linked. Eventually a stimulus that had nothing to do with food (bell ringing) made the animal produce saliva. The dog was **conditioned** to make saliva whenever the bell rang. This very simple type of learning is called **conditioning** or a **conditioned reflex**.

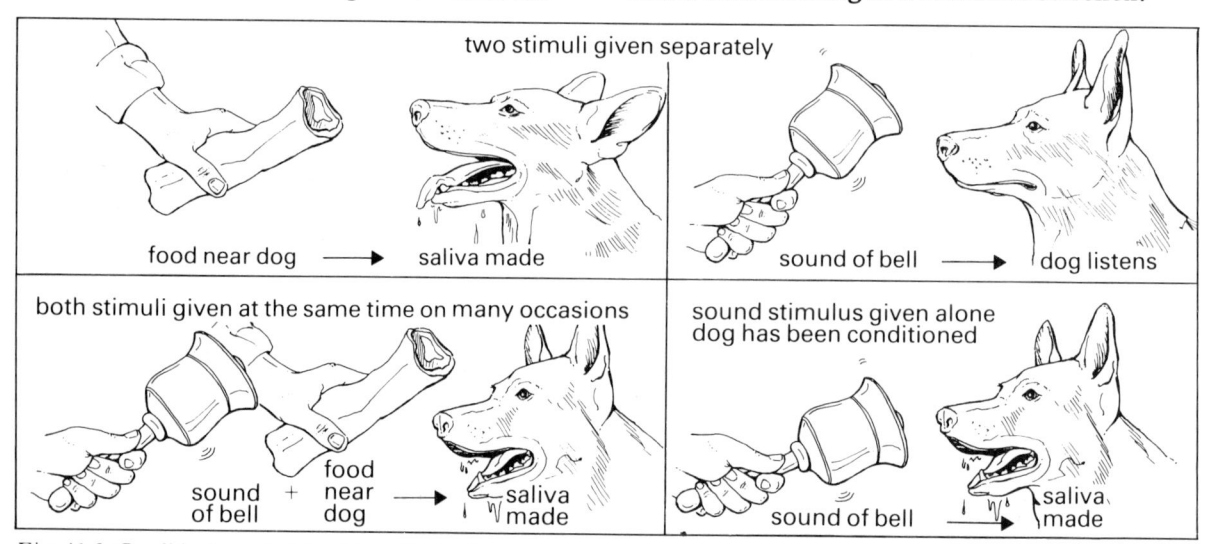

Fig. 41.2 Conditioning a dog's 'making saliva' reflex.

8 Coordination

Conditioning in humans

A puff of air in the eye will make a person blink. If the same person hears a tapping sound, no blinking happens (Fig. 41.3). The two stimuli, the puff of air and the tapping are then given together many times. After a while the person may become conditioned. The tapping sound will cause a blink without the puff of air. This is *learning* because a stimulus makes the person respond in a way he or she did not respond before. However, conditioning does not explain much human learning. It does not explain how you learn responses that are new or the way you work out problems. Most human learning is much more complicated than conditioning.

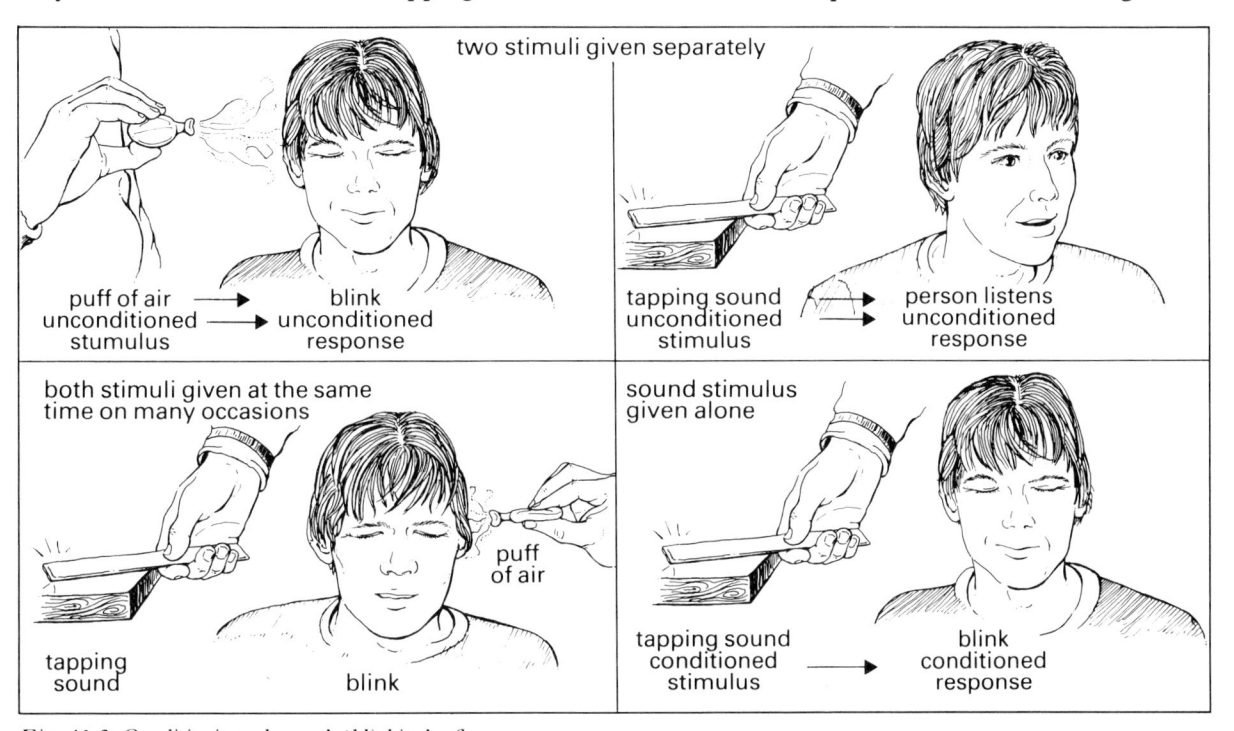

Fig. 41.3 Conditioning a human's 'blinking' reflex.

Fig. 41.4 Praise is a reward to a child and speeds up learning.

Speeding up learning

Learning can be speeded up by giving **rewards** or **punishments**. This is used when training animals. A dog is given a biscuit or patted when it has performed as its owner wanted. This is giving a reward. When the dog does not obey, or does something that is not wanted, the owner will say 'No!' or may even hit the dog. The owner is stopping this behaviour by punishing the dog. Scientists have found that animals learn faster when they are rewarded.

Parents and teachers also use rewards and punishments when teaching children. You probably learn better when you are rewarded by praise rather than punished by having a detention!

8 Coordination

42 Eyes

Two eyes are better than one

The eyes detect light. The two eyes are positioned so that each one gives you a slightly different view of your surroundings. This means you have **binocular vision**. Each eye makes an **image** or picture of what you are looking at (Fig. 42.1). Information about the image in each eye is sent along a nerve to your brain. The brain compares the images from each eye. This makes anything you look at have 'depth' or **three dimensions** (3-D). Your brain can also work out the size of an object and its distance from you.

Keeping the eyes clean

The **eyelids** cover the eyes (Fig. 42.2). The **lashes** flick away dust approaching the eye. The **tear glands** make tears. When you blink, this liquid is spread over the surface of the eye. It washes the eye and stops the surface drying out. Tears drain away through the **tear ducts**.

Moving the eyes

Both eyes can be moved in their hollows or **sockets** in the skull. The movement is brought about by the eye muscles (Fig. 42.3). You can control these muscles. Most people cannot move one eye alone — both eyes move together. They are **coordinated** so that you can see properly.

Light must enter the eyes

Each eye is a liquid-filled ball. The cells that detect light are on the inside of the back wall. The front layers of the eye are **transparent** (clear). This means the light can pass through and get inside the eye.

Light gets to the back of the eye by passing through the **pupil** (Fig. 42.4). This hole is surrounded by the coloured **iris**. The iris contains muscles to change the size of the pupil. When you look at a bright light, the iris muscles work to make the pupil smaller. This cuts down

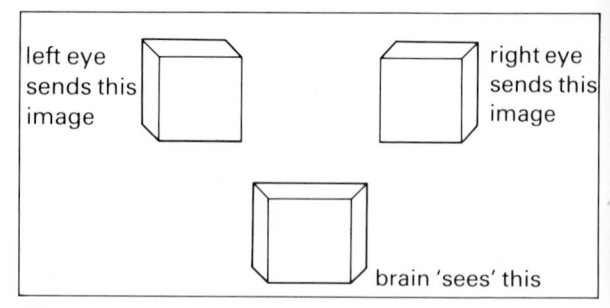

Fig. 42.1 Each eye sends a slightly different image to the brain.

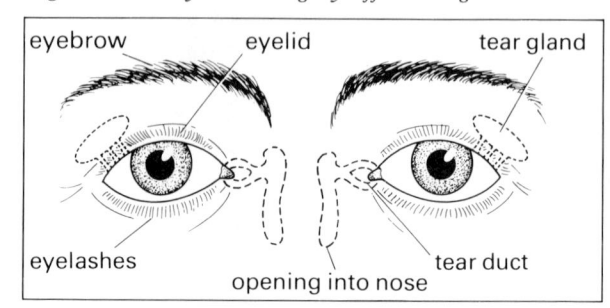

Fig. 42.2 The parts that protect and clean the eye.

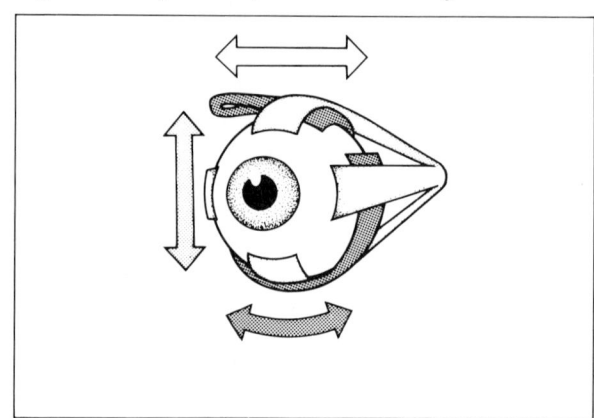

Fig. 42.3 Muscles move the eyeball.

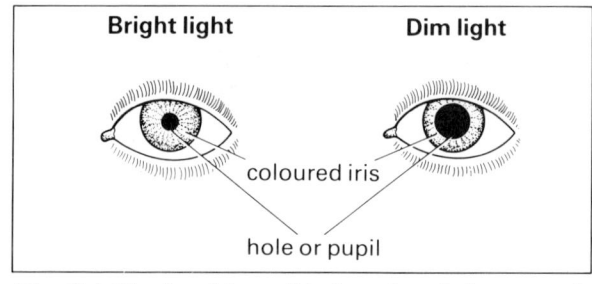

Fig. 42.4 The size of the pupil is changed to suit the amount of light.

the amount of light entering the eye and so protects the sensitive cells. If you are in the dark, the pupil gets bigger to let in more light. The iris muscles work automatically – another reflex.

8 Coordination

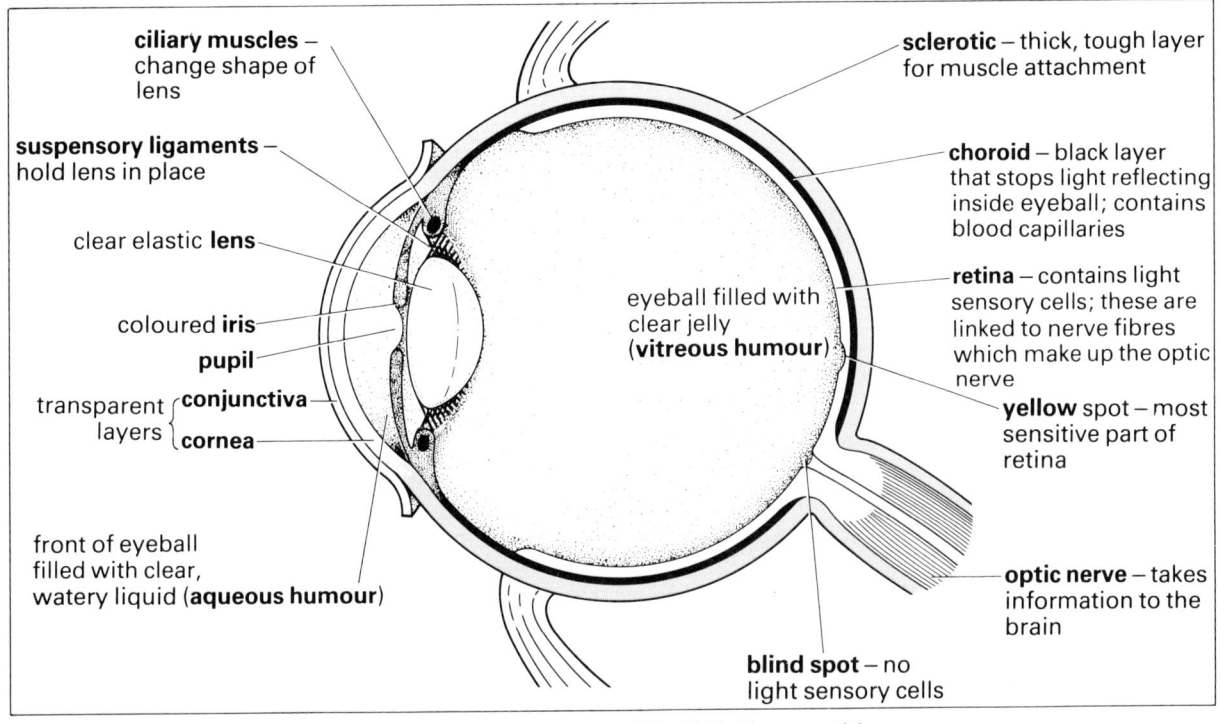

Fig. 42.5 The parts of the eye.

Labels:
- **ciliary muscles** – change shape of lens
- **suspensory ligaments** – hold lens in place
- clear elastic **lens**
- coloured **iris**
- **pupil**
- transparent layers { **conjunctiva**, **cornea** }
- front of eyeball filled with clear, watery liquid (**aqueous humour**)
- **sclerotic** – thick, tough layer for muscle attachment
- **choroid** – black layer that stops light reflecting inside eyeball; contains blood capillaries
- **retina** – contains light sensory cells; these are linked to nerve fibres which make up the optic nerve
- eyeball filled with clear jelly (**vitreous humour**)
- **yellow** spot – most sensitive part of retina
- **optic nerve** – takes information to the brain
- **blind spot** – no light sensory cells

Light sensitive cells

Light enters the eye and hits the **light sensory cells** of the **retina** (Fig. 42.5). The light causes a chemical change in these cells. This chemical change triggers off nerve impulses. The impulses travel through the sensory **optic nerve** to the brain. As the pupil is a tiny hole, the image made on the retina is upside-down. The brain has to correct the image so you see properly.

light ⟶ light sensory cells in retina of eye ⟶ sensory neurons in optic nerve ⟶ brain

Focussing the light

Some of the objects you look at may be near to you; others may be far away. To get a clear image on the retina, **focussing** is needed. A telescope or microscope is focussed by moving the lens nearer to or further away from the object. The eyeball cannot be made longer and shorter. Focussing in the eye is done by changing the shape of the lens. It is elastic and its thickness can change. The thickness of the lens is controlled by the **ciliary muscles** inside the eye. This process is called **accommodation** (Fig. 42.6).

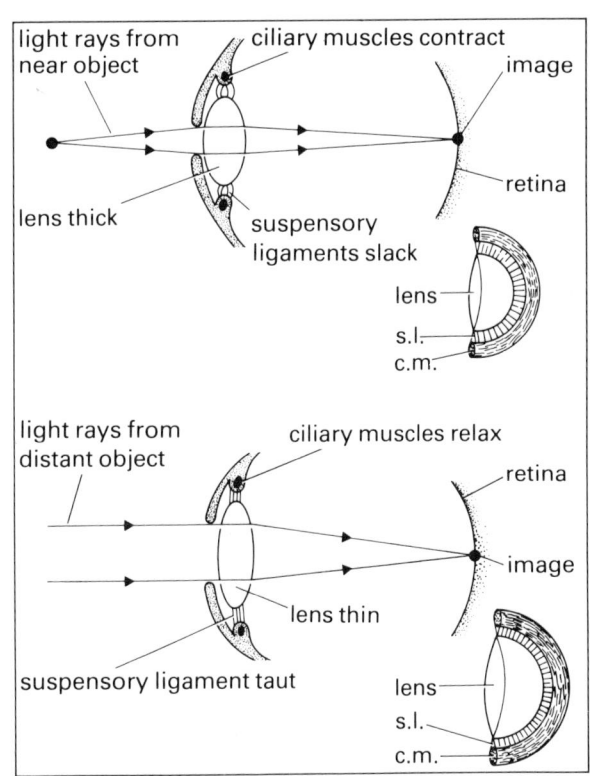

Fig. 42.6 Focussing in the eye.

Labels (near object): light rays from near object; ciliary muscles contract; image; retina; lens thick; suspensory ligaments slack; lens; s.l.; c.m.

Labels (distant object): light rays from distant object; ciliary muscles relax; retina; image; lens thin; suspensory ligament taut; lens; s.l.; c.m.

81

8 Coordination

43 Eye faults

Sometimes the eyes cannot focus properly. There are three kinds of focussing faults.

Astigmatism

Astigmatism is a fault caused by an unevenly curved **cornea**. Anyone suffering from astigmatism cannot focus on upright and sideways lines at the same time (Fig. 43.1). The fault can be helped by putting a lens in front of the eye (Fig. 43.2). The lens can be held in a frame (**spectacles**) or floated on the surface of the eye as a **contact lens** (Fig. 43.3).

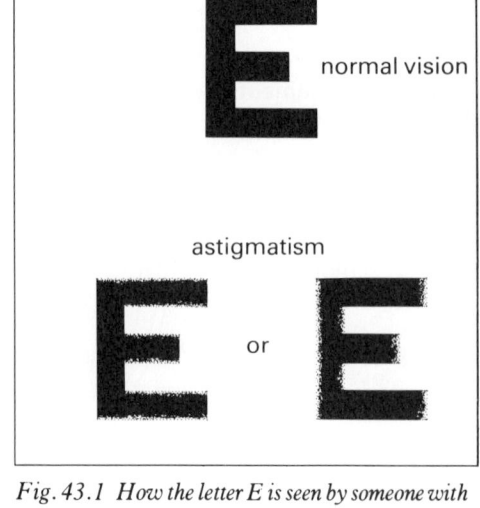

Fig. 43.1 How the letter E is seen by someone with astigmatism.

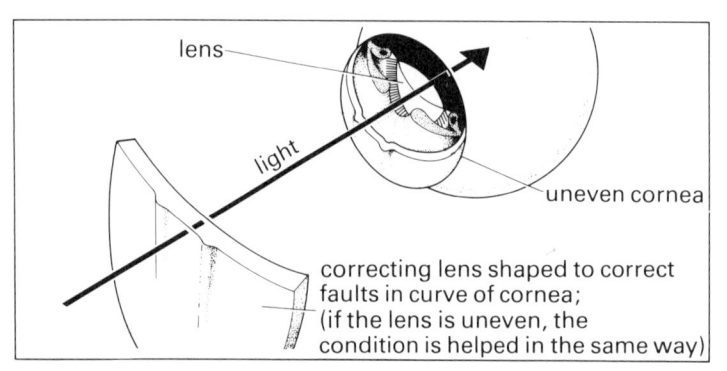

Fig. 43.2 How astigmatism can be helped.

Fig. 43.3 A person putting in a contact lens.

Long and short sight

Some people can see distant objects clearly but cannot focus on objects close by. They are **long-sighted**. Others can see near objects but cannot focus on distant objects. They are **short-sighted**.

Fig. 43.4 A view as seen by three people—someone with normal vision, a long-sighted person and a short-sighted person.

8 Coordination

Curing long sight

Long sight happens if the eyeball has a squashed shape (it is too short). As people get older, the lens loses some of its elasticity and so it cannot be pulled thin. Old people tend to be long sighted. Long-sighted people can be helped when a **convex lens** is put in front of the eye. The lens helps to focus light on the retina (Fig. 43.5).

Curing short sight

Short sight happens if the eyeball is too long. Short-sighted people can also be helped if they have spectacles or contact lenses fitted. The lenses must be **concave** (Fig. 43.6).

There are many other eye faults. Some can be cured and some cannot (Fig. 43.7).

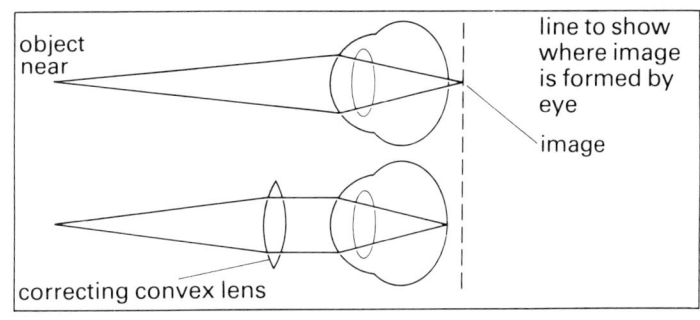

Fig. 43.5 Correcting long sight. Distant objects can be focussed properly; images of near ones cannot. Long sight is corrected by using a lens which bends light rays towards each other – a converging or convex lens.

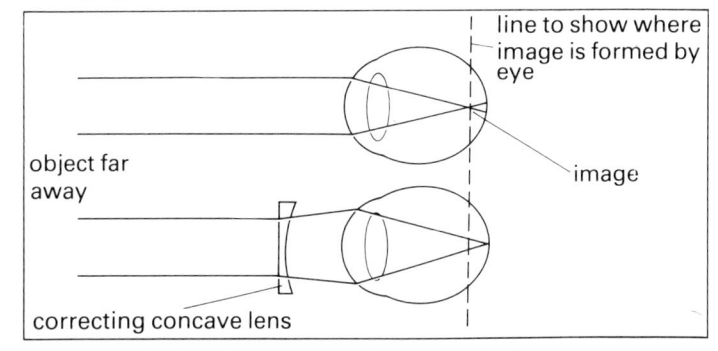

Fig. 43.6 Correcting short sight. Near objects can be focussed properly; images of distant ones cannot. Short sight is corrected by using a lens which bends light rays away from each other – a diverging or concave lens.

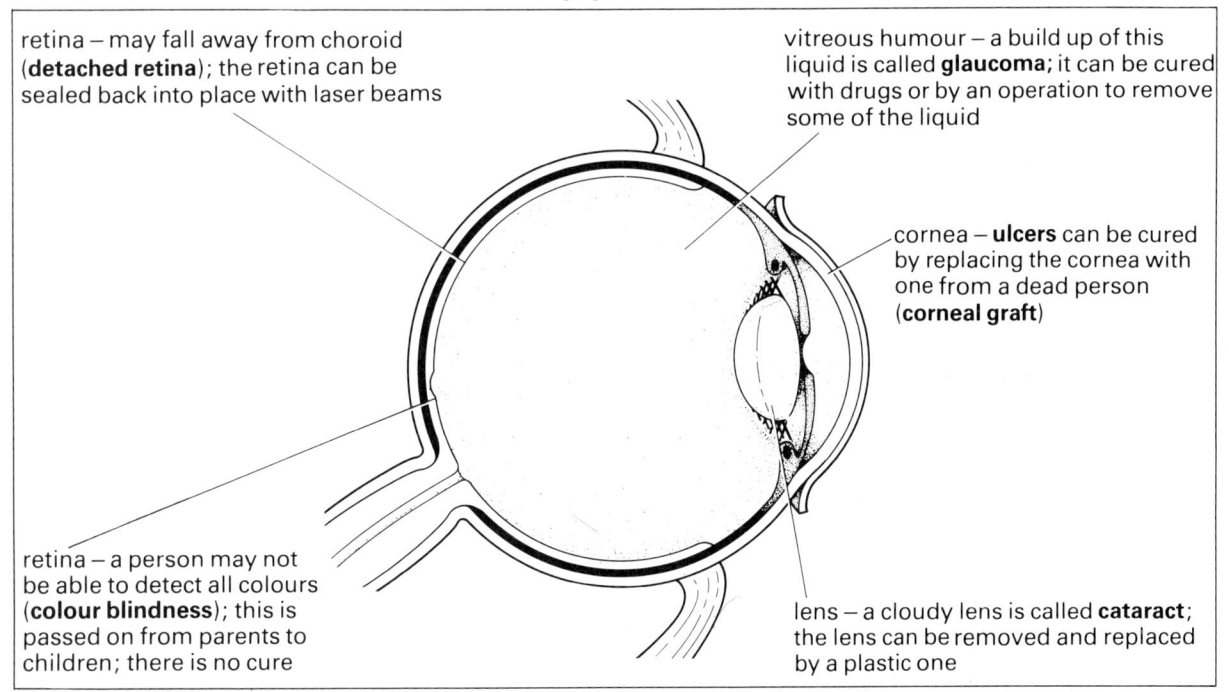

retina – may fall away from choroid (**detached retina**); the retina can be sealed back into place with laser beams

vitreous humour – a build up of this liquid is called **glaucoma**; it can be cured with drugs or by an operation to remove some of the liquid

cornea – **ulcers** can be cured by replacing the cornea with one from a dead person (**corneal graft**)

retina – a person may not be able to detect all colours (**colour blindness**); this is passed on from parents to children; there is no cure

lens – a cloudy lens is called **cataract**; the lens can be removed and replaced by a plastic one

Fig. 43.7 Some other eye faults.

8 Coordination

44 Ears

The ears detect sound energy so that hearing is possible. They are also sensitive to the position and movements of the head. The part of the ear on the outside of the head is only one part of this sense organ. Most of the ear is inside the bone of the skull for protection (Fig. 44.1). Like the eye, the ear is made up of several parts (Fig. 44.2).

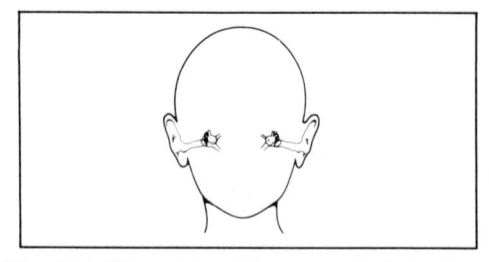

Fig. 44.1 The position of the ears inside the head.

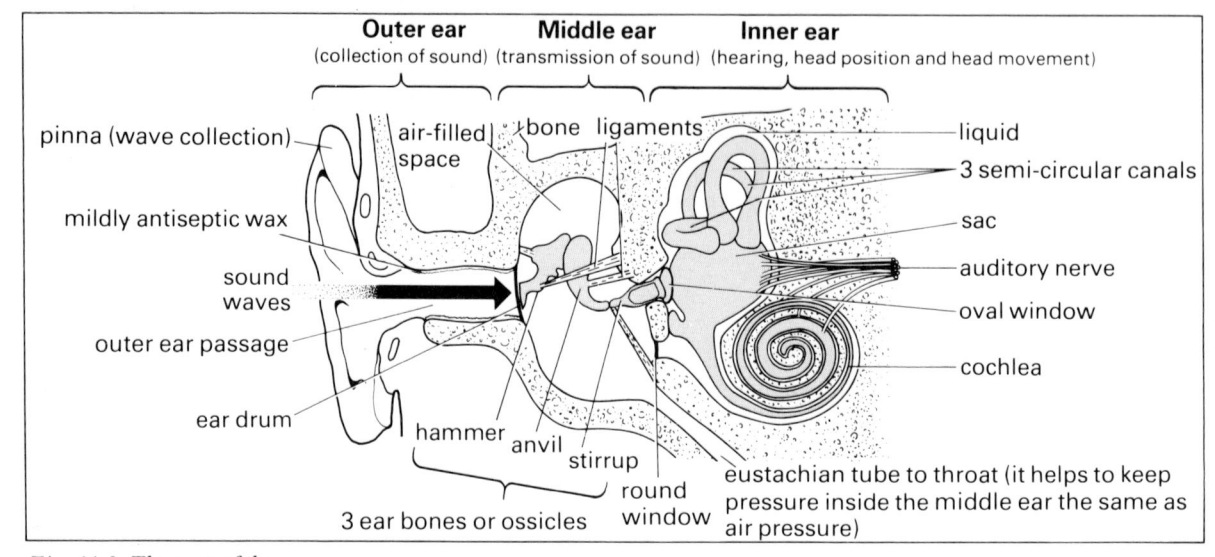

Fig. 44.2 The parts of the ear.

Hearing

Sound energy makes air move or **vibrate**. When the waves of energy reach the **ear drum** it moves backwards and forwards. These vibrations start up movements of the ear bones or **ossicles** (Fig. 44.3). The vibrating ear bones pass on movement to the liquid in the coiled **cochlea** (Fig. 44.4). The sensory cells in the cochlea pick up vibrations of the liquid. These cells pass on the information along the **auditory nerve** to the brain. Here the nerve impulses are interpreted as sounds.

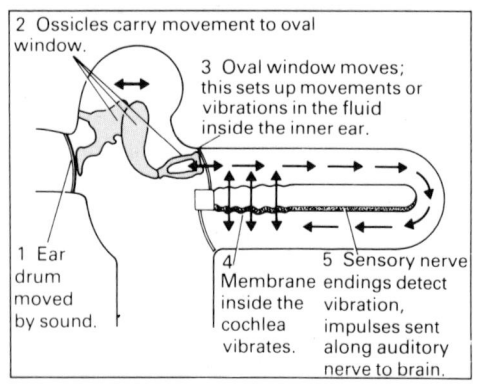

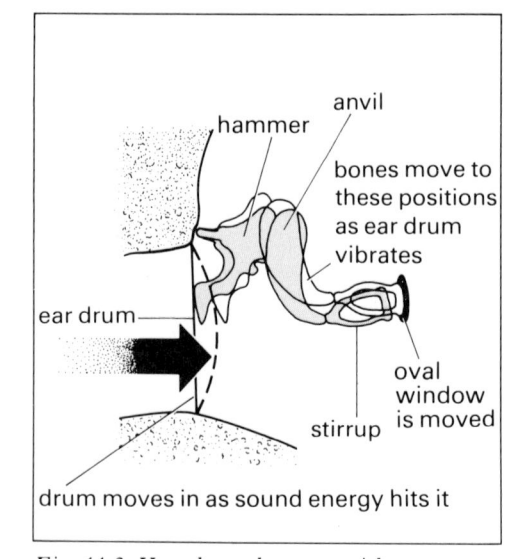

Fig. 44.3 How the ear bones or ossicles move.

Fig. 44.4 Sensory cells in the cochlea detect vibrations.

8 Coordination

Detecting head movements

The three **semi-circular canals** and two **sacs** of the inner ear are filled with liquid (Fig. 44.5). When the head moves the liquid moves (Fig. 44.6). There are sensory cells in the sacs at the end of each canal (Fig. 44.7). The moving liquid moves the hairs from the sensory cells. This causes the cells to send nerve impulses to the brain.

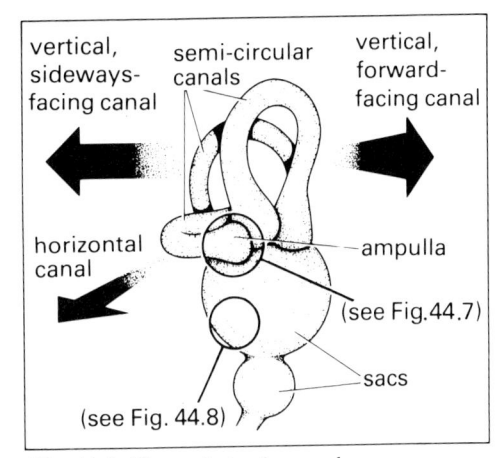

Fig. 44.5 The semi-circular canals.

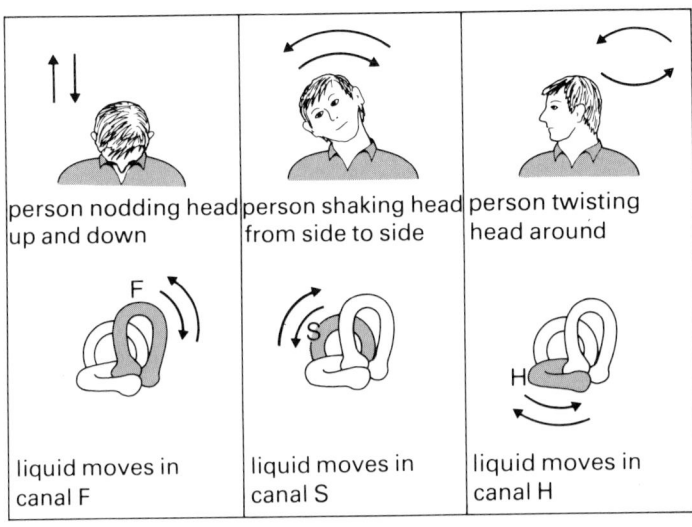

Fig. 44.6 The semi-circular canals and movements of the head. (Also see Fig. 44.5.)

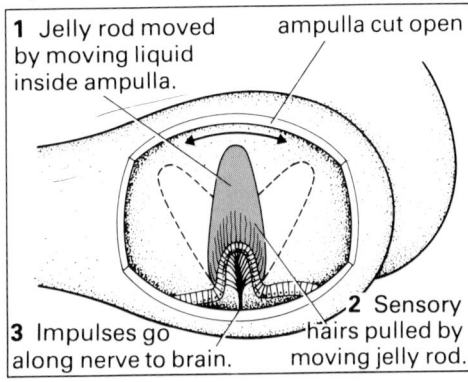

Fig. 44.7 Inside the ampulla sacs of the semi-circular canals.

Dizziness

If you spin around on the spot for some time and then stop, you feel **dizzy**. The liquid in your ears carries on moving even when you have stopped spinning. (In the same way, tea carries on swirling in the cup after you have stopped stirring.) Your *ears* inform the brain that you are moving. Your *eyes* inform the brain that the surroundings are still. This confusing information results in you feeling dizzy.

Detecting the head's position when still

The two sacs tell you about the position of your head when it is still (Fig. 44.8). Inside the sacs, there are groups of sensory cells. They are fixed into particles of chalk. When the head position changes, the chalk particles will move. They will pull on or push down on the cells. These send impulses to the brain.

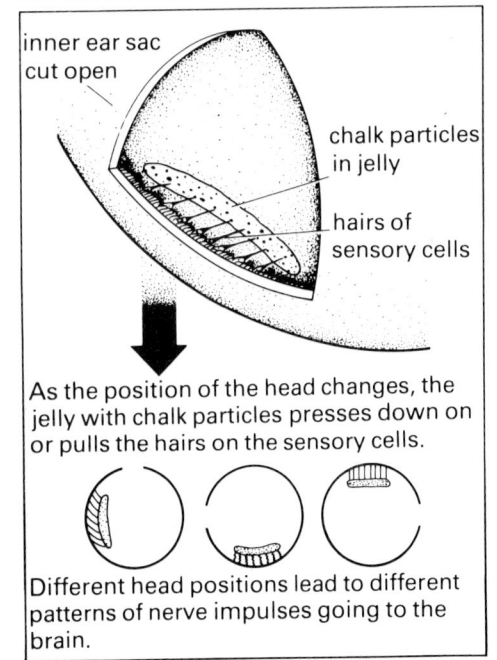

Fig. 44.8 The work of the other inner ear sacs.

85

8 Coordination

45 Ear damage

Sound levels

Sound levels are measured in **decibels** (**dB**). The quietest sound that people with good hearing can hear is tall grass moving in a breeze. This has a sound level of 0 dB. Very intense sound may damage the ears. People who work where sound is intense may gradually lose their hearing. To prevent this, they should wear ear protectors (Fig. 45.1).

Fig. 45.1 Ear protectors should be worn in all jobs with high noise levels.

Deafness

The ear may become faulty and so a person may not be able to hear properly. Some kinds of **deafness** can be helped, others cannot (Fig. 45.2).

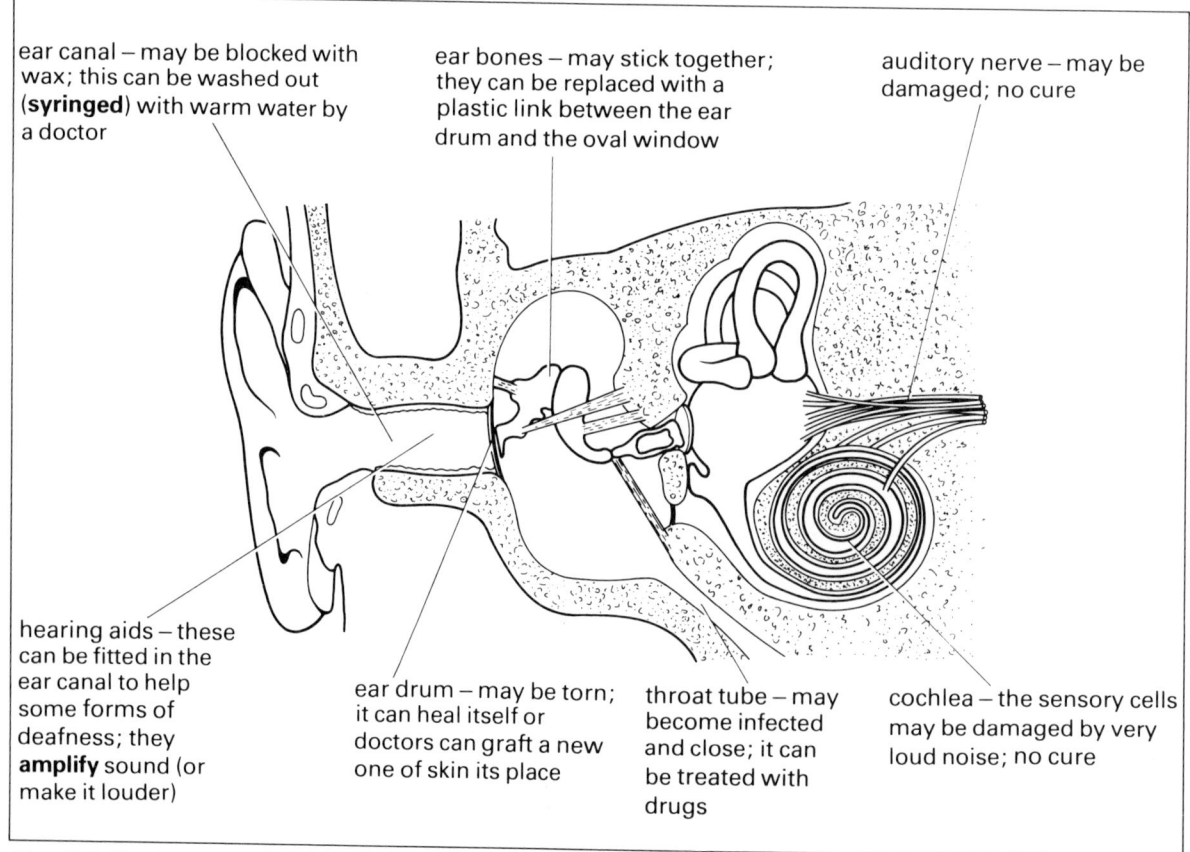

ear canal – may be blocked with wax; this can be washed out (**syringed**) with warm water by a doctor

ear bones – may stick together; they can be replaced with a plastic link between the ear drum and the oval window

auditory nerve – may be damaged; no cure

hearing aids – these can be fitted in the ear canal to help some forms of deafness; they **amplify** sound (or make it louder)

ear drum – may be torn; it can heal itself or doctors can graft a new one of skin its place

throat tube – may become infected and close; it can be treated with drugs

cochlea – the sensory cells may be damaged by very loud noise; no cure

Fig. 45.2 Ear faults.

8 Coordination

46 Other senses

Taste

To taste a substance it must dissolve in the moisture of the mouth. The chemicals in the solution are detected by sensory cells grouped in **taste buds** in the **tongue** (Fig. 46.1). The cells are sensitive to four tastes – sour, sweet, salt and bitter (Fig. 46.2). Most flavours are combinations of these four basic tastes. For instance lemonade contains sugar and lemon. The sugar will have a sweet taste, but the lemon will a bitter taste.

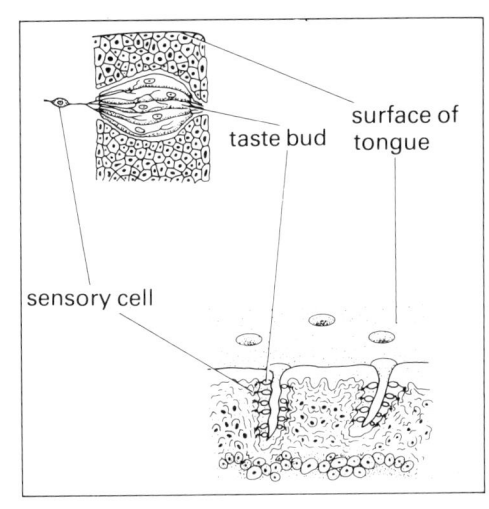

Fig. 46.1 A taste bud on the tongue.

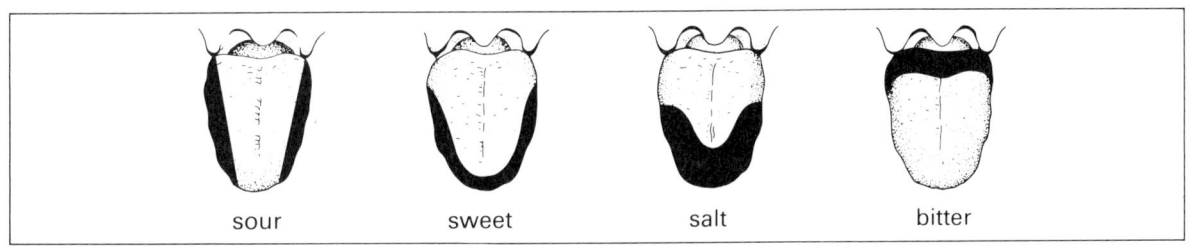

Fig. 46.2 There are taste buds for each of the four basic tastes. They are found in different places on the tongue.

Smell

The senses of smell and taste are linked. If you block off the nose, you may mistake a bite from an onion for an apple. The nose helps produce the sensation of flavours. This is because some of the chemicals in the food can pass into the nose. They travel up the back of the mouth. The cells that are sensitive to smell are inside the nose (Fig. 46.3). They are grouped together in a space about the size of a postage stamp (2 cm^2). Like the sense of taste, these sensory cells respond to chemicals dissolving in moisture.

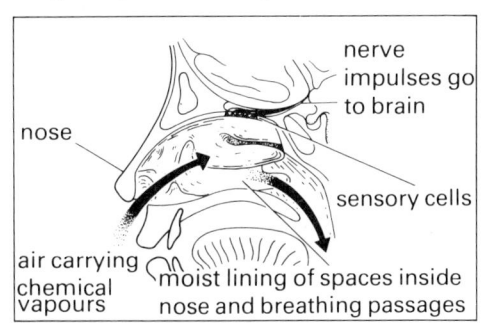

Fig. 46.3 The inside of the nose.

Position of the body •

There are sensory cells scattered through the muscles and tendons of the body (Fig. 46.4). The cells detect if a muscle is contracted or relaxed. They send impulses to the brain. These sensory cells are called **proprioceptors**. They are always sending information to the brain about the movements of your body. If your body is tilting far over to one side, proprioceptors on one side are stimulated more than on the other. The brain receives this information and sends instructions to some muscles. You automatically straighten your back and regain balance.

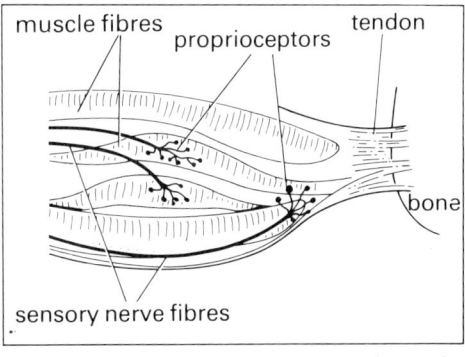

Fig. 46.4 The position of proprioceptors in muscles.

8 Coordination

The skin as a sense organ

The skin is a complicated organ covering the surface of the body. It is made up of many parts and has many jobs or functions (see page 60). One of the skin's functions is being a sense organ. The skin can detect hot and cold, touch and pressure stimuli (Fig. 46.5).

Hot and cold sensory cells

The top layers of the skin are called the **epidermis**. Just below this there are the sensory cells that detect **temperature**. One set of cells detects warmth. Another set detects coldness. Both types are found all over the body. There are more in the fingers and lips than in other places. This means the fingers and lips are best for sensing temperature.

Touch sensory cells

Also near the surface of the skin, there are **touch sensory cells**. Some of them are joined to the **hair follicles**. The touch cells can detect the touch of a feather. There are a great number of these sensory cells in the skin of the fingers. We use these cells to feel the surface of objects.

Pressure sensory cells

The lower layers of the skin are called the **dermis**. Well down in the dermis there are **pressure sensory cells**. These respond to heavier 'touch' than the touch cells. When something is pushing against the skin, the pressure cells will send nerve impulses to the brain.

The feeling of pain

Some sensory cells in the skin and inner parts of the body may only work when they sense a very strong stimulus. These may send impulses to the 'pain centre' of your brain.

If a very strong stimulus starts thousands of the ordinary sensory cells working at once, this may cause you to feel pain. Pain is 'useful'. It lets us know when something is wrong with a part of the body.

Type of sensory cell	Type of stimulus detected
 cold	 iced drink
 pain	 drawing pin
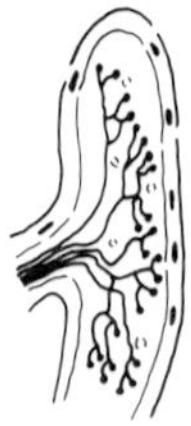 heat	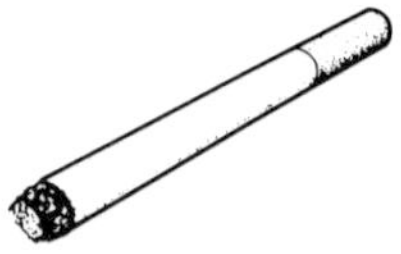 cigarette tip
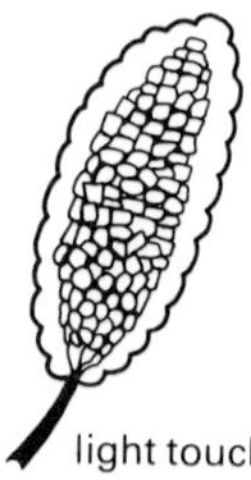 light touch	 cat's fur
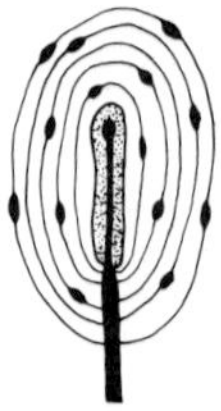 pressure	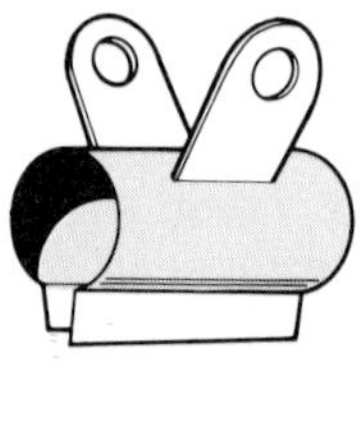 strong clip

Fig. 46.5 The sensory cells of the skin.

8 Coordination

47 Glands

Glands are groups of cells that make substances needed elsewhere in the body. The cells of the gland release the substances called **secretions**. There are two main types of glands – **exocrine** and **endocrine** glands.

Exocrine glands

Exocrine glands pour their juices or secretions into tubes or **ducts**. In this way the secretions go to the outside of the body or into a space inside one of the body's organs. (See Fig. 21.1 on page 38 and Fig. 47.1.)

Endocrine glands

Other glands pour their secretions into the blood. These glands are **endocrine** glands. Their secretions are called **hormones** (Figs. 47.2 and 47.3). Hormones are transported quickly round the body by the blood. Hormones affect many processes but some affect just one part of the body. This part is the **target** (Fig. 47.4). Endocrine glands are important in coordinating the activities of the body.

Example of exocrine gland	Name of secretion	Secretion goes to
sweat gland	sweat	skin surface
salivary gland	saliva	inside of mouth
mammary gland	milk	outside of nipple

Fig. 47.1 The secretions of some exocrine glands.

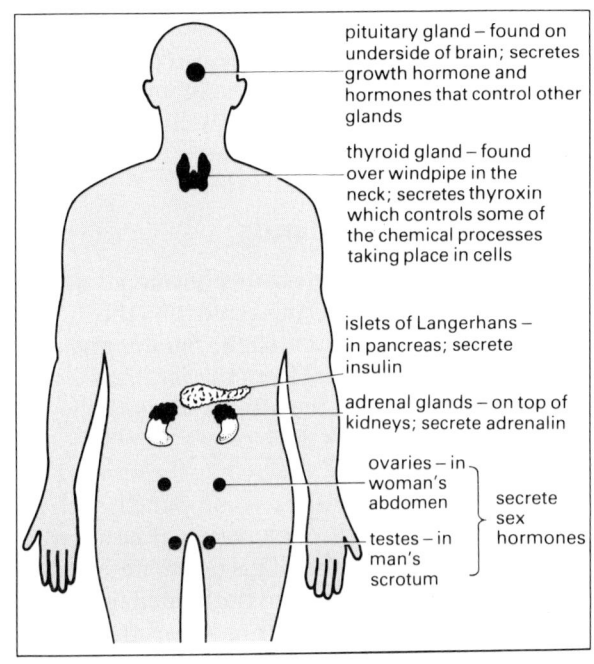

Fig. 47.2 The position of the endocrine glands, and their secretions.

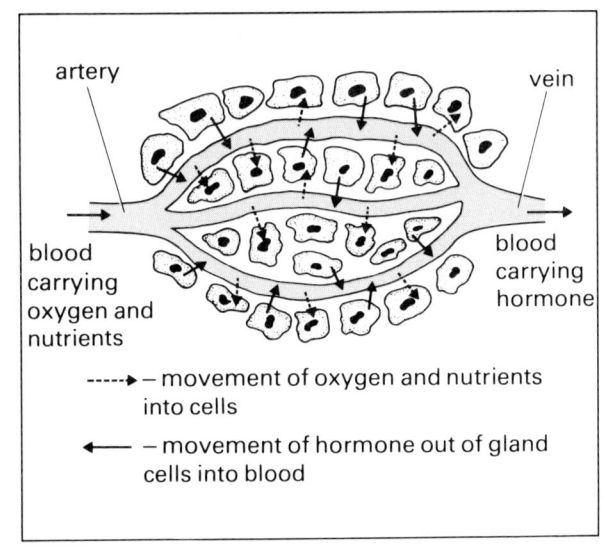

- pituitary gland – found on underside of brain; secretes growth hormone and hormones that control other glands
- thyroid gland – found over windpipe in the neck; secretes thyroxin which controls some of the chemical processes taking place in cells
- islets of Langerhans – in pancreas; secrete insulin
- adrenal glands – on top of kidneys; secrete adrenalin
- ovaries – in woman's abdomen } secrete sex hormones
- testes – in man's scrotum

Fig. 47.3 How an endocrine gland works.

- - - ▶ — movement of oxygen and nutrients into cells
◀—— — movement of hormone out of gland cells into blood

Hormones	Target(s)
growth	all body cells
thyroxin	all body cells
insulin	liver cells
adrenalin	heart and liver
sex hormones	sex organs

Fig. 47.4 The parts of the body affected by some hormones.

8 Coordination

48 Hormones at work

The wrong amount of hormone

Hormones change the activity of some of the body's organs or tissues. Our knowledge of the way hormones work has been gained by studying what happens when a gland is not working correctly. A gland may become **over-active** and secrete too much hormone, or **under-active** – secreting too little. **Growth hormone** is secreted by the **pituitary gland** during childhood. The pituitary gland is about the size of a pea and is attached to the underside of the brain. If the pituitary gland goes wrong, growth is affected (Fig. 48.1).

Controlling the glands

The pituitary also secretes other hormones which control different endocrine glands. So the pituitary is sometimes called the **master gland**. For example, hormones from the pituitary control the activity of the **sex glands** and the **thyroid gland** (Fig. 48.2).

The pituitary can be affected by the brain. The brain can also directly affect some glands, such as the adrenal glands, through nerves. The adrenal glands secrete **adrenalin**. This hormone speeds up the heart beat. If you are frightened or angry, your heart beats faster. This increases the blood supply to your muscles so you can run away or fight back! The brain has instructed the adrenal glands to secrete adrenalin to help you cope with the emergency.

Two coordinating systems

The endocrine system and the nervous system work together to control the activities of the body. This means they are both involved in coordination. A comparison of the two systems is shown in Fig. 48.3.

Fig. 48.3 Comparing the nervous and endocrine systems.

Fig. 48.1 At the age of 21, this man's height was 2·38 m (7 ft 10 in). His body made too much growth hormone.

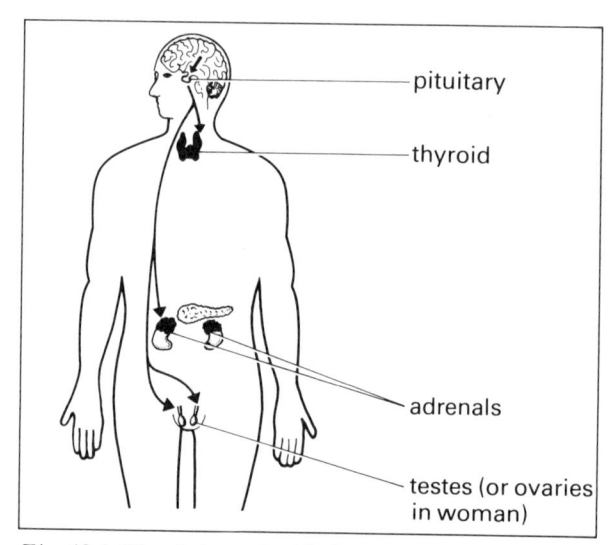

Fig. 48.2 The pituitary gland is the master gland. It controls many other endocrine glands.

Nervous control	Hormonal control
message is electrical/chemical impulse	message is a chemical
message travels along nerve cells	message is carried in blood
response usually quick and in one part of body	response is usually slow and over many parts of the body
effect lasts for a short time	effect usually lasts a long time
controlled by brain or spinal cord	most controlled by pituitary gland

8 Coordination

The liver and sugar levels

The amount of sugar (**glucose**) in the blood must stay *steady* if the body is to work properly. The level tends to go up just after a meal and fall between meals. There is a store of sugar in the liver which can top up the blood if the level drops. If the sugar level in the blood is too high, then extra sugar is removed from the blood. It is stored (as **glycogen**) in the liver (Fig. 48.4).

The sugar hormone

A hormone which affects the liver cells is made by groups of cells in the **pancreas**. These groups or 'islands' of cells were discovered by Paul Langerhans in 1867, so they are called **Islets of Langerhans** (Fig. 48.5). The cells make a hormone called **insulin**. If insulin is not produced, sugar will not be stored in the liver. Instead it is passed out of the body in the urine. The person may feel weak and sleepy as their blood sugar level changes. Fats and muscle proteins have to be used to supply the body with energy. So the person loses weight because the body wastes away. This condition is called **diabetes**.

Treating diabetes

Insulin is a protein. If the hormone is given to a patient to swallow as a pill, then the digestive juices will break it down. So, to replace the hormone they cannot make, diabetics have daily injections of insulin (Fig. 48.6). The insulin is obtained from the pancreases of animals like the cow. Scientists have recently developed a type of insulin which is not digested. Now some diabetics are helped by daily tablets of insulin.

The main points about hormones

All hormones are:
1 made by endocrine glands,
2 made from protein or fat,
3 transported by the blood,
4 able to change the activity of cells,
5 destroyed by the liver.

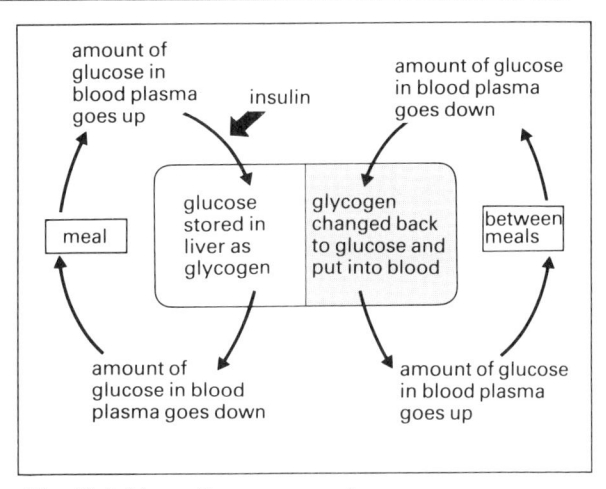

Fig. 48.4 Liver cells can store or release sugar.

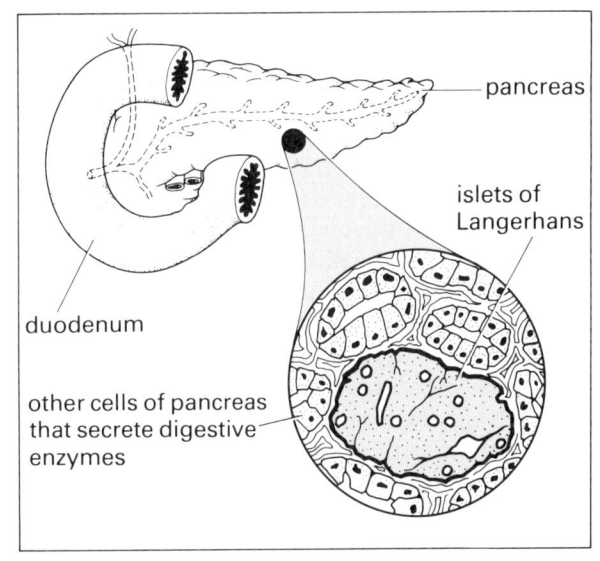

Fig. 48.5 The islets of Langerhans in the pancreas.

Fig. 48.6 Diabetics must receive insulin to keep them well.

8 Coordination

49 Sex hormones

Puberty

As anyone grows up, their body changes as they become **sexually mature**. This means they are able to **reproduce** (or have children). The changes are known as **puberty**. It is a time when the body grows quite quickly (see page 134). Puberty is brought about by hormones produced by the pituitary glands and the **gonads** (Fig. 49.1). The gonads are the sex glands – the **ovaries** in the female and the **testes** in the male. The changing levels of hormones can mix-up the emotions during these years. Some teenagers find their mood changes quickly. During puberty and a few years afterwards, a teenager's behaviour changes. This time can be called **adolescence**.

Boys

Male puberty starts at about 11 or 12 years. It can be earlier or later for some boys without there being anything wrong. Hormones from the pituitary gland start the testes working. The testes grow larger and make the male sex hormone, **testosterone**. This makes the penis grow, the voice deepen and makes hair grow around the sex organs, under the arms and eventually on the face. The shoulders broaden and the body becomes more muscular (Fig. 49.2). Testosterone also causes the growth of the male sex cells or **sperms**. At puberty a boy will start being able to have **erections** of the penis. He may also have **wet dreams** while asleep. This is when some liquid containing sperms is released from the erect penis.

Girls

Puberty in girls usually starts at about 9 or 10 years. As in boys, puberty may start earlier or later without there being anything to worry about. The ovaries produce two female sex hormones, **oestrogen** and **progesterone**. These make the hip bones widen, the nipples get larger and makes the hips and buttocks fatter. Breasts gradually develop (Fig. 49.3). The internal sex organs start to mature; the female sex cells, **eggs** or **ova**, start growing and changes in the womb or **uterus** have started.

Fig. 49.3 The changes of the female at puberty.

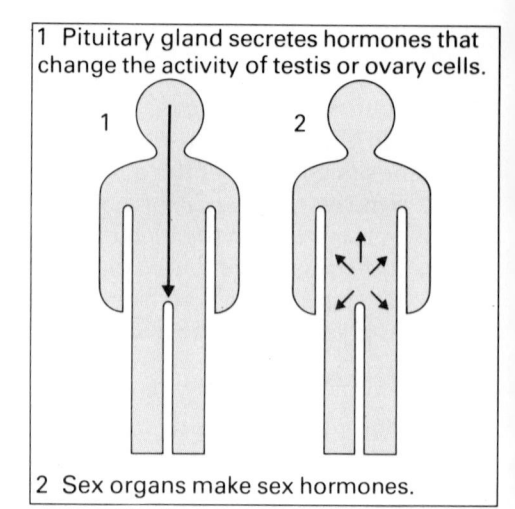

Fig. 49.1 Hormones from the pituitary and gonads cause puberty.

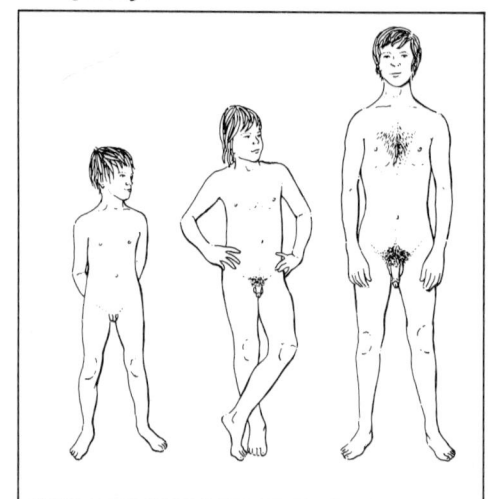

1 Pituitary gland secretes hormones that change the activity of testis or ovary cells.
2 Sex organs make sex hormones.

Fig. 49.2 The changes of the male at puberty.

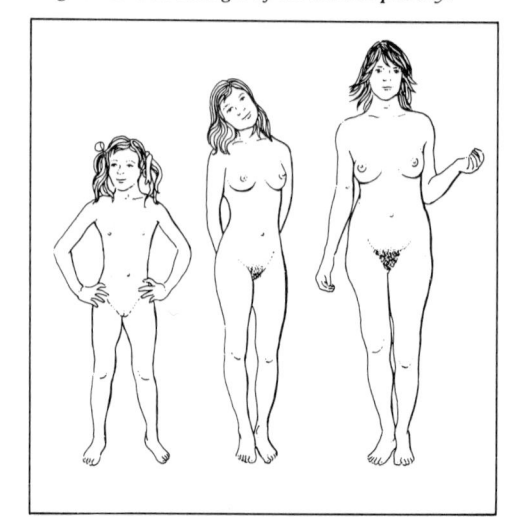

8 Coordination

1 A hormone from the pituitary gland causes the ripening of one egg in one ovary and causes other cells in the ovary to make oestrogen. This makes the uterus lining thicken by about 6 mm.

2 When the egg is ripe, a hormone from the pituitary gland causes the release of the egg. The egg bursts out of the follicle at ovulation.

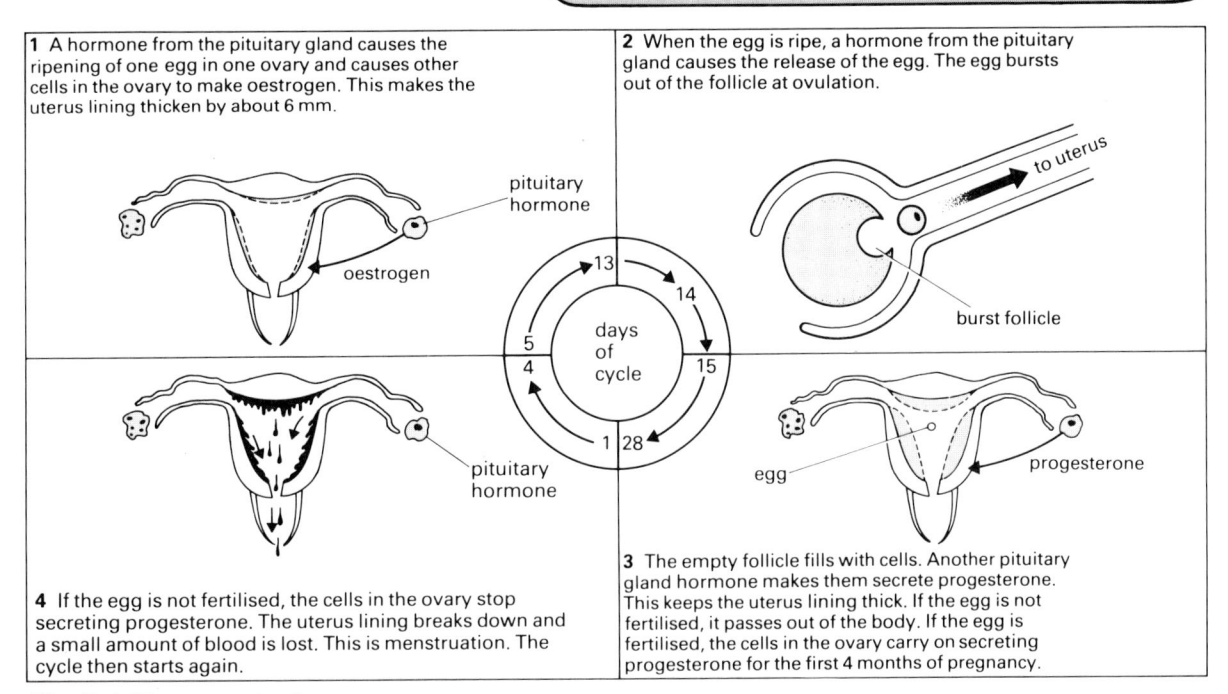

3 The empty follicle fills with cells. Another pituitary gland hormone makes them secrete progesterone. This keeps the uterus lining thick. If the egg is not fertilised, it passes out of the body. If the egg is fertilised, the cells in the ovary carry on secreting progesterone for the first 4 months of pregnancy.

4 If the egg is not fertilised, the cells in the ovary stop secreting progesterone. The uterus lining breaks down and a small amount of blood is lost. This is menstruation. The cycle then starts again.

Fig. 49.4 The menstrual cycle.

Menstruation

One change experienced by girls at puberty is the start of **periods** or **menstruation**. A small amount of blood is lost each month, as the womb's lining breaks down (Fig. 49.4). The period is a sign of the changes that take place inside a woman's body each month. These changes are linked with the release of the egg from the ovary. The release of the egg is called **ovulation**.

At ovulation, the body temperature rises slightly. A woman can find out the time of egg release by taking her temperature in the morning before she gets up. The bleeding starts about two weeks after ovulation. The period usually happens once every four weeks and lasts for 3–6 days. However the timing of periods can be different in different girls.

Summary: Coordination

* Coordination of the body is carried out by the nervous system and the endocrine system.
* Changes in the surroundings (stimuli) are detected by sense organs.
* Responses to changes are made by effectors (glands and muscles).
* The nervous system links sense organs and effectors.
* The nervous system is made up of three types of nerve cells (neurons) – sensory, connector and motor neurons.
* A reflex action uses very few neurons, is quick, cannot be controlled and the response made to a stimulus is always the same.
* The brain is a large organ protected by the skull. The brain has many jobs. Its main job is to coordinate many of the body's activities.
* Conscious actions and learning are controlled by the brain.
* Groups of cells that detect stimuli form the sense organs.
* The eye is the sense organ that detects light.
* The sensitive cells are in a layer called the retina.
* The ear detects sound and head movements.
* The sensitive cells are in the inner ear.
* Other sense organs are the tongue, nose, muscles and skin.
* The skin detects temperature, touch and pressure.
* There are two types of glands, exocrine and endocrine.
* Endocrine glands secrete hormones into the blood.
* The most important endocrine gland is the pituitary as it controls other glands.
* Hormones from the sex organs cause the changes at puberty that lead to sexual maturity.

9 Reproduction

50 Making gametes

Each month a woman releases a single cell from one of her ovaries. This cell is an **egg** or **ovum**. A man makes cells called **sperms**. Eggs and sperms are the sex cells or **gametes** (Fig. 50.1).

The sex organs and fertilisation

If an egg and sperm meet, the nucleus from each may join. This is **fertilisation**. The single, fertilised cell formed begins to divide making many cells. After a short time the collection of cells will become organised into a baby. These changes take place while the egg is inside the body of the woman. So she has organs in which the baby will develop (Fig. 50.2). Development can only start if a sperm meets an egg and fertilises it. So the man has organs for passing sperm out of his body and placing them in the woman (Fig. 50.3).

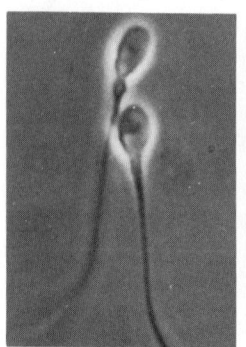

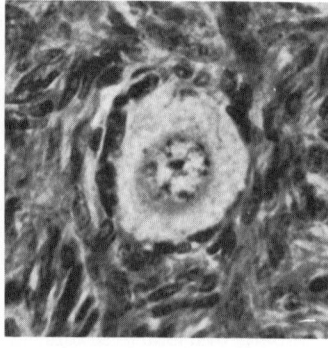

Fig. 50.1 The human gametes: sperms are shown on the left ($\times 1500$); an ovum inside the ovary is shown on the right ($\times 350$).

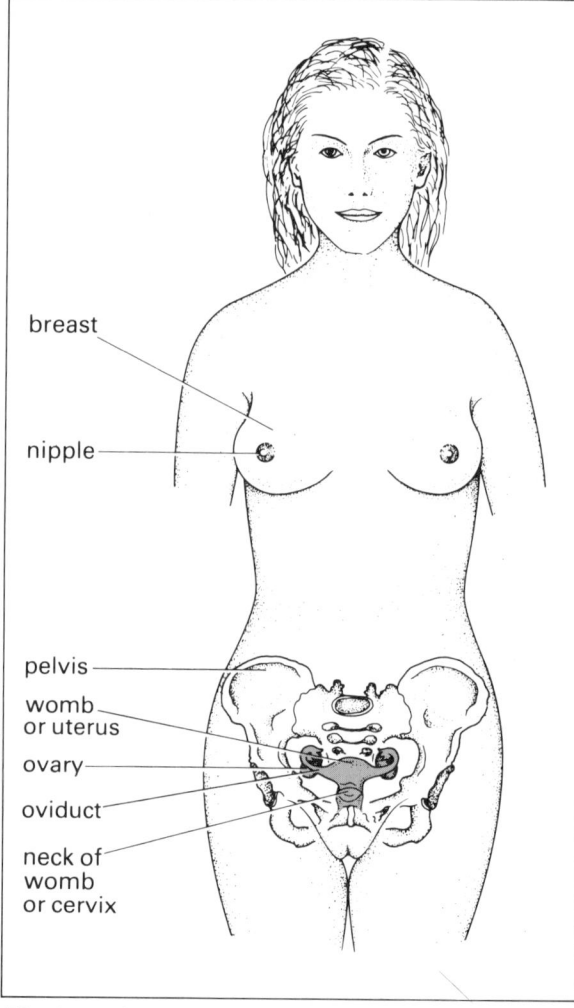

Fig. 50.2 The human female reproductive organs.

9 Reproduction

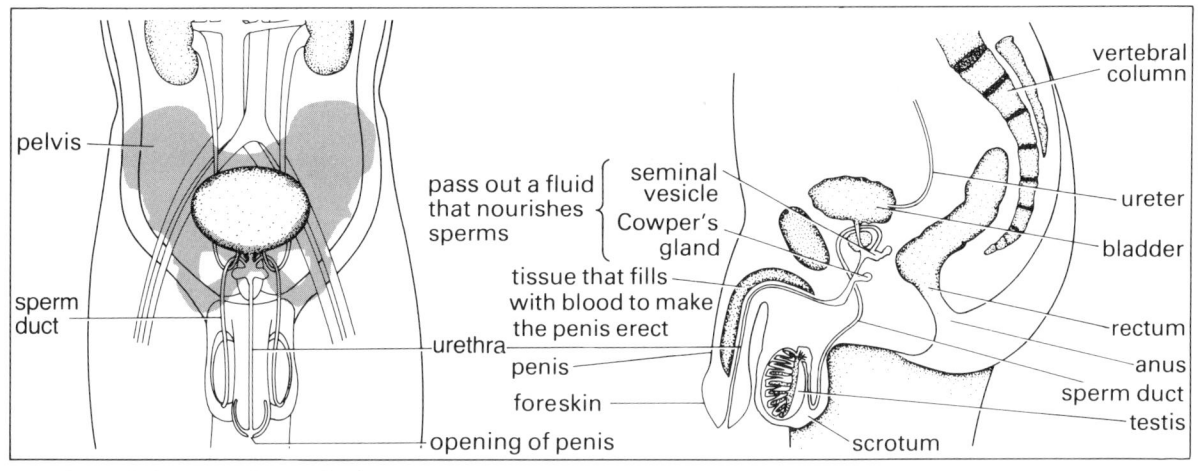

Fig. 50.3 The human male reproductive organs.

When reproduction is possible

Men and women can release gametes after puberty. The male sex hormone is **testosterone**. It is produced by the **testes** throughout an adult man's life. This means he can produce active sperms all his life.

The female sex hormones are **oestrogen** and **progesterone**. These control the release of eggs from the ovary from puberty until a woman is middle-aged. A woman has reached **menopause** when she stops releasing eggs and having periods. This means she can no longer have children. Until that time a woman will have released one egg each month (sometimes more). The egg travels down the **oviduct** and into the **uterus** or womb. The egg will pass out of the body if it is not fertilised (Fig. 50.4).

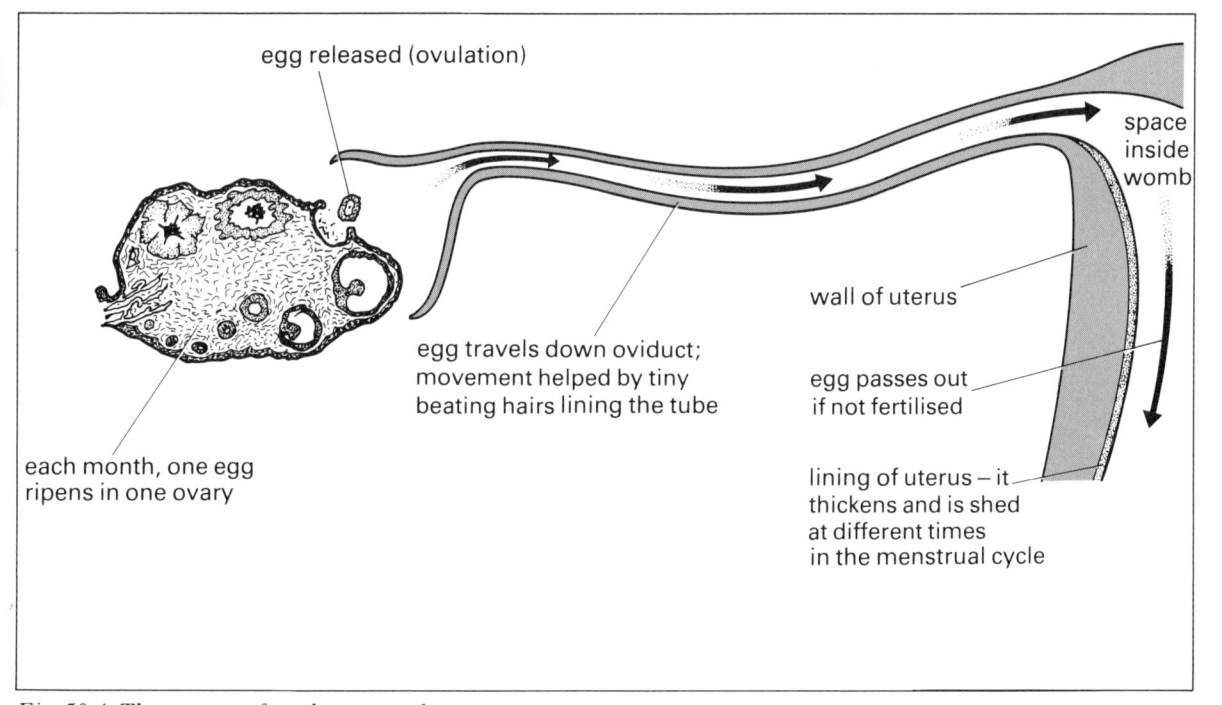

Fig. 50.4 The egg moves from the ovary to the uterus.

9 Reproduction

51 Conceiving

Sexual intercourse

To start a baby growing, the male and female gametes must meet. Sperms must be put into the woman's body at around the time when an egg is released from the ovary (**ovulation**). The sperms pass into the woman's body during **sexual intercourse** (or **copulation**, Fig. 51.1).

Sexual intercourse is when the man's **penis** is inside the woman's **vagina**. Two things make this possible. The tip of the penis and the vagina's entrance are sensitive to touch. If these are stroked, the penis will fill with blood and become stiff (an **erection**); the vagina becomes moist. When the penis is moved up and down in the vagina, **orgasm** may occur. At this time a teaspoonful of milky-white liquid called **semen** is pumped or **ejaculated** out of the penis. The semen contains about 100 million sperms. The walls of the vagina and uterus move in and out. This helps to suck the sperms towards the opening of the uterus.

Once inside, the sperms swim towards the egg – if one is there. The sperm and egg usually meet in the oviduct. Only one sperm will fertilise the egg. The sperms make a great effort to reach the egg. It has been compared to the effort needed if a person tried to swim through a sea of treacle the size of the Atlantic Ocean! If a sperm fertilises an egg, **conception** has happened (Figs. 51.2 and 51.3).

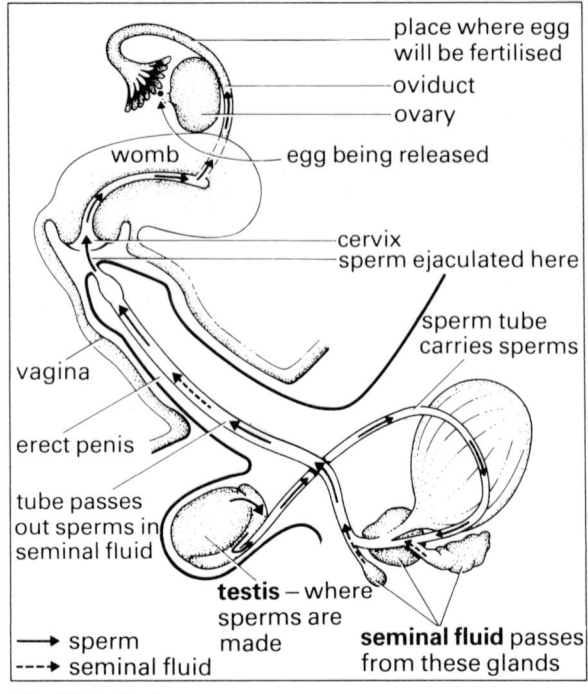

Fig. 51.1 Getting sperms near an egg.

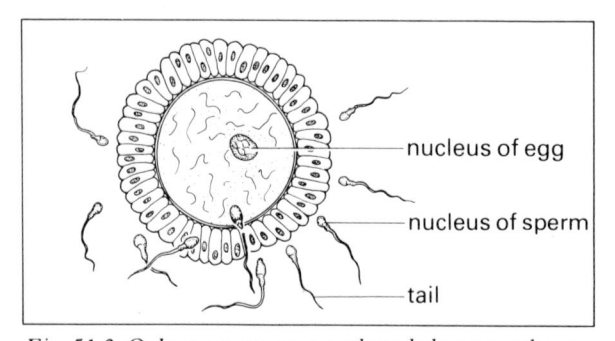

Fig. 51.2 Only one sperm can pass through the egg membrane.

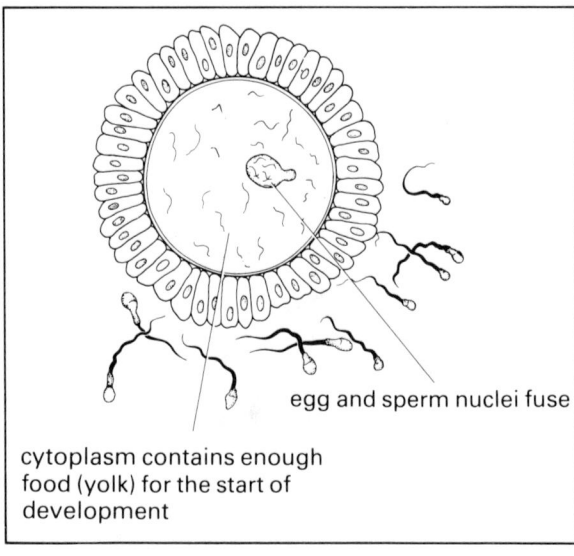

Fig. 51.3 When the nucleus of the sperm joins up with the egg nucleus, fertilisation has happened.

Arriving in the womb

The first sperm to reach the egg passes through the **egg membrane**. The two nuclei fuse or join together (fertilisation). The egg membrane immediately changes and stops other sperms

9 Reproduction

entering the egg. The fertilised egg takes about a week to pass down the oviduct and reach the uterus. The egg divides many times to make a ball of cells called the **embryo** (Fig. 51.4). The embryo sinks in the soft lining of the uterus (**implantation**).

Feeding the growing embryo

The embryo begins to get nourishment from the mother once it is in the uterus wall. It needs food and oxygen to grow. At first, these come directly from the uterus wall. After a couple of weeks an organ starts growing from the tissues of the embryo and the mother. This is the **placenta** (Fig. 51.5). It acts as a 'life support system'. By this stage the embryo is more than just a ball of cells. It is beginning to look more like a baby. At about three months, bone starts to develop. The embryo is now called a **foetus**. In the placenta chemicals are exchanged between the mother and the baby. The blood of the mother and the blood of the baby flow close together in the placenta. Chemicals can pass across from one to the other by diffusion (see page 65). The umbilical cord is the 'lifeline' that connects the baby to the placenta. It contains blood vessels (Fig. 51.6). The capillaries of one of these picks up oxygen and food chemicals from the mother and carries them into the baby. The other vessel takes carbon dioxide and other waste chemicals from the baby to the mother. The placenta is a barrier between the two blood supplies. This means that most dangerous chemicals and bacteria cannot pass across the placenta into the baby.

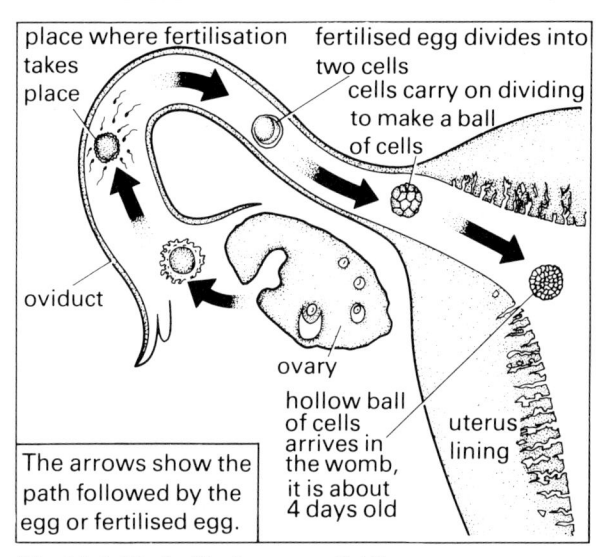

Fig. 51.4 The fertilised egg starts dividing.

Hormone levels in pregnancy

Like the ovaries, the placenta makes the hormones oestrogen and progesterone. The amounts of these sex hormones in the blood are very different in pregnant and non-pregnant women. The level of progesterone is high and oestrogen is low during pregnancy. These hormone levels stop the woman's periods, so she does not ovulate or menstruate. The hormones also make the uterus grow at the same speed as the baby and make the breasts grow and start making milk.

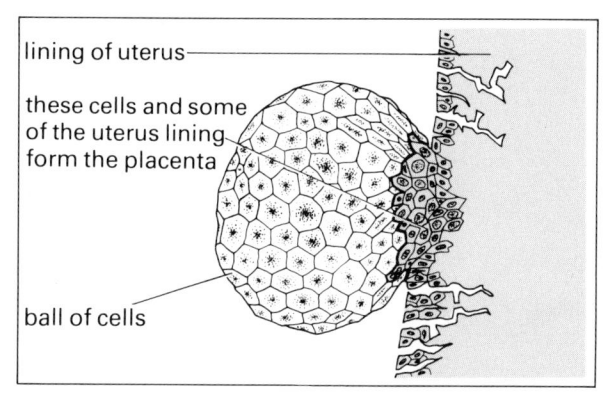

Fig. 51.5 The implanted embryo and growth of the placenta.

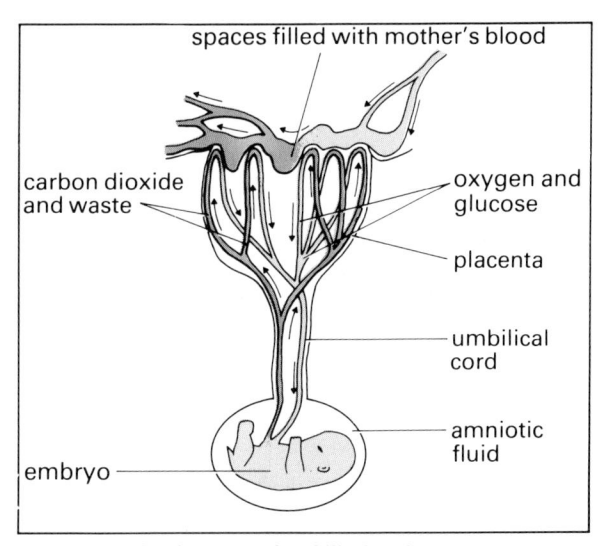

Fig. 51.6 The placenta and umbilical cord.

9 Reproduction

52 Growth of the baby

The foetus grows inside a bag of watery liquid. This is the **amniotic fluid** surrounded by a membrane called the **amnion** (Fig. 52.1). The fluid protects the developing baby from knocks. The baby develops inside the mother for about nine months (38 weeks). This is the **gestation period**. The changes that occur are shown below (Fig. 52.2).

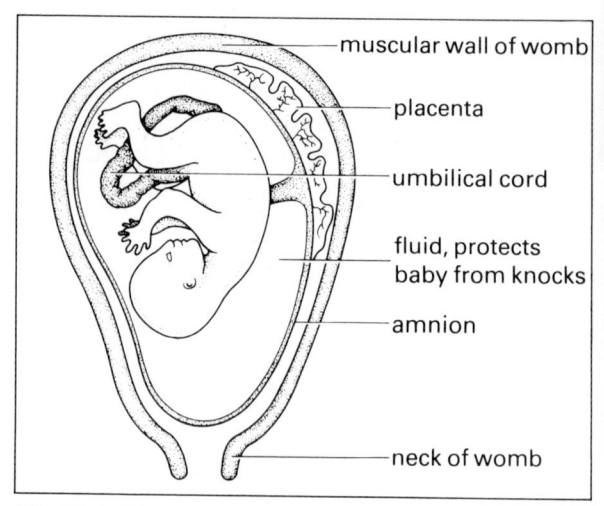

Fig. 52.1 The embryo in the amnion.

The stages of growth of the baby

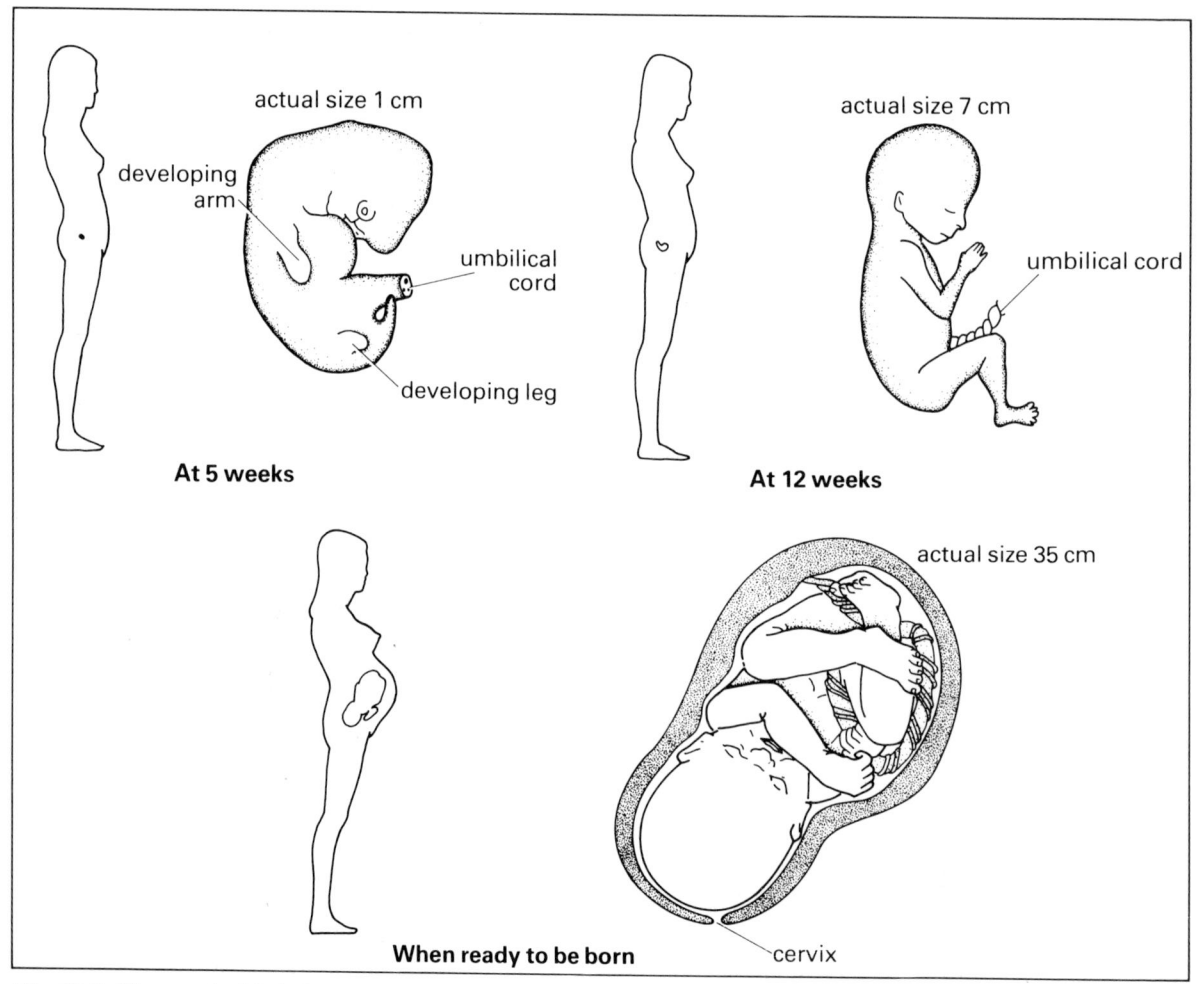

Fig. 52.2 The growth of the baby during pregnancy.

9 Reproduction

A healthy pregnancy

As the baby grows, it needs more food and oxygen. To help supply these, the amount of blood in the mother increases by half. Nutrients, like sugar, stay in her blood for longer than usual. This gives them more time to pass into the baby. Pregnancy makes many demands on the mother's body. If she does not eat properly, the baby will suffer. She needs plenty of **iron** to make more blood for herself and the baby needs iron to make its own blood. A lack of iron in her diet may make the mother become **anaemic** (see page 11). Some substances in the mother's blood can pass through the placental barrier and may damage the baby. Drugs such as alcohol and chemicals from cigarette smoke slow the growth of the baby (Fig. 52.3). The German measles virus and X-rays can interfere with the baby's growth. The AIDS virus can be passed from mother to baby.

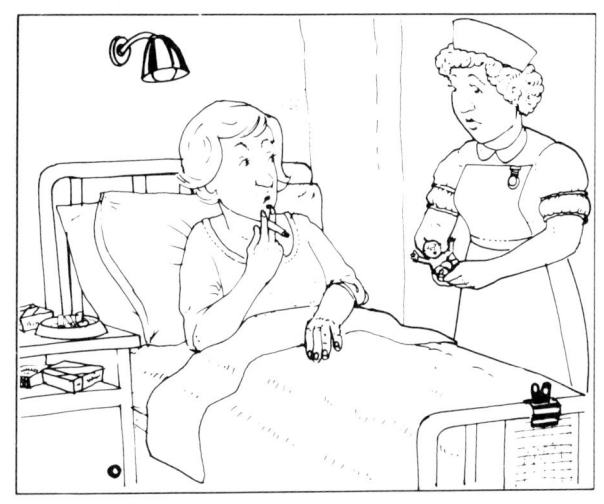

Fig. 52.3 Smoking during pregnancy slows the growth of the baby.

Ante-natal classes

Regular check-ups by a doctor during pregnancy, help to make sure that mother and baby are well. The mother should go to **ante-natal** classes (Fig. 52.4). (Ante-natal means 'before birth'.) The mother will be taught exercises that help her to strengthen and control the muscles of her body ready for child-birth. At the classes she will learn about the changes taking place in her body, the birth itself, and how to care for herself while she is pregnant.

During pregnancy, a woman gets very tired. She must learn to rest and relax. She will then be physically and mentally ready for the birth.

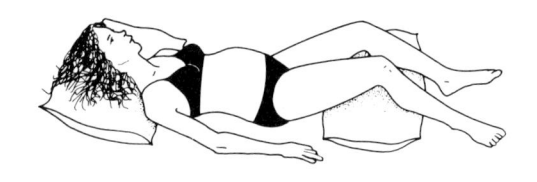

At ante-natal clinics, a pregnant woman learns how to control and build up some muscles. These are the muscles she will use during the birth of the baby.

Fig. 52.4 Ante-natal exercises.

9 Reproduction

53 Birth

A baby is born about 38 weeks after fertilisation. The baby usually weighs about 3–3·5 kg (6–8 lbs). During the last few days of pregnancy, the baby positions itself so its head is near the opening of the uterus (Fig. 53.1). If its feet are here, the birth is a **breach delivery**. The baby is pushed out of the mother's body by the action of the muscles of the womb. The process is called **labour** (Fig. 53.2).

Life outside

At birth, a baby comes from a dark, warm, wet, quiet world. In the womb it had a steady supply of food and oxygen. It is born into a world which is light, dry, cooler and more noisy. Lengths of thread are tied in 2 places around the umbilical cord. The cord is cut between the two tied threads. This separates the baby from the mother, the baby has to change the way it breathes, feeds and gets rid of waste. It also has to start controlling its temperature.

About 15 minutes after the baby has been born, the placenta, umbilical cord and membranes are pushed out of the mother's body. This is the **afterbirth**.

In 95 out of every 100 births, the baby's head is in the neck of the womb as shown. In 5 out of every 100 births, the baby sits in the neck of the womb – the **breach** position.

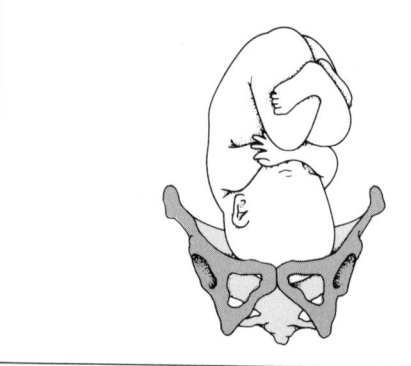

Fig. 53.1 The baby positioned for birth.

The muscle walls of the uterus begin to contract. This is **labour**.

The baby's head is pushed through the cervix.

The baby's head passes through its mother's pelvis.

The baby's head is born.

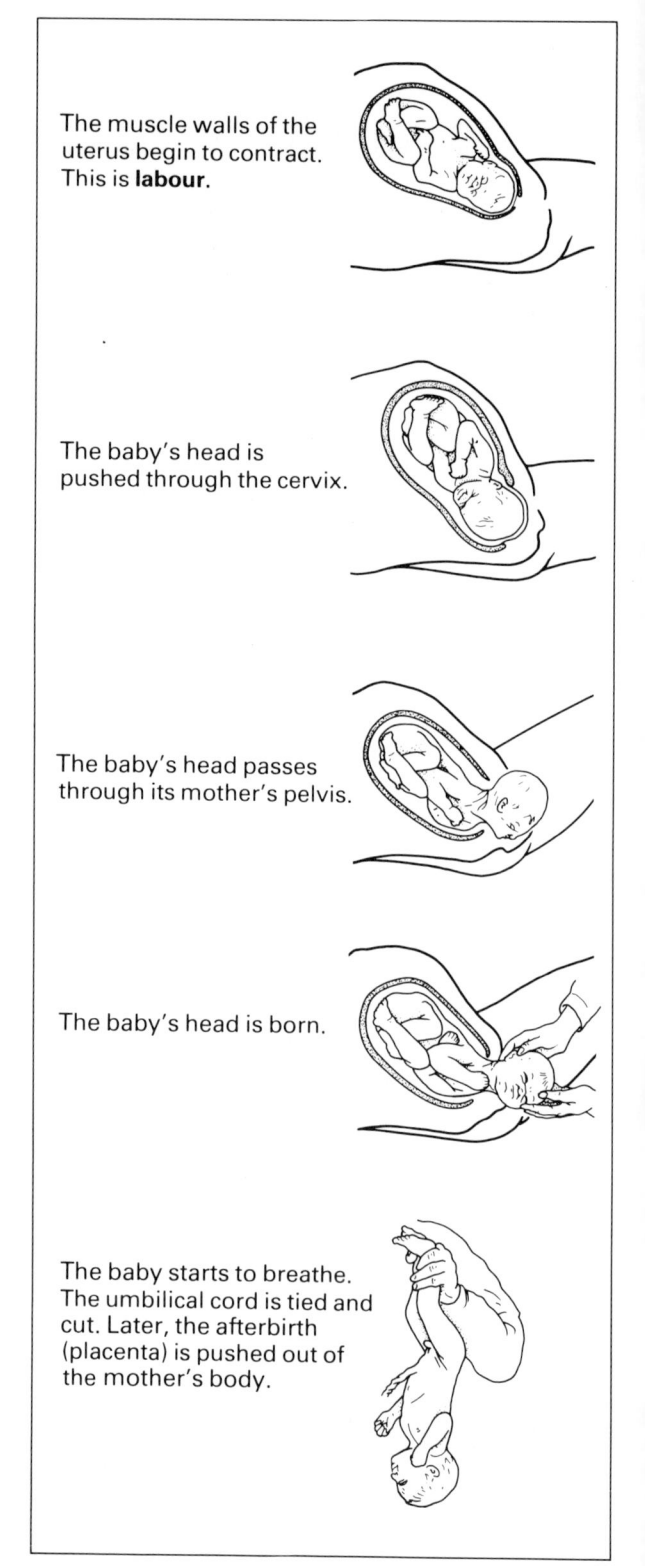

The baby starts to breathe. The umbilical cord is tied and cut. Later, the afterbirth (placenta) is pushed out of the mother's body.

Fig. 53.2 The stages of giving birth.

9 Reproduction

54 Post-natal care

The few months after birth are called the **post-natal** period. During this time the baby needs a lot of attention. The mother may get tired easily. The father and other people can be a great help at this time. (Fig. 54.1).

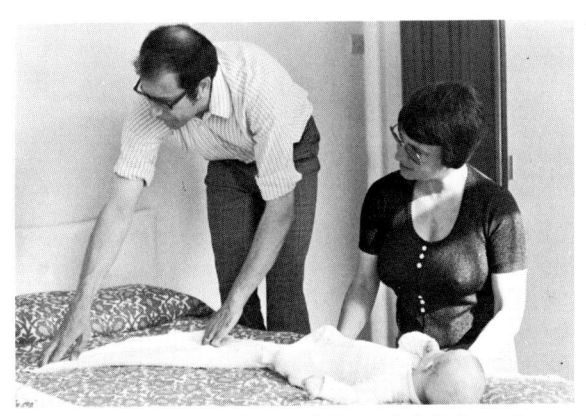

Fig. 54.1 A mother with a new baby needs help from others.

Feeding the baby

Most mothers **breast-feed** or **suckle** their babies. The milk is produced in the **mammary glands** in the breasts (Fig. 54.2). Milk production or **lactation** is controlled by hormones. The breasts make as much milk as the baby needs. This is about 1–2 litres (3–4 pints) a day. The baby has small amounts at frequent intervals.

Human milk is best for the baby. It goes straight from mother to baby so there is little chance of infection. It contains chemicals that protect the baby from some diseases for a while. (The chemicals are **antibodies**, see page 161.) Also human milk contains less protein and fat than cow's milk. This makes it easier for the baby to digest.

Some mothers cannot breast feed their babies. They use a dried substitute which is made up with water and fed to the baby from a bottle. The dried milk is made from cow's milk which has been treated to remove some of the protein and fat. The mother must **sterilise** all the containers in which this milk is prepared or stored. This makes infection of the baby less likely.

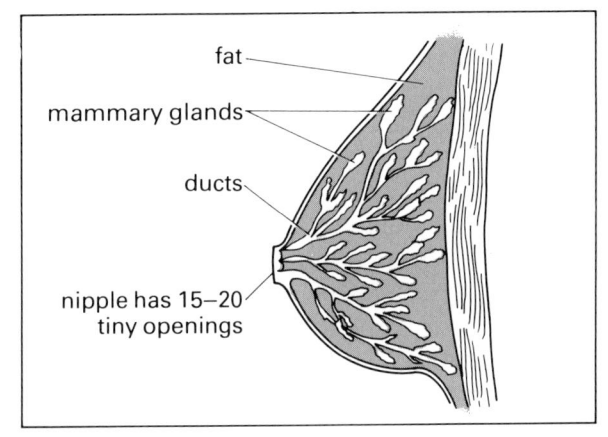

Fig. 54.2 The mammary glands in the breast.

Post-natal exercises and check-ups

After the birth, the mother's body starts to get back to the normal size and shape. When the baby was born the uterus was 160 times bigger than normal. It has to shrink! Exercises help the muscles get back to normal (Fig. 54.3). This takes about 8 weeks. Both mother and baby will have regular check-ups to make sure they are both healthy. A qualified nurse, a **health visitor**, will do these checks. The nurse can also advise the mother about any problems she may have.

Fig. 54.3 Two post-natal exercises which help to get the abdomen back into shape.

9 Reproduction

55 Multiple births

A woman usually releases one egg from an ovary each month. It is usual to have one baby at each pregnancy. Occasionally a woman may give birth to more than one baby at a time. This is a **multiple pregnancy**. If a woman has two babies at once, she has **twins**. If three, these are **triplets** and if four, these are **quadruplets**.

Identical twins

Sometimes a single, fertilised egg will split in half as it is dividing to form an embryo (Fig. 55.1). If it splits into two, it will form two embryos. These embryos have come from the same fertilised egg. This means that the cells of each embryo contain exactly the same **genes** (see page 107). The genes control the development of the embryos. Both babies that develop will be the same sex and have the same features. Inside the womb they share the same placenta. They are **identical twins**.

Fig. 55.1 How identical twins are formed.

Fraternal twins

Sometimes a woman will release two eggs from her ovaries at about the same time (Fig. 55.2). These eggs may both be fertilised by separate sperms. They then become implanted in the womb. Each will develop into an embryo having its own placenta. Each embryo develops from different eggs and sperms, containing different genes. The two babies may be of different sexes and will be no more alike than brothers and sisters. These are **fraternal twins**.

Fertility drugs

Some women do not release eggs from their ovaries. They cannot have babies and are **infertile**. Some can be helped by treatment with hormones (**fertility drugs**). This treatment may cause a woman to release several eggs at once. She may even give birth to five or six babies at once!

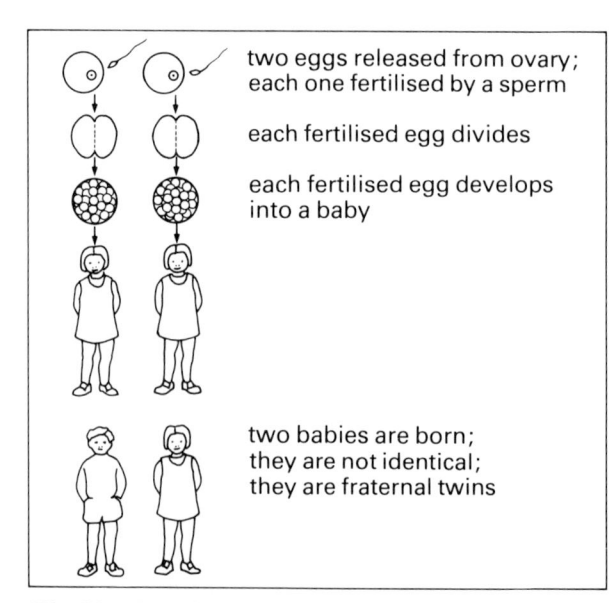

Fig. 55.2 How fraternal twins are formed.

9 Reproduction

56 Population change

World population

The number of people alive in the world is increasing very quickly (Fig. 56.1). It took 200 years, from 1650 to 1850, for the **population** to double. It only took 100 years, from 1850 to 1950 to double again!

Population of Britain

Fig. 56.2 shows how the population in Britain has changed between 1700 and 1972. In the last 20 years, the population increase has begun slowing down.

Population of India

The population of India is increasing very quickly (Fig. 56.3). It has not slowed down in recent years, as it has in Britain. Occasionally diseases and **famine** (shortage of food) may affect millions of people in countries like India. These will slow down population increase for a short time. This happened in India in 1920 as can be seen on the graph.

Changing population growth

Many things affect the rate of growth of a population. Improved housing, **sanitation**, diet and medicine are important. These factors will lead to the following:
1 More babies are born alive each year. (**Birth rate** goes up.)
2 More babies survive to become adults. (**Infant mortality rate** goes down. Fewer babies under a year old die from disease.)
3 The adults live longer. (**Death rate** goes down.)
4 The adults reproduce and so the population increases quickly.

These four things have happened in industrialised countries like Britain so their populations have increased. One reason why the population increase in Britain is slowing down is **contraception**. People in industrialised countries have ways of controlling how many children they have. In under-developed countries like India, few people use contraception so the birth rate there is not yet slowing down.

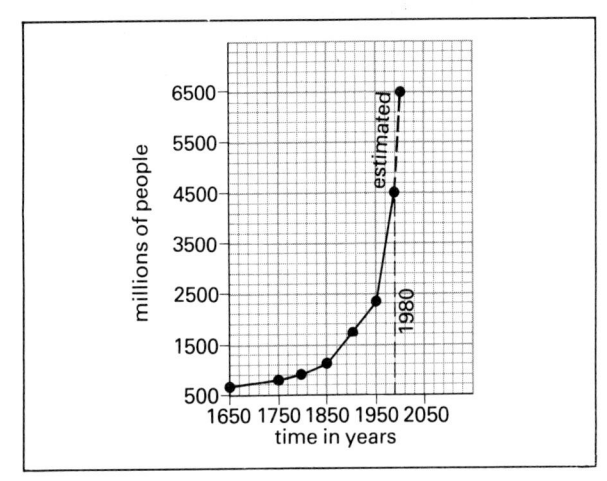

Fig. 56.1 World population graph.

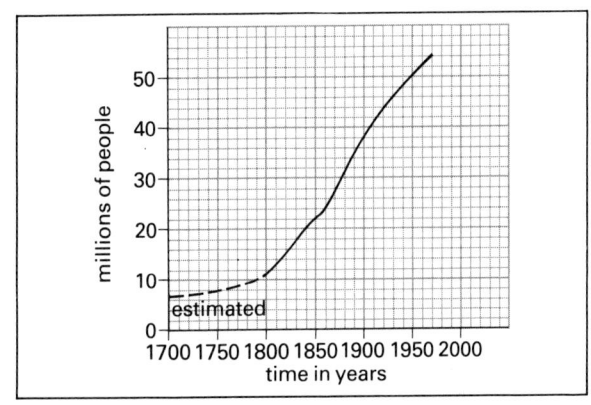

Fig. 56.2 Growth of population of England, Wales and Scotland (1700–1972).

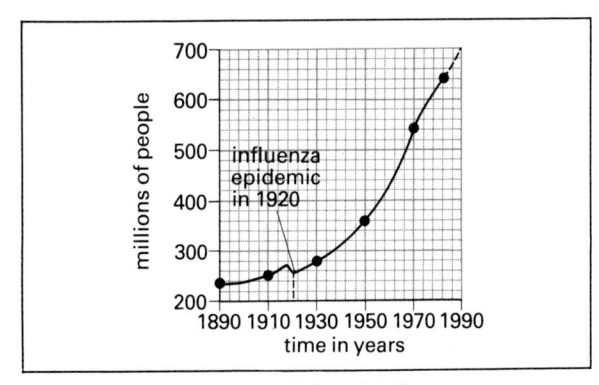

Fig. 56.3 The growing population of India.

9 Reproduction

57 Contraception

Contraceptives are ways of stopping a baby being conceived. One old method, mentioned in the Bible is **coitus interruptus**. This is when the man pulls his penis out of the vagina before the sperms are ejaculated. It is not a reliable method of stopping conception. The methods available nowadays are explained below (Figs. 57.1 and 57.2).

Contraceptive pill

The most common type of pill is taken by the woman once a day for 21 days. She then stops taking it for 7 days during which time she has a 'period'. The pill contains hormones which stop eggs being released from the ovary. Some women cannot take the pill for medical reasons.

Intra-uterine device or IUD

This is a piece of plastic or metal placed in the women's uterus by a doctor. It is usually left in permanently. It may come out accidently, or can be removed by a doctor when the woman wants to get pregnant. The IUD may work either by stopping fertilisation or by stopping implantation of the fertilised egg in the womb.

Sterilisation

This is an operation which stops the sex cells passing down the tubes of the sex organs. In the man the sperm ducts are cut or tied. In the woman the oviducts are cut or tied. The operations cannot usually be reversed.

Rhythm method

At the time of ovulation a woman's temperature is higher than normal. If she does not want to become pregnant, she must avoid sex during these days. She must take her temperature every morning before she gets up. She should then know when she is 'safe'. This method is not very reliable as many women have irregular periods and the woman must never forget to check her temperature.

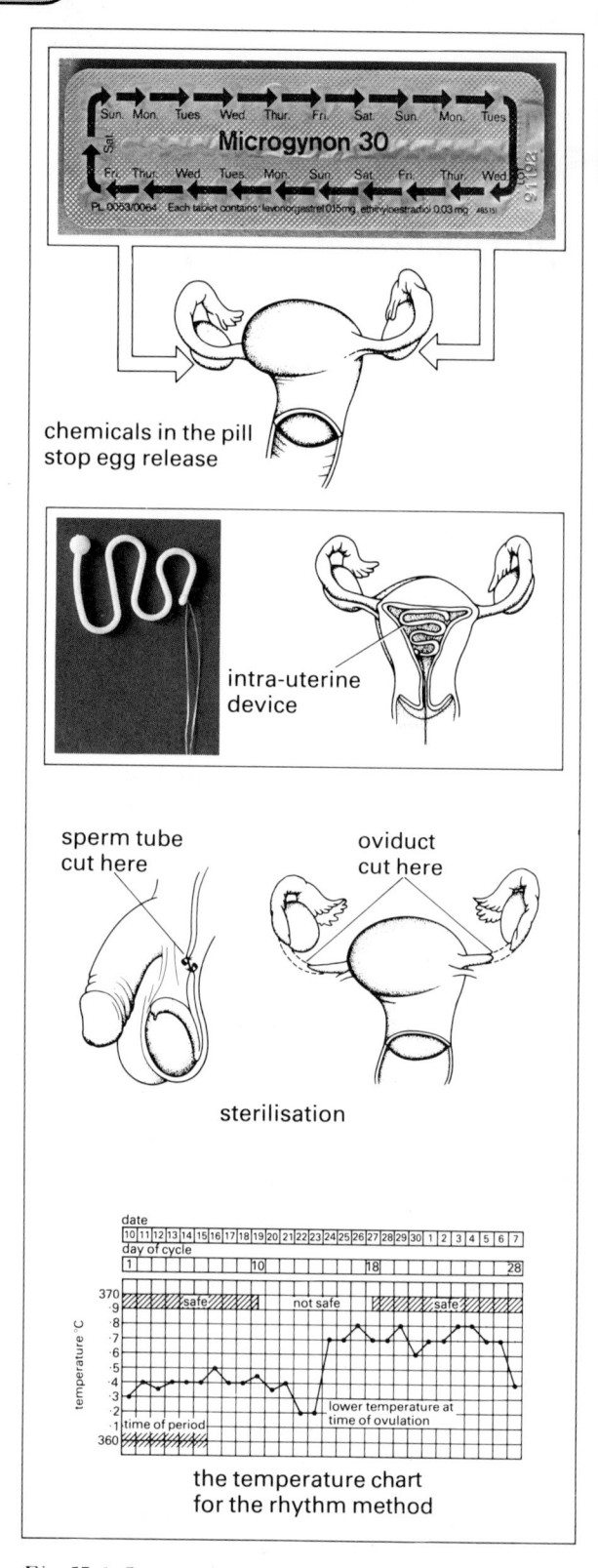

Fig. 57.1 *Some methods of contraception.*

9 Reproduction

Spermicidal creams

This is cream which kills sperms. The woman puts it high up in her vagina before having sex. It is not a safe method when used alone. However it should be used with a sheath or cap to make those methods safer. Spermicidal cream can be bought from the chemist.

Sheath or condom

This is like a 'glove' of thin rubber that the man puts on his erect penis. The sperms are caught inside it and so cannot get into the woman's womb. It is not a very safe method as sperms may get out. However, the condom will act as a barrier to the transfer of microbes, like the AIDS virus, from one sexual partner to another. Using spermicidal cream increases the safety. Sheaths can be bought from chemists.

Cap or diaphragm

This is a thin, rounded sheet of rubber that covers the opening into the womb. A cap of the right size is needed and it must be fitted by a doctor. The women puts it up into her vagina before having sex. It must be left in for 8 hours afterwards. A cap must be used with spermicidal cream if it is to be safe.

Effectiveness

Some methods are more **effective** or 'safer' than others (Fig. 57.3).

Fig. 57.2 Other methods of contraception.

Contraceptive method	Pregnancy rate
contraceptive pill	0·2
intra-uterine device	2·0
rhythm method	25·0
spermicidal cream	4·1
sheath or condom	12·5
cap or diaphragm (with creams)	2·2
no contraceptive used	80·0
sterilisation	0·0

Fig. 57.3 How good are contraceptives?

Summary: Reproduction

* Male and female sex organs produce gametes.
* The male sperms and female egg are brought together during sexual intercourse.
* The nucleus of one sperm fuses with the nucleus of an egg at fertilisation.
* This usually takes place in the oviduct.
* The fertilised egg divides to form an embryo.
* The embryo is implanted in the uterus wall.
* A placenta develops to supply the baby with food and oxygen, to get rid of its waste and to act as a barrier to harmful materials. Some substances can pass across and may affect growth.
* The placenta secretes progesterone which stops the pregnant woman ovulating or menstruating.
* The baby takes about 38 weeks to develop and after this time is pushed out by the muscles of the womb.
* A mother can have care before and after the birth to make sure she and the baby are healthy.
* Some women have more than one baby at a time.
* Reproduction has caused the world population to increase.
* Preventing conception is a way of controlling the increasing population.

10 Inheritance

58 Variation

Any large group of normal human adults will show the human **characteristics**. These include a body covering of fine hair, two hands that can grasp, arched feet and nails on the fingers. But if you look at the group more closely, you will see that each person is different.

Continuous variation

Some adults are tall and some are small. If they were put in a line their heights would go up steadily from 'small' to 'tall'. People **vary** (or differ) in height. This characteristic is an example of **continuous variation** (Fig. 58.1).

Discontinuous variation

There are some characteristics where there are clear-cut differences between individuals (Fig. 58.2). For example, some people can roll their tongues and others cannot; some people have ear lobes which hang freely and others have ones which are joined to the head along one side; you either have a white blaze in your hair or you do not. These are called **discontinuous characteristics**. They can be studied to find out how they are passed on from parents to their children. The way these characteristics are passed on is called **inheritance**.

Fig. 58.1 Variation in height in a group of people.

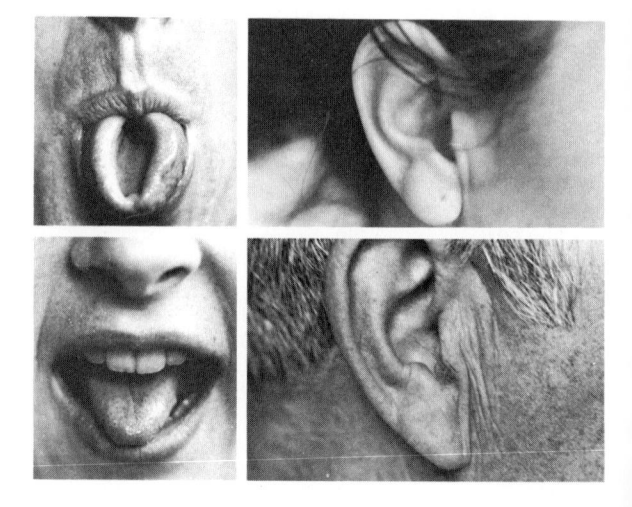

Fig. 58.2 Two discontinuous characteristics in humans.

10 Inheritance

Inside the nucleus

Only the egg made by the mother and the sperm made by the father go towards the making of a baby. So the egg and the sperm must carry all the information needed to control how the baby forms. This information is carried in the **nucleus** of each cell.

The nucleus of body cells

All human cells (except red blood cells) have a nucleus. A cell can be removed from the body and treated so the inside of the nucleus can then be seen with a microscope (Fig. 58.3). Each nucleus contains twisted threads. These are the **46 chromosomes**. The chromosomes can be paired. So in every body cell of humans, there are 23 pairs of chromosomes. 46 is the normal or **diploid (2N)** number for humans.

The nucleus of a gamete

In a sex cell or gamete there is *half* the normal number of chromosomes (Fig. 58.4). So in a sperm or an egg cell there are **23 chromosomes**. This is the **haploid (N)** number. In a gamete, each chromosome has 'lost' its partner.

Information on chromosomes

Each chromosome is made up of a long chain of **genes**. A gene is an instruction for the development and working of one bit of the cell. Chromosomes in a sperm carry genes from the father. Egg cell chromosomes carry genes from the mother. When the nuclei of the sex cells join at fertilisation one new nucleus is formed. It will have some of the genes of both parents. The baby will have some of the characteristics of its mother and some of its father (Fig. 58.5). Studying the way characteristics are inherited means studying how the genes are passed on. Studying inheritance is called **genetics**.

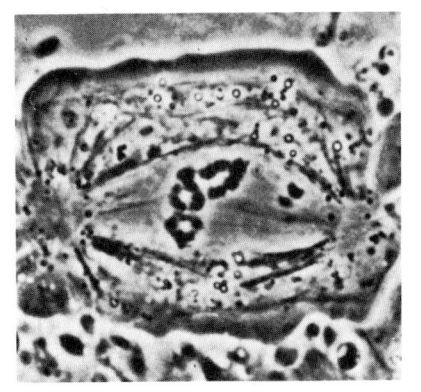

Fig. 58.3 A cell dividing into two ($\times 1500$).

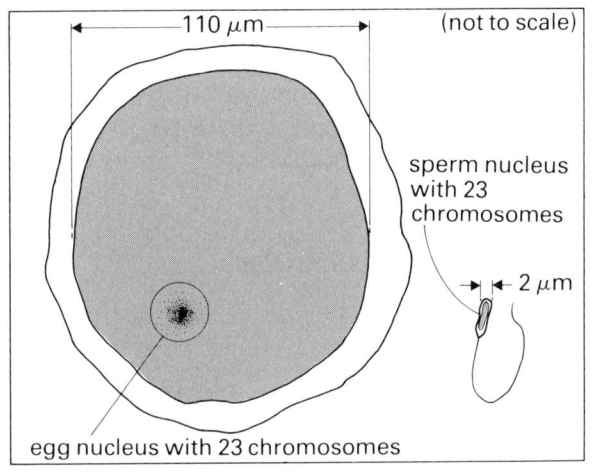

Fig. 58.4 The sperm and the ovum each contain 23 chromosomes.

Each man and woman have their own set of genes in each cell.

Gametes are made in the ovaries or testes. The gametes carry genes of the father or the mother.

The fertilised egg cell grows and divides. The cells of the child will have genes from the mother and father.

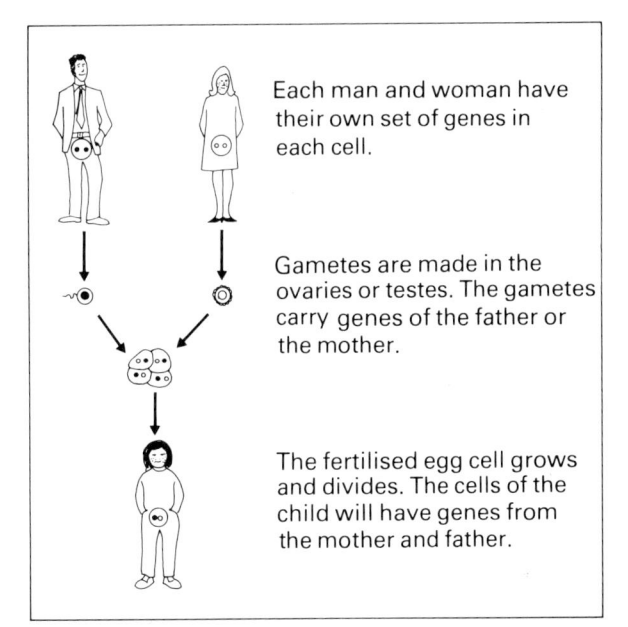

Fig. 58.5 Genes are passed on from parents to their children.

10 Inheritance

59 Cell division

To find out how characteristics are passed on you must know how cells divide to make new cells.

Making gametes

Gametes are the sperms and egg cells. They are made by cells in the testis or ovary. Cells in the testis or ovary have 46 chromosomes (23 pairs). When an egg or sperm is made the number of chromosomes is *halved* (Fig. 59.1). A gamete has only 23 chromosomes and they are not in pairs. Sperms and egg cells are made by a type of cell division called **meiosis**. Meiosis happens only in the ovaries and testes.

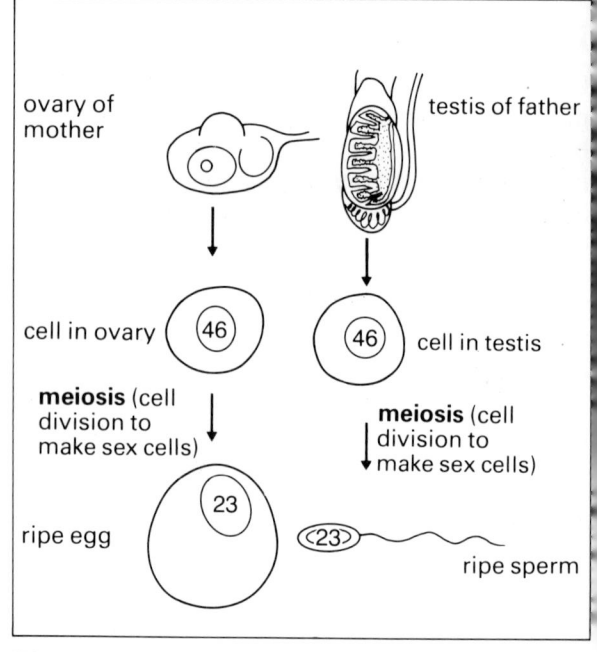

Fig. 59.1 Meiosis makes gametes. The numbers in the cells show that the number of chromosomes in the cells is halved.

The stages of meiosis

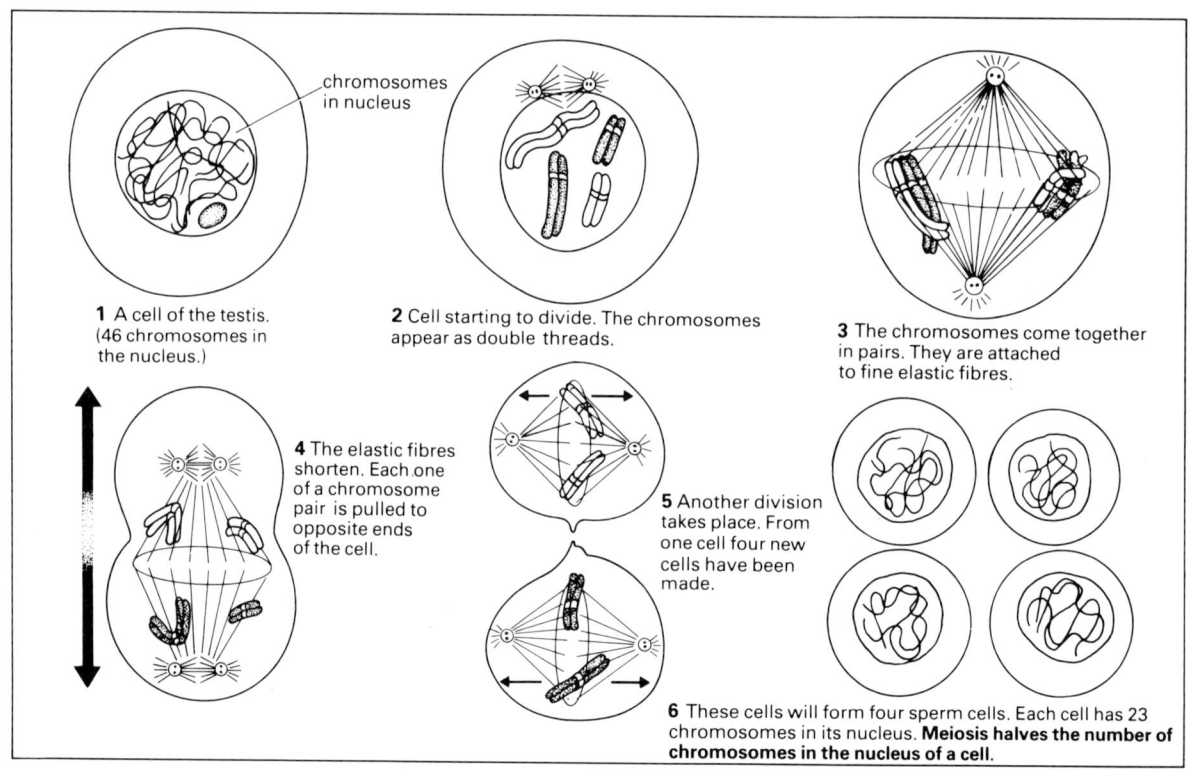

1 A cell of the testis. (46 chromosomes in the nucleus.)

2 Cell starting to divide. The chromosomes appear as double threads.

3 The chromosomes come together in pairs. They are attached to fine elastic fibres.

4 The elastic fibres shorten. Each one of a chromosome pair is pulled to opposite ends of the cell.

5 Another division takes place. From one cell four new cells have been made.

6 These cells will form four sperm cells. Each cell has 23 chromosomes in its nucleus. **Meiosis halves the number of chromosomes in the nucleus of a cell.**

Fig. 59.2 Meiosis – the way sex cells are made. The diagrams show a cell in the testis dividing to form sperms. Only 4 chromosomes (2 pairs) are shown to make the process easy to follow. There would really be 46 chromosomes (23 pairs) in the testis cell. The same stages take place in the ovaries when the eggs (ova) are made.

10 Inheritance

Fertilisation

When a sperm fertilises an egg a single cell is made. This cell nucleus has 46 chromosomes, 23 from the sperm and 23 from the egg. Each chromosome has a partner again. In each pair of chromosomes one will be a chromosome from the father and the other will be from the mother (Fig. 59.3). The chromosomes carry genes to control the development of the baby. So the new human inherits genes from both parents.

Fig. 59.3 Fertilisation brings the number of chromosomes back to 46. In each pair of chromosomes, one has come from the mother and one from the father. (To make the diagram simple only two chromosomes are shown in each sex cell.)

Making cells of the body

The human body is made up of many cells. The fertilised egg cell must divide many times to form a human. The division of body cells is called **mitosis**. In mitosis one cell with 46 chromosomes divides to form two identical cells, each with 46 chromosomes. Mitosis provides new cells during growth (Fig. 59.4).

Fig. 59.4 Mitosis makes body cells. The numbers show that the cell nucleus still has 46 chromosomes after division.

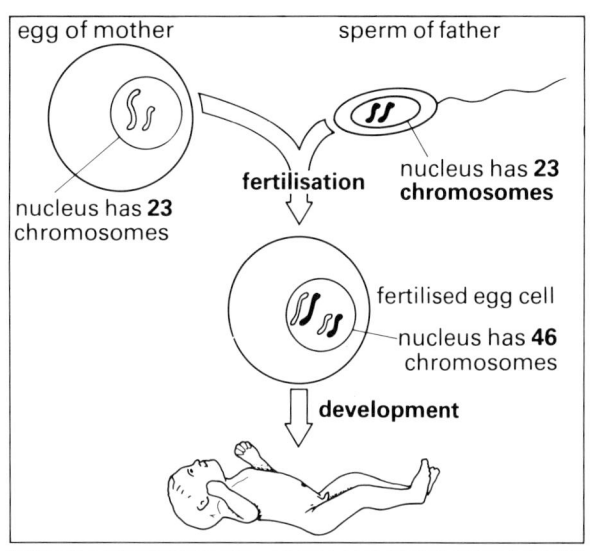

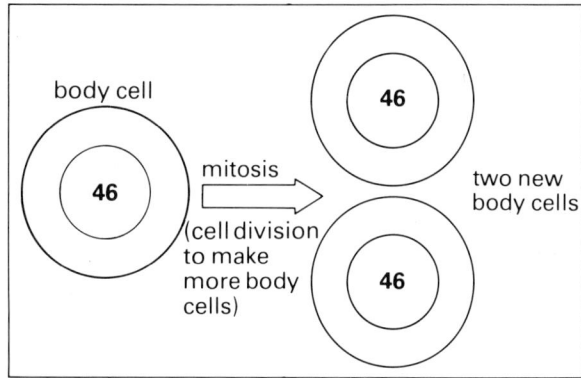

The stages of mitosis

1 A body cell about to divide. (46 chromosomes in the nucleus.)

chromosomes in the nucleus

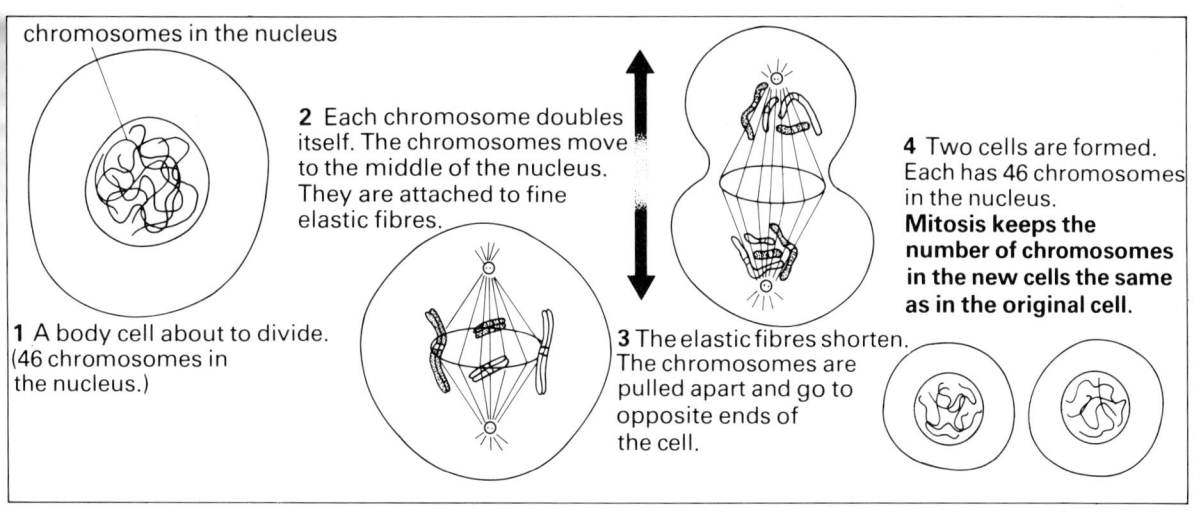

2 Each chromosome doubles itself. The chromosomes move to the middle of the nucleus. They are attached to fine elastic fibres.

3 The elastic fibres shorten. The chromosomes are pulled apart and go to opposite ends of the cell.

4 Two cells are formed. Each has 46 chromosomes in the nucleus. **Mitosis keeps the number of chromosomes in the new cells the same as in the original cell.**

Fig. 59.5 Mitosis – the way new body cells are made. The diagrams show a body cell dividing to form new body cells. Only 4 chromosomes (2 pairs) are shown to make the process easy to follow. There would really be 46 chromosomes (23 pairs) in the body cell.

10 Inheritance

60 The work of Mendel

An Austrian monk called Gregor Mendel was one of the first people to work out how characteristics are passed on. He worked over 120 years ago when nobody knew about chromosomes and genes. He studied plants but his results also help explain inheritance in humans and other animals.

Using peas to study inheritance

Mendel chose to breed pea plants rather than humans! The breeding of pea plants can be controlled and the offspring mature in one year. Human breeding cannot be controlled in the same way and it takes a long time to get the results! The reproductive organs of peas are in their flowers (Fig. 60.1). Each flower makes male sex cells inside **pollen** and female sex cells called **ovules** (egg cells). Mendel could decide which plants were **crossed** or allowed to breed with each other.

Mendel's experiments

Mendel studied inheritance of discontinuous characteristics such as pod colour. He had one set of plants that always produced green pods when crossed with others from this set. He called this group **pure-breeding** for green pods. He had another pure-breeding set that always produced yellow pods. He crossed these two types and then crossed their offspring. The results are shown in Fig. 60.2.

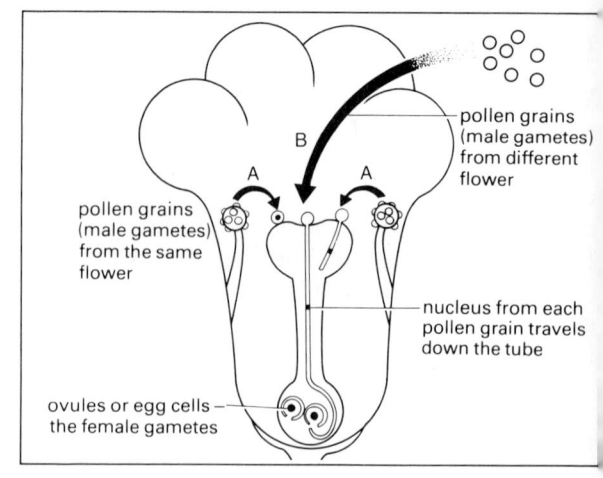

Fig. 60.1 The reproductive parts of a flower. **Self-fertilisation** *is shown by arrow A;* **cross-fertilisation** *is shown by arrow B.*

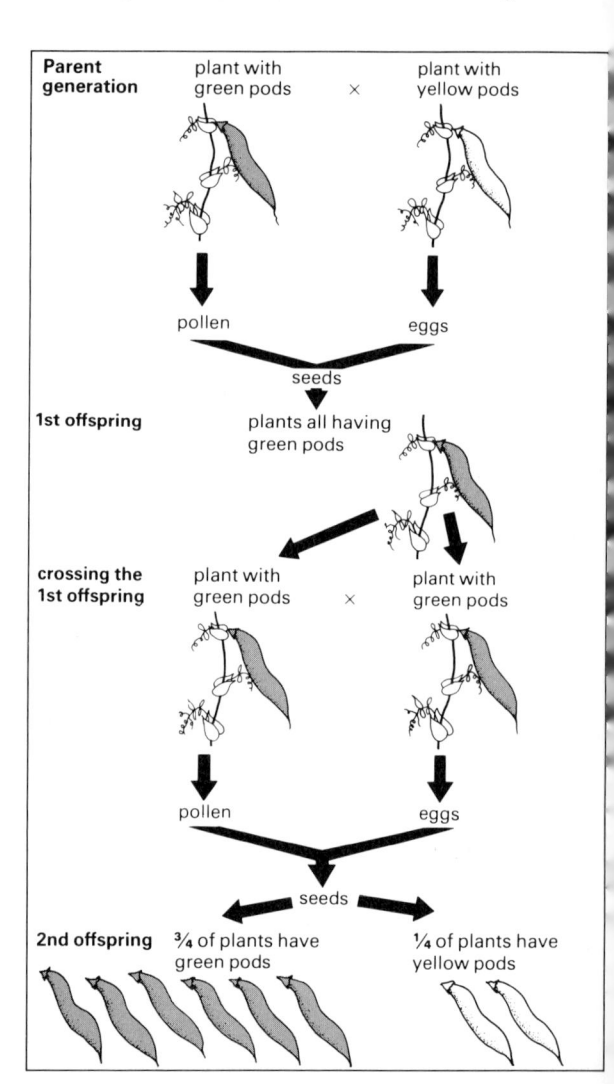

Fig. 60.2 The inheritance of pod colour in pea plants.

10 Inheritance

Explaining Mendel's results

Mendel said that each cell in the parent plant had a pair of 'factors' to control pod colour. These factors are now known to be genes. Mendel saw that pure-bred green pod plants crossed with pure-bred yellow pod plants produced green pod offspring. But some of the second offspring had yellow pods – they must have inherited this from the parent generation. The first offspring must have had one green factor from one parent and one yellow factor from the other parent. Opposite factors of the same characteristic are called **alleles**. The first offspring had green pods so 'green' is **dominant** over 'yellow' – the recessive factor. A dominant factor can 'over-rule' a **recessive** factor when they come together.

In peas there is a pair of factors controlling the pod colour. There is one factor or allele on each of the chromosomes in the pair. Letters are used for the alleles. A dominant allele is given a capital letter. A recessive allele for that characteristic is given the same letter but written small. In this experiment, the dominant allele for green pods is shown as **G**; the recessive allele for yellow pods is shown as **g** (Fig. 60.3).

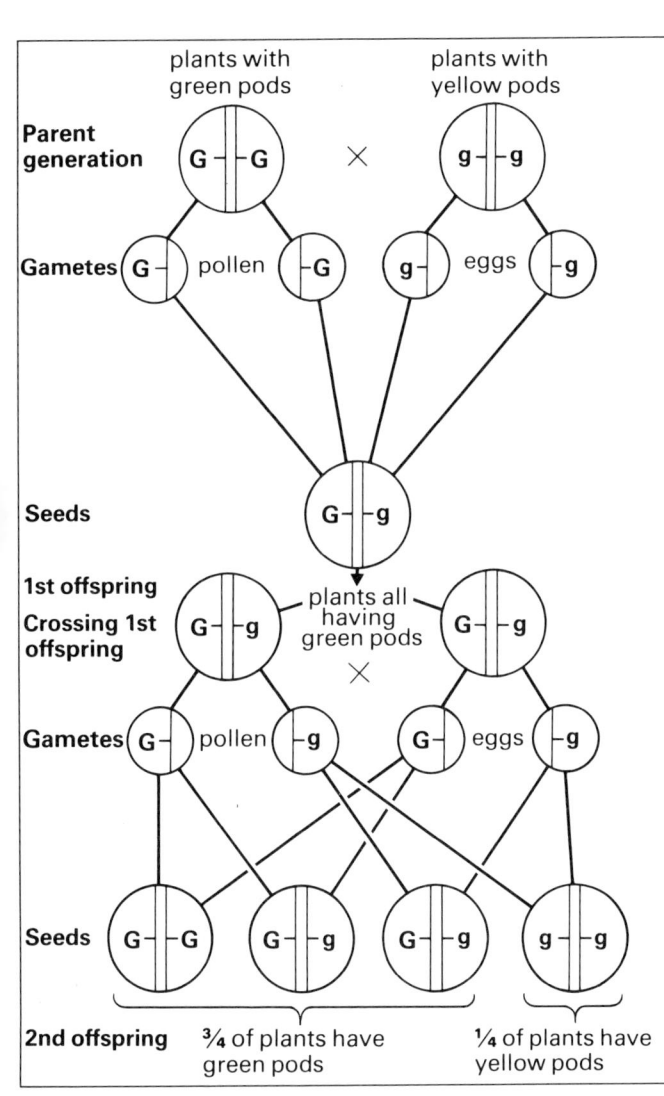

Pure-breeding plants have the same alleles on the chromosome pair. They are **homozygous**, either **GG** (green) or **gg** (yellow).

Each plant can make only *one* type of gamete, containing only one allele of the pair. Green pod plants make gametes containing **G**. Yellow pod plants make gametes containing **g**.

Only *one* combination is possible at fertilisation – **G** with **g**.

All plants are **heterozygous** meaning they have two different genes – **Gg**. All plants are green because **G** is **dominant** over the yellow **recessive** gene **g**. Their **phenotype** or appearance, is green pods. The genes carried by the chromosomes is the plant's **genotype** – here the genotype is **Gg**.

Each heterozygous plant can make *two* types of gametes – **G** or **g**.

There are four possible combinations at fertilisation. All combinations are equally likely.

¾ of plants have at least one dominant allele so have green pods. ¼ of plants have two recessive alleles, and no dominant gene, so they have yellow pods. From this cross, there are three green podded plants to every one with yellow pods. **The phenotype ratio is 3 : 1.**

Fig. 60.3 How the genes of pod colour are inherited.

10 Inheritance

61 Inheritance in families

Dominant	Possible genotype	Recessive	Possible genotype
white blaze in hair	WW or Ww	no white blaze	ww
ear lobes joined to head	EE or Ee	ear lobes not joined	ee
can roll tongue	RR or Rr	cannot roll tongue	rr
freckles	FF or Ff	no freckles	ff

Fig. 61.1 Some human phenotypes and their genotypes.

Dominant and recessive alleles are known to exist in humans. The discontinuous characteristics mentioned on page 106 are inherited in the same way as pod colour in peas. Having freckles or not is another phenotype (appearance) controlled by a dominant allele. The possible genotypes for these characteristics are shown in Fig. 61.1.

Inheritance of freckles in families

The diagrams below show how freckles would be passed on in different families. The genes are shown by letters alone. The way the gametes could combine is shown in a chequer-board (Fig. 61.2). We cannot be sure of a freckled person's genotype. The 'freckle' allele is dominant, they could be **FF** or **Ff**. One without freckles must not have the dominant allele present, so they must be **ff**.

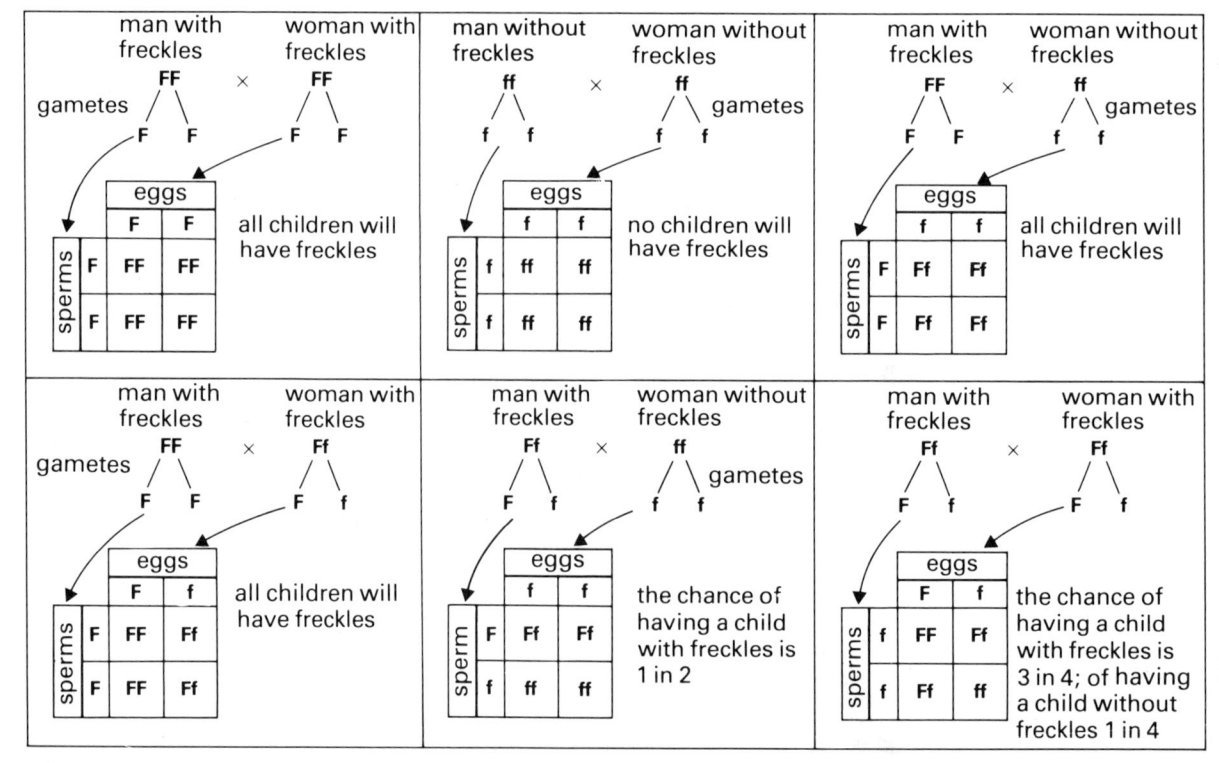

Fig. 61.2 The six possible ways of inheriting the genes that control whether freckles develop or not.

10 Inheritance

Short fingers

It is possible for some people to have genes which cause unusual development. This can be a disadvantage for these people. Luckily such genes are quite rare. One example is the dominant allele causing **brachydactyly**. This is when a person has unusually short fingers. The bones in the fingers are short and may have no joints in them or the fingers may be completely missing. The photos show the difference between normal hands and the short form (Figs. 61.3 and 61.4). The diagram (Fig. 61.5) shows how the condition could be inherited. The woman's chromosomes have one allele causing brachydactyly. (She is heterozygous.) Her genotype is written **Bb**. Her husband has normal fingers, which means his chromosomes have two recessive alleles, so his genotype is written **bb**.

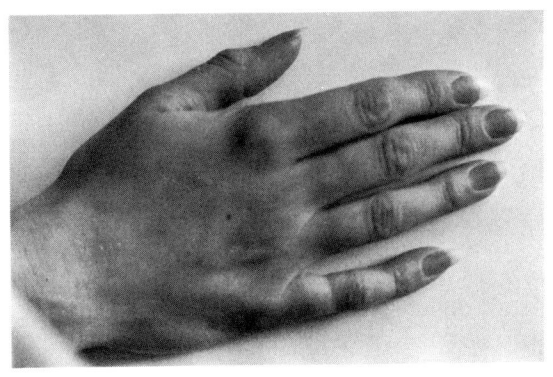

Fig. 61.3 A normal hand.

Inheritance and chance

Inheriting genes is a matter of **chance**. We would expect the couple to have equal numbers of children with normal and short fingers. But imagine that they have three children. All three could be born with normal fingers or all three could be born with short fingers. It depends on which sort of egg (**B** or **b**) meets the sperms. This *cannot* be forecast. Everytime these parents have a child, the chance of having a normal child stays the same (1 in 2).

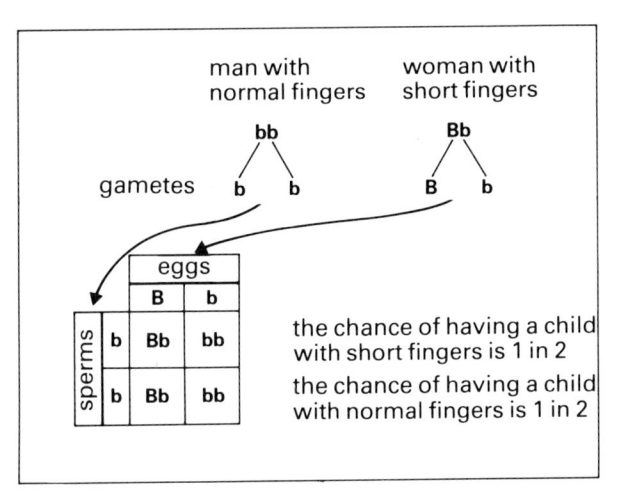

Fig. 61.5 The possible inheritance of short fingers (brachydactyly).

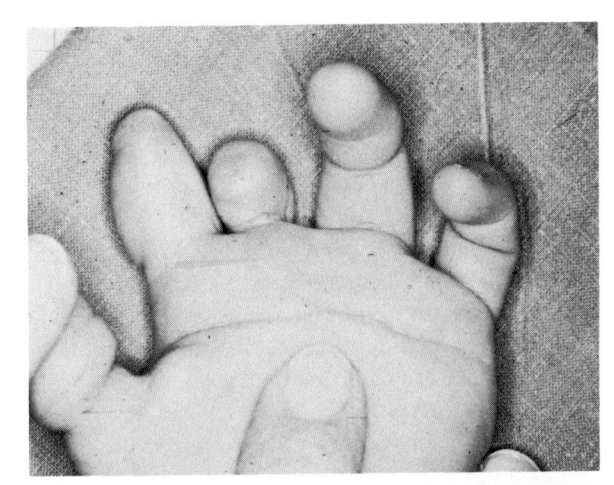

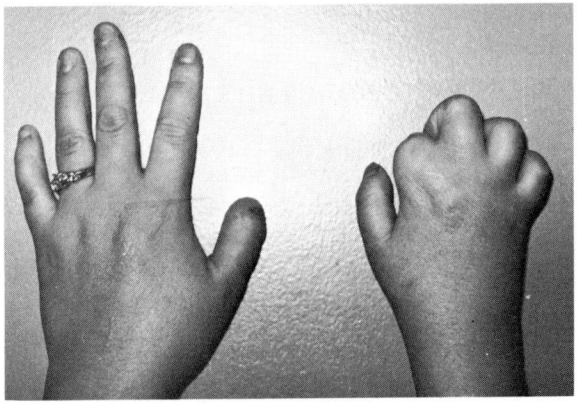

Fig. 61.4 Hands of people suffering from brachydactyly. The child's hand (top picture), being held by a nurse, shows some fingers more seriously affected than others. The lower photo shows both hands of one person. The left hand is almost normal but the right hand has very short fingers that are curled over.

10 Inheritance

62 Male and female

The sex chromosomes

If a photograph is taken of a cell during its division, the chromosomes can be cut out of the photo and put in order of size and shape. Comparing the sets of male and female human chromosomes shows one important difference (Fig. 62.1). In the woman, both of the chromosomes in the marked pair are the same. They are called the **XX** chromosomes. In the man one of the chromosomes in the marked pair is much smaller than the other. These are called the **XY** chromosomes. The **XX** and **XY** chromosomes are the sex chromosomes. They carry the genes that control whether a fertilised egg will develop into a male or female.

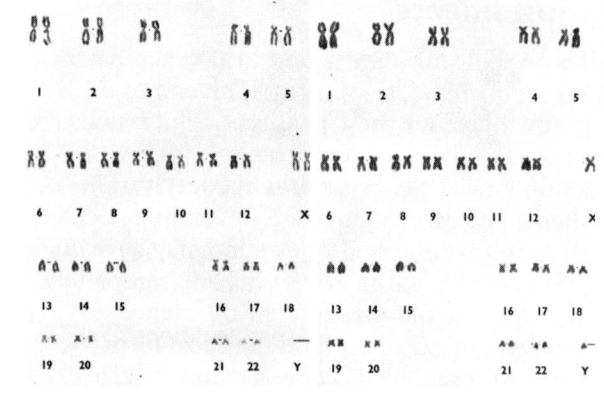

Fig. 62.1 The chromosomes in a body cell of a woman and man.

Will the baby be a boy or a girl?

Whenever a baby is born there is a 1 in 2 chance that it will be a boy and a 1 in 2 chance that it will be a girl. A man makes two sorts of sperms. Half of his sperms will have an **X** chromosome in the nucleus; the other half will have a **Y** chromosome. All the woman's egg nuclei will have an **X** chromosome. The sex of the child will depend upon which sort of sperm meets the egg (Fig. 62.2).

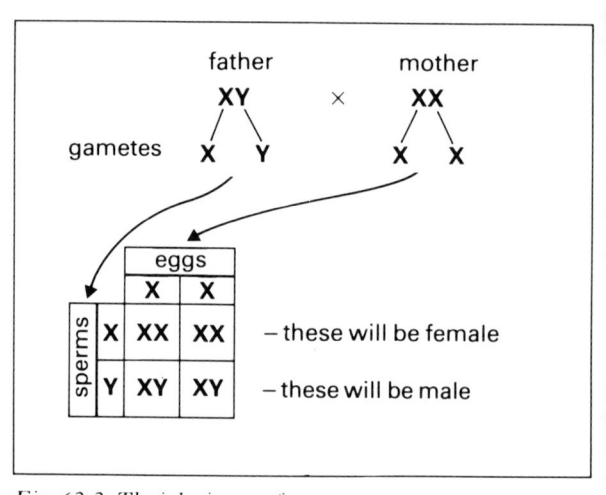

Fig. 62.2 The inheritance of sex.

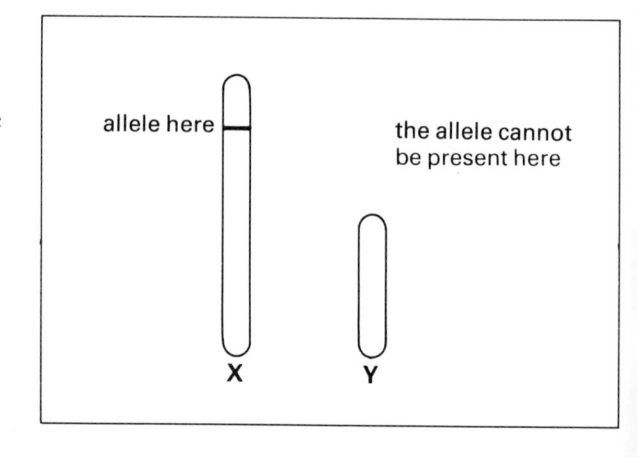

Sex chromosomes and genes

The sex chromosomes also carry genes that control other things apart from the sex of an individual. The alleles on the sex chromosomes are called **sex-linked** alleles. The **X** chromosome is large; the **Y** chromosome is much smaller. An allele on the **X** chromosome may not have a partner on the **Y** chromosome where there is no room for it. So in a male (**XY**) there may be just one gene present to control a sex-linked characteristic (Fig. 62.3).

Fig. 62.3 The sex chromosomes of the male. The Y chromosome is much smaller than the X chromosome.

10 Inheritance

Colour-blindness

Some people cannot see much difference between certain shades of red and green. They are **colour-blind**. It is a rare complaint but occurs more often in men than women. The alleles for normal colour vision are dominant (**N**). The alleles for colour-blindness are recessive (**n**). They are carried on the **X** chromosome.

As a woman is **XX**, she must have two alleles present. If she is colour-blind she is $X^n X^n$. If she has normal vision she can be either $X^N X^N$ or $X^N X^n$. A man is **XY** and the allele is only on the X chromosome. So he must be $X^N Y$ if he has normal vision or $X^n Y$ if he is colour blind.

A woman can have normal vision but may have the recessive allele present in her cell ($X^N X^n$). She can pass on the complaint to her children. She is a **carrier**. The inheritance of colour vision is shown in Figs. 62.4 and 62.5. Fig. 62.5 shows a **family tree** or **family pedigree**.

Colour-blindness is an example of a sex-linked complaint. Another is **haemophilia**, a disease in which blood does not clot properly. Wounds heal slowly. The gene for haemophilia is recessive.

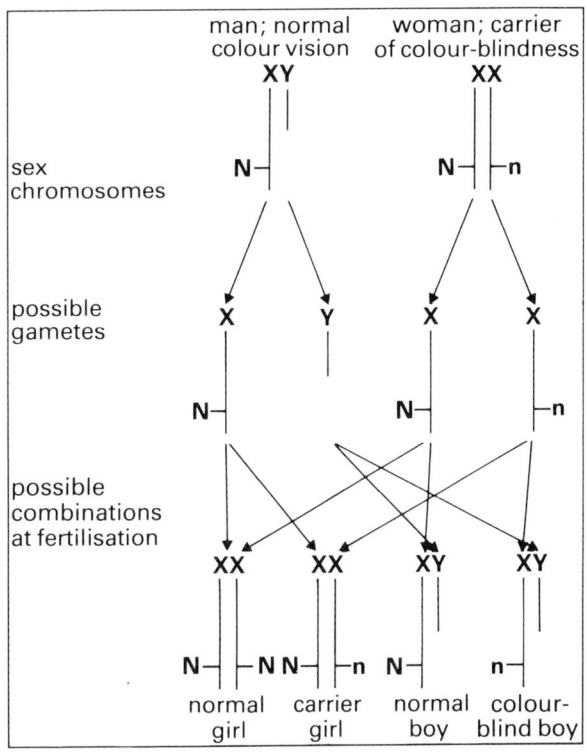

Fig. 62.4 The inheritance of colour vision.

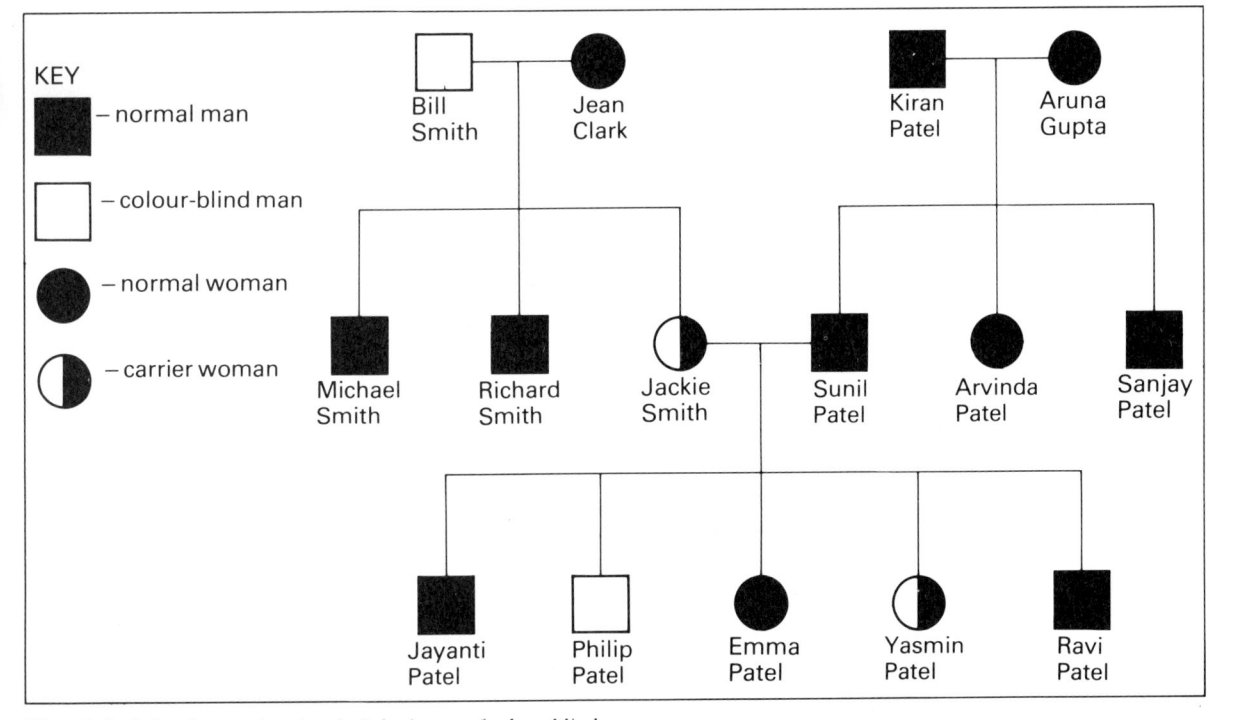

Fig. 62.5 A family tree showing the inheritance of colour-blindness.

10 Inheritance

63 Faulty inheritance

The wrong number of chromosomes

Sometimes a fertilised egg may have the wrong number of chromosomes. This will often affect the development of the baby. In **Down's syndrome** or **mongolism** each cell of the body has one chromosome too many. There are 47 chromosomes instead of 46 (Fig. 63.1). This happens because either the sperm from the father or the egg from the mother was made incorrectly. No one knows why it happens. A child with Down's syndrome could be born into a family where no other child with this condition is known. The extra chromosome affects development in many ways (Fig. 63.2).

Faulty genes

Sometimes an allele on a chromosome may be altered. The gene may be damaged and stop working or its position on the chromosome may change. This will affect the way the cell works. The altered allele can be passed on to the next generation. Queen Victoria's children were affected by an altered allele. Queen Victoria's parents did not suffer from haemophilia but some of her children did. The genes for wound healing are carried on the **X** chromosome. In this case the gene that controls wound healing had changed in the sperm or the egg. When the egg was fertilised, it contained the faulty allele. As Queen Victoria did not have the disease, she must have been $X^H X^h$ (H = normal blood clotting, h = haemophilia.) The sudden appearance of a new characteristic is called a **mutation**.

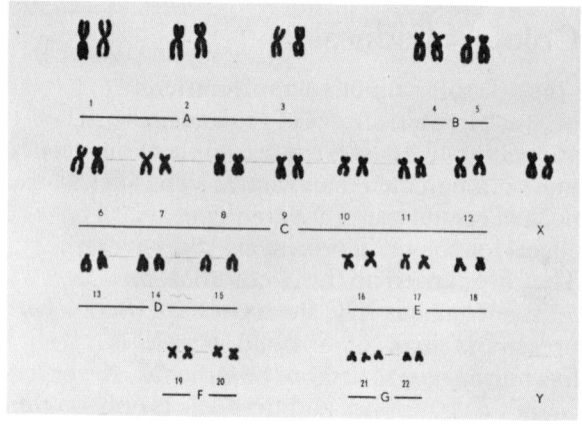

Fig. 63.1 The chromosomes of a girl with Down's syndrome. The extra chromosome is shown at G21.

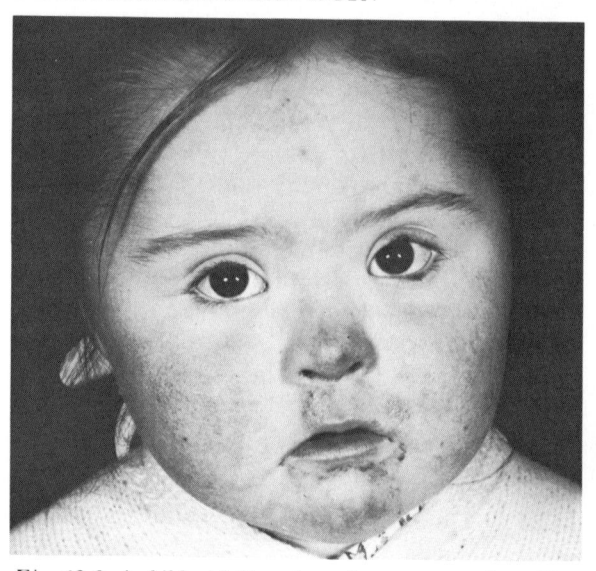

Fig. 63.2 A child with Down's syndrome or mongolism. The characteristics are folded skin on the eyelids (giving a Mongoloid appearance), coarse skin and low intelligence. Also, the heart and kidneys may not grow properly.

Fig. 63.3 Queen Victoria (seated in the middle of the picture) was a carrier of haemophilia. This was passed on to several of her offspring.

10 Inheritance

Causing mutations

No one knows what caused the mutation that produced Queen Victoria's altered gene. It is known that certain chemicals like mustard gas, used in World War I, and some types of **radiation**, can damage genes and chromosomes. Radiation means energy in the form of rays. X-rays have enough energy to pass through flesh and can damage dividing cells. Human sex organs should not be X-rayed (Fig. 63.4). If they are, the X-rays may damage the chromosomes in the sex cells and cause mutations.

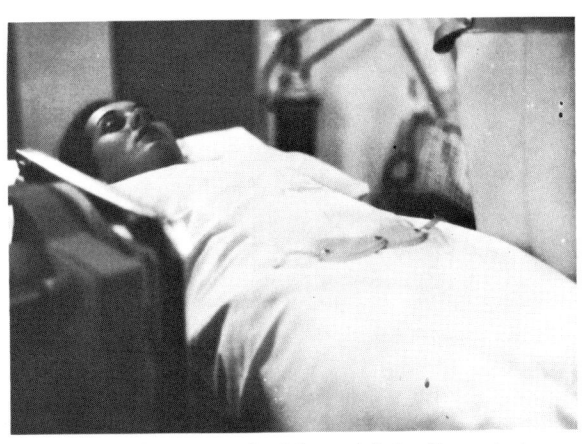

Fig. 63.4 When a person's abdomen is being X-rayed, the sex organs are protected by pieces of lead.

Discovering abnormalities

When a baby is developing inside its mother's womb, cells from its body flake off into the liquid around it (the amniotic fluid). If doctors suspect a growing baby to be abnormal, tests can be made. Some of the liquid is removed and the cells from the baby are collected and treated, so that their chromosomes show up. They can be studied by an expert who can tell if anything is wrong. The parents can be given advice about their unborn baby. This is **genetic counselling**.

Summary: Inheritance

* Humans vary in their characteristics; variation can be continuous or discontinuous.
* The passing on of characteristics from parents to children is inheritance.
* The nuclei of body cells have 46 chromosomes (23 pairs), the diploid (2N) number.
* The nuclei of sex cells (gametes) have 23 chromosomes, the haploid (N) number.
* The chromosomes carry many genes.
* The study of how genes pass on inherited information is genetics.
* Cell division that makes gametes is meiosis.
* This produces cells with unpaired chromosomes.
* It halves the chromosome number.
* When an egg is fertilised by a sperm, the chromosome number becomes normal (diploid) again.
* Cell division of the fertilised egg and all body cells is mitosis. This makes identical cells (all diploid).
* Gregor Mendel, the founder of genetics, studied inheritance in peas; human inheritance works in a similar way.
* Genes are units that pass on information.
* Genes occur in pairs in all body cells. 'Opposite' aspects of a gene are alleles.
* Genes occur singly in sex cells.
* An allele can be dominant or recessive.
* Homozygous body cells contain 2 dominant or 2 recessive allele.
* Heterozygous body cells contain one dominant and one recessive gene.
* The genotype is the genes contained by an individual; the phenotype is the individual's appearance.
* The X and Y chromosomes control an individual's sex; a female human has XX, a male has XY.
* The X chromosome carries some other genes not related to sex; these are sex-linked characteristics.
* An individual may differ from normal if (a) there are more than 46 chromosomes in each body cell or (b) a gene changes.
* The sudden appearance of a new, changed characteristic is a mutation.

11 Support and movement

64 The skeleton

Bones

Bone is a hard material which supports parts of the body and protects some delicate organs. The bones are joined together in a way that makes movement possible. Muscles joined to the bones cause movement. Bones come in many shapes and sizes. The bones of the body are called the **skeleton** (Fig. 64.3).

Calcium makes bones strong

Bone remains long after other parts of the body have decayed after death. It lasts so long because it is made of **calcium** salts – the material similar to that in chalk and limestone rocks. The main salt in bone is **calcium phosphate**. Calcium salts are hard and brittle. So, to stop the bones breaking, bone has tough elastic fibres going through it (Fig. 64.2).

Cartilage

The ears on your head need support. Otherwise they would be limp and floppy. But if they were supported by bone they might snap off! In such places **cartilage** (gristle) is used. It is tough but flexible. Other parts of the body, like the guts and liver, are supported by sheets of **fibres**.

Bone, cartilage and fibres are **connective tissues**. They support and connect the soft parts of the body.

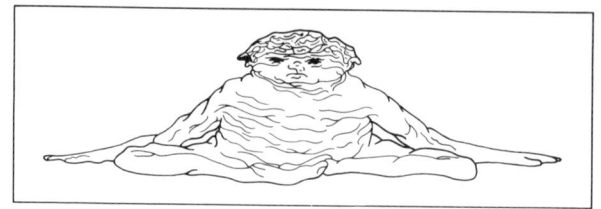

Fig. 64.1 If all the bone was taken out, the human body would be like jelly.

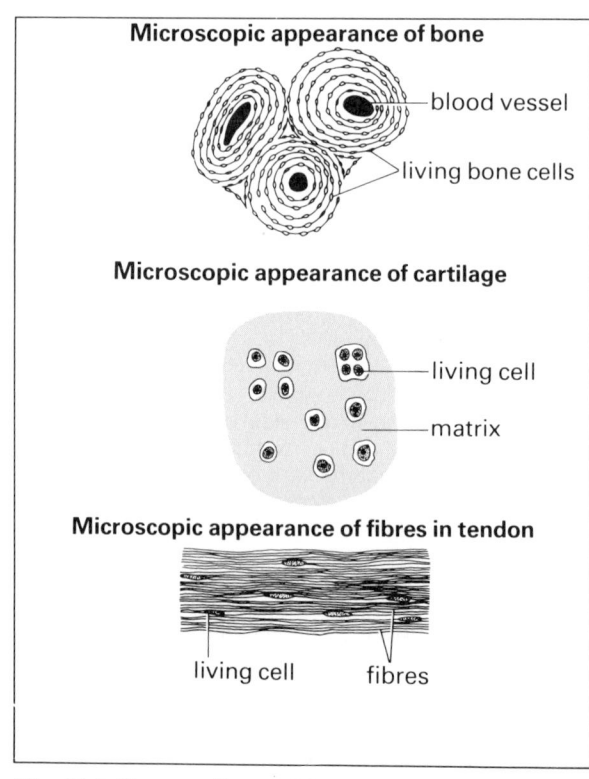

Fig. 64.2 Bone, cartilage and fibres support the body.

11 Support and movement

The skeleton and its work

The five functions of the skeleton are support, protection, movement, making blood cells and transmitting sound in the ear. Each part of the skeleton is specialised to do one or more jobs as shown below.

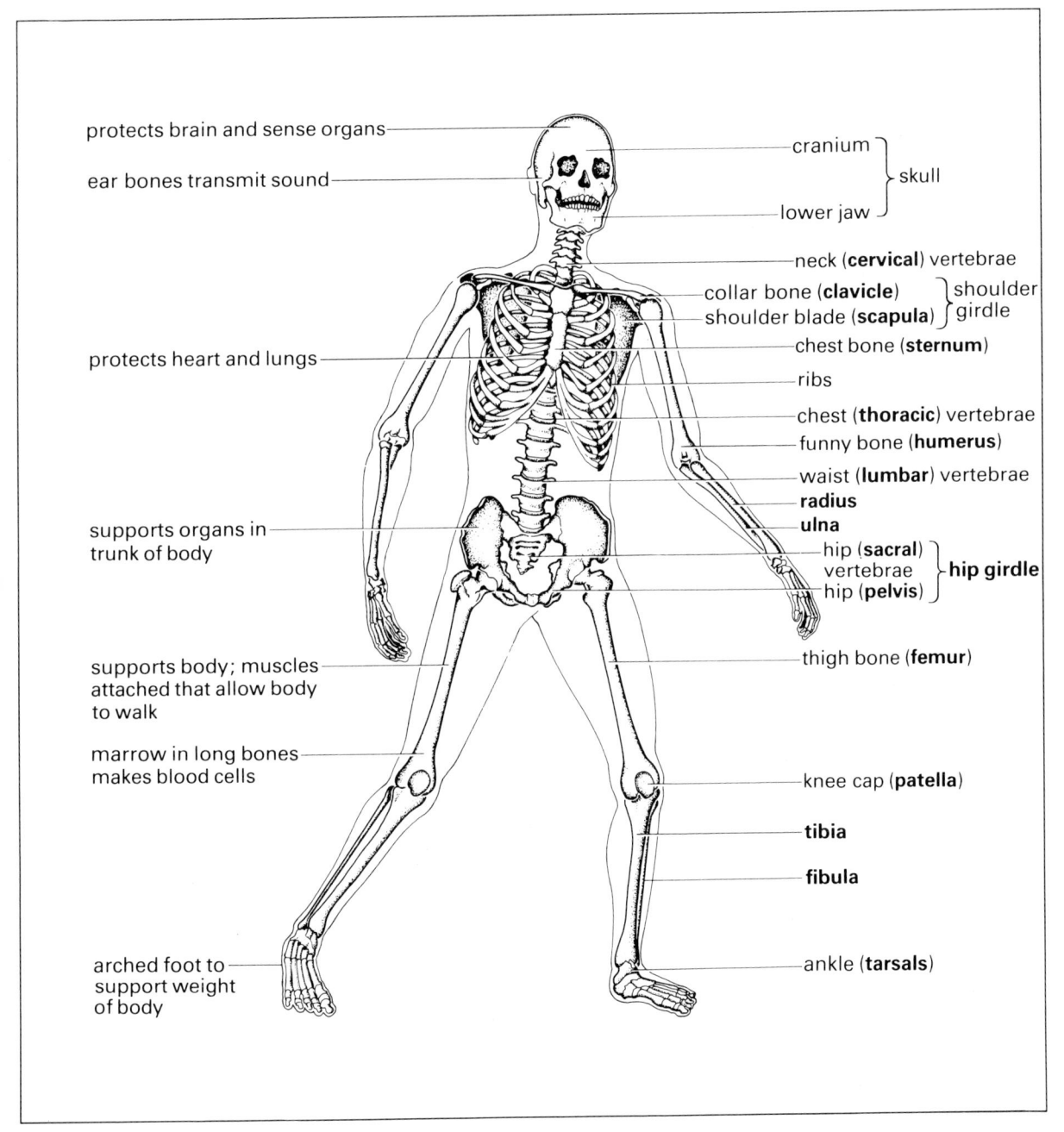

- protects brain and sense organs
- ear bones transmit sound
- cranium ⎫
- lower jaw ⎭ skull
- neck (**cervical**) vertebrae
- collar bone (**clavicle**) ⎫ shoulder
- shoulder blade (**scapula**) ⎭ girdle
- chest bone (**sternum**)
- protects heart and lungs
- ribs
- chest (**thoracic**) vertebrae
- funny bone (**humerus**)
- waist (**lumbar**) vertebrae
- **radius**
- **ulna**
- supports organs in trunk of body
- hip (**sacral**) vertebrae ⎫ hip girdle
- hip (**pelvis**) ⎭
- thigh bone (**femur**)
- supports body; muscles attached that allow body to walk
- marrow in long bones makes blood cells
- knee cap (**patella**)
- **tibia**
- **fibula**
- arched foot to support weight of body
- ankle (**tarsals**)

Fig. 64.3 The bones of the skeleton and the work they do.

11 Support and movement

65 Skull and backbone

The skull

Your head is made up from several bones called the skull. The **cranium** protects the brain and sense organs of the head. The **jaws** are used in feeding and speaking. The nose is needed for breathing (Fig. 65.1).

The backbone

The backbone or **spine** is 33 bones joined to form a strong, fairly flexible rod in the middle of the body. Each bone is a **vertebra** so the whole spine can be called the **vertebral column** (Fig. 65.2). Each part of the three types of vertebra is designed to suit a certain job (Figs. 65.3, 65.4 and 65.5).

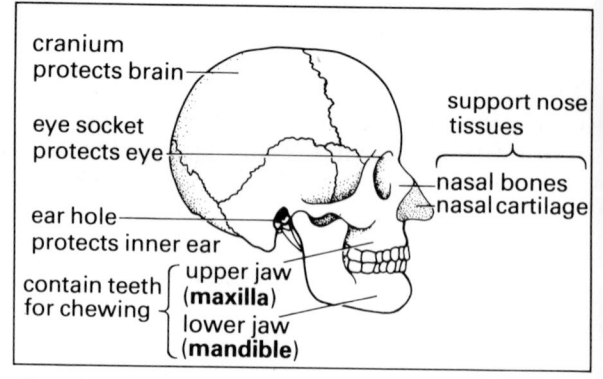

Fig. 65.1 The skull and its work.

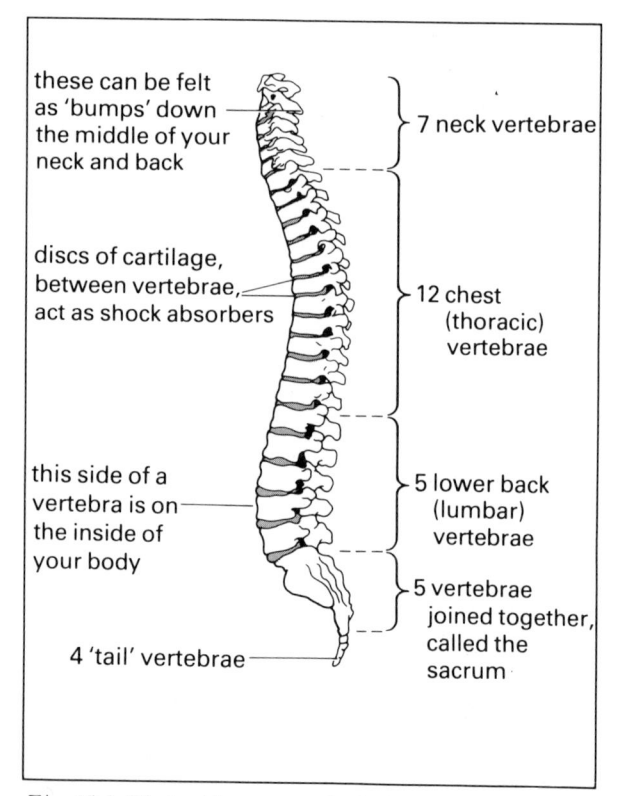

Fig. 65.2 The backbone or vertebral column.

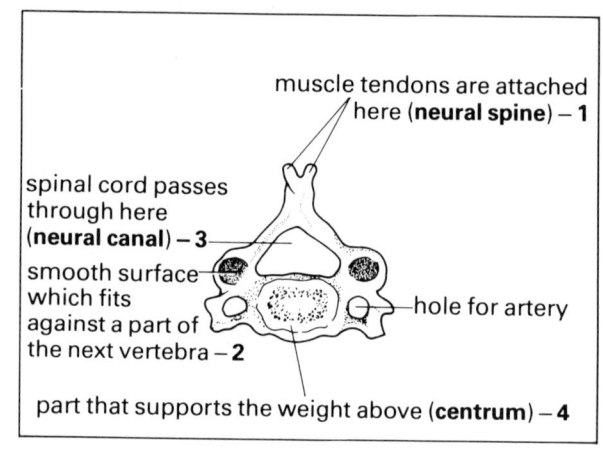

Fig. 65.3 A neck or cervical vertebra.

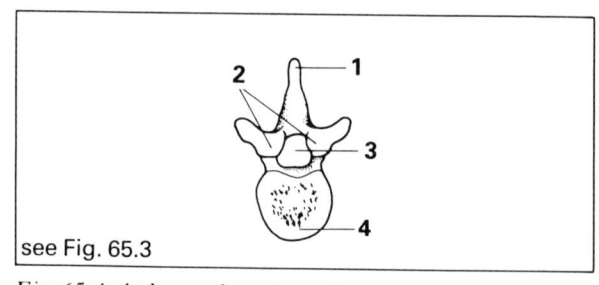

Fig. 65.4 A chest or thoracic vertebra.

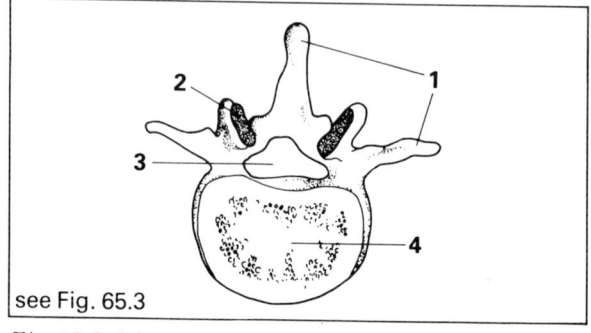

Fig. 65.5 A lower back (waist) or lumbar vertebra.

11 Support and movement

66 Growth of bones

The hardening skeleton

In the mother's womb, the skeleton of the growing baby starts as cartilage. During the third month of growth, cells in the cartilage start trapping calcium. The cartilage slowly becomes more like bone. At birth the baby's skeleton is still fairly soft bone. This allows the baby to pass more easily down through the birth canal. In the years after birth the cartilage is steadily replaced by bone (Fig. 66.1). Growth continues and the bones become longer, thicker and stronger. The cartilage is just left as a cap on the ends of the bones. Toddlers often fall over as they learn to walk and run. Their bones are not as rigid and hard as an adult's so the bones do not break as easily. In old age, more calcium is trapped in the bones so they become brittle. The bones of old people break easily, and take a long time to mend.

Damage to bone growth

Bones will not grow properly if a child does not have enough calcium in the diet. Vitamin D is also needed for proper growth of bones and a lack of it leads to rickets (see page 11). Growing bones can be squeezed out of their normal shape by tight shoes (Fig. 66.2). Young children should always try on shoes that are bought for them. Their feet should be measured and they should walk and run in the shoes they try on. As the feet will grow the shoe must be about 18 mm longer than the longest toe (Fig. 66.3). If a shoe is too narrow or too short, the toes will be bent out of shape. The joints at the base of the big toe will become swollen and painful. This is a **bunion**. If the shoes rub against the skin, a painful **corn** may form. A corn is a thickened part of the skin.

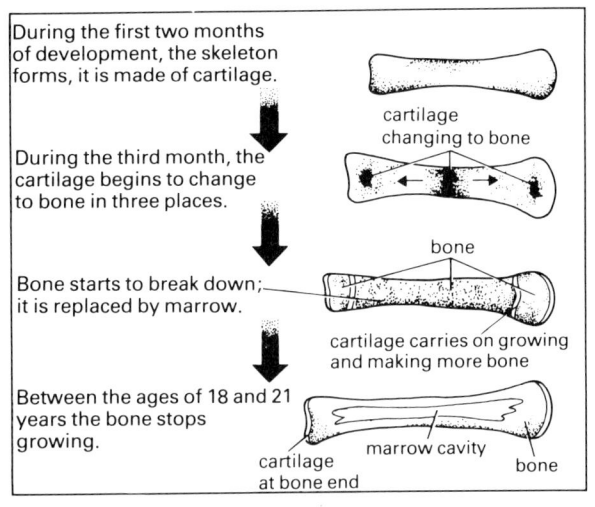

Fig. 66.1 How bones grow.

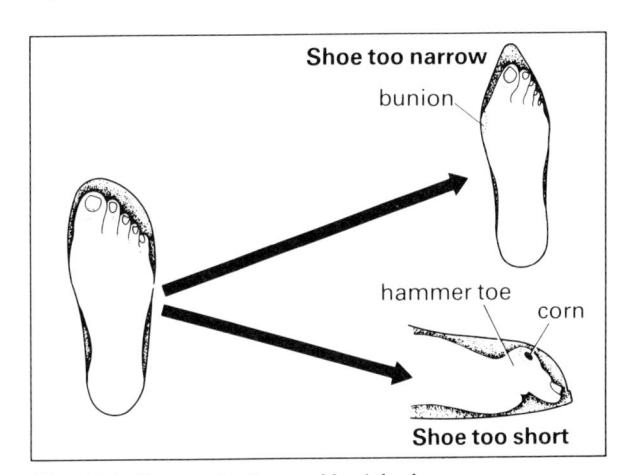

Fig. 66.2 Feet can be damaged by tight shoes.

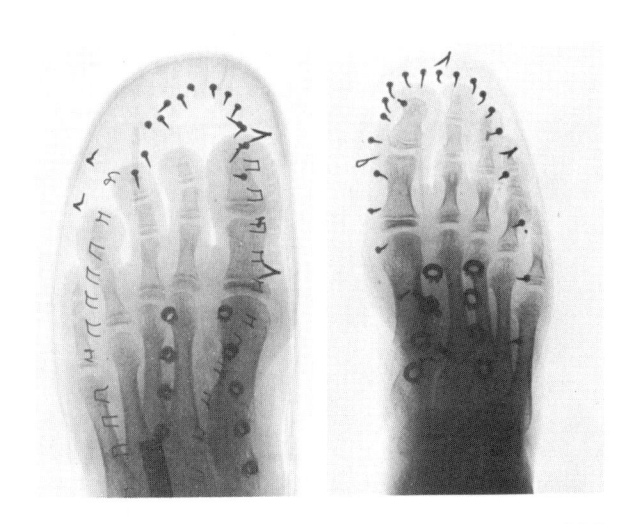

Fig. 66.3 X-rays of feet inside shoes.

11 Support and movement

67 Bones and joints

Inside bones

There are two kinds of bone tissue. **Spongy bone** is a mesh of connecting strips. **Compact bone** has cells so closely packed together that a mesh cannot be seen (Fig. 67.1). In the long bones of limbs spongy and compact bones are arranged to form a tube (Fig. 67.2). The spaces in the spongy bone are filled with red **marrow**. This is where the red and some of the white blood cells are made. If the limb bones were solid, they would be heavy for the body to move.

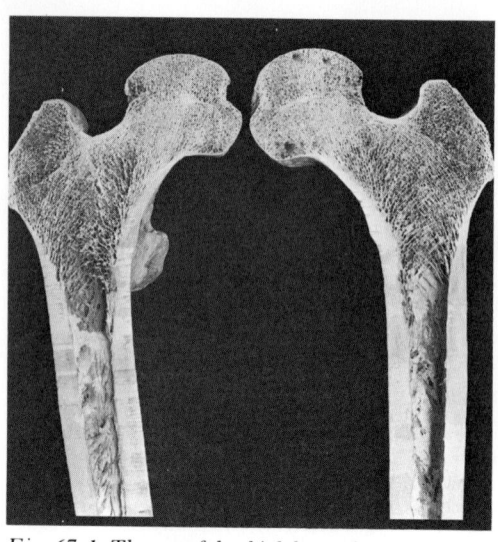

Fig. 67.1 The top of the thigh bone (femur) cut in half to show the two types of bone.

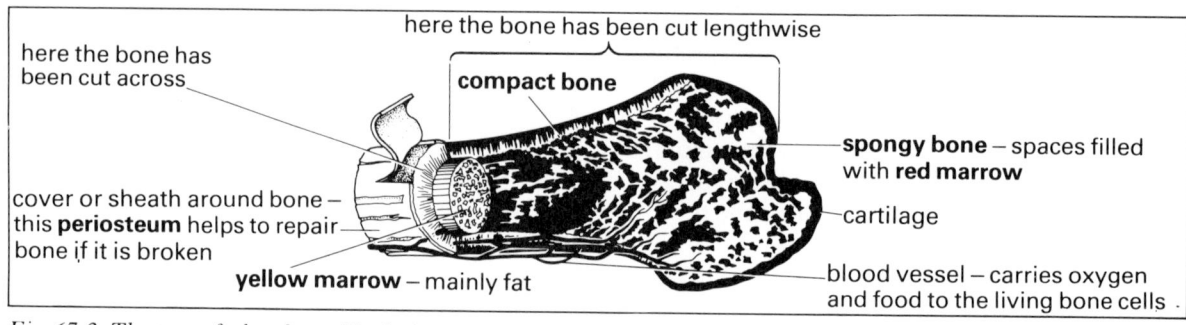

Fig. 67.2 The parts of a long bone, like the femur.

Holding bones together

Over 200 bones make up the human skeleton and they must be held together. A strong flexible material is used so movement is possible. The non-stretching fibres are a connective tissue bundled together as a ligament. Bones are held together by ligaments (Figs. 67.3 and 67.4).

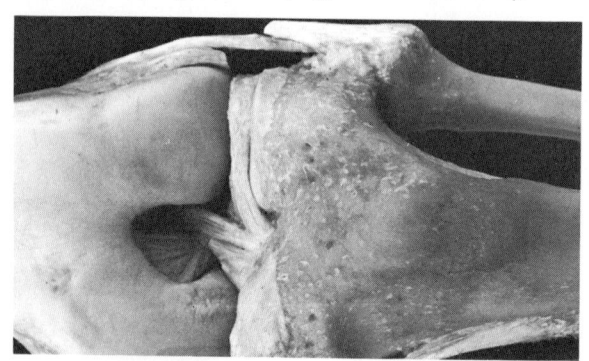

Fig. 67.3 Ligaments at the knee.

Fixing muscles to bones

Muscles cause movement when they pull on bones. Muscles must be attached to bones. Muscles are joined to bones by **tendons**. A tendon is also made from non-stretching fibres. Bones sometimes have special parts for the attachment of tendons (Fig. 67.4).

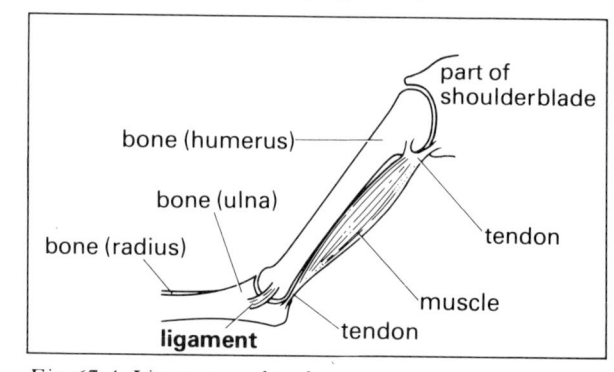

Fig. 67.4 Ligaments and tendons.

122

11 Support and movement

Joints

A joint is where two or more bones meet. There are five main types of joint (Fig. 67.5). Joints move in different ways and some do not move at all.

Free-moving, synovial joints
1 Ones that allow movement in several directions:
a) ball-and-socket joint, b) pivot joint

hip joint

joint between neck and skull

2 Ones that allow movement in one direction – hinge joint

knee joint

3 Slightly movable joint

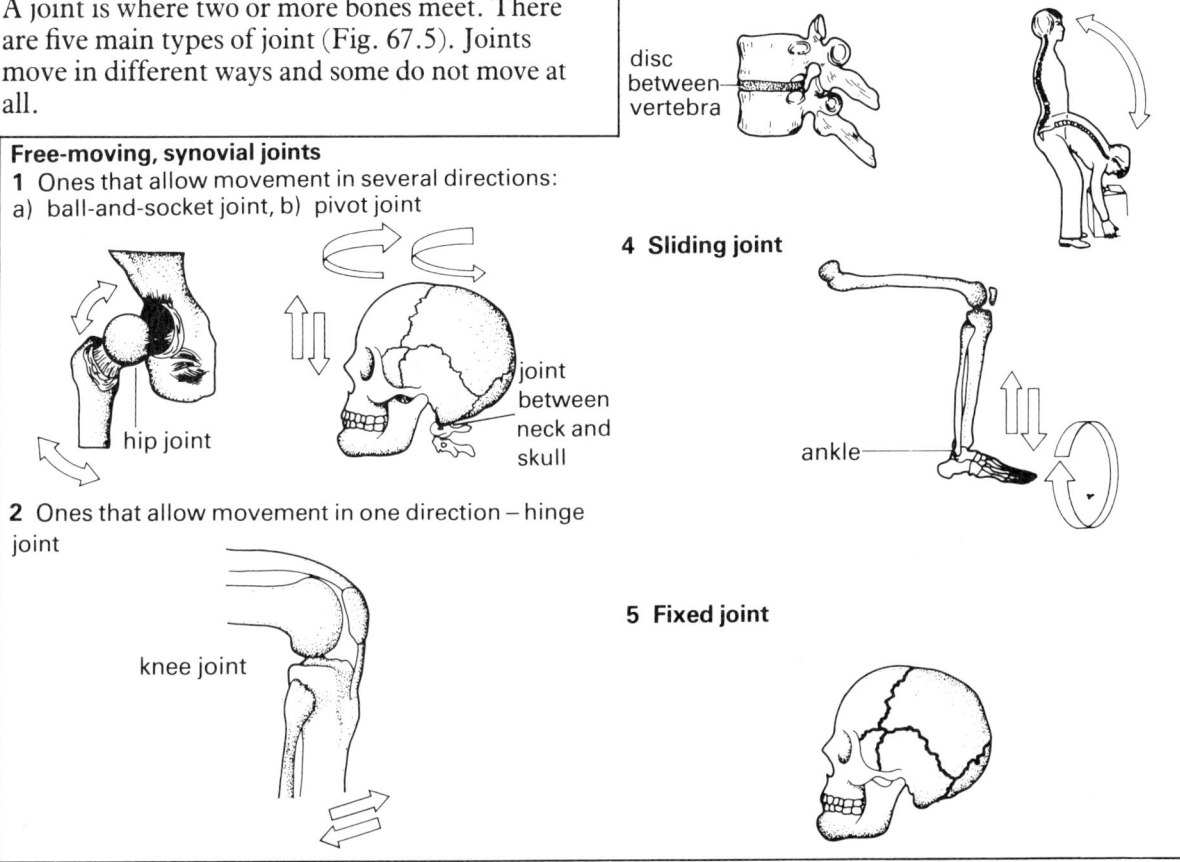

disc between vertebra

4 Sliding joint

ankle

5 Fixed joint

Fig. 67.5 *The five types of joint.*

Oiling the joints

To make the joint move easily it must be **lubricated**. Also, joints must not wear out quickly. A joint has layers between the bones to help the movement. These **movable** or **synovial** joints (e.g. the elbow or knee) have a special design (Fig. 67.6). As people get older, a joint may stop moving freely. The cartilage may wear and the joint can sometimes be replaced (Fig. 67.7).

- bone cut lengthwise
- bone sheath
- spongy bone
- **capsule** (envelope) that surrounds the joint
- bag of liquid (**synovial fluid**) which works like a cushion; it helps the joint move smoothly
- **cartilage** to form a smooth end to the bone

Fig. 67.6 *The parts of a synovial or freely-movable joint.*

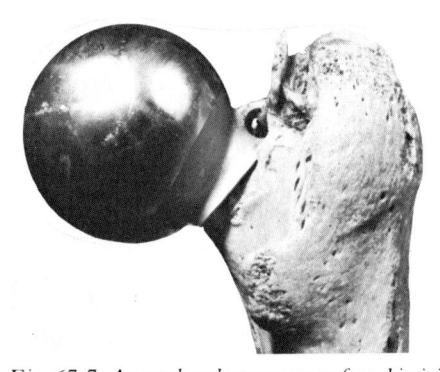

Fig. 67.7 *A metal replacement part for a hip joint.*

123

11 Support and movement

68 Muscles

Muscle cells

Movements of your body are caused by muscle. Muscle cells work by **contracting** or getting shorter. When they stop contracting they **relax** and return to normal. Muscle contraction needs energy and so uses up food and oxygen. There are three kinds of muscle tissue.

Fig. 68.1 Smooth muscle.

Smooth muscle

The cells of **smooth muscle** do not have any markings on them. Their shape is shown in Fig. 68.1. Smooth muscle is found in the walls of the gut and blood vessels. The intestines need muscular walls to squeeze on the food, moving it on through the tube. You do not have to think about moving your gut muscles. It is controlled automatically by the nervous system. So smooth muscle is also called **involuntary muscle**.

Heart muscle

Heart or **cardiac muscle** looks rather different as shown in Fig. 68.2. Cardiac muscle is found only in the heart. The muscle fibres are linked so that when one contracts, they all do. The fibres of heart muscle beat or contract at their own rhythm. They will carry on beating for a while even when taken out of the body!

Fig. 68.2 Cardiac muscle.

Striped muscle

The cells of **striped muscle** have dark and light bands so they look striped (Fig. 68.3). Striped muscle is also called **skeletal muscle** because it moves the bones. Striped muscle can be controlled by you in a conscious way. You can decide when and how to move your arm. So another name for striped muscle is **voluntary muscle**. Nerve impulses are sent to the muscle and they make the muscle cells contract. Striped muscle cells are grouped together in bundles to form one muscle.

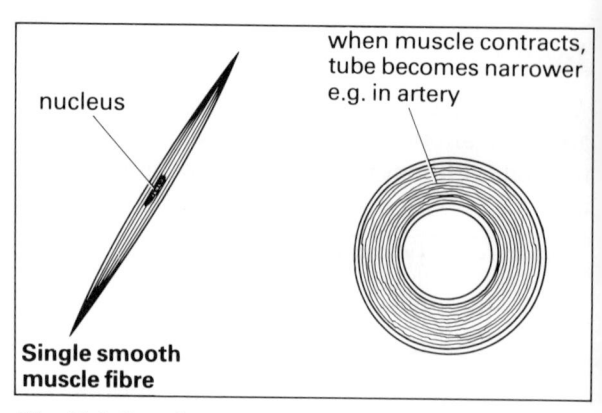

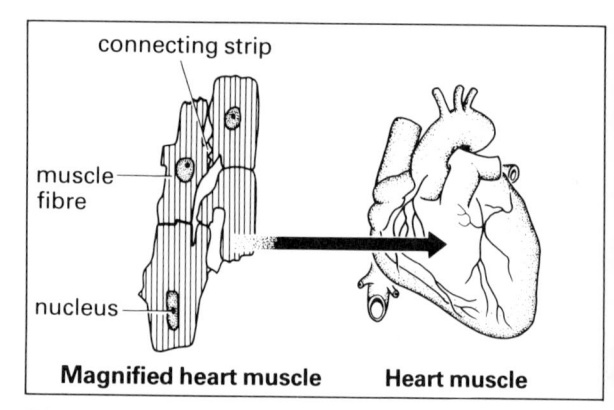

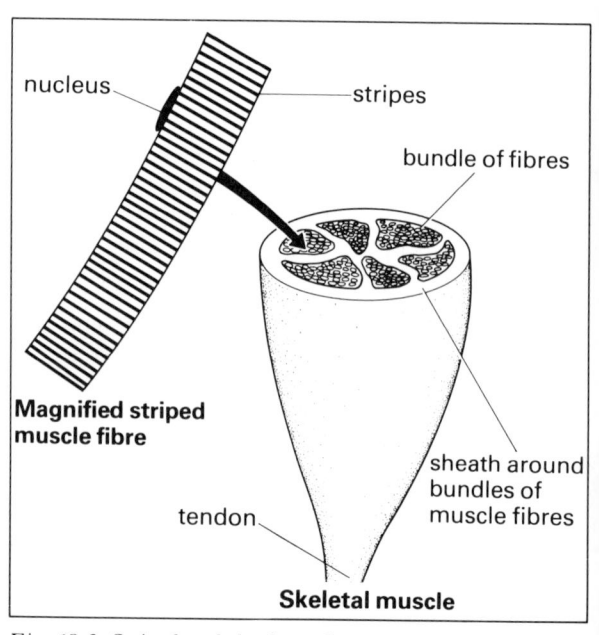

Fig. 68.3 Striped or skeletal muscle.

11 Support and movement

Moving the body

The body needs hundreds of muscles to bring about all the movements it can do (Fig. 68.4). If you eat red meat, such as a steak, you are eating an animal's skeletal muscles. When a muscle contracts (shortens) it pulls on a bone causing movement at a joint. A muscle is joined to a different bone at each end. One bone stays still. The attachment here is called the **origin** of the muscle. The other end of the muscle is fixed to the bone that moves. This is the **insertion** of the muscle (Fig. 68.5).

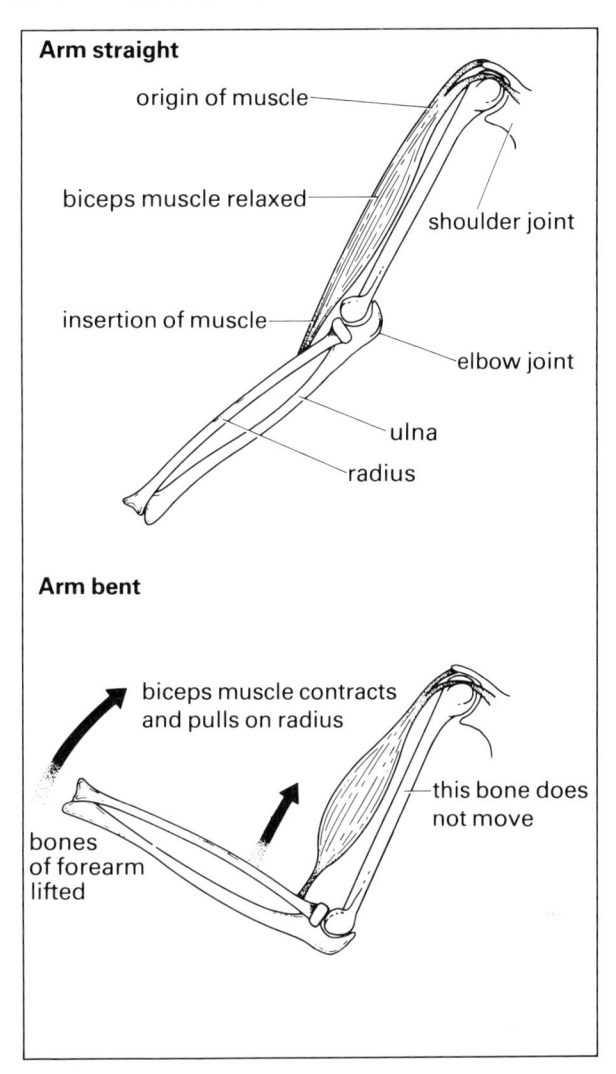

Fig. 68.5 *A muscle pulls on a bone.*

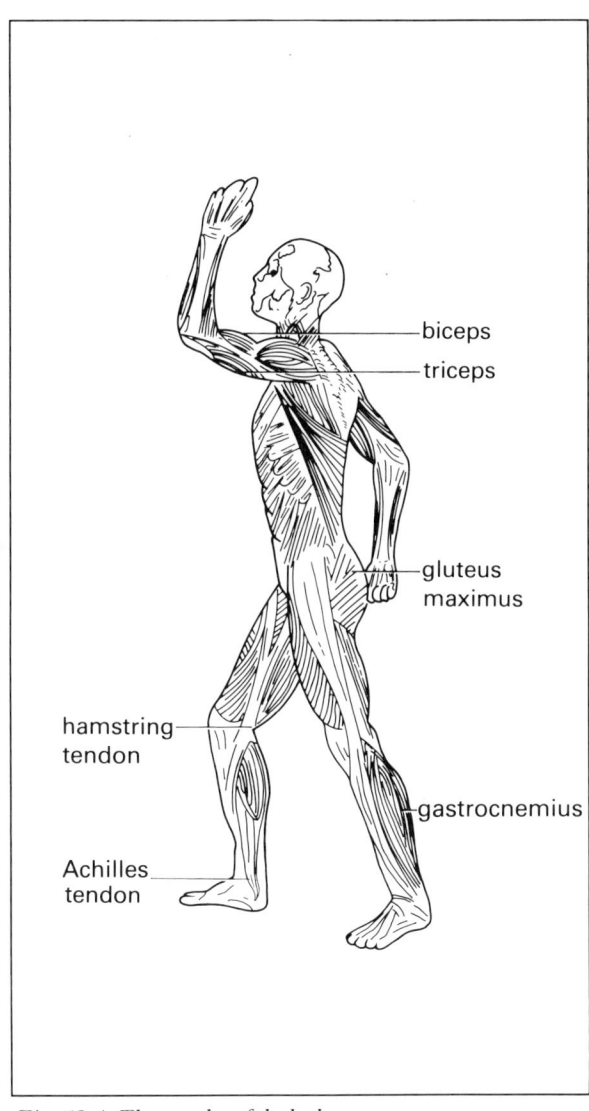

Fig. 68.4 *The muscles of the body.*

Fig. 68.6 *With practice, the body can be moved into strange positions.*

11 Support and movement

69 Muscles, bones and levers

Pairs of muscles

Muscles often work in pairs as at a hinge joint. A muscle moves the bone one way and another muscle is needed to move the bone the other way. A pair of muscles that have *opposite* effects are called **antagonistic** muscles. The **biceps** and the **triceps** are two antagonistic muscles that raise and lower the forearm (Fig. 69.1). As one muscle (biceps) contracts and bends the limb, the other (triceps) must relax. The muscles receive their instructions from the impulses in motor nerves. When one muscle is 'told' to contract, the other is 'told' to relax.

Many movements of the body are brought about by antagonistic pairs of muscles. The muscle that bends or **flexes** a joint is a **flexor**. The muscle that straightens or **extends** a joint is an **extensor** (Fig. 69.2).

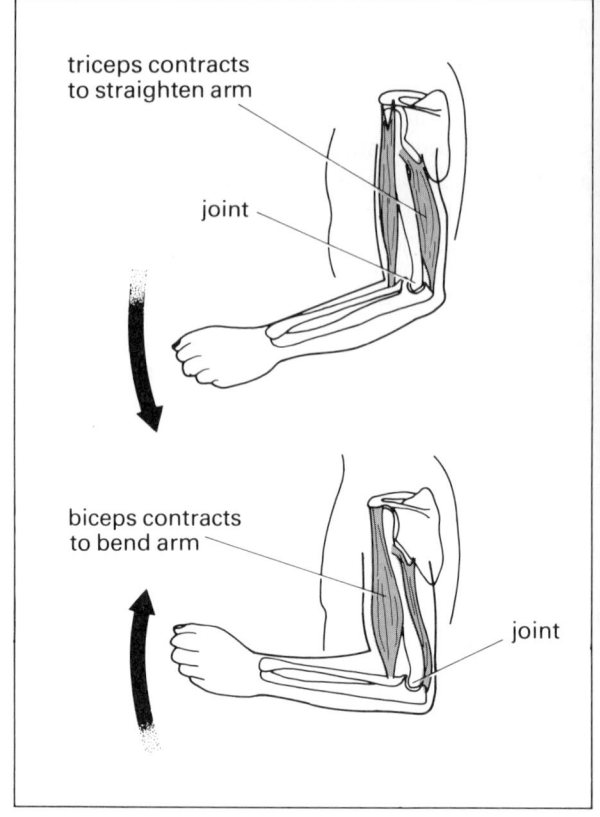

Fig. 69.1 Muscles that move the forearm.

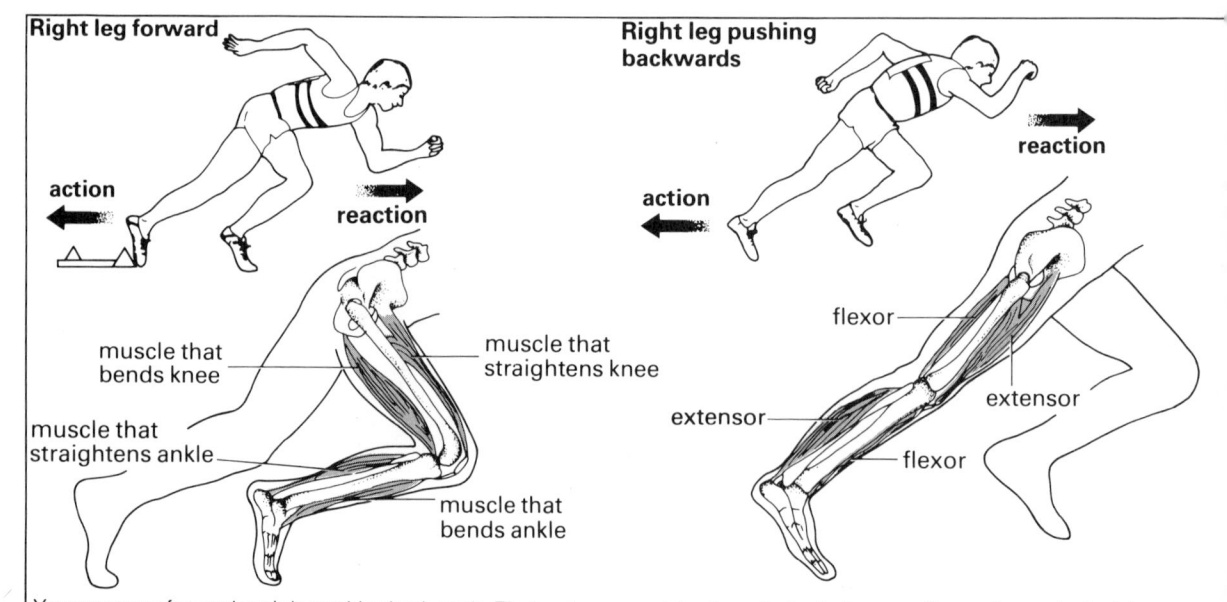

You can move forwards only by pushing backwards. The harder you push backwards, the faster you will move forwards. Sprinters use blocks to give them a better start. The diagrams show how the leg muscles work during the first two strides of a race.

Fig. 69.2 How the leg muscles work during the first two strides of a race.

11 Support and movement

Levers

Levers are 'machines' that make light work of many jobs. For instance, a lever is used to take the lid off a paint tin. Using a lever involves three things – the **load** to be moved, the **effort** or force used to move the load, and a **fulcrum** or balance point (Fig. 69.3). The further the distance of the effort from the fulcrum, the easier it is to lift the tin lid load. There are three kinds of lever.

the tin lid is lifted here (**load**)

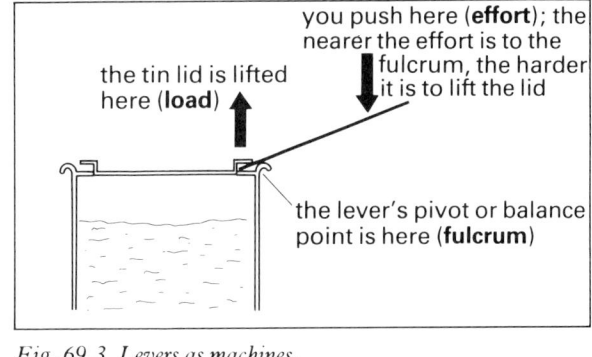

you push here (**effort**); the nearer the effort is to the fulcrum, the harder it is to lift the lid

the lever's pivot or balance point is here (**fulcrum**)

Fig. 69.3 Levers as machines.

First order

Lifting a child on a see-saw is a **first order lever**. The order is 'load – fulcrum – effort'. In the body, nodding the head is an example of a muscle moving a load in this way (Fig. 69.4).

See-saw
load   effort   fulcrum

Lifting the chin; the neck muscles contract and pull down the back of the skull.

load   fulcrum   effort

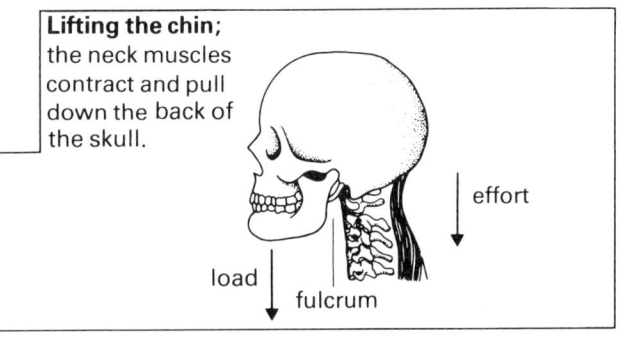

Fig. 69.4 First order levers.

Second order

A wheelbarrow is a **second order lever**. The order is 'fulcrum – load – effort'. When you are standing on tip toe, the calf muscle lifts the body like a second order lever (Fig. 69.5).

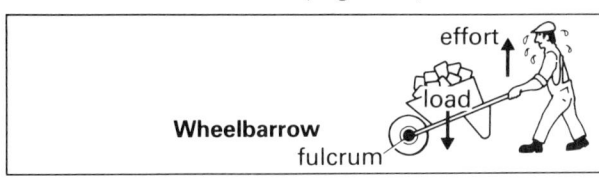

Wheelbarrow
effort   load   fulcrum

Standing on tiptoe
effort — calf muscle contracts and pulls on tendon
fulcrum   load – weight of body presses down here

Fig. 69.5 Second order levers.

Third order

Some car accelerator pedals are **third order levers**. The order is 'fulcrum – effort – load'. There are many third order levers in the body. In these the muscle pulls the 'near' end of the bone up by a short amount. The 'far' end moves a much greater distance (Fig. 69.6).

Accelerator pedal on some cars
fulcrum   effort   accelerator cable (load)   pedal

Bending the arm at the elbow
effort – the biceps muscle tendon pulls up the forearm   load   fulcrum

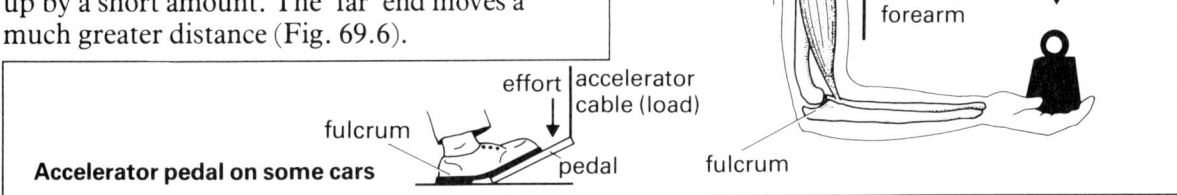

Fig. 69.6 Third order levers.

127

11 Support and movement

70 Broken bones

Bones are strong but they can be damaged. If you fall awkwardly or jump off a wall and land without bending your legs, your leg bones are put under a lot of stress. They may break or **fracture**.

Types of fractures

When a bone breaks cleanly into two, it is a **simple** fracture. If the skin is not damaged it is a **closed**, simple fracture. If the skin is damaged by the broken bone, it is an **open**, simple fracture. When a bone breaks on one side only, it is a **greenstick** fracture. If there is more than one break in a bone, the fracture is **compound**. If the broken ends of the bone tear into blood vessels or nerves, then it is a **complicated** fracture (Fig. 70.2).

The signs of a fracture

Some people think that if a person can move an arm or a leg, then it is not broken. This is not true. Someone with a broken bone may have:
Pain.
Unusual shape to the limb.
Lost the use of the limb.
Swollen and tender flesh near the break.
Extra movement in the limb.
For the signs of a fracture, remember – **P.U.L.S.E!**

Fig. 70.1 Parachutists are taught how to fall so that they do not break their bones.

Fig. 70.3 This person may have a broken humerus or upper arm.

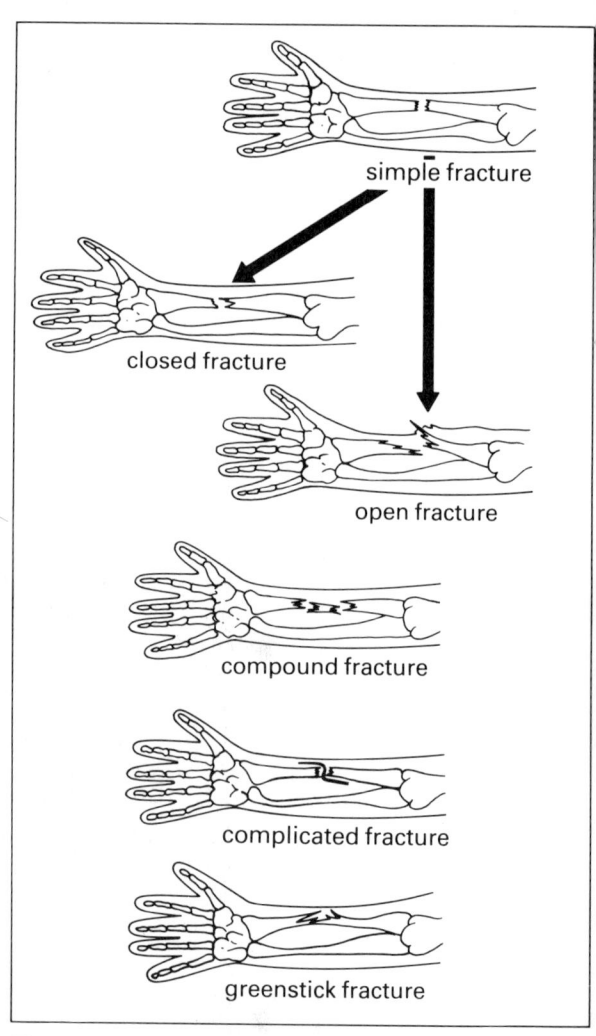

Fig. 70.2 Different types of fractures.

11 Support and movement

Finding the fracture

Doctors check for breaks using **X-rays** (Fig. 70.4). Like light, these rays cause changes in photographic plates. When an X-ray hits such a plate, the plate goes black. X-rays pass through the soft parts of the body but not through bone. Where the parts of the body are soft, the X-ray will look black or grey. Where there is bone, the X-ray will look white (Fig. 70.5).

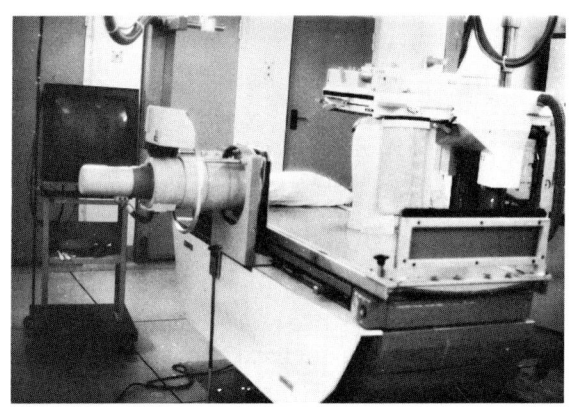

Fig. 70.4 An X-ray machine.

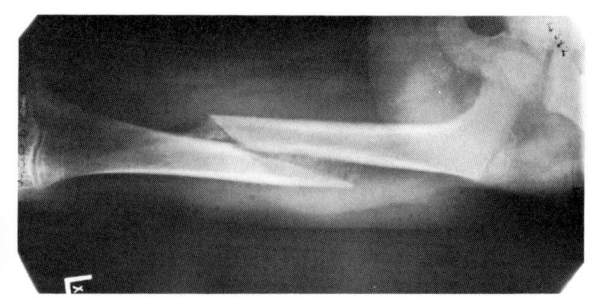

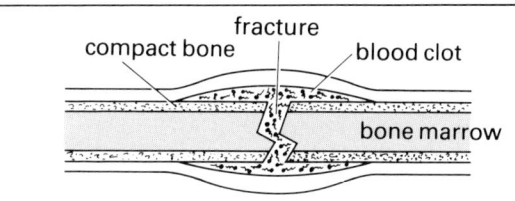

Fig. 70.5 This X-ray shows a simple fracture of the thigh bone or femur.

Mending broken bones

Broken bones heal themselves (Fig. 70.6). If broken bones are to mend, the ends of the bones must be put into place. This is **setting** the bones. The parts must be kept still. Today this is done by putting the limb in **plaster** (Fig. 70.7).

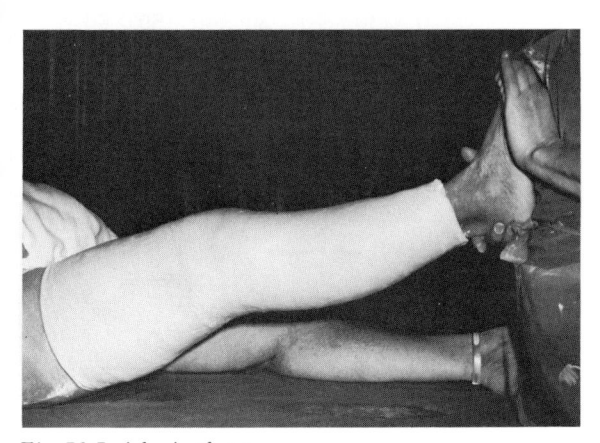

1 A blood clot forms between the broken ends of the bone.

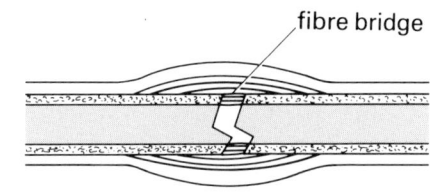

2 Fibres are laid down in the clot.

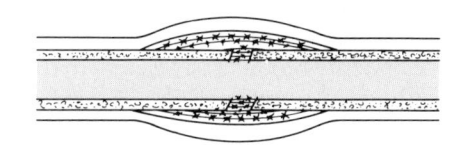

3 Bone cells pass amongst the fibres.

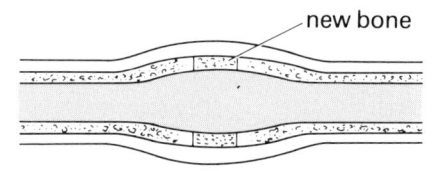

4 The new bone gets stronger. In children, the broken bone will get back its smooth shape in about one year. In adults, a tiny bump will remain at the break.

Fig. 70.7 A leg in plaster.

Fig. 70.6 Bones repair themselves.

11 Support and movement

71 Exercise and fitness

Moving the body keeps it healthy

Exercise brings many parts of the body into action. Regular exercise is good for you as parts of the body that are not used tend to waste away. A broken arm or leg is held in a plaster cast to stop it moving. When the cast is taken off, the muscles will not be as bulky as those of the unbroken limb. They will also be weaker.

In space, very little effort is needed to support and move the body (Fig. 71.1). This can have unusual effects as was discovered in a study of astronauts in the 1960s. During a 14-day space flight they lost up to 15 per cent of their **bone mass**. By the time Skylab was launched in 1973, the astronauts had a special bicycle on which to exercise. On lengthy flights astronauts spend up to 1½ hours a day on the bicycle. This stops them losing bone mass and keeps their muscles in good condition.

Exercise and energy

When you exercise, the muscle cells need energy to work. Energy is released when the cells break down glucose. To do this oxygen is needed by the cells. As you exercise you breathe faster and more deeply (Fig. 71.2). To get oxygen and glucose to the cells, the tiny blood vessels going to the heart and body muscles widen and the heart beats

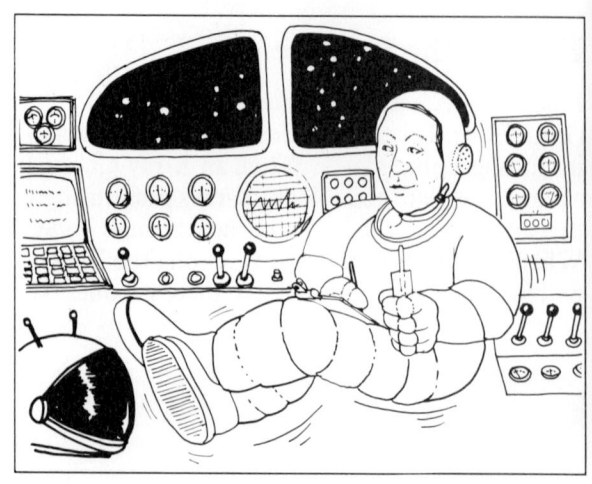

Fig. 71.1 In space astronauts' muscles do not get much exercise.

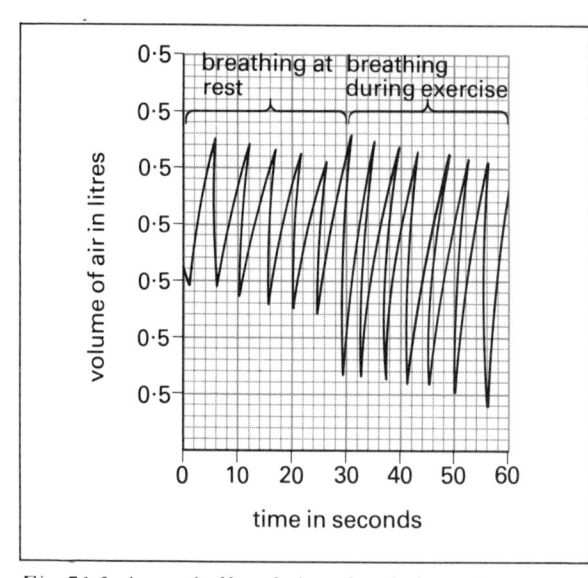

Fig. 71.2 A record of breaths in and out before and during exercise.

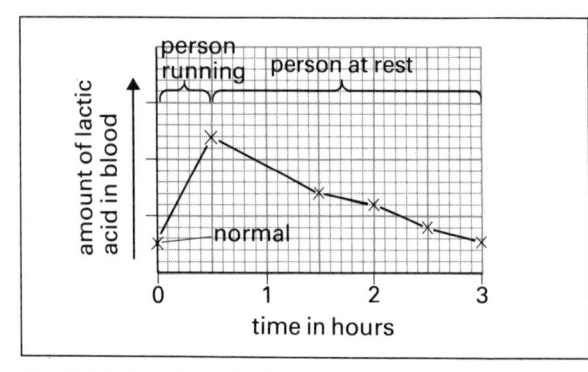

Fig. 71.4 The change in the amount of lactic acid in the blood during exercise.

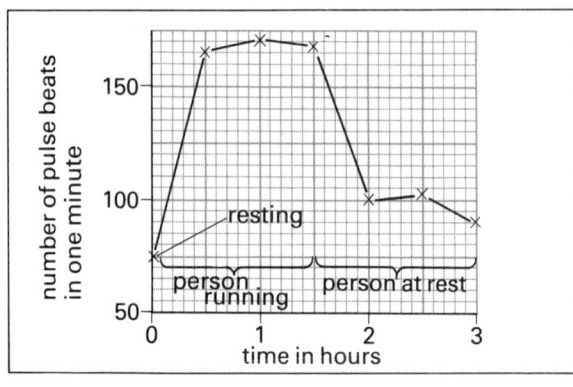

Fig. 71.3 The change in pulse beats during exercise.

11 Support and movement

faster (Fig. 71.3). If the heart does not work fast enough, the cells do not get enough oxygen for respiration. The food will not be 'burned' properly and a substance called **lactic acid** is made (Fig. 71.4). If lactic acid builds up, the muscles stop working properly. This is why a runner who is not fit may have to stagger across the finishing line. After exercise, the lactic acid is broken down as oxygen reaches the cells again.

Fitness

The average heart beats about 72 times each minute. Some fit athletes have hearts that pump as slowly as 40 times a minute. Athletes **train** and this makes the heart work harder (Fig. 71.5). The heart gets bigger so it pumps more blood at each stroke and rests longer between beats. When the athlete is at rest, the trained heart beats more slowly than normal – but it is still working properly. A slow heart rate is one sign of **fitness**.

Fig. 71.5 Exercise helps keep the body fit. There are many types of training. A few examples are jogging, cycling, swimming, walking, doing physical jerks and working in a gym.

Lack of exercise

The tiny blood vessels in the body may close if blood is not pushed through them by exercise. If a large vessel gets clogged by fat the blood can pass the blockage by going through smaller vessels. If these are closed, the detour cannot take place. This can lead to heart attacks.

If you are not used to exercise working up a sweat can be dangerous. As a person gets hotter, the blood vessels in the skin surface get wider and carry more blood. Your muscles do not get enough blood for them to work. The heart may be strained. Running or cycling until you can go no further can be **fatal** for a person who is normally not very active. Cold showers do not keep people fit. They may be refreshing, but if the body is put in very cold water, the blood vessels narrow. This can happen to the blood vessels of the heart and it may stop working properly.

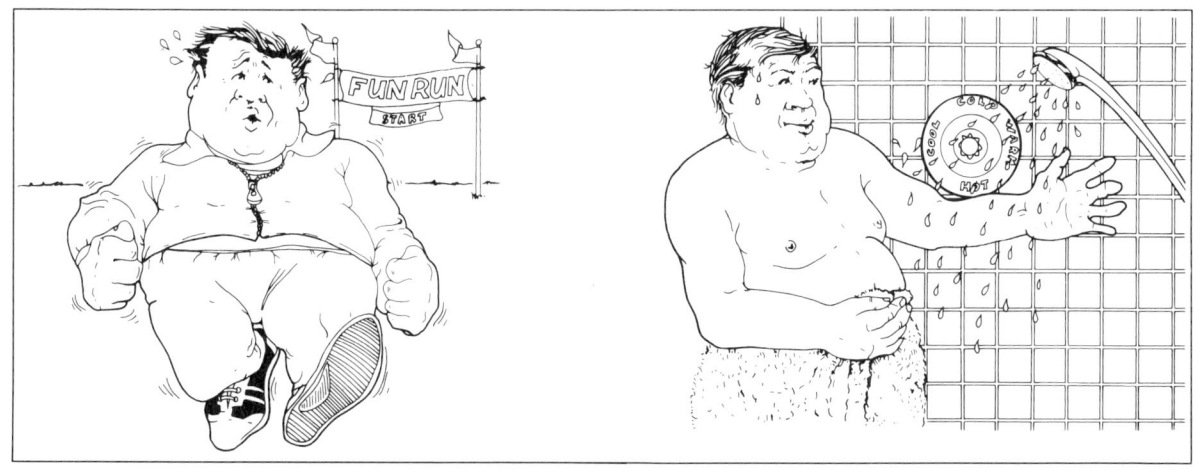

Fig. 71.6 Working up a sweat can be dangerous for someone who is not fit.

Fig. 71.7 Cold showers do not keep people fit.

11 Support and movement

72 Lifting and posture

Lifting a weight

You do not have to be an athlete to be fit. Common activities like lifting or carrying heavy objects, making beds, twisting and stretching, all help keep you fit. They strengthen muscles and stop joints becoming stiff. If parts are not moved or used properly, they may be damaged. Up to 50 000 people in Britain are off work each day suffering from **backache**. Some of this damage may be due to lifting and bending in the wrong way (Fig. 72.1). For instance, if you lift heavy objects wrongly, you may suffer from a slipped disc. One of the discs of cartilage between the bones of the back has burst, not slipped. It is worth learning how to pick up an object without straining the spine.

Lifting is work

The amount of work done by the body during exercise can be measured. Work is measured in units called joules. If the exercise is lifting a sand bag on to a table, the work done to lift it can be calculated:

work (joules) = force (newtons) × distance (metres)

In Fig. 72.2 the sand bag needs a force of ten newtons to lift it, and the table is one metre high. The work done is:

10 N × 1 m = 10 joules

Posture

In many body positions, the skeletal muscles are not fully relaxed or contracted. They are in **tone**. For example, standing upright uses several pairs of muscles in the legs and back. Both muscles of each pair will be contracting slightly at the same time to keep you standing. If you do not hold the body properly when standing or sitting, your **posture** is wrong. Sitting or standing with your back bent over is **slouching** (Fig. 72.3). If you

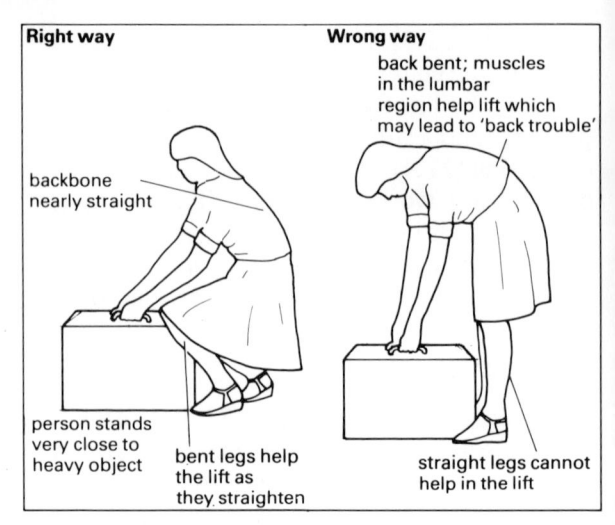

Fig. 72.1 The right and wrong way to lift a heavy object.

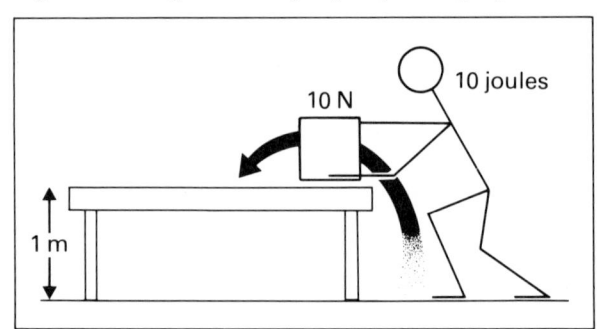

Fig. 72.2 Lifting an object is work.

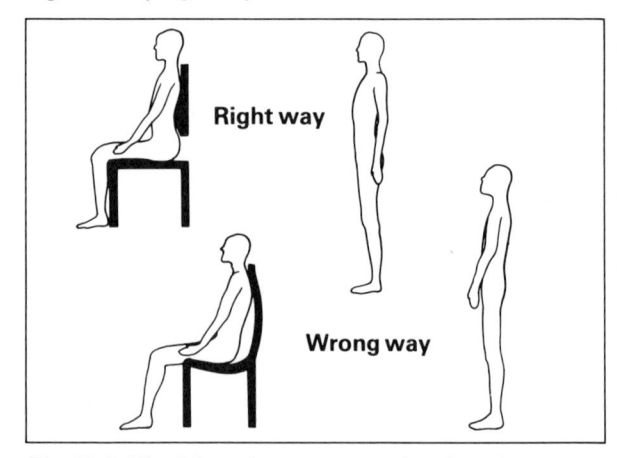

Fig. 72.3 The right and wrong ways to sit and stand.

slouch, your chest organs and gut may be cramped and not work at their best. Pregnant women sometimes get backache in the later stages of pregnancy. This is because the developing baby pulls the body forwards and strains the back muscles.

11 Support and movement

73 Sleep

The amount of sleep we need

On average a man aged 60 will have spent 20 years of his life asleep. Yet until recently nobody really understood why we need sleep. People who are stopped from sleeping become quick-tempered and after two days they cannot concentrate on even the simplest tasks. It is important to get the right amount of sleep. The amount needed varies with age (Fig. 73.1).

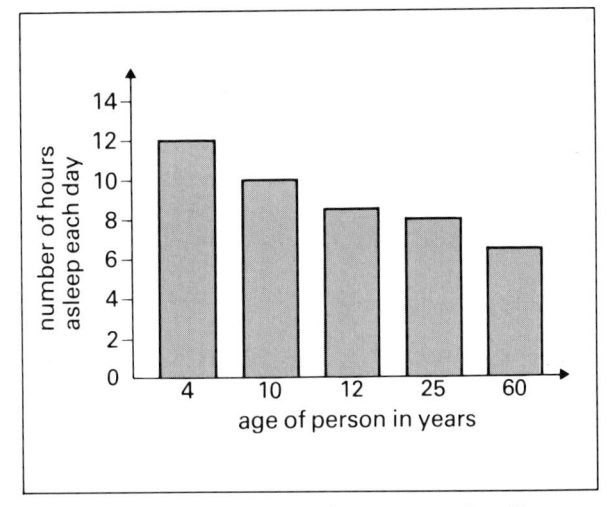

Fig. 73.1 A histogram showing the average number of hours that people sleep.

Resting and repairing the body

In sleep, the body's activities slow down and the muscles relax to give the body a rest. During sleep some of the body's energy can be used in other ways. Worn out or damaged cells can be replaced by new ones. This is important for old or ill people. There is more growth hormone in the blood when you are asleep. So cells grow more quickly. Carrying your body around during the day compresses the back and leg bones and the discs between your vertebrae. You are slightly shorter in the evening than you are in the morning! Sleep allows bones and discs to return to their correct size. This is important for young children whose bones are quite soft and still growing.

Even though your body is at rest, it still moves. A sleeper changes position between 20 and 40 times each night. And the brain is definitely active at night. The **electroencephalogram** machine (or **EEG**) can record the activity of the brain when a person is awake or asleep (Figs. 73.2 and 73.3). In sleep the eyes are still most of the time. A person wakened during this time will say he has been 'thinking'. About five times a night there are **rapid eye movements** or **REM sleep**. A person wakened during this time will say he has been **dreaming**. Scientists think that dreams are needed for health. In dreams the brain may sort out the day's events and slot them into the right places in our memory.

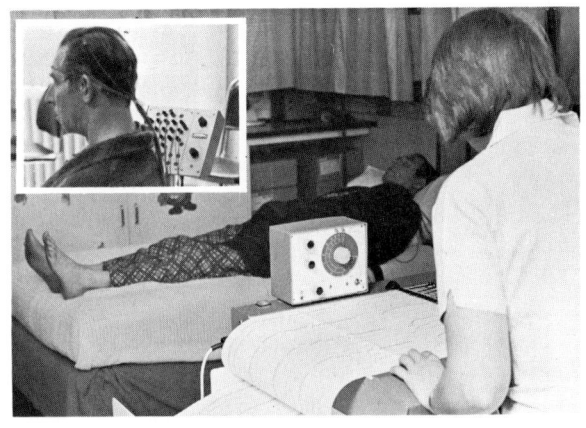

Fig. 73.2 Recording brain waves using an electroencephalogram (EEG).

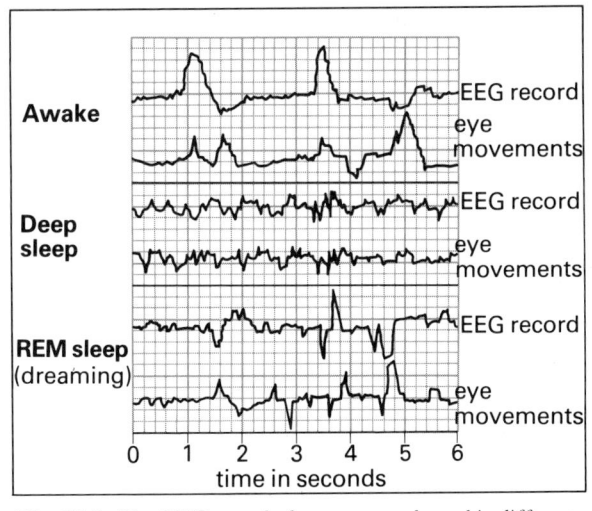

Fig. 73.3 The EEG record of a person awake and in different stages of sleep.

11 Support and movement

74 Growing up and growing old

Rates of growing

At birth your head, compared to the rest of your body, is much larger than when you are adult. As you grow, parts of your body grow at different speeds (Fig. 74.1). While in your mother's womb you grow very quickly. Another time of fast growth is when you are a teenager – that is during puberty (Fig. 74.2 and see page 92). Different individuals also vary in how quickly they grow. One boy may be full grown by the age of sixteen and another may not be fully grown until he is twenty.

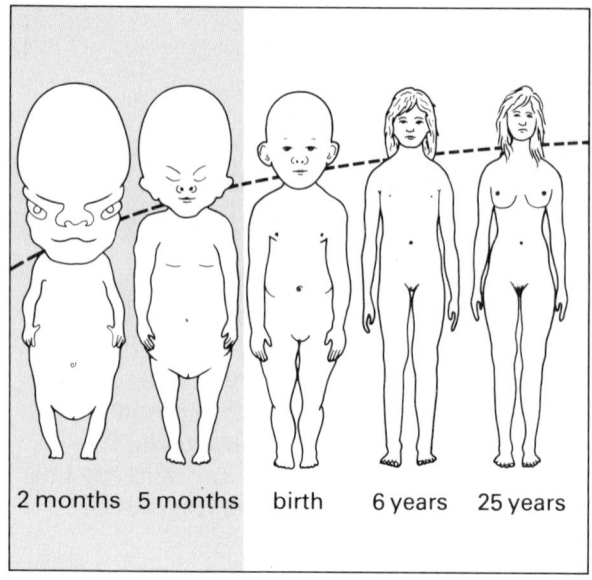

2 months   5 months   birth   6 years   25 years

Fig. 74.1 *Different parts of the body grow at different speeds. Before birth the head grows most quickly. After birth the legs grow quickly and the shoulders widen.*

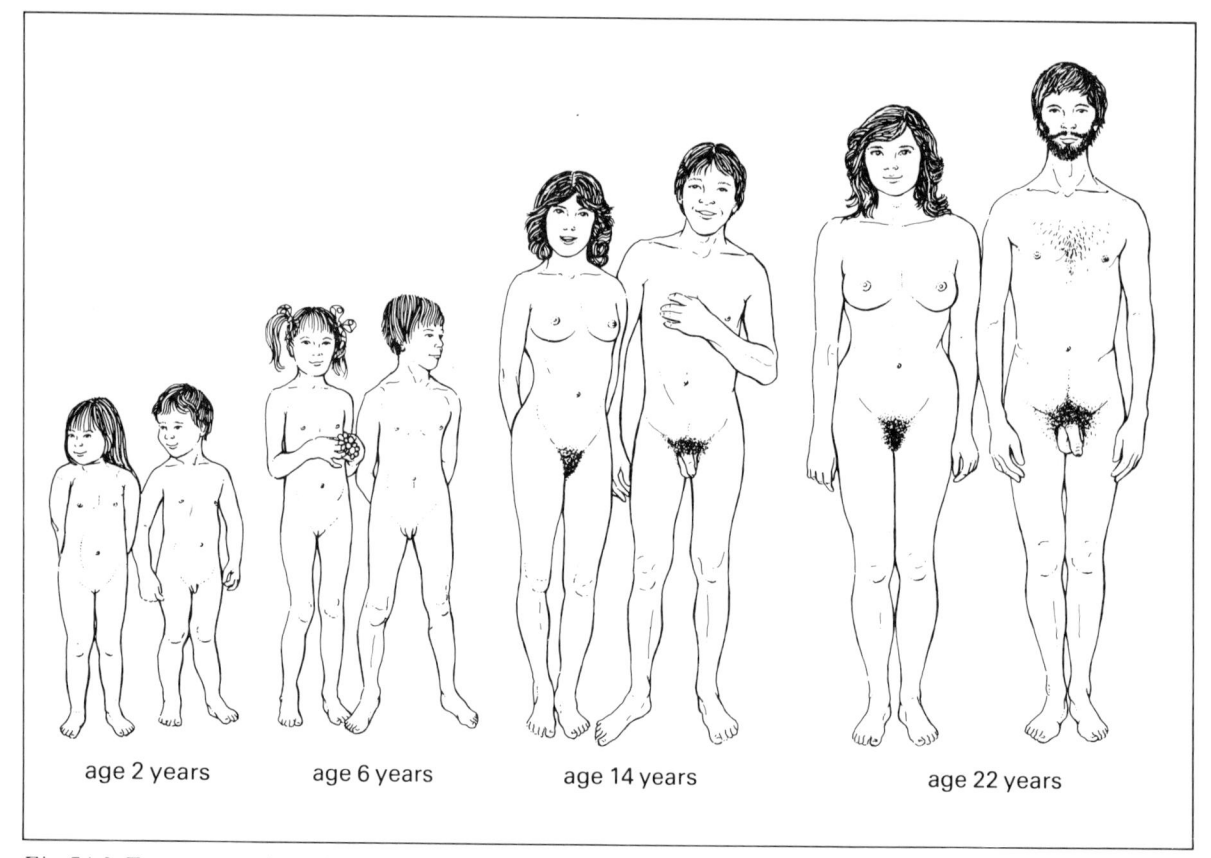

age 2 years   age 6 years   age 14 years   age 22 years

Fig. 74.2 *Twenty years of growth for boys and girls.*

11 Support and movement

Growing older

Growing older can be called **ageing**. It is difficult to say when ageing begins. For instance, a cut heals more quickly in a baby than in a child of three years old. Ageing speeds up when a person is fully grown at about 20 years of age.

Many body cells only live a certain length of time (Fig. 74.3). They then die and must be replaced by new cells. As a person ages this renewal becomes slower and the body works less well. Some cells cannot be replaced, such as nerve cells. So an old person may not see and hear as well, movements may be slower and less precise, and the memory may be less accurate. Old people may not be able to make enough heat to keep the body temperature at 37 °C. So old people in cold rooms may die from **hypothermia** (see page 63). Ageing is more rapid and obvious in some people than others.

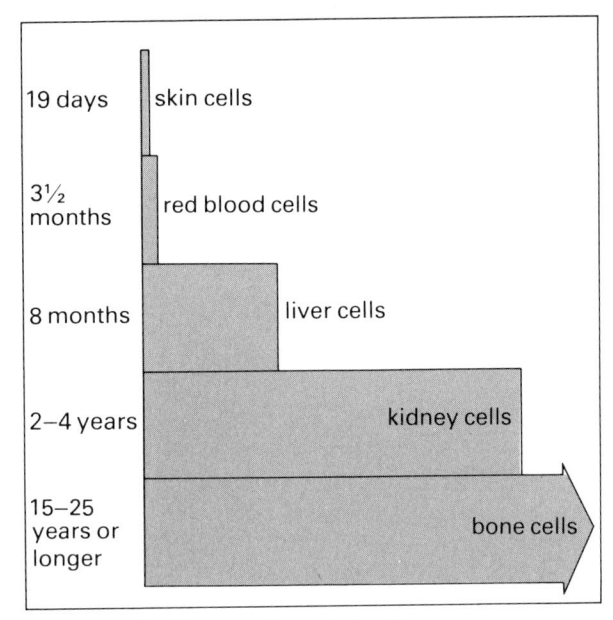

Fig. 74.3 The life span of some body cells.

Cell type	Life span
skin cells	19 days
red blood cells	3½ months
liver cells	8 months
kidney cells	2–4 years
bone cells	15–25 years or longer

Fig. 74.4 Growing older.

Summary: Support and movement

* The body is supported by bone, cartilage and fibres.
* The bone of the skeleton contains calcium phosphate.
* The skeleton has 5 functions. These are support, movement, protecting delicate organs, making blood cells and transmitting sound in the ear.
* The skeleton is made of cartilage at first. Its cells trap calcium phosphate and gradually it changes to bone.
* Bones of children are soft; in old people they are brittle.
* Different parts of the skeleton grow at different rates.
* Bone can be compact or spongy.
* Bones are moved by muscles. Tendons attach muscles to bone. Bones are held together by ligaments.
* Joints are formed where bones meet. There are 5 kinds of joint. A moving joint is cushioned by synovial fluid.
* There are 3 kinds of muscle; smooth or involuntary muscle, cardiac muscle and skeletal (striped) or voluntary muscle.
* At hinge joints, muscles work in antagonistic pairs.
* Parts of the body work like levers.
* If bones break they can repair themselves if set.
* Muscles need oxygen to work. If there is a shortage of oxygen, the cells make lactic acid when they release energy.
* Exercise keeps the body working properly. Rest is needed for health.
* The amount of work done by the body can be measured.

12 Disease and its causes

75 Disease

Parasites

There are many living things that either feed on us or make their homes in or on us. An **organism** (living thing) that lives on or in the human body is called a **parasite**. The human is its **host**. Parasites can damage the body and cause **disease**. Parasites come in many shapes and sizes. Some are so small they can be carried in air, water or on our bodies, without being seen. Many of the parasites that live inside us have complicated lives. This makes sure that some of their offspring pass out of a host's body and get to another.

Feeling ill

When you have a cold, you do not feel well. You could be suffering from a disease. The word disease means 'not at ease'. When a person has a disease there are signs that a doctor can see or detect. These signs or **symptoms** include things like a high temperature, a skin rash or the wrong chemicals in the urine.

Types of diseases

It is hard to explain what a disease is as there are so many different kinds (Fig. 75.1). Some diseases are caused by **microbes**. Such microbes are **pathogens**. These can be passed on or **transmitted** from one person to another (Fig. 75.2). There are other diseases which cannot be passed on from one person to another – these are diseases linked with diet or growing old. Some diseases may be inherited.

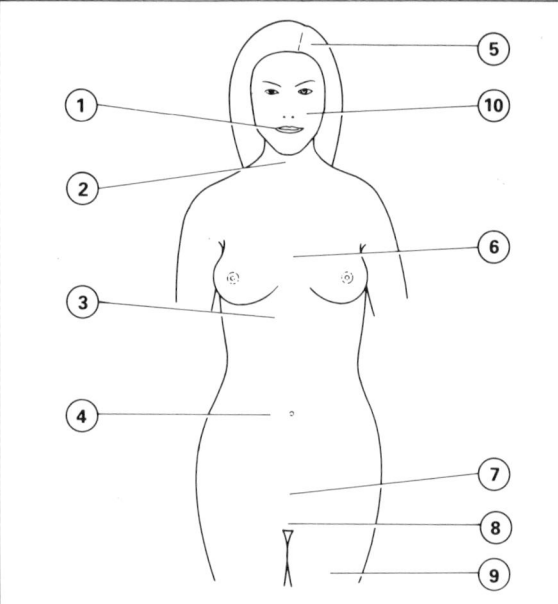

1 Infectious diseases (German measles, impetigo, pp. 141, 143).
2 Hormones out of balance (diabetes, p. 91).
3 Tumours (lung cancer, p. 185).
4 Diseases linked with food and diet (scurvy, p. 13, food poisoning, p. 166).
5 Mental illness (schizophrenia, p. 203).
6 Diseases of the blood system (thrombosis, p. 54).
7 Inherited diseases (colour blindness, haemophilia, p. 115).
8 Sexually transmitted infectious diseases (syphilis, p. 149).
9 Diseases of old age (arthritis, p. 123).
10 Diseases linked with the surroundings (asbestosis, p. 187).

Fig. 75.1 The main types of diseases.

12 Disease and its causes

Ways of passing on disease

A person who has a disease is **infected** by one type of parasite. An infectious disease can be transmitted when the parasites move from one person to another through the air or in our drinking water. **Contagious** diseases are passed from one person to another when people make contact or touch (Fig. 75.2). In the world as a whole, about 60 million people die each year. About 15 million of these deaths are caused by infections.

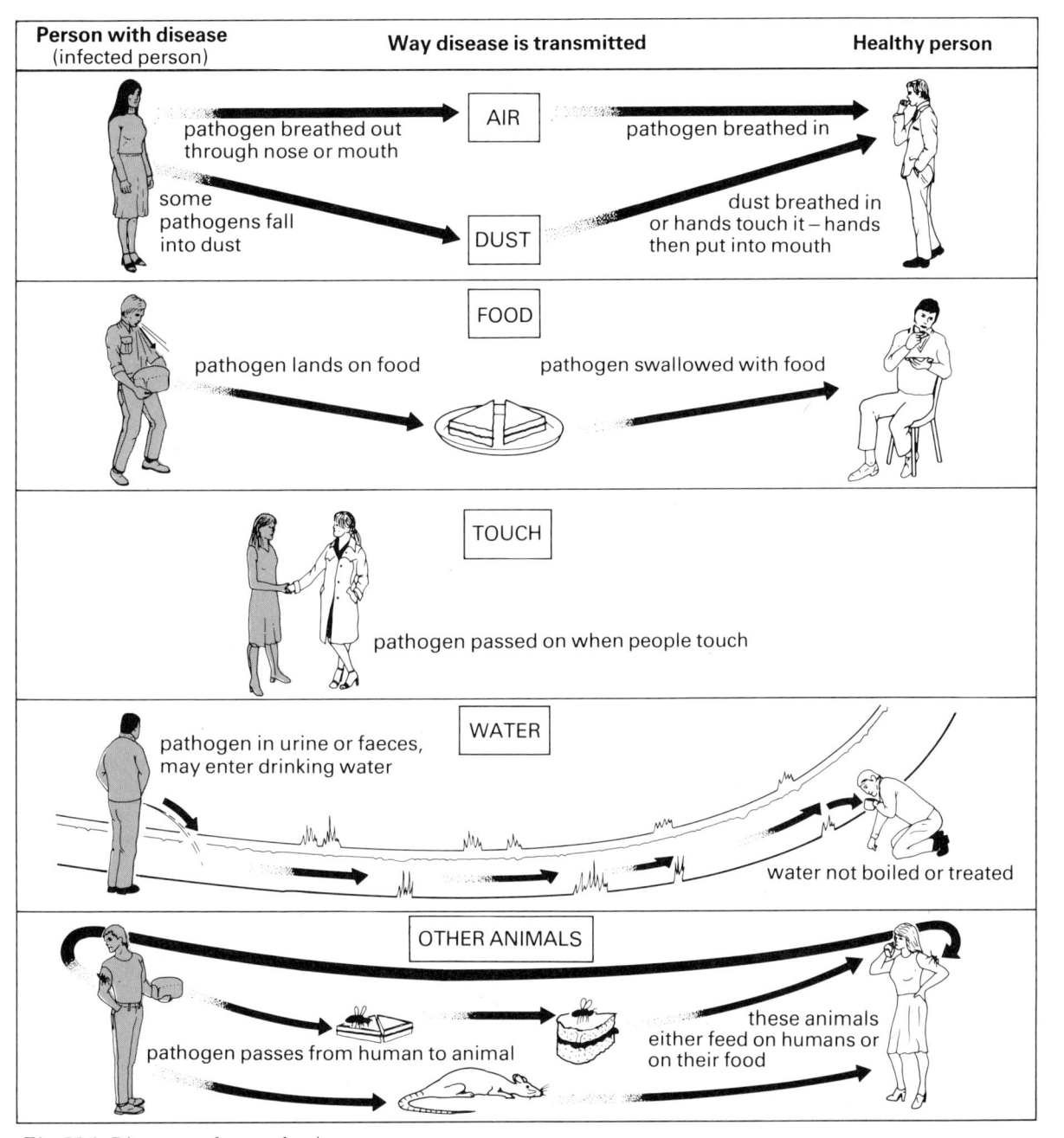

Person with disease (infected person)	Way disease is transmitted	Healthy person
	AIR — pathogen breathed out through nose or mouth / pathogen breathed in	
	DUST — some pathogens fall into dust / dust breathed in or hands touch it – hands then put into mouth	
	FOOD — pathogen lands on food / pathogen swallowed with food	
	TOUCH — pathogen passed on when people touch	
	WATER — pathogen in urine or faeces, may enter drinking water / water not boiled or treated	
	OTHER ANIMALS — pathogen passes from human to animal / these animals either feed on humans or on their food	

Fig. 75.2 Diseases can be passed on in many ways.

12 Disease and its causes

76 The cause of disease

Up to 100 years ago, scientists were always trying to find out the cause of disease with little success. In those days no one knew about the real causes of diseases like measles, flu or cholera. The connection between disease and microscopic organisms (microbes) was worked out by scientists like **Spallanzani** and **Louis Pasteur** in the nineteenth century (Fig. 76.1). Pasteur heard about the problems of some silk farmers. Many of their silk moths were suffering from a disease and were not producing much silk. Pasteur began studying the silk moths to try and find out what caused the disease (Fig. 76.2). He then did an experiment to test his idea (Fig. 76.3).

Fig. 76.1 Louis Pasteur (1822–1895).

Pasteur studied healthy and diseased silk moths

1 Pasteur found a healthy silk moth. He killed it and crushed up the body.

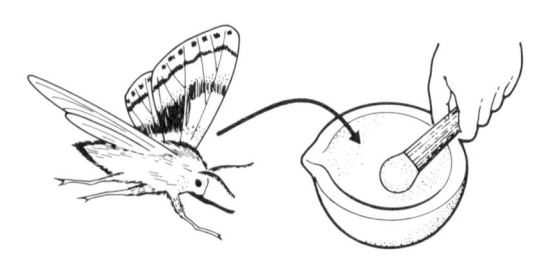

2 He looked at it under a microscope. He saw only the cells of the moth's body.

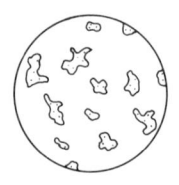

3 He found a diseased silk moth. He killed it and crushed up the body.

4 He looked at it under a microscope. He saw tiny particles mixed up with the cells of the moth. He decided these particles must be causing the disease. To prove this he carried out an experiment.

Fig. 76.2 Pasteur looked at cells from healthy and diseased silk moths.

12 Disease and its causes

Pasteur's experiment

1 Pasteur crushed up the body of a diseased moth.

2 He collected some of the liquid that came from the crushed up body.

3 He put the liquid from the body of the diseased moth into the body of a healthy moth. This moth became diseased. He did the experiment many times. Every time, the healthy moth became ill.

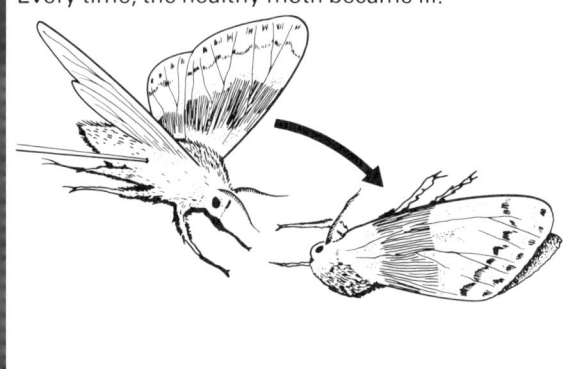

4 He crushed up the bodies of the ill moths and looked at the cells under the microscope. Every time he saw the tiny particles. These were **bacteria** and they caused the disease.

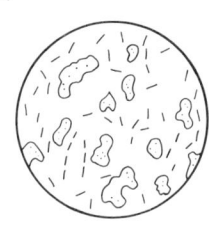

Fig. 76.3 Pasteur carried out an experiment. This was a test to find out if his idea was correct.

Robert Koch's rules

Robert Koch was the first person to give some rules to guide anyone working on the cause of disease. His most important work was done just after Pasteur had discovered that microbes were the cause of silkworm disease. Koch worked out how to remove microbes from a diseased animal and grow them in a dish of jelly-like material (**agar**). This is called **culturing** the microbe (Fig. 76.4). Koch's rules are given below.

1 The same microbe must be found in every case of the disease that is studied.
2 When the microbes are removed from the diseased animal, it must be possible to grow them in *pure* culture. A pure culture contains one type of microbe only.
3 If microbes from the pure culture are given to a healthy animal, this animal must develop the disease.
4 When microbes from the newly-infected animal are removed and grown in a pure culture, they must be the same type of microbe as found in other animals with the disease.

These rules also work for plant diseases. Today it is known that there are four main groups of microbes that cause disease – **viruses**, **bacteria**, **protozoa** and **fungi**. But there are other living things that can damage the body.

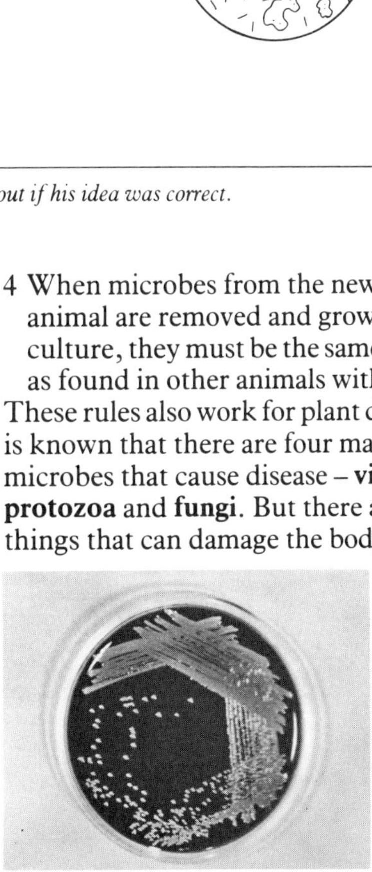

Fig. 76.4 A culture of microbes on a dish of agar jelly.

12 Disease and its causes

77 Viruses

Viruses are so small they can only be seen with the help of an electron microscope (Fig. 77.1). Viruses can only live inside living cells. Once inside the cell, a 'battle' starts between the virus and the body's defences (Fig. 77.2). Either the virus is overcome or it survives and damages the host's cells. The host will be diseased. Just as there are many different animals and plants there are many viruses. When inside the cells they cause different diseases. It may take some time between the arrival of the virus in the cells of the body and the start of the disease. This time is called the **incubation period**.

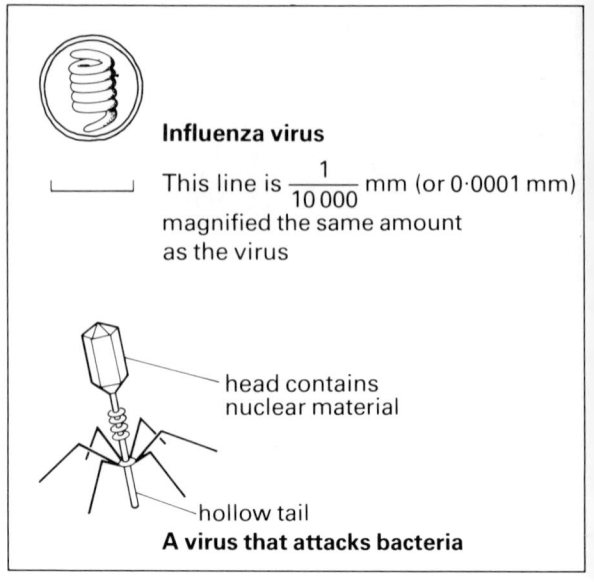

Influenza virus

This line is $\frac{1}{10\,000}$ mm (or 0·0001 mm) magnified the same amount as the virus

- head contains nuclear material
- hollow tail

A virus that attacks bacteria

Fig. 77.1 Two viruses.

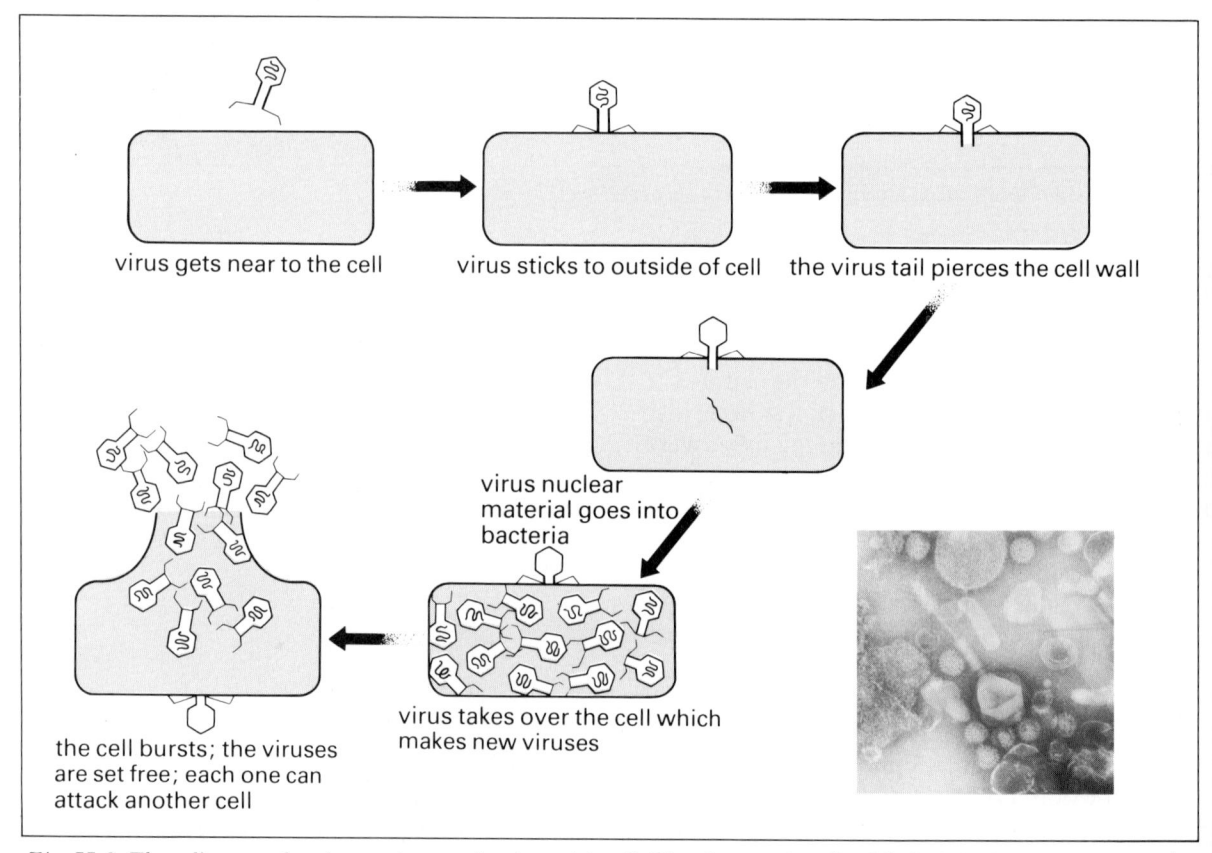

- virus gets near to the cell
- virus sticks to outside of cell
- the virus tail pierces the cell wall
- virus nuclear material goes into bacteria
- virus takes over the cell which makes new viruses
- the cell bursts; the viruses are set free; each one can attack another cell

Fig. 77.2 These diagrams show how a virus attacks a bacterial cell. They damage the cells of the body in the same way. The photo shows two types of virus ($\times 20\,000$).

12 Disease and its causes

Diseases caused by viruses

The symptoms and incubation periods of some diseases caused by viruses are given below. Viruses can enter the body in different ways (Fig. 77.3). The photos show the viruses and symptoms of two diseases (Figs. 77.4 to 77.7).

Mumps

The virus lives in the cells of the salivary glands. These swell. Incubation period = 12–20 days.

Measles

The virus lives in the cells of the skin and breathing tubes. It causes a rash, swollen glands and swollen eyes.
Incubation period = 8–13 days.

German measles or rubella

The virus lives in the blood and the skin. Fine pink spots develop on the face and neck, and may spread over the whole body.
Incubation period = 14–21 days.

Common cold

The virus lives in the cells of the breathing tubes. It causes these cells to make a lot of mucus.
Incubation period = 3 days.

Poliomyelitis

The virus lives in the cells of the gut and spinal cord. It may stop the body moving (paralysis). Incubation period = 10 days.

Chicken pox

The virus lives in the cells of the skin and blood, causing spots. Incubation period = 17 days.

Smallpox

The virus lives in the cells of the skin and blood. It causes spots and these leave scars on the skin. Incubation period = 14 days (see page 206).

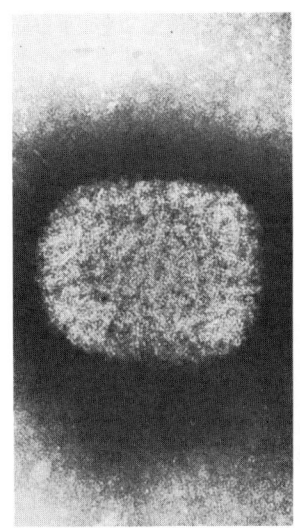

Fig. 77.4 The smallpox virus (× 300 000).

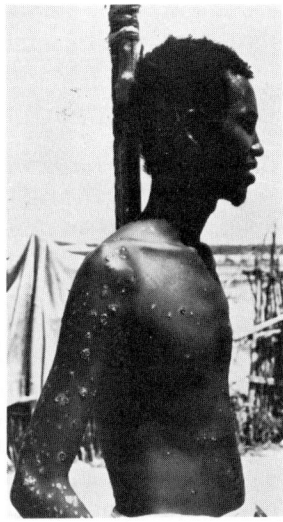

Fig. 77.5 The symptoms of smallpox. This man is the last recorded case of naturally-occurring smallpox (Somalia, 1977).

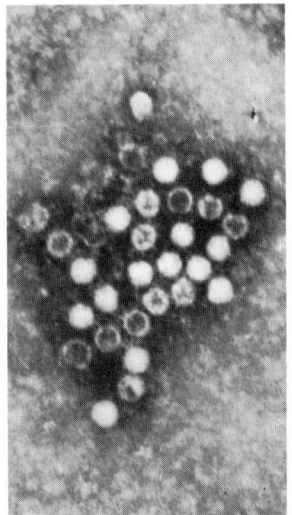

Fig. 77.6 Polio viruses (× 20 000).

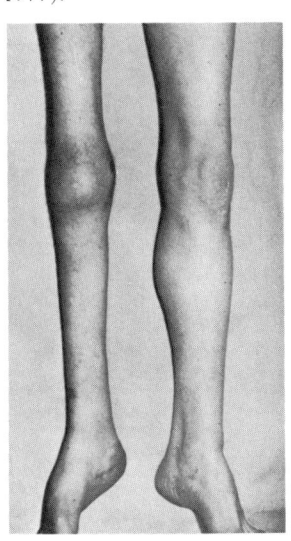

Fig. 77.7 The symptoms of polio.

Disease	How the virus enters the body
mumps measles German measles common cold chicken pox	the virus is breathed in with air
poliomyelitis	the virus is breathed in or is in the food or water that someone eats or drinks
smallpox	the virus enters through the skin

Fig. 77.3 Viruses can enter the body in different ways.

12 Disease and its causes

78 Bacteria

Different shaped bacteria

Bacteria are very small cells. They have many different shapes. Some have a spiral shape, some are round, some are rod-shaped and some have threads to help them move (Fig. 78.1 and 78.2).

Bacteria reproduce quickly

Bacteria reproduce by dividing into two (Fig. 78.3). In the right conditions some can divide every 20 minutes. So in one day a single bacterium could make 1000 million, million, million offspring! There are more bacteria on your body than there are people on the earth yet they could all be packed into a soup tin! Bacteria live most easily in warm, damp places like the armpits and between the toes. Most of the bacteria are harmless. Harmful bacteria cause disease either by destroying our cells or making poisons called **toxins**.

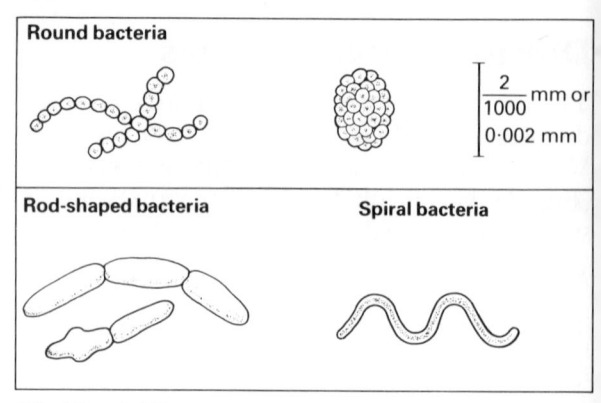

Fig. 78.1 Different types of bacteria.

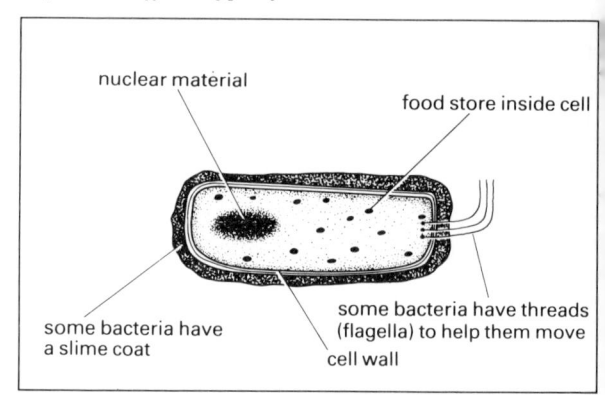

Fig. 78.2 The parts of one bacterium.

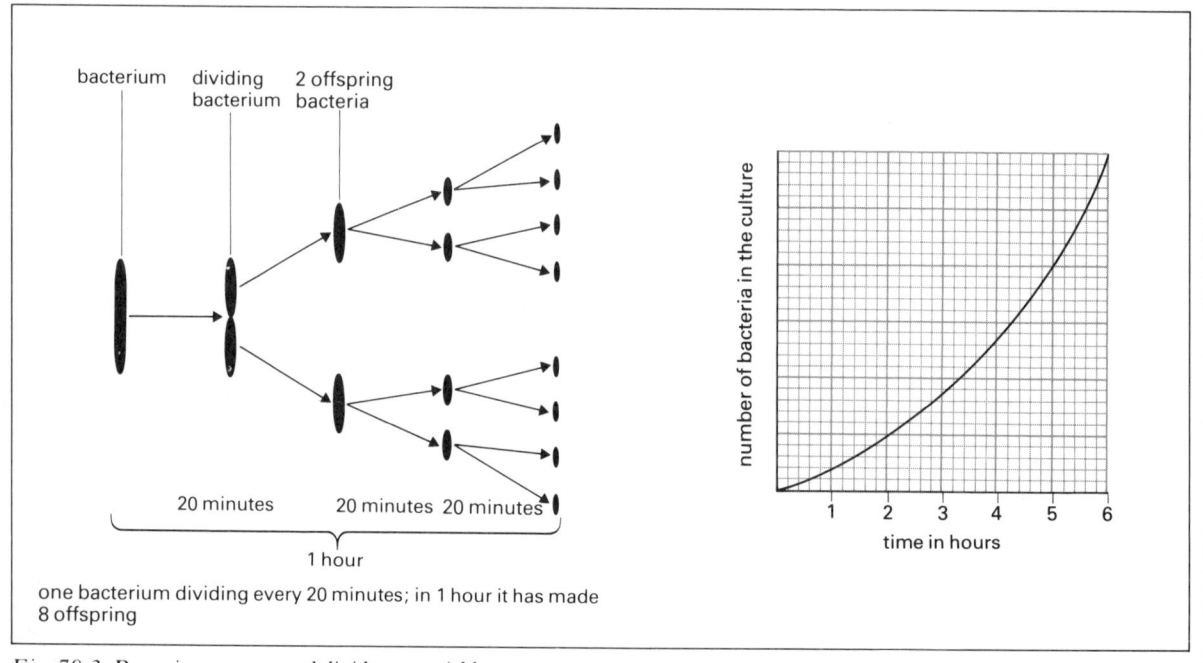

Fig. 78.3 Bacteria can grow and divide very quickly.

12 Disease and its causes

Diseases caused by bacteria

Some of the symptoms and incubation periods of a few diseases caused by bacteria are given below. The photos show the bacteria and symptoms of two of the diseases (Figs. 78.4 to 78.7).

Impetigo
The bacteria live on the cells of the skin. These cause red patches on the skin.
Incubation period = 1–4 days.

Cholera
The bacteria live in the blood. The symptoms are diarrhoea, sickness, cramp, thirst and exhaustion. Incubation period = 1–5 days.

Typhoid
The bacteria feed on the gut. They cause a high fever and constipation or diarrhoea.
Incubation period = 14 days.

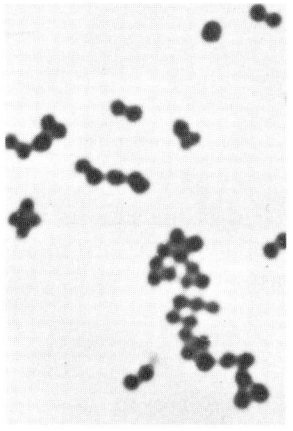

Fig. 78.4 The bacteria that cause impetigo ($\times 2000$).

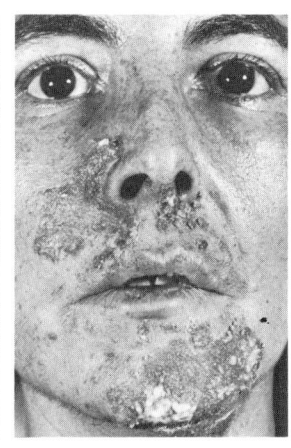

Fig. 78.5 A person suffering from impetigo.

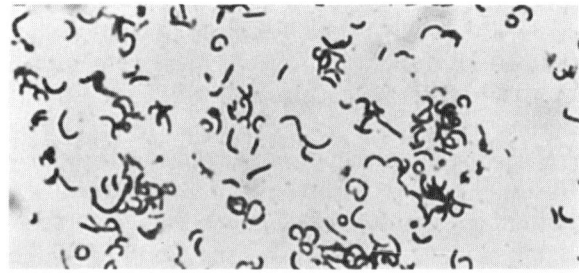

Fig. 78.6 Cholera bacteria ($\times 3000$).

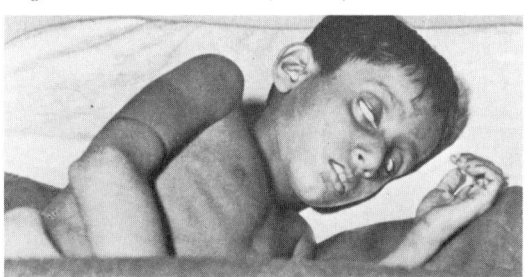

Fig. 78.7 This child is seriously ill with cholera.

Isolation

Sometimes the person who is ill must be kept away from other people or **isolated** (Fig. 78.8). This prevents the disease from spreading. If you have been near a person with a disease, the microbe may have entered your body. You may have to be isolated until the end of the incubation period.

You may be a **carrier** of the microbe. Carriers do not suffer from the disease but can pass it on to others. Possible carriers of dangerous diseases are kept in **quarantine**, away from others. This prevents the disease spreading further.

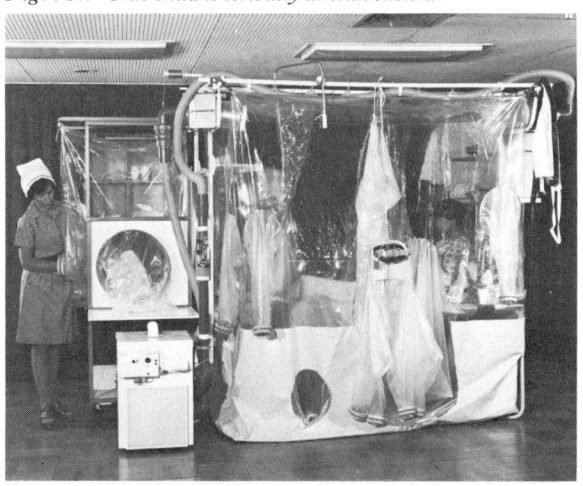

*Fig. 78.8 A patient with a highly dangerous infectious disease may be treated in an **isolator**.*

12 Disease and its causes

79 Protozoa

These are small, single-celled animals found in water or soil. Some are found living in the human body and may cause disease.

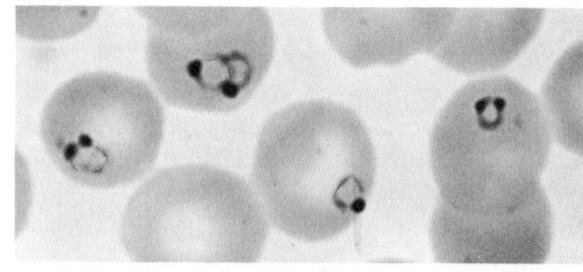

Fig., 79.1 These red blood cells are infected by Plasmodium, *the protozoan that causes malaria* ($\times 2000$).

Malaria

Plasmodium is a **protozoan** that lives in the human liver or red blood cells (Fig. 79.1). Some types of female mosquitoes feed on blood by biting through the skin and sucking up blood. A mosquito may eat blood cells that contain the parasite. If it then feeds on a healthy person the mosquito passes the microbe into the second person's body (Fig. 79.2). The parasite, *Plasmodium*, makes poisons at certain stages in its life. These toxins give the person a **fever**. A high temperature or fever at regular intervals is one symptom of the disease malaria (Fig. 79.3). Preventing the mosquitoes from breeding or feeding on humans will reduce the spread of malaria.

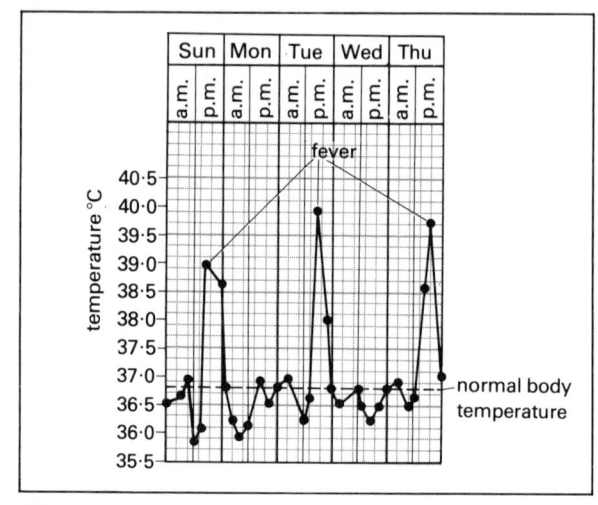

Fig. 79.3 The temperature chart of a person suffering from malaria.

Amoebic dysentery

Entamoeba is a protozoan found in water (Fig. 79.4). If water containing the animal is drunk, the animal will get into the gut. *Entamoeba* starts to feed on the bacteria that are usually there. It may also feed on the cells lining the gut, causing bleeding and diarrhoea. These are the symptoms of **amoebic dysentery**. This disease can be prevented if drinking water is treated and the parasite is killed.

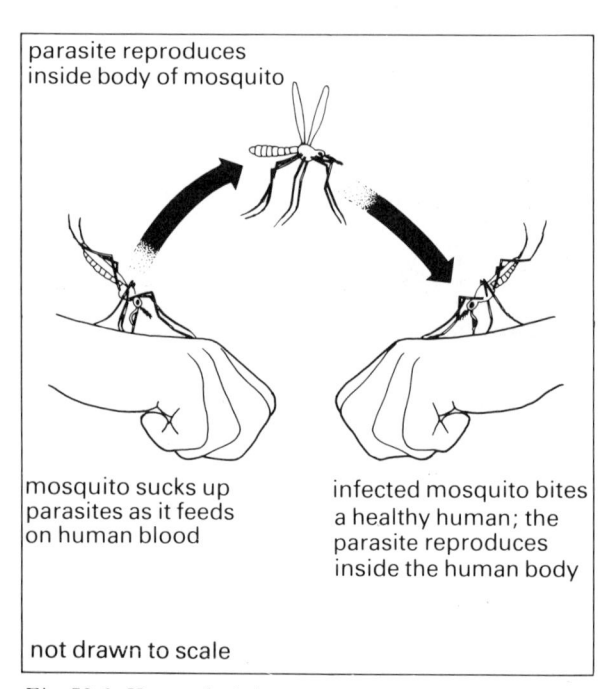

Fig. 79.2 How malaria is spread by the mosquito.

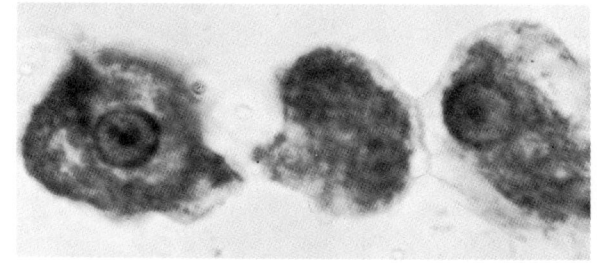

Fig. 79.4 Entamoeba *is the protozoan that causes amoebic dysentery* ($\times 2500$)

12 Disease and its causes

80 Fungi

How fungi feed

Fungi are plants that are not green (Fig. 80.1). Fungi do not contain the green pigment **chlorophyll**. This means they are not able to make their food by photosynthesis. They need a ready made supply of food. Most fungi get their food from dead and decaying remains of animals and plants. (Fig. 80.2). However, some fungi use other living things for food. These fungi are parasites. Fungi which are parasitic on man are rare. They cause skin diseases.

Fig. 80.1 Fungi in a wood.

Ringworm

Ringworm is caused by a fungus. The plant sends out feeding threads or **hyphae** into the skin and the hair around this part falls out. If this fungus is feeding on the cells in the scalp, the person has true ringworm (Fig. 80.3). If it is in the groin, then it is '**dhobie itch**' and between the toes, it is called '**athlete's foot**'.

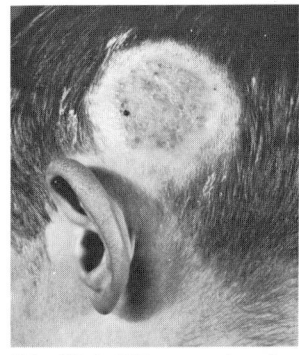

Fig. 80.3 This person has ringworm.

Thrush

Another fungus, called *Candida* may be found inside openings of the body like the mouth and vagina. If the body is weak, the fungus may grow and form white areas around the mouth. The infection is called **thrush** (Fig. 80.4).

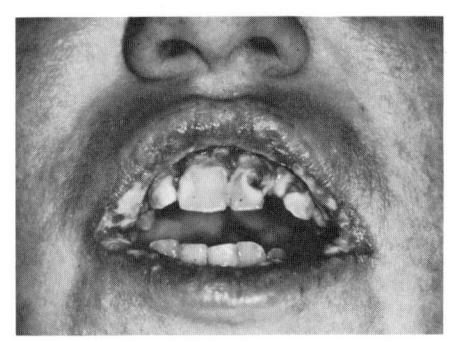

Fig. 80.4 This person is suffering from thrush around the mouth.

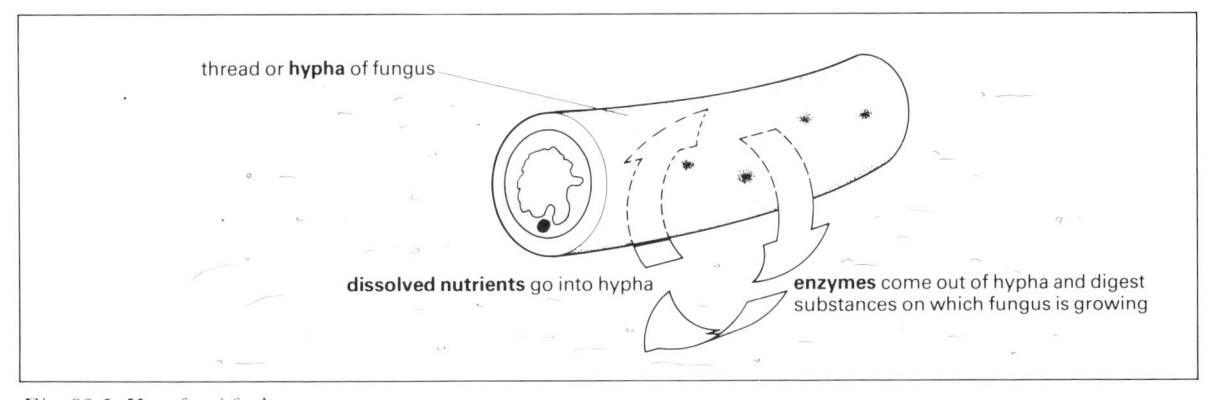

thread or **hypha** of fungus

dissolved nutrients go into hypha

enzymes come out of hypha and digest substances on which fungus is growing

Fig. 80.2 How fungi feed.

12 Disease and its causes

81 Worms

Most people are hosts at some time or another to parasitic **worms**. There are several types.

Roundworms

One type of **roundworm** that causes disease is the **hookworm**. They have cutting edges around the mouth. These burrow into the skin from the soil. When inside the body, they feed on blood and cells. A person with hookworm disease may have anaemia and be weak.

Another type of roundworm is the **pinworm** or **threadworm**. These get into and develop in the gut when the eggs are swallowed. The worms and their eggs are passed out in the faeces of humans and dogs (Fig. 81.1).

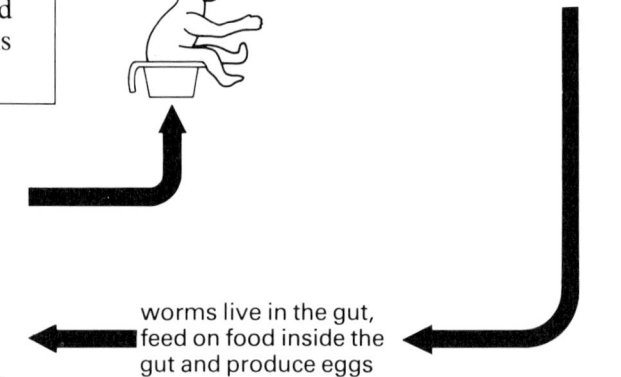

Fig. 81.1 *The life history of a roundworm (human pinworm).*

Tapeworms

Tapeworms are flat, ribbon-like animals that are able to live inside the human gut. The broad **fish tapeworm** may be over one centimetre wide and can reach over thirty metres in length. Humans get the parasite when they eat raw fish (Fig. 81.2). It is quite common in Japanese people. The parasite damages the gut.

There are other tapeworms which are passed on to humans when they eat meat containing the young stages. These are **beef** and **pork tapeworm**.

The spread of tapeworms can be controlled by inspecting raw fish and meat. Thorough cooking of fish and meat will kill the young stages.

Flatworms

One of the most devastating diseases in underdeveloped countries is **snail fever** or **bilharzia**. It affects over 250 million people. The disease is caused by a flatworm called *Schistosoma*, so the disease is also called **schistosomiasis**. The flatworms live in a person's blood. At first they cause a fever. Later, as they grow, they block important blood vessels which may damage various organs. Bilharzia exhausts the victim. It may shorten a person's life by twenty years. The flatworm lives part of its life in a human and the rest in a fresh-water snail. The disease is common in countries where agricultural land is **irrigated** by channels of water (Fig. 81.3).

146

12 Disease and its causes

How a human gets fish tapeworm

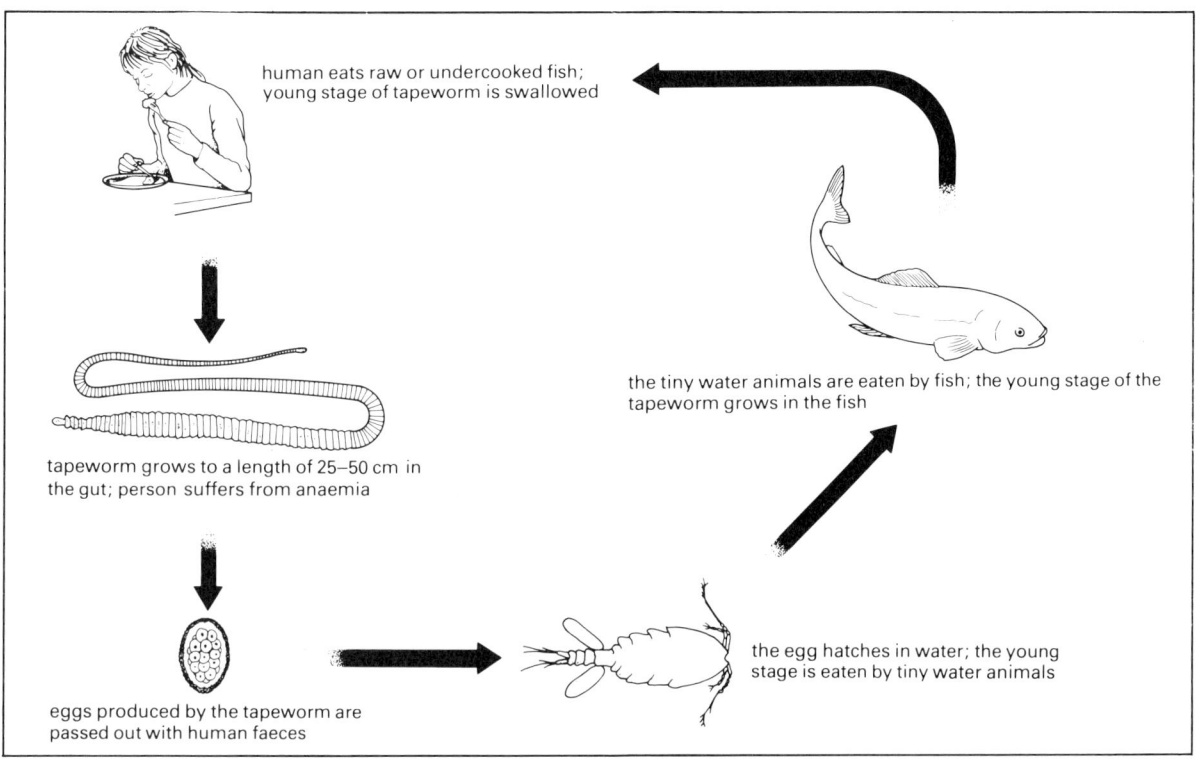

human eats raw or undercooked fish; young stage of tapeworm is swallowed

tapeworm grows to a length of 25–50 cm in the gut; person suffers from anaemia

eggs produced by the tapeworm are passed out with human faeces

the egg hatches in water; the young stage is eaten by tiny water animals

the tiny water animals are eaten by fish; the young stage of the tapeworm grows in the fish

Fig. 81.2 The life history of the fish tapeworm.

How bilharzia is spread

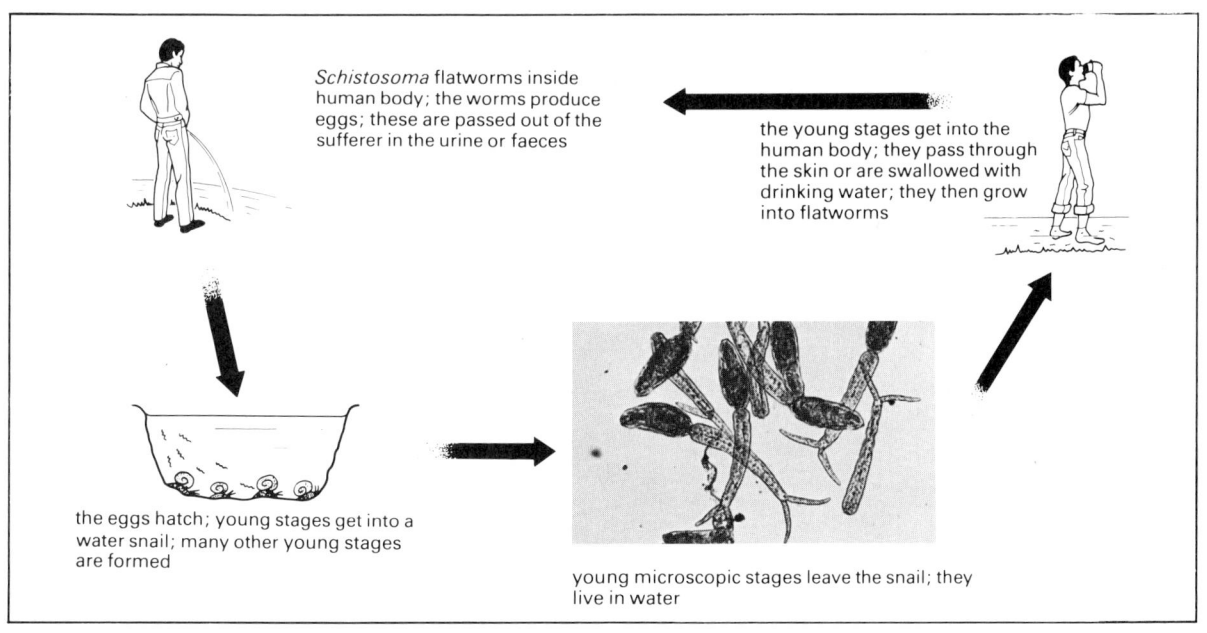

Schistosoma flatworms inside human body; the worms produce eggs; these are passed out of the sufferer in the urine or faeces

the eggs hatch; young stages get into a water snail; many other young stages are formed

young microscopic stages leave the snail; they live in water

the young stages get into the human body; they pass through the skin or are swallowed with drinking water; they then grow into flatworms

Fig. 81.3 The life history of the Schistosoma *flatworm.*

147

12 Disease and its causes

82 Sexually transmitted diseases

Diseases that can be passed from one person to another during love-making used to be called **venereal diseases** (**VD**). They were named after Venus, the goddess of love. Today they are called **sexually transmitted diseases**.

Types of disease

During love-making (sexual intercourse or petting), many microbes can be passed from one person to another. Some of these cause disease. These microbes die quickly when they are away from the warmth and moisture of the body. This means they can be caught only by close contact with the body of someone already infected. The three most well known diseases are **gonorrhoea** (sometimes called 'clap'), **AIDS** and **syphilis** (or 'pox'). There are others. As sexual contact between unmarried people is increasing so is the number of people suffering from these diseases (Fig. 82.1).

Gonorrhoea

Gonorrhoea is caused by bacteria. Within 2 to 10 days after contact with an infected person the first symptoms may show. A man may suffer pain when passing urine and have a yellow pus at the tip of the penis. A woman may not notice any change (Fig. 82.2). After some time the microbe will reproduce, spread through the body and reach the sex organs. These will be damaged. A man or a woman could become **sterile** (unable to have a child). If a woman has a child while she is infected the baby may be harmed. It could be born blind.

Year	Number of males and females in the U.K. that were new patients for treatment
1961	68 068
1966	82 979
1971	139 472
1978	169 804

Fig. 82.1 The increase in the number of people suffering from sexually transmitted diseases.

A new disease was identified in the late 1970s. This disease, Acquired Immune Deficiency Syndrome is caused by a virus. At present there is no cure. It has many symptoms, as someone with AIDS can catch infections the body normally resists. The total number of AIDS cases reported in the UK up to 30 April 1987 was 750, and the number of deaths due to AIDS was 420.

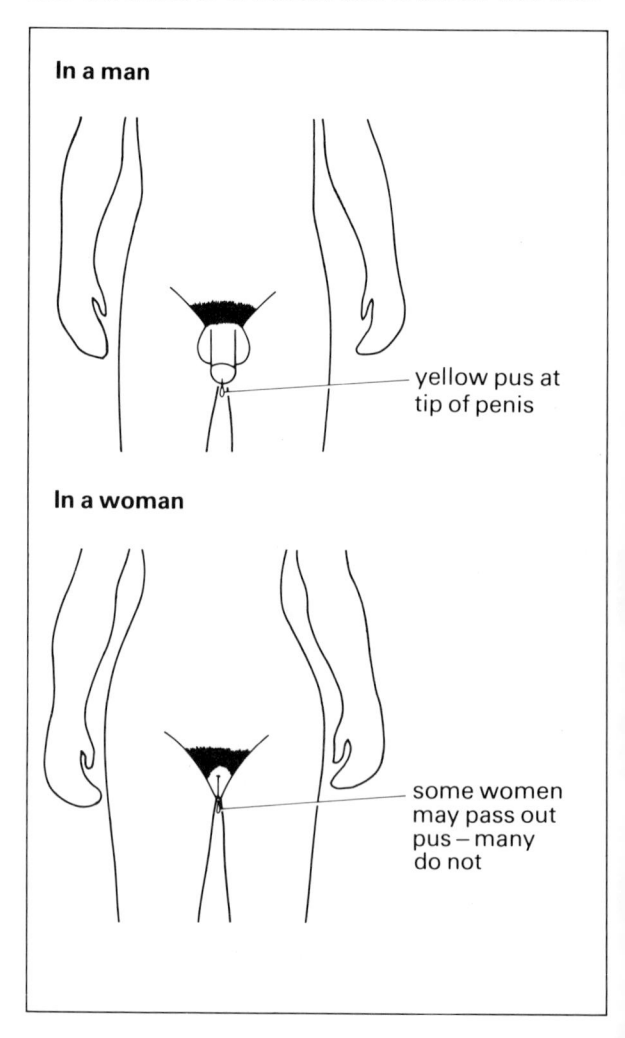

Fig. 82.2 The first symptoms of gonorrhoea.

12 Disease and its causes

Syphilis

Syphilis is caused by a bacterium called *Treponema*. The first sign of the disease is a painless sore or **chancre** (Fig. 82.3). It appears on the sex organs 3 to 6 weeks after contact with an infected person. In men the sore is on the penis; in women it may be inside the body and not be seen. The sore heals and weeks or months later, the body is covered by a rash. This is the second stage (Fig. 82.4). If untreated, then in 10 to 20 years after the contact the third stage develops (Fig. 82.5). The microbe will have seriously damaged the heart, the brain and the joints. If a woman with the disease has a baby, she can pass the disease to the child.

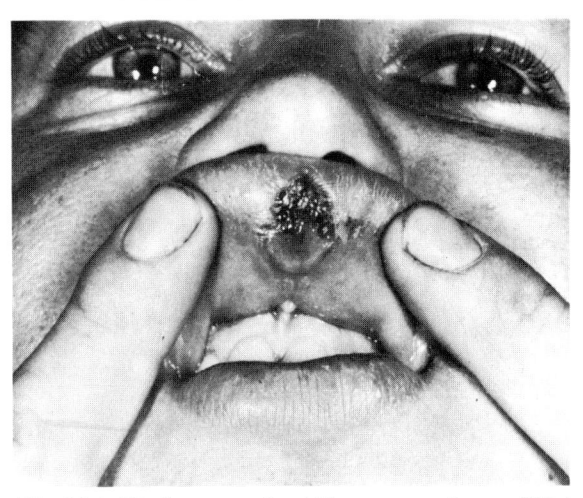

Fig. 82.3 The first stage of syphilis – a spot or chancre. This is usually on the sex organs but occasionally it may appear on the lips.

Treating sexually transmitted diseases

In 1917, a law was passed that meant treatment for sexually transmitted diseases could only be given by qualified doctors. The law forbids anyone else from offering treatment. The different diseases can be identified in laboratory tests that are carried out by **special clinics**. Many general hospitals now have special clinics. The treatment is free and no appointment is necessary. Many of the diseases can be cured by the use of **antibiotics**, but some of the microbes are becoming resistant. Larger doses are having to be used to control the diseases.

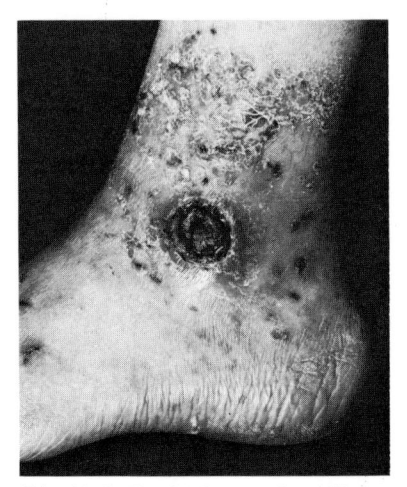

Fig. 82.5 The third stage of syphilis – an ulcer.

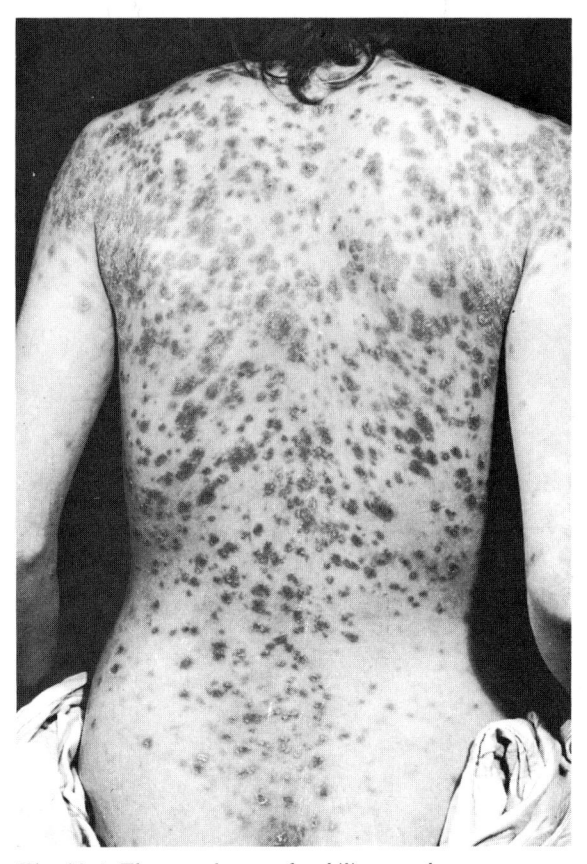

Fig. 82.4 The second stage of syphilis – a rash.

12 Disease and its causes

83 Vectors of disease

Animals which pass pathogens from one living thing to another are called **vectors**.

Insects

The mosquito is the vector of malaria. The insect passes on the parasite, *Plasmodium*, from one person to another (see page 144). There are many other insects that act as vectors of disease. For instance the **tsetse fly** spreads **sleeping sickness**. **Fleas** feed on blood (Fig. 83.1). The human flea may spread disease as it feeds on one person and then another. The rat flea and human flea both helped to spread **bubonic plague** (the Black Death) during the Middle Ages.

The **housefly** may pass on several diseases of the gut and even polio. A housefly is attracted to food and animal faeces. If a fly feeds on food, microbes from its feeding tube and body may be left on the food (Fig. 83.2). If a person eats this food, infection may follow.

Lice are small insects that may live in human hair. They lay eggs and stick these to the hair as **nits** (Fig. 83.1). Lice can spread diseases such as **typhus** and **relapsing fever**.

Mammals

Rats live in sewers, on ships, in warehouses, on tips and in some houses. **Mice** live in some houses. Like houseflies, rats and mice feed on human food and rubbish. They have microbes on their fur and may pass other microbes out with their faeces. These microbes may not harm the rats and mice, but, if they pass from them to our food and into the human body, they might cause **food poisoning** (Fig. 83.3). Rats have fleas. These caused the spread of bubonic plague (see above).

Dogs, bats and **foxes** are vectors of **rabies**. An infected dog can pass on the rabies virus when it bites a human.

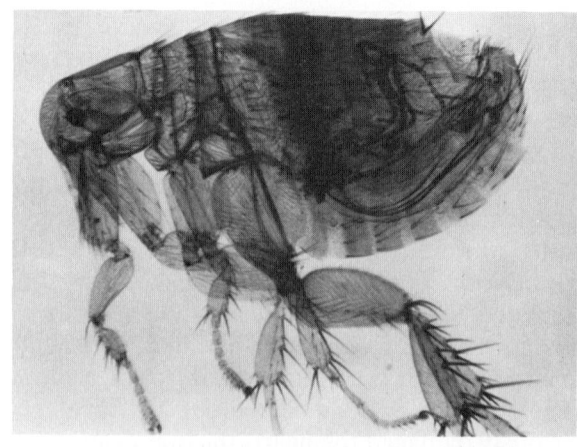

Fig. 83.1 Fleas and lice can both spread human diseases.

Fig. 83.2 A housefly using its feeding tube.

Fig. 83.3 Rats spread diseases such as food poisoning.

Fig. 83.4 Birds can be vectors of disease.

Birds

Birds can also pass on disease. Many of the **pigeons** in large cities can pass on the disease **ornithosis** to humans (Fig. 83.4).

12 Disease and its causes

Name of disease	Type of organism causing disease	Symptoms	How does it spread
AIDS	virus	many, depends on infection	direct contact with infected body fluids, e.g. as a result of sexual intercourse
amoebic dysentery	protozoan (Entamoeba)	diarrhoea, bleeding of gut	in water and in wastes passed into the toilet
bilharzia	flatworm (Schistosoma)	fever and weakness	young stage burrows into skin from water of ponds and streams
chicken pox	virus	skin becomes covered with 'pock' marks; temperature rises	in air in droplets of moisture from the nose
cholera	bacterium	sickness, diarrhoea, stomach pains, and severe thirst	in water and in wastes passed into the toilet
common cold	virus	sneezing, runny nose	in air in droplets of moisture from the nose
diphtheria (mainly in very young children)	bacterium	severe pains in the throat and high temperature; lining of throat may swell and prevent breathing	in air in droplets of moisture, produced when coughing
impetigo	bacterium	rash around the mouth; scab like sores on the skin	by contact
German measles (rubella)	virus	slight temperature, possibly a slight rash; causes serious eye damage to unborn babies during the first three months of pregnancy	in air in droplets from the nose
gonorrhoea (also called 'clap', 'pox', or 'a dose')	bacterium	in men, pain on passing water and pus in the urine; in women there may be no symptoms	by having sexual intercourse with someone who is infected; cannot be caught from lavatory seats, towels or underwear
malaria	protozoan	weakness; alternate bouts of fever and shivering	by mosquito
measles	virus	skin rash; swollen glands and eyes	in air in droplets of moisture from the nose
mumps	virus	temperature develops; neck swells and becomes painful	in air in droplets of moisture from the nose, or in spit
plague (or 'black death')	bacterium	high fever, swellings on skin	carried by fleas living on rats
polio (or 'infantile paralysis')	virus	mild fever in very young children; can cause permanent paralysis in older children or adults	in droplets from the nose and in the wastes passed out into the toilet; can then spread in water
ringworm	fungus	maybe between toes, in scalp or in groin; skin becomes painful	by touch, by sharing infested clothing or walking barefoot on wet floors
smallpox	virus	skin becomes covered with 'pock' marks; high fever	in air in droplets of moisture from nose
syphilis	bacterium	small pimple on the sex organs; later, there may be a rash	by having sexual intercourse with someone who is infected; cannot be caught from lavatory seats, towels or underwear
thrush	fungus	white patches around mouth; in women, some white patches around vagina	by touch or by sharing infected clothes
tuberculosis ('T.B.' or consumption)	bacterium	cough, with fever and blood-stained spit	in spit brought up from lungs; the bacteria are carried in the air
typhoid fever	bacterium	high temperature, diarrhoea	in water, in food, or in toilet wastes

Fig. 83.5 Diseases – a summary.

Summary: Disease and its causes

* Parasites are animals and plants that live on or in other living things.
* Some organisms are so small that they are only seen when magnified. These are microbes.
* Microbes that cause disease are pathogens.
* Diseases caused by microbes can be passed from one person to another.
* Louis Pasteur worked out the link between bacteria (one type of microbe) and disease.
* Robert Koch worked out the rules for finding out the cause of disease.
* Microbes can be organisms from the virus, bacteria, protozoa or fungi groups.
* When microbes enter the body they may cause disease.
* Each disease has different features or symptoms.
* In many diseases there is a short time between the entry of the microbe into the body and the showing of the first symptoms.
* To prevent the spread of disease, people who may be infected are kept away from others.
* Larger animals, such as roundworms, flatworms and tapeworms, also cause disease.
* A few diseases are passed on during sexual contact.
* Some animals help to spread disease. These animals are vectors.

13 Using and fighting microbes

84 Useful microbes

Many people think that all microbes, like bacteria and fungi, are harmful. This is not true. Most microbes are harmless. We make use of many kinds of microbes.

Microbes of decay

Without microbes the countryside would be piled up with dead plants and animals. In the soil, there are microbes which cause **decay** or **rotting**. The soil microbes feed on the dead plants and animals and release chemicals from them (Fig. 84.1). As the bodies are broken down, the chemicals mix with and improve the soil. This also improves the texture of the soil. Rotting plants (or **compost**) help to make soil fertile (see page 21).

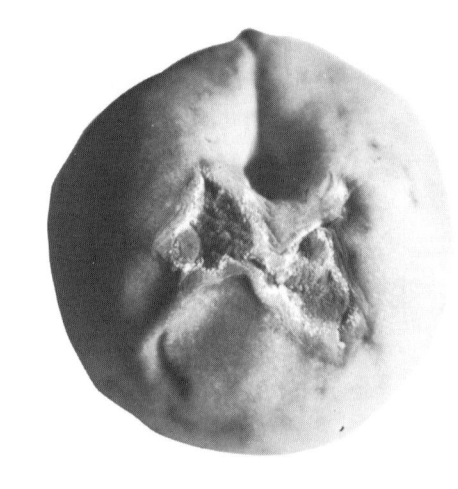

Fig. 84.1 This peach is decaying because microbes are feeding on it.

Sewage

In a **sewage works** waste water is cleaned before it is allowed to flow into rivers or the sea. The water passes through **filter beds** containing stones and gravel. These are covered by microbes which feed on the sewage as it passes over them. The sewage is broken down (Fig. 84.2 and see page 172).

Fig. 84.2 This is a filter bed at a sewage works. Microbes help clean the water by breaking down the waste material.

13 Using and fighting microbes

Using microbes to make food and drinks

Some of our food and drinks are made with the help of microbes.

Bread

Yeast is a fungus which is used in bread-making. Yeast cells can release energy from food without using oxygen (**anaerobic respiration**, see page 30). The cells make two waste products in this process: they are **carbon dioxide** gas and **ethanol**. In bread-making, the yeast cells feed on sugar in the dough mixture. Carbon dioxide is given off and this makes the dough 'rise'. The bread dough will be packed with bubbles and have a light texture (Fig. 84.3).

Wine, beer and cider

Yeast is also used to make wine. The yeast cells feed on the sugars in grapes. The carbon dioxide is given off as bubbles. The ethanol that is made stays in the liquid yeast and grape mixture. Ethanol is the chemical in 'alcoholic drinks'. Ethanol affects our nervous system, so it can be called a **drug**. Yeast can be fed with other fruits to make different drinks. If hops and barley are used, beer is made. Apples are used to make cider (Fig. 84.4).

Cheese and yogurt

Different types of bacteria are used to make the various cheeses and yogurt. The bacteria are allowed to grow and reproduce in warm milk. They affect the milk in two ways They make parts of the milk solid (**curdling**) and produce chemicals which give the curdled milk a particular flavour (Fig. 84.5).

Other useful microbes

The skins of dead animals are cleaned by microbes before being turned into leather. This is called **curing** the leather. Microbes can be used in the production of vinegar and to make some important medicines (see page 155). Some microbes are used to extract metals from ores. The acids made by bacteria dissolve the metals out of their ores. The valuable metal uranium can be extracted in this way.

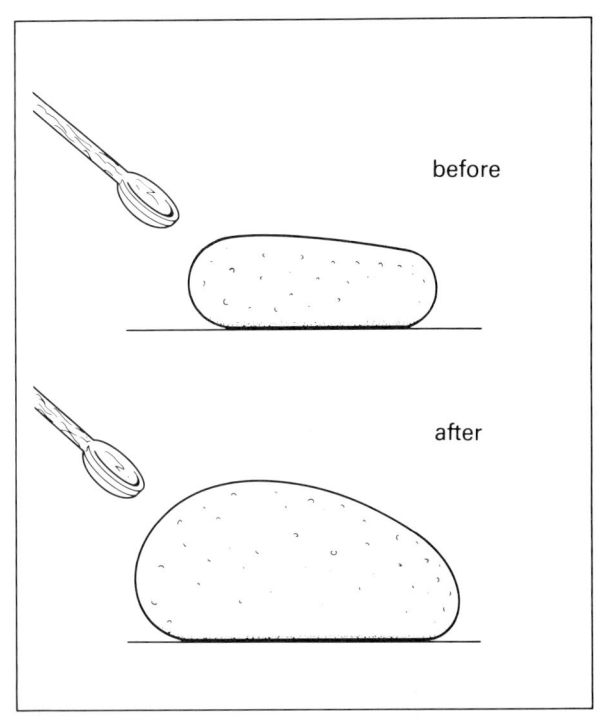

Fig. 84.3 Bread dough before and after it has risen.

*Fig. 84.4 This pool of beer is **fermenting** – the yeast cells in it are making ethanol and carbon dioxide.*

Fig. 84.5 Microbes are used to make cheese from milk.

13 Using and fighting microbes

85 Controlling microbes

Microbes, such as bacteria, grow well if given the following. They need a supply of food, moisture, warmth and air in the surroundings. We can stop microbes growing if we make conditions unsuitable for them. Microbes can be killed by burning any item that might have microbes on it or by boiling it for about one hour (Fig. 85.1). There are some chemicals which kill microbes or stop them growing.

Disinfectants

Disinfectants are chemicals that kill bacteria. Disinfectants were discovered by **Joseph Lister** (Fig. 85.2) who was working as a surgeon in a hospital. In those days many patients died from operations because their bodies became infected. Louis Pasteur (1822–1895) had just shown how microbes were carried in the air. Lister realised that microbes could get into the body through wounds and make them go **septic** (poisoned). He found that **carbolic acid** killed microbes. During his operations Lister made sure all the knives, operating table, and clothes were sprayed with the disinfectant. Lister then found that fewer of his patients became infected after operations. However, carbolic acid not only kills microbes it stops the cells near the wound growing properly to repair the wound.

Some disinfectant chemicals are **phenol** (another name for carbolic acid), **iodine**, **chlorine**, **formalin** and **sodium hypochlorite**. Very weak disinfectants are called **antiseptics**. These do not kill microbes, but they stop them from multiplying (Fig. 85.3).

Fig. 85.1 An autoclave in a hospital. Instruments are sterilised in 'super-heated' steam.

Fig. 85.2 Joseph Lister (1827–1912).

Fig. 85.3 Bottles of disinfectant.

13 Using and fighting microbes

Antibiotics

Some microbes produce **antibiotics** which are chemicals which kill or stop the growth of some disease-causing microbes. Antibiotics interfere with the processes going on inside bacteria. Or they may break open the walls of the bacteria (Fig. 85.4). Antibiotics are very useful because they do not damage human cells.

Penicillin

One of the most famous antibiotics, **penicillin**, is made by the fungus *Penicillium*. Its effect was discovered by **Alexander Fleming** while he was working with bacteria that cause boils (Fig. 85.5). He was growing these bacteria in jelly cultures in his laboratory. In one of his dishes he found a mould had got in by accident. Around this mould, no bacteria were growing. The *Penicillium* was passing out a chemical that stopped the bacteria growing (Fig. 85.6). He called the chemical penicillin. Today the fungus is grown in large vats and the penicillin is extracted. Many other antibiotics have been discovered and include **streptomycin** and **aureomycin**. Some of these chemicals can be made in chemical factories without using microbes. They can be produced in large amounts.

Sulphonamides

Another group of chemicals that affect bacteria are the **sulphonamides**. They are made by man in chemical factories. They also interfere with the growth of the bacteria.

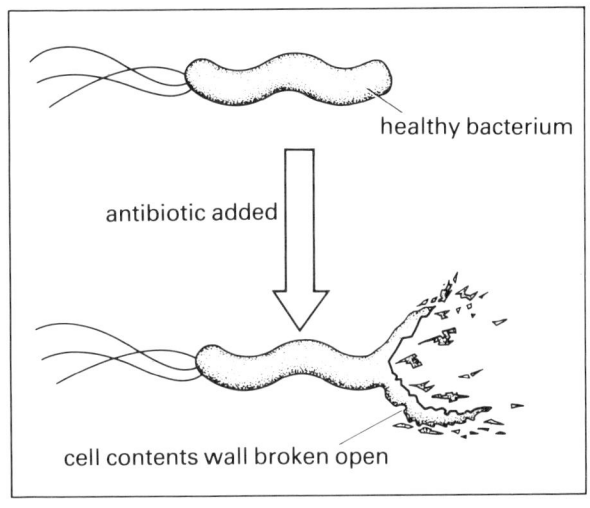

Fig. 85.4 A healthy bacterium and one that has been damaged by an antibiotic.

Fig. 85.5 Alexander Fleming (1881–1955).

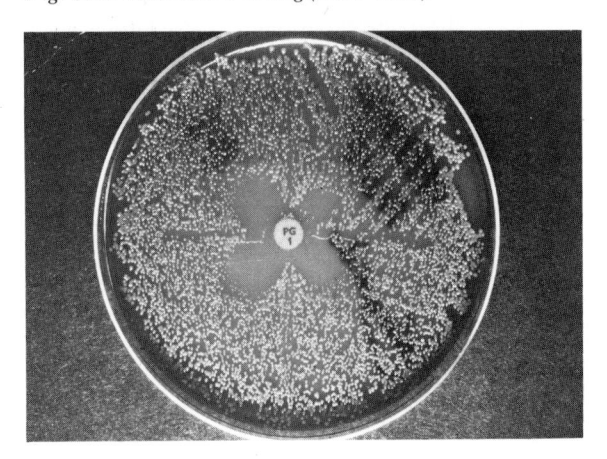

Fig. 85.6 The tablet in the middle contains an antibiotic which spreads outwards through the jelly. The clear patches show that the antibiotic has stopped the growth of bacteria near the centre.

13 Using and fighting microbes

86 Keeping clean

You can cut down the chances of becoming diseased by taking care of your body.

Personal hygiene for men

1. **Hair** Wash at least once a week. Use shampoo and rinse thoroughly.

2. **Eyes** Do not strain by trying to read or work in dim light.

3. **Ears** Wash the back and front of the pinna with water each day. Never poke things down the ear canal.

4. **Note** Use a clean handkerchief each day. Blow the nose to remove dirt trapped in mucus.

5. **Food** Eat a balanced diet for health.

6. **Teeth** Clean with a toothbrush every morning and night to remove plaque. If possible clean teeth after each meal. Visit the dentist regularly.

7. **Hands** Always wash the hands before handling food and after going to the lavatory. Keep the nails short and clean out dirt trapped under the nails.

8. **Armpits** Wash each day. Some people use a deodorant to stop body odour. Only washing will remove body odour.

9. **Crotch** Wash with warm, soapy water each day. Always wipe the opening of the anus with paper after defaecating.

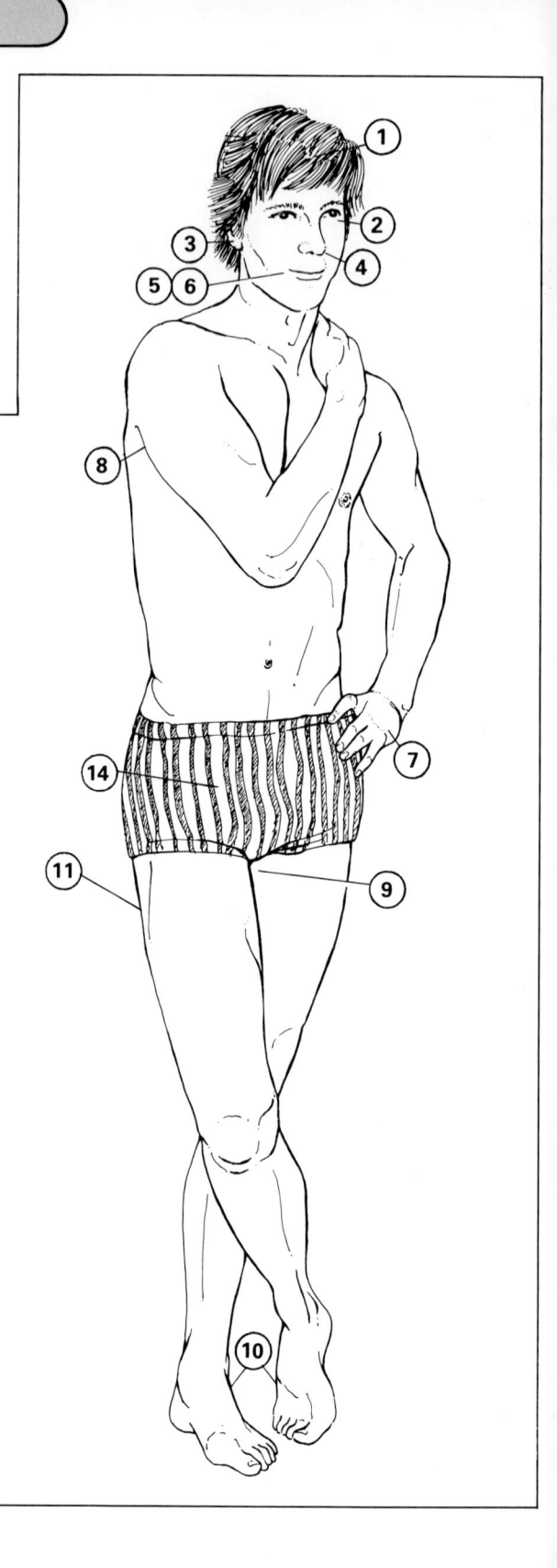

Fig. 86.1 Keeping clean – boys.

13 Using and fighting microbes

Personal hygiene for women

⑩ **Feet** Wash each day. Dry between the toes. Cut nails straight across to avoid ingrown toe nails. Do not wear shoes or socks/tights that cramp the feet. Wear clean socks or tights each day.

⑪ **Body** Wash all over at least once a week.

Women only

⑫ Wear clean underwear every day. During a period, sanitary towels or tampons must be changed every few hours. Wash the crotch as often as possible during a period.

⑬ If a bra is worn, put on a clean one regularly.

Men only

⑭ Wear clean underpants every day. Men who have not been circumcised should wash under the foreskin of the penis each day.

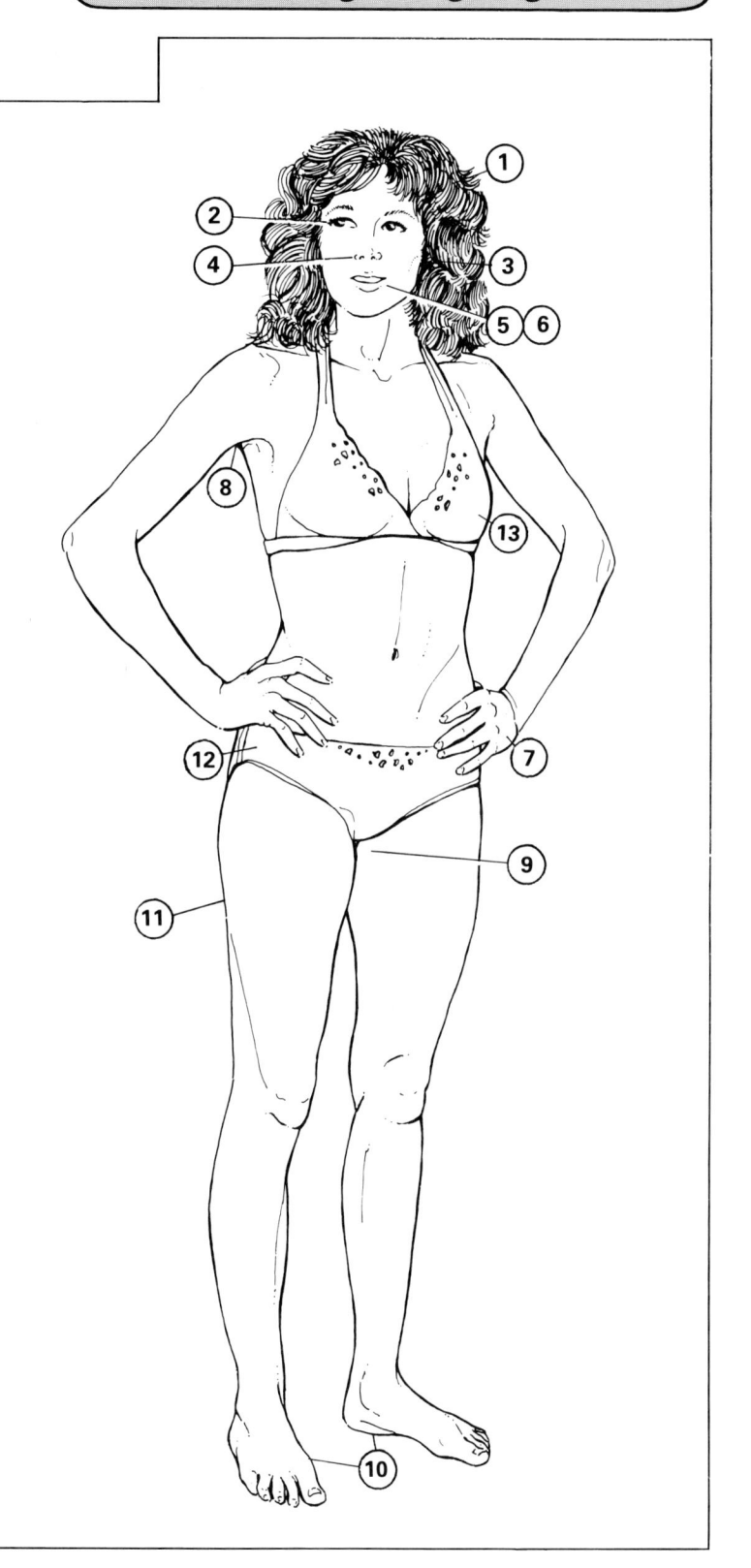

Fig. 86.2 Keeping clean – girls.

13 Using and fighting microbes

87 Protecting the body

The body is always 'under attack' from microbes. To stay healthy the body has ways of keeping microbes out and ways of dealing with microbes if they enter. The body's 'first lines of defence' against invasion by bacteria and viruses are the skin, the breathing tubes and the stomach (Fig. 87.1).

The skin is a barrier

The skin acts as a barrier against microbes. The dead cells of the outer layer are always being replaced by cells from a living layer deeper down. This dead layer is kept moist and flexible by an oily and antiseptic fluid called **sebum**. This is made by the **sebaceous glands** near the **hair follicles** (see page 60).

Air passages

Dust and microbes can enter the body through the nose and mouth. In the breathing tubes, these are trapped in a slimy, sticky substance called **mucus** which lines the walls. Tiny hairs (**cilia**) in the tube move the layer of mucus towards the throat, where dirt and slime are swallowed (see page 27).

Acid in the stomach

Microbes may be swallowed in the food we eat. They enter the stomach and most are killed by the digestive juices and acid. These are secreted by glands in the wall of the stomach.

Blood clotting

Another line of defence is in the blood. If the skin is cut or broken, blood vessels could be damaged. A lot of blood could be lost. The wound would also be an entry place for microbes. A blood **clot** forms at the wound to stop the loss of blood and

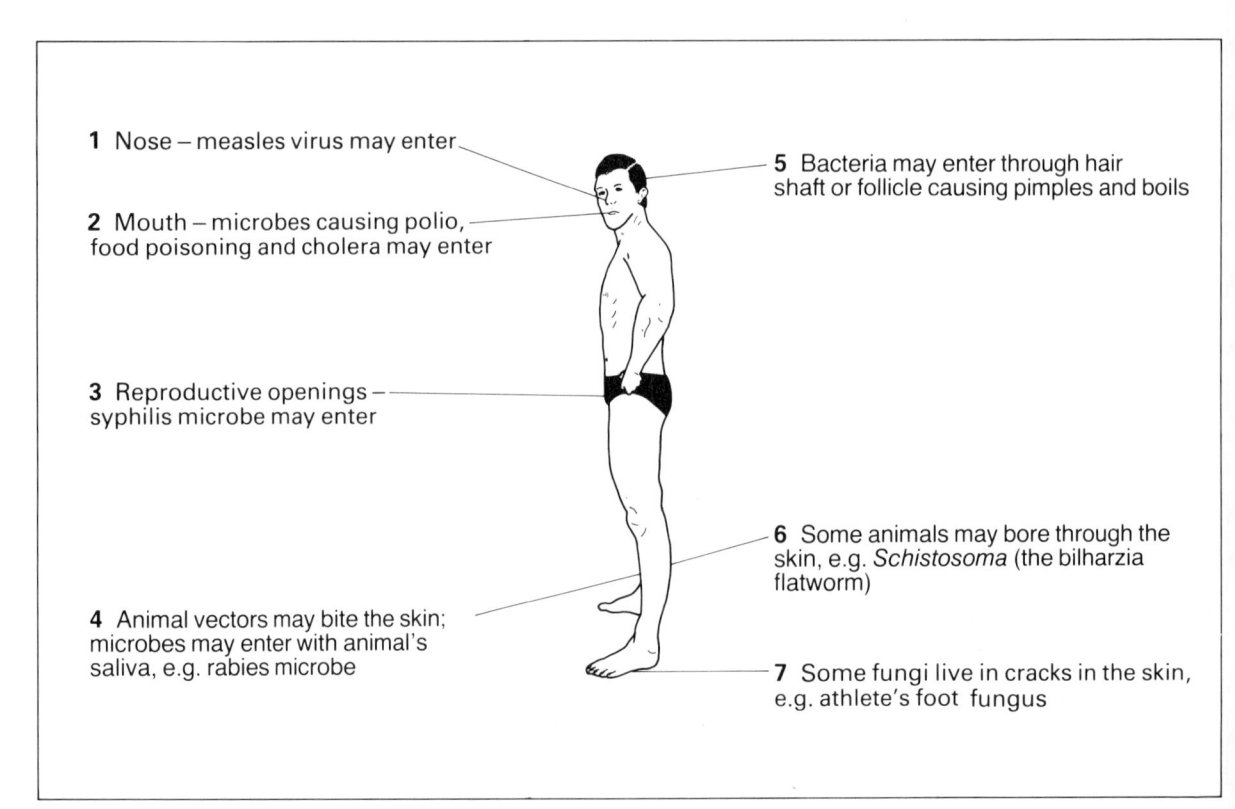

1 Nose – measles virus may enter

2 Mouth – microbes causing polio, food poisoning and cholera may enter

3 Reproductive openings – syphilis microbe may enter

4 Animal vectors may bite the skin; microbes may enter with animal's saliva, e.g. rabies microbe

5 Bacteria may enter through hair shaft or follicle causing pimples and boils

6 Some animals may bore through the skin, e.g. *Schistosoma* (the bilharzia flatworm)

7 Some fungi live in cracks in the skin, e.g. athlete's foot fungus

Fig. 87.1 How microbes may enter the body.

13 Using and fighting microbes

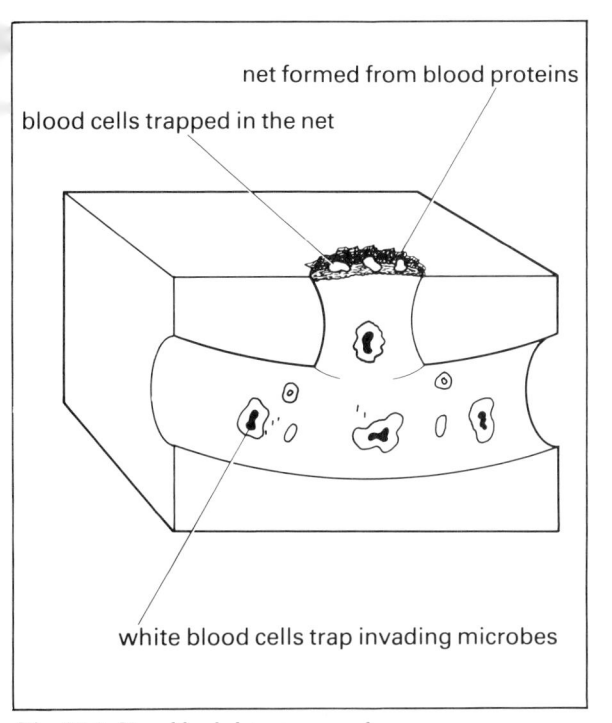

Fig. 87.2 How blood clots at a wound.

White blood cells feed on microbes

Once microbes get into the body, they are attacked by a group of white blood cells called **phagocytes**. These destroy microbes by taking them into themselves. They break down the microbes by digestion (Fig. 87.4). The phagocytes are produced in the **red bone marrow** and the **lymph nodes**. Sometimes these nodes swell when they are working to make phagocytes (Fig. 87.3).

the entry of microbes. At a wound, the blood cells and platelets are open to the air. This triggers off a chain of chemical changes in the blood. The proteins in the blood plasma form a sticky net. This soon gets plugged with red blood cells. When the plug dries it forms a **scab** and new skin grows underneath to form a seal (Fig. 87.2).

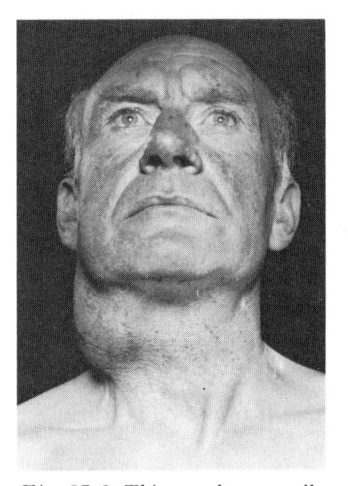

Fig. 87.3 This man has a swollen gland (lymph node) in his neck.

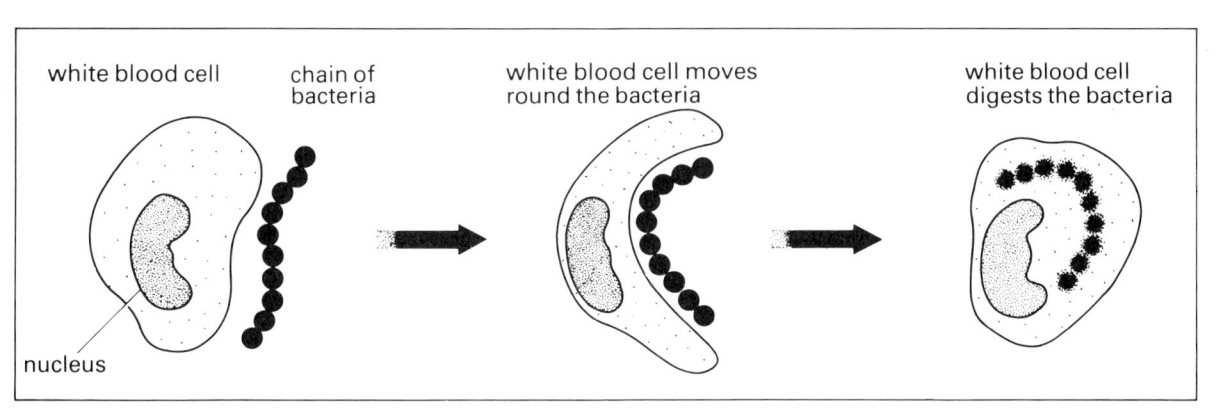

Fig. 87.4 A white blood cell taking in microbes.

13 Using and fighting microbes

88 Blood and immunity

Fighting infection

An infected wound sometimes feels hot and pus may be seen around the scab that forms (Fig. 88.1). Heat or **inflammation** is caused when more blood comes to the area. This allows more white blood cells to leave the capillaries and attack the bacteria. Some of the white cells are killed by poisons or toxins from the bacteria. The pus is made up of dead and some living white cells and damaged skin cells. As the chemistry of the body is working hard to overcome infection, heat is produced. The body temperature may rise and this causes a fever (see Fig. 79.3, page 144).

Immunity

There are some microbes that cause disease in animals. For example, a virus that attacks cattle causes a disease called 'foot and mouth' disease. This virus cannot grow inside the cells of the human body. This means we cannot catch this disease. We are **naturally immune** to this disease.

Immunity and how it works

There is another protection system in the blood. Some microbes, such as bacteria and viruses, will cause disease if they get into the blood. These microbes are 'foreign' protein. The white blood cells can 'recognise' that these are not normal human protein. The invading or foreign protein is called an **antigen**. An antigen in the blood starts the white cells making defence chemicals called **antibodies**. Some antibodies break up the antigens. Others make the antigens stick together. This stops the antigen entering the body cells and makes it easier for the phagocytes to attack them. Some bacteria produce toxins inside the body. Our white blood cells can also make **antitoxins** to destroy the poison. Antibodies and antitoxins help prevent microbes damaging the body. They help us 'fight off' the disease, giving us **immunity** to the disease (Fig. 88.2).

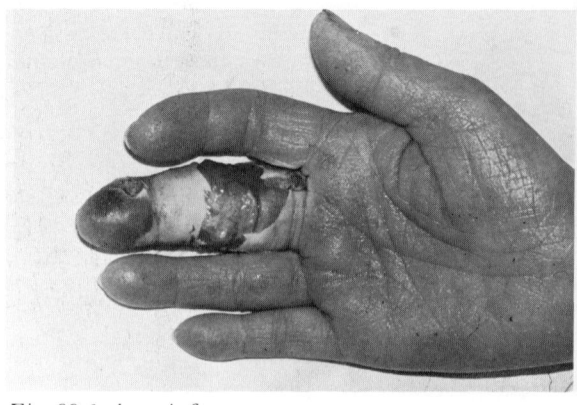

Fig. 88.1 A septic finger.

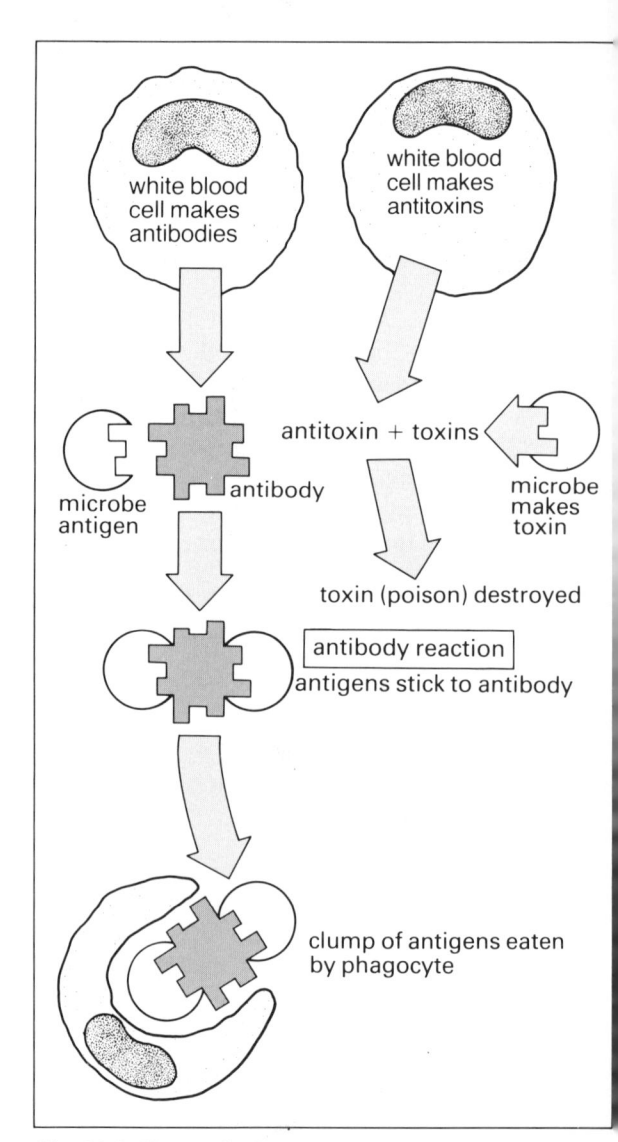

Fig. 88.2 How antibodies work.

13 Using and fighting microbes

Immunity and a second attack of a disease

The type of antibody made depends on the type of antigen invading. An invading measles virus (protein) will make the body produce 'measles antibodies'. These antibodies will stay in the blood for some time (Fig. 88.3).

A boat-builder can make many identical glass fibre boats from one mould. The body works in a similar way. Once an antigen has been recognised many antibodies of the same kind can be made. If the measles virus attacks again, the body is ready to resist the disease. The antibodies remaining in the blood will be ready immediately to attack the viruses. If large numbers of measles viruses invade the body, more antibodies may be needed. The white blood cells already have the 'plan' needed to make these antibodies, so more are made quickly. If you have measles antibodies in your blood you are immune to measles. You will not suffer from the disease even if measles viruses enter your body.

SLOW REACTION

A type of microbe enters the body for the first time.

White blood cells captures microbe.

White blood cells makes antibodies.

Information about microbe antigen passed to another white blood cell.

Antibodies released.

As the reaction is slow, some microbes may cause the disease.

Antibody traps antigen.

Antibody stays in blood.

Clump of antigens eaten by white blood cells.

QUICK REACTION

The same type of microbe enters the body for a second time.

White blood cell recognises the antigen. The cell makes antibodies quickly.

Some antibodies already in blood.

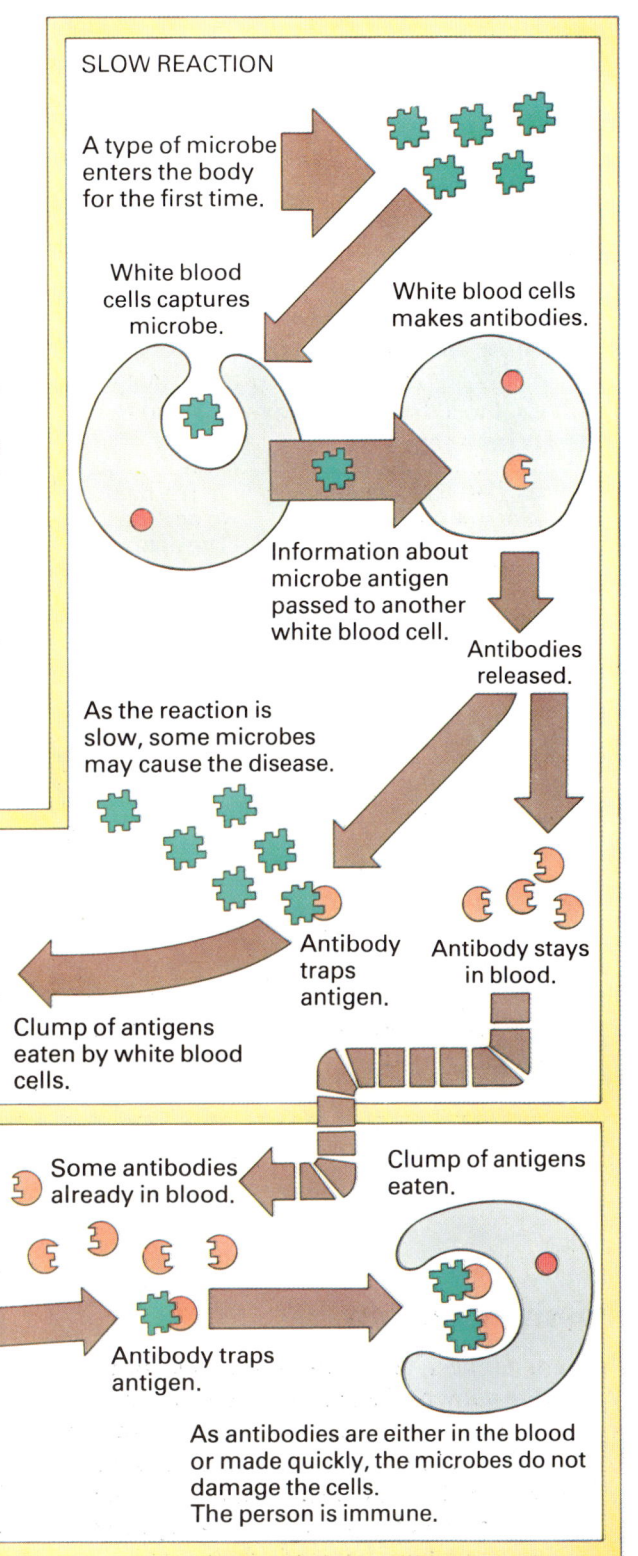

Clump of antigens eaten.

Antibody traps antigen.

As antibodies are either in the blood or made quickly, the microbes do not damage the cells.
The person is immune.

Fig. 88.3 Antibodies and immunity.

13 Using and fighting microbes

Active immunity

We can help the body resist attack by pathogens. Giving the body immunity can be done in several ways (Fig. 88.4). A small dose of weakened living microbes, dead microbes or poisons can be put in the body. This is **immunisation** or **vaccination**. The dose may be injected into our muscles or blood. Sometimes it may be put into the mouth and swallowed. The small dose makes the body produce the antibodies that fight the infection (Fig. 88.5). As the body is working to make antibodies to a disease, the person is said to be **actively immune**.

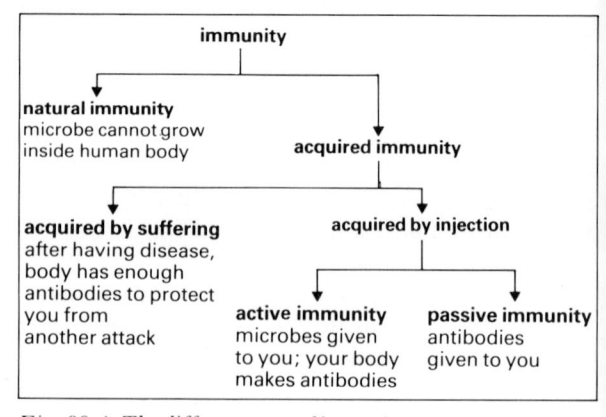

```
                        immunity
                           │
             ┌─────────────┴─────────────┐
      natural immunity              acquired immunity
      microbe cannot grow                │
      inside human body       ┌──────────┴──────────┐
                      acquired by suffering   acquired by injection
                      after having disease,        │
                      body has enough      ┌───────┴───────┐
                      antibodies to protect  active immunity  passive immunity
                      you from              microbes given   antibodies
                      another attack        to you; your body given to you
                                            makes antibodies
```

Fig. 88.4 *The different types of immunity.*

1 A six month old baby is given a dose of weak polio virus. The virus multiplies slowly inside the baby's cells.

2 The baby's cells make antibodies to destroy the polio viruses. The antibodies stay in the blood plasma.

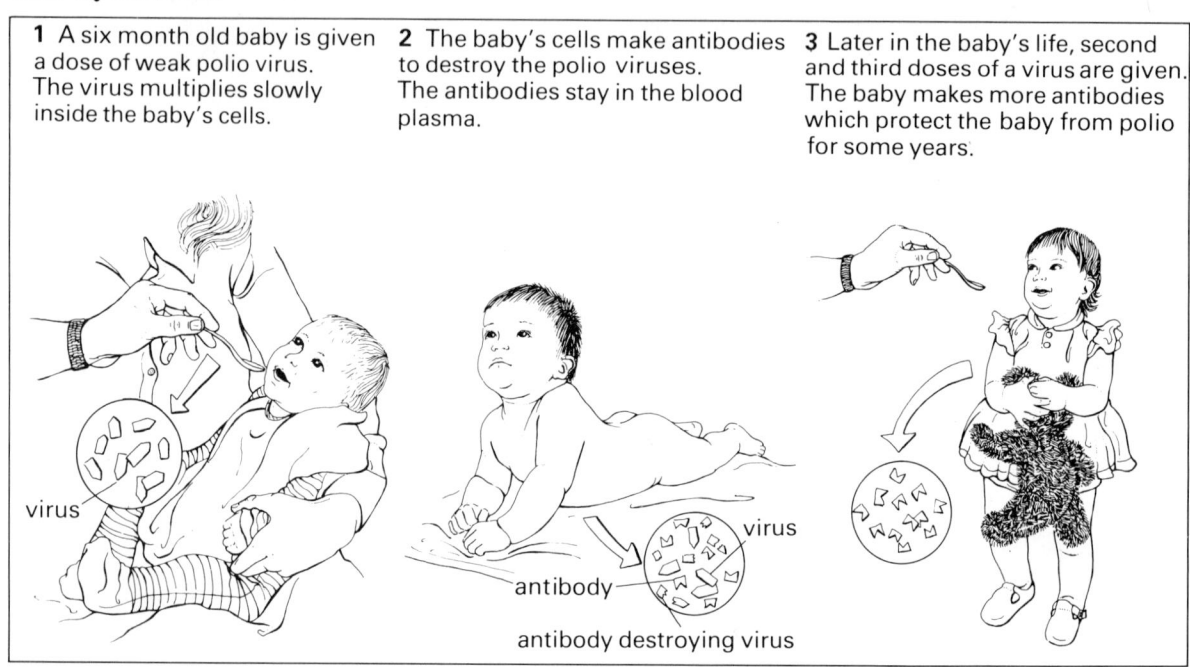

3 Later in the baby's life, second and third doses of a virus are given. The baby makes more antibodies which protect the baby from polio for some years.

Fig. 88.5 *Giving a baby immunity to polio.*

Passive immunity

If there has been an outbreak of a dangerous disease in a town, the people need protection quickly. They can be injected with ready-made antibodies or antitoxins. These chemicals may have been made in and extracted from the body of another person or an animal. As the people receiving them have not made their own antibodies this is called **passive immunity**.

Edward Jenner (1748–1823) was the first person to put pathogens into someone's body and make them actively immune. He was a doctor working on **smallpox**. Jenner knew that the mild disease **cowpox** had similar symptoms to smallpox. He also knew that in country places, people with cowpox sores rubbed these into scratches on another person's body. This protected the 'scratched' person from smallpox. By 1880, this method of protection was being used, in a more scientific way, throughout the country. Jenner did his work before Pasteur had shown that microbes existed.

13 Using and fighting microbes

89 Blood transfusions

Blood loss

If a person is badly injured, they may lose a lot of blood. One-sixth of the total amount of blood in the body can be lost without suffering serious damage. If more is lost, the body will stop working properly. Blood can be made inside the body to replace any that is lost, but this takes time. A badly-wounded person can be given blood from another person.

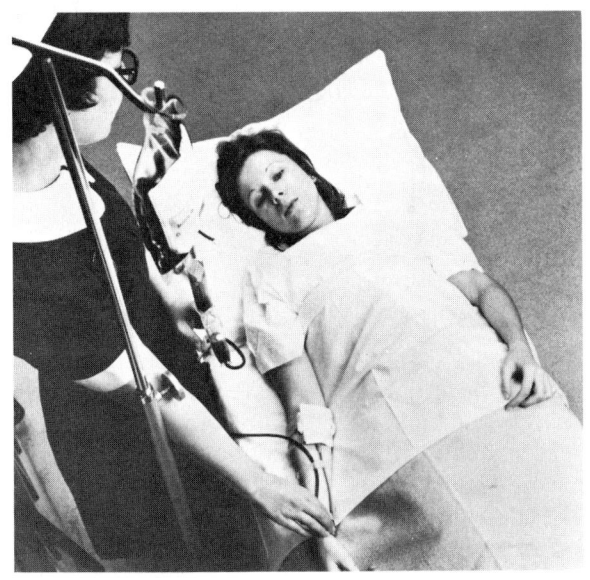

Blood transfusions

Receiving blood from someone else is called a **blood transfusion** (Fig. 89.1). The person receiving blood is a **recipient**. The person who gives blood is a **donor**. When blood is taken from one person and given to another, foreign protein is being put into the recipient. So that the recipient's body does not 'fight' the foreign protein, blood must be checked to make sure it can be mixed.

Blood groups

There are different types of blood. Blood is **grouped** by the chemicals (antigens) carried on the outside of the red cells. The best known groups are those of the **ABO system** and the **Rhesus system**. The name of the group depends on the antigen on the red blood cells.

The ABO blood groups

In the ABO system there are two types of antigens, **A** and **B**. The different groups and their antigens are shown in Fig. 89.2. The plasma may contain some antibodies. If a person has antigen **A** on their blood cells, their plasma will contain antibody **b**. Groups A and O are the most common groups in Britain (Fig. 89.3).

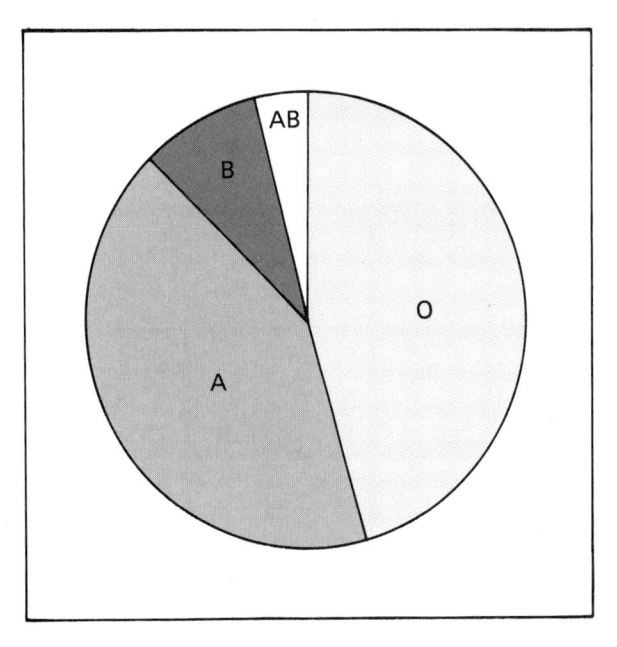

Fig. 89.1 A person receiving a blood transfusion.

Blood group	Antigen on red blood cells	Antibody in plasma
A	A	anti-B (b)
B	B	anti-A (a)
AB	A and B	none
O	none	anti-A and anti-B

Fig. 89.2 The ABO blood groups.

Fig. 89.3 A pie chart showing how common the different ABO groups are in England.

13 Using and fighting microbes

Mixing different blood groups

If red cells with antigen **A** on them are mixed with plasma containing antibody **a**, the cells stick together. If this happened in the body, the **clumps** of cells would block the capillaries (Fig. 89.4).

Safe transfusions

The donor's blood must not contain antigens that match the antibodies in the recipient. If they did match, the blood cells would clump. This can lead to death. Fig. 89.5 shows which blood can be given to patients of different blood groups.

Blood of group O can be given to people of any of the four groups. A person who is blood group O is a **universal donor**. A person who is AB can receive any of the other groups and so is a **universal recipient**.

The Rhesus system

The Rhesus blood groups work in a similar way to the ABO groups. In Britain, 85% of the population are **Rhesus positive** and 15% are **Rhesus negative** (Fig. 89.6).

Rhesus blood grouping is controlled by a dominant gene (see page 111). Rhesus positive is dominant (**R**), Rhesus negative is recessive (**r**). The Rhesus group could be a problem if a Rhesus negative woman (**rr**) has a child by a Rhesus positive man (**RR** or **Rr**, Fig. 89.7).

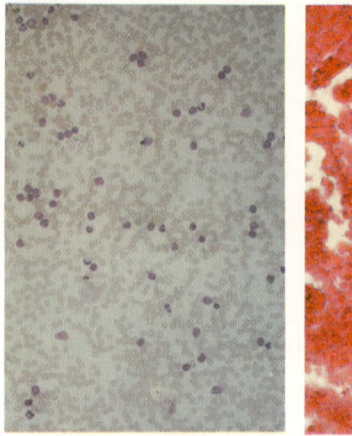

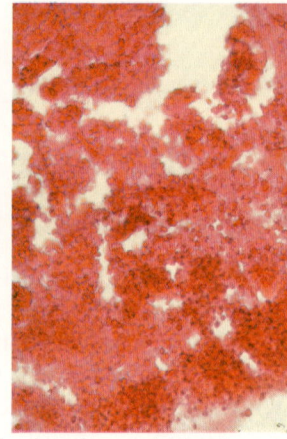

Fig. 89.4 Two blood smears that have been stained and magnified (× 200). The smear on the right shows clumping.

Blood group of recipient / antibodies in plasma	Blood group of donor / antigens on red blood cells			
	A / A	B / B	AB / A and B	O / none
A / b	✓	✗	✗	✓
B / a	✗	✓	✗	✓
AB / none	✓	✓	✓	✓
O / a and b	✗	✗	✗	✓

(AB row = universal recipient; O column = universal donor)

Fig. 89.5 In this chart a tick means a safe transfusion; a cross means a transfusion would be dangerous.

Blood group	Antigen on red blood cells	Antibody in plasma
Rhesus positive (Rh+)	Rhesus	none
Rhesus negative (Rh−)	none	Rhesus

Fig. 89.6 The Rhesus blood groups.

Rhesus positive father   Rhesus negative mother
RR × rr
↓
Rr
Rhesus positive
All children will be same blood group

Rhesus positive father   Rhesus negative mother
Rr × rr
↓
Rr   or   rr
Rhesus positive   Rhesus negative
Children could be either blood group

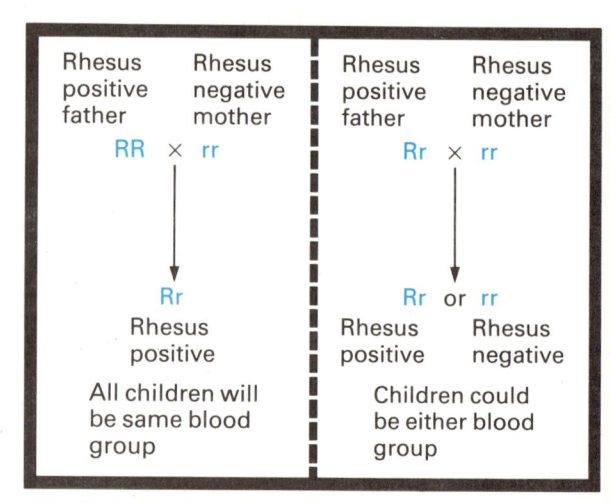

Fig. 89.7 Inheriting Rhesus blood groups.

13 Using and fighting microbes

Damage to an unborn baby

When the Rhesus negative mother has a Rhesus positive baby, problems can occur. During the pregnancy, some of the baby's blood will leak across the **placenta** into the mother's blood (Fig. 89.8). If this happens with the first child, the mother will only make a few antibodies. However, if the second baby is Rhesus positive, the mother's blood will produce more antibodies. The antibodies will then pass across the placenta and cause some of the baby's red cells to clump together. This may give the baby **jaundice** or cause it to be born dead. Nowadays a transfusion, given to the baby before birth, stops this happening.

Baby's red blood cells carrying antigens, leaking into mother's blood.

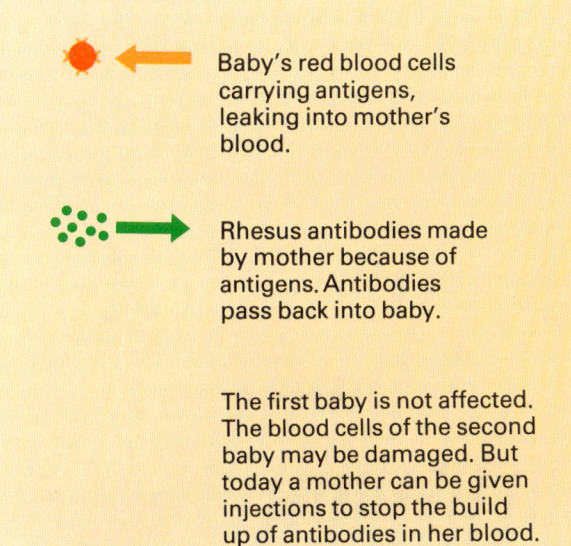

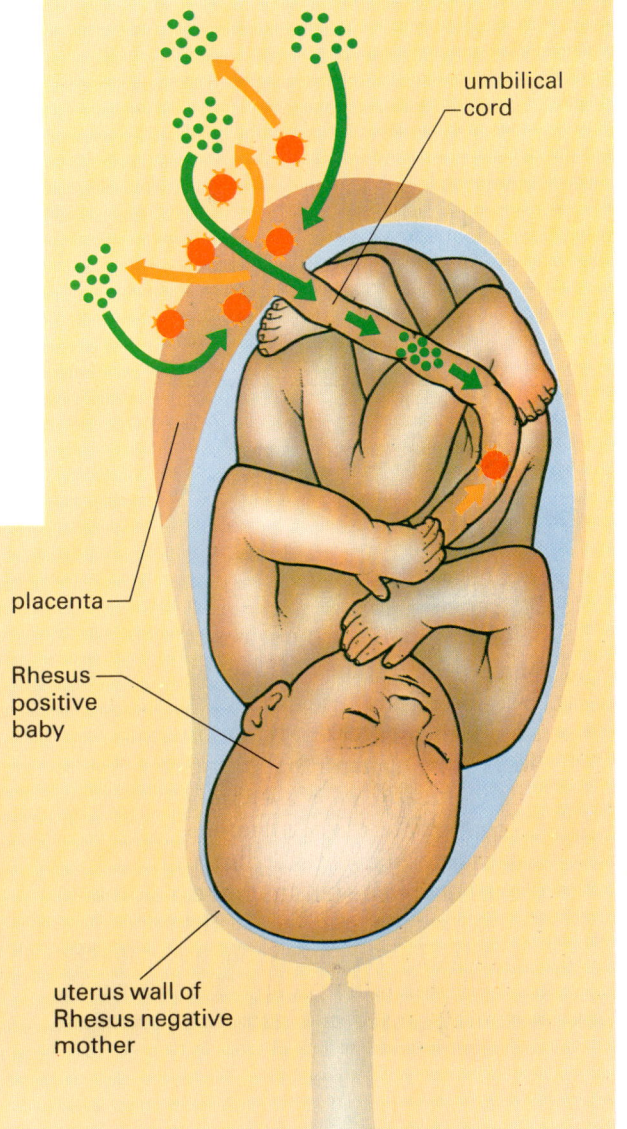

Rhesus antibodies made by mother because of antigens. Antibodies pass back into baby.

The first baby is not affected. The blood cells of the second baby may be damaged. But today a mother can be given injections to stop the build up of antibodies in her blood.

Fig. 89.8 *A Rhesus positive baby may be affected in the womb if its mother is Rhesus negative.*

Summary: Using and fighting microbes

* Many microbes are used by man. Uses include rotting of waste, cleaning sewage and making some foods and drinks.
* The spread of microbes can be stopped by using disinfectants, antiseptics and antibiotics.
* Many antibiotics are made by microbes. Penicillin is made by a fungus.
* Personal hygiene helps prevent microbes entering the body.
* The body has defences. These include the skin, the air passages and the stomach.
* If a blood vessel is broken, the wound is healed. The first stage of healing is the clotting of blood.
* White blood cells can attack invading microbes.
* The body reacts to invading microbes or foreign protein (antigens) by making chemicals called antibodies. This is immunity.
* Doctors can help people to become immune. This giving of immunity can be active or passive.
* The immune reaction plays a part in blood grouping.
* The most well known blood grouping systems are ABO and Rhesus.

14 Clean food and water

90 Kitchens and cooking

Food poisoning

The food we prepare for ourselves can also be food for microbes. Some of these microbes are harmless. Some can cause disease, such as food poisoning, if they enter our bodies in food (Fig. 90.1). The bacteria that cause food poisoning include *Salmonellae*, *Staphylococci* and some *Clostridia*. The most dangerous type of food poisoning is caused by a bacterium called *Clostridium botulinum*. This microbe makes a toxin that is the most poisonous substance known to man. Two or three spoonfuls would be enough to kill 100 million people! **Botulism** is the food poisoning caused by *Clostridium botulinum*.

Food hygiene

Food must be stored, prepared and cooked in a hygienic way. This will cut down the chances of microbes growing in food. A kitchen should:
1 be well ventilated so that smelly, greasy air can escape and fresh air enter,
2 have no corners that are hard to clean,
3 have table tops and draining boards that are easy to clean,
4 have a supply of hot water and drinking water,
5 have a washable bin, with a tight-fitting lid, for food scraps,
6 have a place for drying tea towels and cloths,
7 have a refrigerator for storing food at low temperatures,
8 have cupboards for storing food that is not kept in a refrigerator,
9 have containers with tight-fitting lids in which food can be kept,

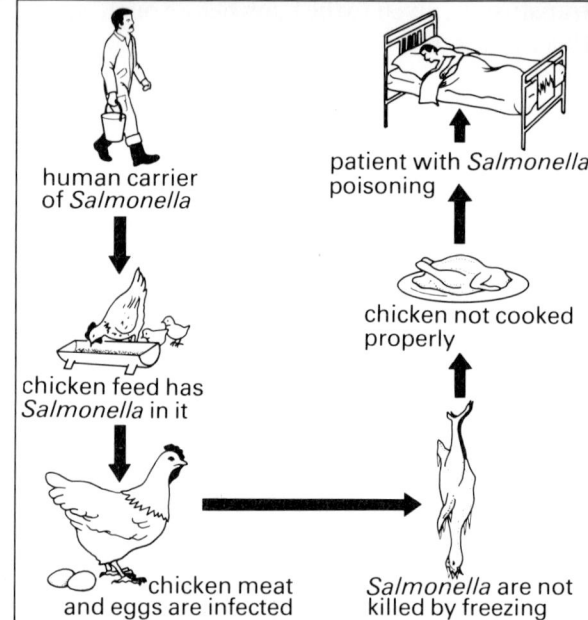

Fig. 90.1 How food poisoning bacteria can be spread.

10 have separate storage for cooked and uncooked meats,
11 be a place where pets are not allowed.

When preparing and cooking foods remember to:
1 tie back long hair,
2 wash your hands before handling food,
3 clean working surfaces before use,
4 wash fresh foods to remove microbes or chemicals,
5 use clean cooking utensils,
6 cook thoroughly, especially meat and fish,
7 wash cooking utensils after use and allow to dry by draining,
8 clean up any food scraps on working surfaces and the floor.

14 Clean food and water

91 Preserving food

When microbes grow on our food, they change and spoil it. Some of our foods, like oranges and meat, are produced in another part of the world and must be transported to this country (Fig. 91.1). The food must be preserved to kill microbes or make them **inactive** during long journeys. Food produced here must also be **preserved**. It may take a few days for food to be moved from where it was produced to shops in other parts of the country. Also we may want to eat the food out of the season when it is produced. Stopping microbes growing can be done in several ways. These include freezing, heating to high temperatures, cutting off the supply of oxygen, **dehydration** (removing water), and adding certain chemicals. The ways different food preserving methods work is shown in Fig. 91.2.

Fig. 91.1 These carcasses of meat were frozen to preserve them during their journey to this country.

Method of preservation	Effect of preservation on:				
	bacteria	fungi	oxygen	water	acidity
cooking	kills most types	kills most types			
chilling	slows down growth	slows down growth			
vacuum packing	slows down growth	slows down growth	removes and keeps out the gas		
canning and bottling	kills all types	kills most types	removes and keeps out the gas		
freezing	kills up to ¾ of all types	stops them growing		turns solid	
dehydration	stops them growing	stops them growing		removes	
curing	slows down growth	slows down growth			
pickling	makes them inactive	stops them growing			makes it more acid
adding chemicals	stops them growing	stops them growing			may change

Fig. 91.2 The different methods of preserving foods. Each method kills microbes or prevents them growing.

14 Clean food and water

How common are the methods?

Some methods of preserving can be used with more foods than others. Nearly all 'wet' foods like meat, fish, vegetables, soups and fruits, can be preserved by **canning**. The foods are boiled in liquid in the can and then it is sealed. This means there is no room for air inside and microbes will not grow. Some roast meat which was canned in 1823 was still edible when opened in 1958!

Freezing is another very common method. Meat, fish, some vegetables and fruits can be frozen easily (Fig. 91.3). **Drying** or dehydration can be used for foods that can be cut into small pieces or powdered. Examples are dried meat and onion pieces in a packet of soup, or dried mashed potato. **Vacuum-packing** is a way of wrapping fresh foods. It removes the air and so stops the growth of microbes. This increases the 'shelf-life' of food in supermarkets.

Curing changes the flavour of food as well as preserving it. **Salting**, **pickling** and **smoking** are ways of curing food today. They were all in use a long time ago. All three methods add chemicals to the food which slow down the decay. Examples are smoked bacon and fish (kippers), pickled onions and gherkins, and salted herrings.

Fig. 91.3 Modern methods of preserving foods.

Milk

Milk from cows is an important and cheap food. It can be preserved in several ways (Fig. 91.4).

Fig. 91.4 Ways of preserving milk.

14 Clean food and water

92 Processing food

Many foods are **processed** (treated in various ways) to make them pleasant to eat (Fig. 92.1). Some processed foods are then preserved.

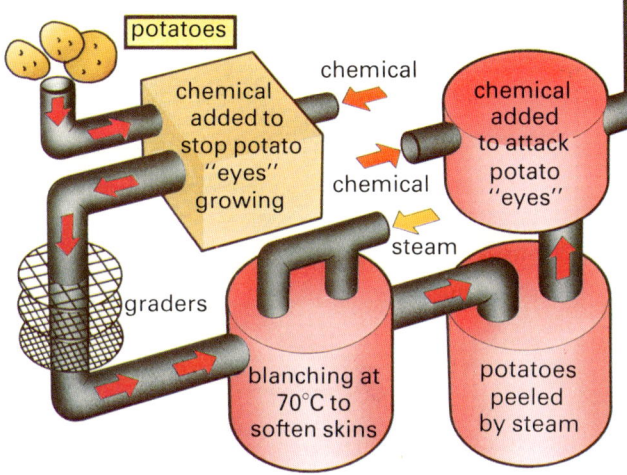

Fig. 92.1 Processing and preserving potatoes.

Chemicals used in processing

Some chemicals, such as **sodium nitrite**, are added to foods to preserve them. But other chemicals may be added to foods. These may be nutrients. White bread has calcium, iron and some of the B-group vitamins added. Some foods, like dessert mixes, have chemicals added to give 'body' to the prepared food. Substances that change the texture include **emulsifier**, **lecithin** and **sodium caseinate**.

Other chemicals change the colour. In Britain in the nineteenth century, copper was used in beer and antimony salts were used to colour sweets. These substances are now known to be poisonous and their use is banned. Today there are many regulations linked to the chemicals that are added to food. The **Public Analyst** does chemical tests on food on sale in shops (Fig. 92.2). Any chemicals added (**additives**) must be shown on food labels (Fig. 92.3).

Fig. 92.2 A public analyst at work in a laboratory.

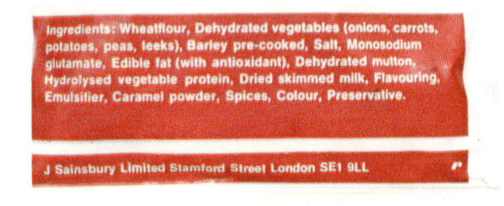

Fig. 92.3 A label on processed food must list all the chemicals it contains.

14 Clean food and water

93 Supplying clean water

Industry	Item made or treated	Amount of water used to make item (litres)
brewing	1 litre of beer	350
papermaking	1 kg of paper	900
steelmaking	1 kg of steel	20
laundering	1 kg of clothes	150

Fig. 93.1 *The amounts of water used in some industries.*

The uses of water

We need water to drink but we also need it for washing ourselves, our clothes and for processes in factories (Fig. 93.1). It has been shown that in Britain the amount of water used each day works out at 180 litres for every person (Fig. 93.2).

Where water comes from

Most of us get our water out of a tap. This water has been pumped to our homes from the **water works**. The water is piped to the water works from rivers, springs, wells, reservoirs and dams. These are always being topped up by rain (Fig. 93.3). The water will be carrying soil or rock particles and possibly larger pieces of rubbish. Many microbes may be carried in the water that goes to the water works. Typhoid and cholera are diseases that can be spread by drinking infected water. So at the water works, the water must be cleaned and treated to kill pathogenic microbes.

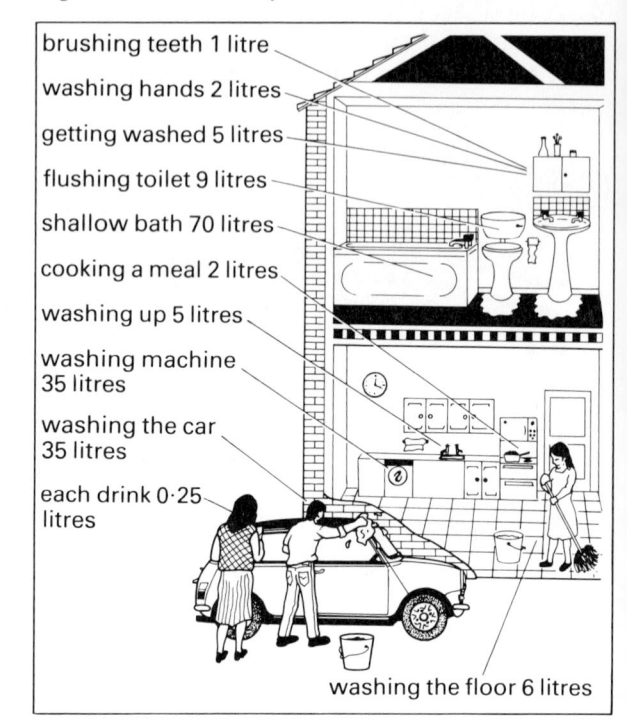

Fig. 93.2 *The amounts of water used in various activities in the home.*

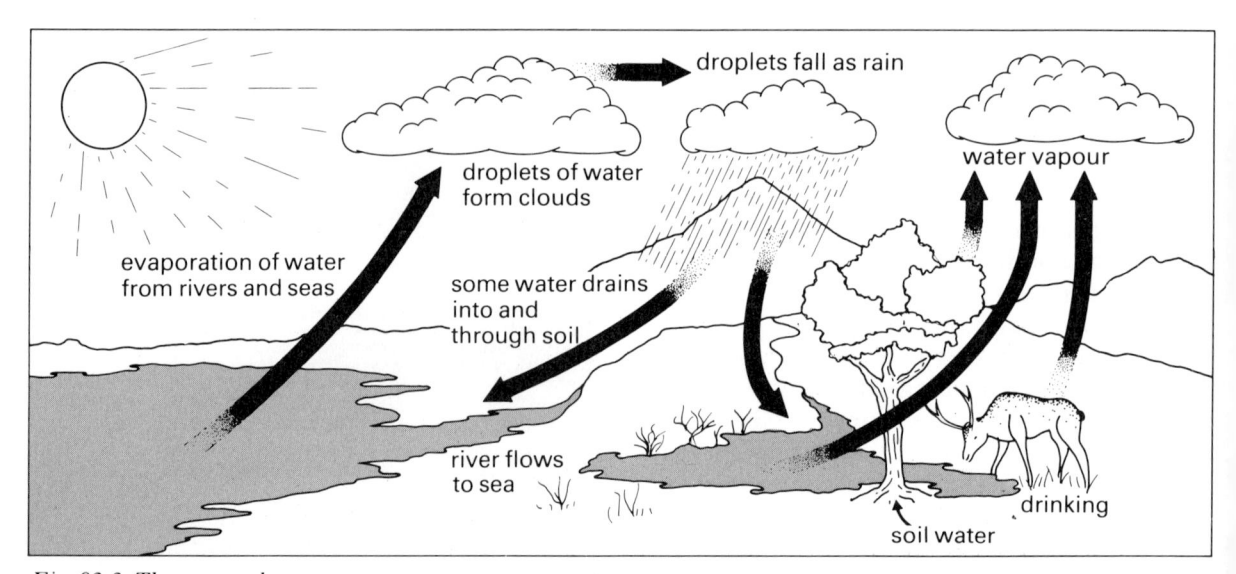

- brushing teeth 1 litre
- washing hands 2 litres
- getting washed 5 litres
- flushing toilet 9 litres
- shallow bath 70 litres
- cooking a meal 2 litres
- washing up 5 litres
- washing machine 35 litres
- washing the car 35 litres
- each drink 0·25 litres
- washing the floor 6 litres

Fig. 93.3 *The water cycle.*

14 Clean food and water

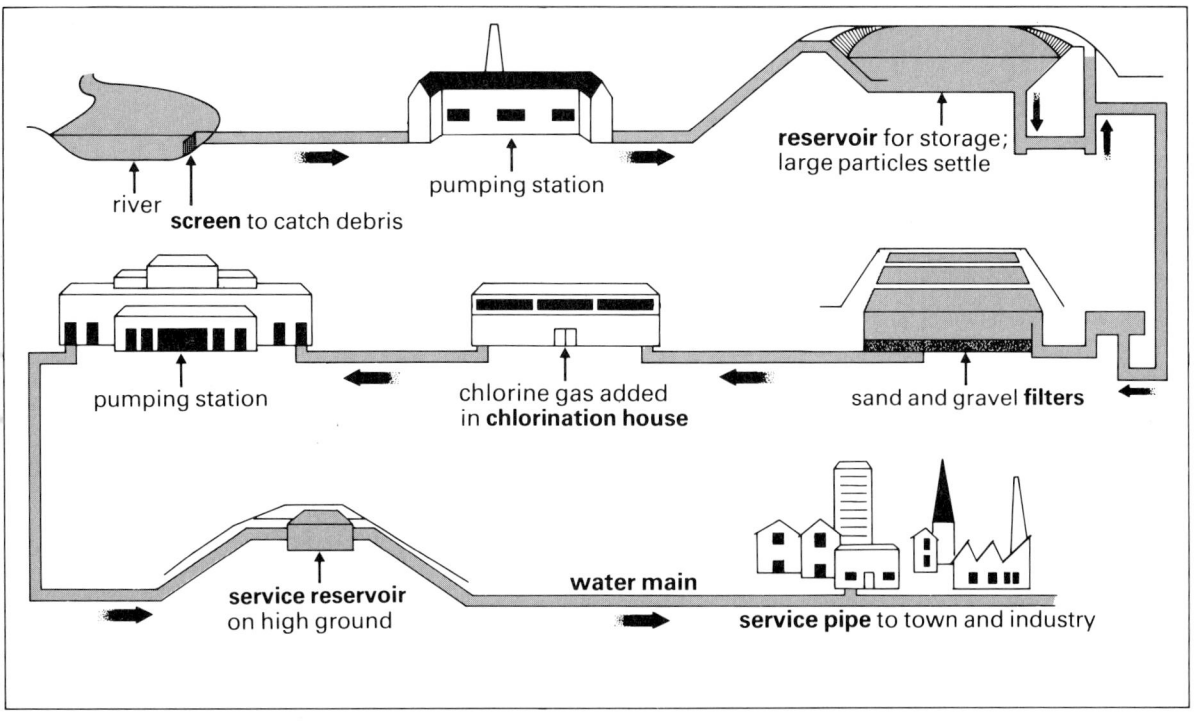

Fig. 93.4 Cleaning water and getting it to homes.

Cleaning the water

At the water works, water is cleaned (Fig. 93.4). It is **filtered** through sand and gravel. The disinfectant, **chlorine**, is added to kill off any harmful microbes. In some parts of the country, **fluoride** is added. This substance helps to harden the enamel in the natural teeth of the people who drink it. So fluoride cuts down tooth decay. The clean water is stored in small local reservoirs. Water is pumped from here to our homes.

Water in our homes

A **water main** brings water to a house. The mains are pipes beneath the streets. Inside a house, the **rising main** branches off the water main and carries water up to the **cold water storage tank** (Fig. 93.5). Pipes take this water to the bath, wash-basins, lavatories, and to the hot water system. The cold water is heated by a **boiler** and stored in the **hot water tank**. Pipes lead from this tank to all the hot taps in the house. One pipe comes directly from the rising main to the cold tap in the kitchen. As this water has not been stored in a tank, it is fresher and should be used for drinking and cooking.

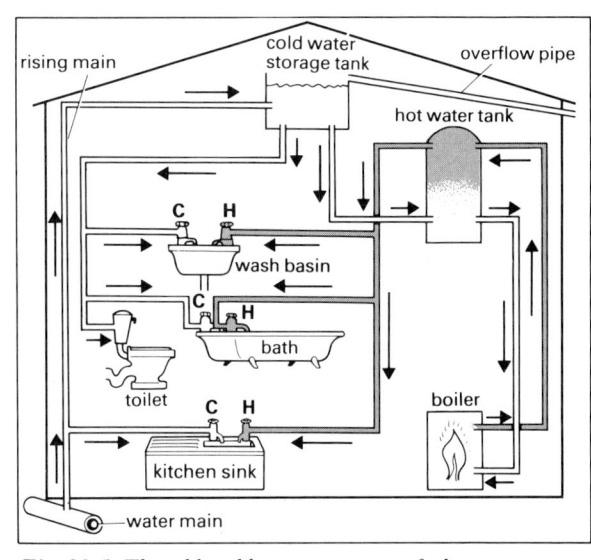

Fig. 93.5 The cold and hot water systems of a house.

In some parts of the world, it is not possible for people to get pure water from taps. These people must be taught to treat their water to kill any harmful microbes.

171

14 Clean food and water

94 Treating sewage

Waste water

People used to throw their dirty water straight into rivers and streams. Londoners put their waste in the River Thames. This helped make the river unsuitable for drinking and killed fish. Now in many places water is cleaned before it is put into rivers so the river water may be used again.

Waste water may contain many substances that must be removed (Fig. 94.2). Water from factories may contain chemicals like detergents. Waste water from baths and wash-basins will contain dirt and microbes from our skin. Water from the kitchen sink may contain potato peelings, oil, tea leaves and other cooking scraps. This water flows away down waste pipes or **drains**.

Waste lavatory water is made up of waste chemicals, microbes and undigested food from the human body. It is important to get rid of it carefully. **Flushing** a lavatory sends a large amount of clean water into it. This pushes the waste away rapidly to large, underground pipes called **sewers**. Some of the clean water stays in the lavatory, trapped in a bend in the pipe. This is a **water seal**. It stops the smells of the sewers getting into the house (Fig. 94.3).

Sewage

All this waste water is **sewage**. The drains lead to the sewers. The sewers take all the waste to a **sewage works** where the sewage is treated. The waste is removed and the cleaned water goes into rivers (Fig. 94.4).

Fig. 94.1 A stagnant river.

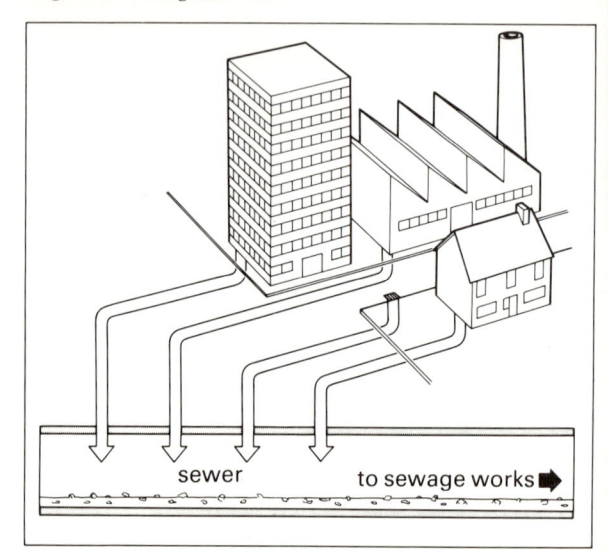

Fig. 94.2 Waste water flows through pipes into sewers.

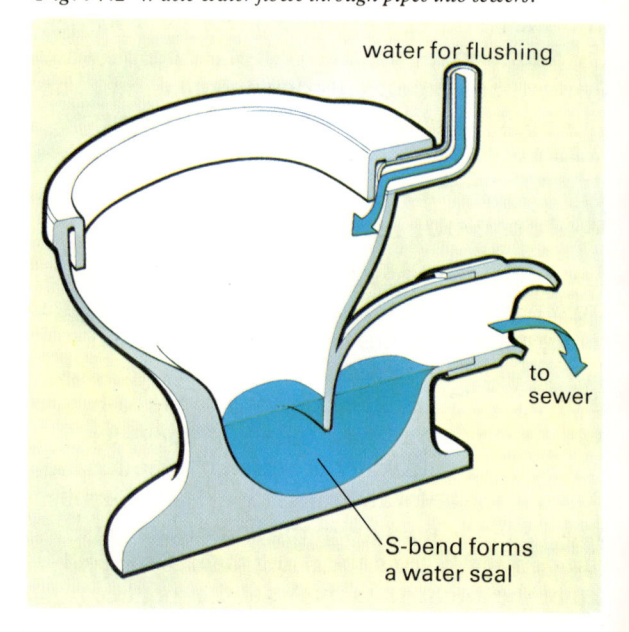

Fig. 94.3 A water seal in a lavatory.

14 Clean food and water

Cleaning waste water

The sewage arrives at the sewage works. Rubbish, such as broken glass and rags, is filtered off. Sewage then goes to **grit tanks**. Here grit and gravel sinks to the bottom.

The sewage without rubbish and gravel goes to **sedimentation tanks**. Here tiny particles settle as **sludge**. The waste water can be treated in two ways.

1 or 2

The waste water from the sedimentation tank is sprinkled over stones that are coated with harmless microbes. Very slowly, these break down the waste particles in the water. This is a **biological filter bed**. (Also see Fig. 84.2, p. 152.)

The waste water is mixed with air in tanks. Harmless microbes break down waste quickly. This is the **activated sludge** way of cleaning water.

The water is clean enough to go to rivers. Some of the microbes in the river finish off the cleaning process.

The sludge from the sedimentation tank goes to a **digester**. Here microbes feed on the sludge. A gas (**methane**) is given off and can be used as a fuel. When the sludge is harmless it is dried. Some is used as a **fertiliser** on land. Most is dumped at sea.

Fig. 94.4 How sewage is treated at a sewage works.

14 Clean food and water

95 Getting rid of rubbish

Natural waste

The natural waste of gardens and the countryside is made up of dead leaves and the remains of animals and plants. These are slowly broken down as microbes in the soil help them to decay. Chemicals that are released by the decay can be used again. The chemicals are re-used or **cycled**. All plants need nutrients from the soil. The nutrients get into the soil dissolved in rainwater and through the slow breaking up of underlying rocks. When plants and animals die and rot, the nutrients are returned to the soil (Fig. 95.1).

Household waste

Some household waste is made up of naturally produced substances, such as potato skins, pea pods and vegetable oils. If left in the ground, these would gradually break down. But most of our domestic waste is made up of material which cannot be broken down. Examples are cans, glass and most plastics. All household waste should be stored in a dustbin with a well-fitting lid. This stops flies and other pests entering. In the summer, a dustbin that is not kept in a reasonable state, may contain hundreds of **maggots**. These have hatched from flies' eggs. Flies may carry microbes of disease (see page 150). The bacteria which cause cholera, poliomyelitis, typhoid and dysentery may all be carried by flies (Fig. 95.2).

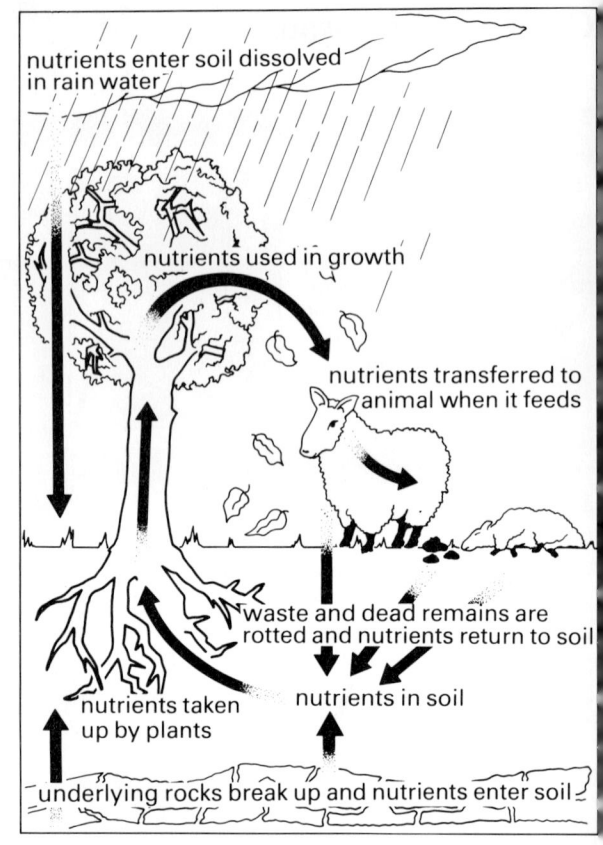

Fig. 95.1 The nutrient cycle.

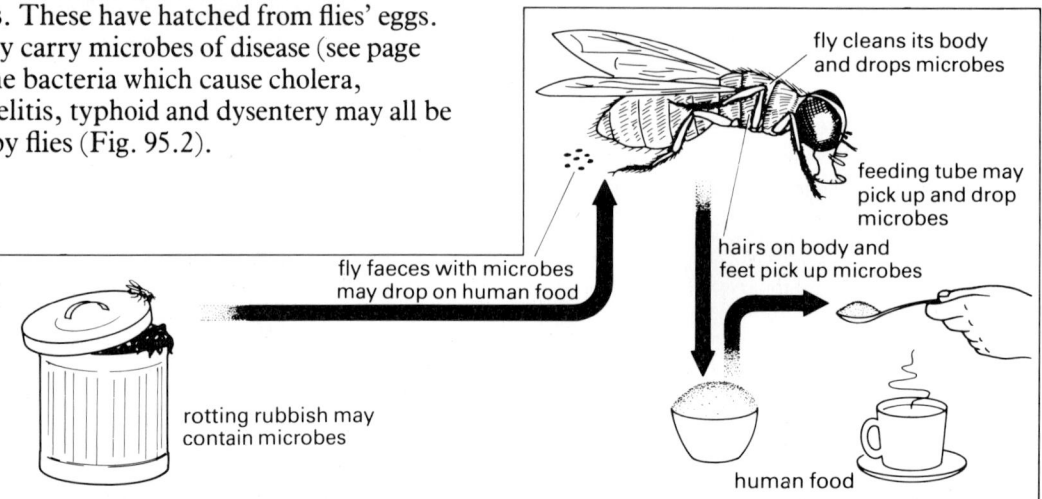

Fig. 95.2 Flies and open dustbins can lead to the spread of disease.

14 Clean food and water

Collecting and disposing of rubbish

Local councils employ people to collect our rubbish every week. It is disposed of in different ways (Fig. 95.3). Some rubbish is dumped at **tips**. Sometimes fires start in tips because of the heat given off by bacteria breaking down some of the waste. Some rubbish is burned in large **incinerators** or crushed into fine particles (**pulverising**).

Recycling rubbish

Today people are realising that many of the things they throw away can be treated and used again or **recycled**. Paper can be shredded and made up into paper again. Some kinds of waste can be formed into sticks that can be used for fuel (Fig. 95.4). Tipping can be used to claim land back from the rivers or sea. Recycling helps to save some of the world's valuable materials or **resources**, that might otherwise run out.

Fig. 95.4 Fuel sticks made from some of our household waste.

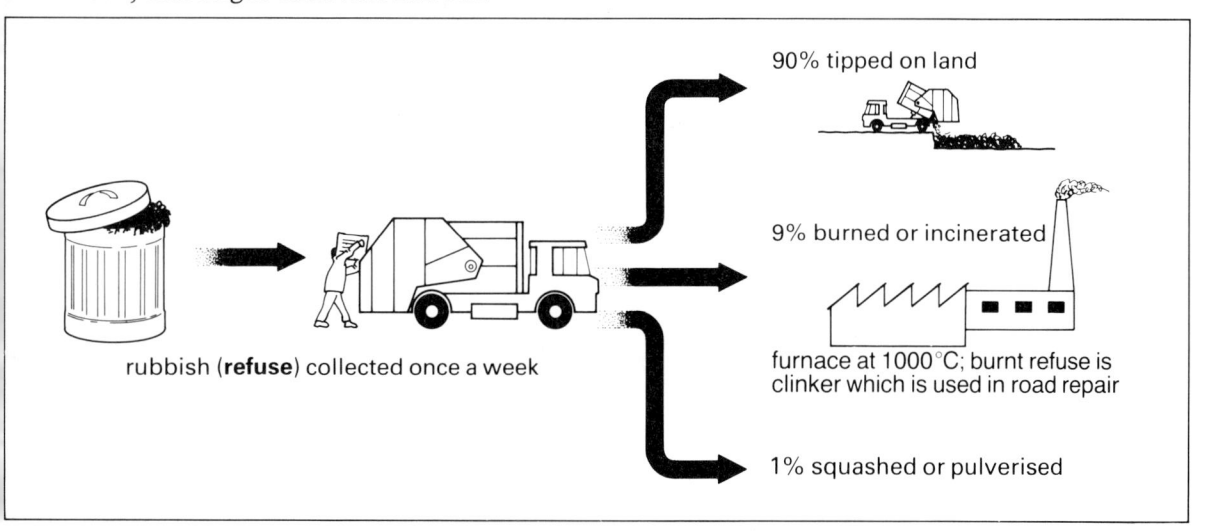

rubbish (**refuse**) collected once a week

- 90% tipped on land
- 9% burned or incinerated
  furnace at 1000°C; burnt refuse is clinker which is used in road repair
- 1% squashed or pulverised

Fig. 95.3 Disposing of rubbish.

Summary: Cleaning food and water

* Microbes can enter the body in the food we eat and cause food poisoning.
* Food must be stored, prepared and cooked in a hygienic way.
* Food can be preserved so it can be transported long distances or eaten out of season.
* Food can be processed to improve its taste or change its appearance.
* Chemicals may be added to food.
* The Public Analyst checks food additives.
* Microbes can enter the body in drinking water.
* Water is purified at the water works.
* Waste water (sewage) is treated at a sewage works before it is sent back to rivers.
* Many materials are cycled naturally.
* Household rubbish is collected and may be tipped, burned or turned into fuel.
* Some rubbish is being recycled to conserve supplies of natural materials that may run out.

15 Homes

96 House construction

Houses and flats are not just buildings, they are places where people live. They should be designed to give **shelter** and **comfort** to those living inside. Each person should have enough **space**. **Over-crowding** is unpleasant and allows disease to spread more easily. Homes must not be places where pests (or vectors) can flourish. When houses are built or **constructed** there are many other features included to make them safe.

Building materials

Natural, local materials such as stone, wood and clay were used in the past. In some tropical countries, bamboo and palm leaves can give enough protection from the weather (Fig. 96.1). Today local materials are in short supply so man-made products are used. Man learnt how to make **bricks** from clay about 6000 years ago. They are still one of the most widely used building materials (Fig. 96.2.). Bricks are held together by **mortar**. Other man-made materials that are used include **concrete**, **steel** and **glass**. Wood is still needed for roof supports, doors and window frames.

Site

Choosing the right place or **site** to build a house is important. Damp soft ground can only be used if the house can be raised above it in some way (Fig. 96.1).

Fig. 96.1 A house in Malaysia built from local materials. It is raised off the wet surface by pillars which are sunk into firm ground underneath.

Fig. 96.2 A house being built from bricks.

Foundations

Before a house is built **foundations** are laid. These form a firm layer in the ground and support the weight of the building. Foundations are usually made from broken rocks and stones covered with a thick layer of **concrete**.

15 Homes

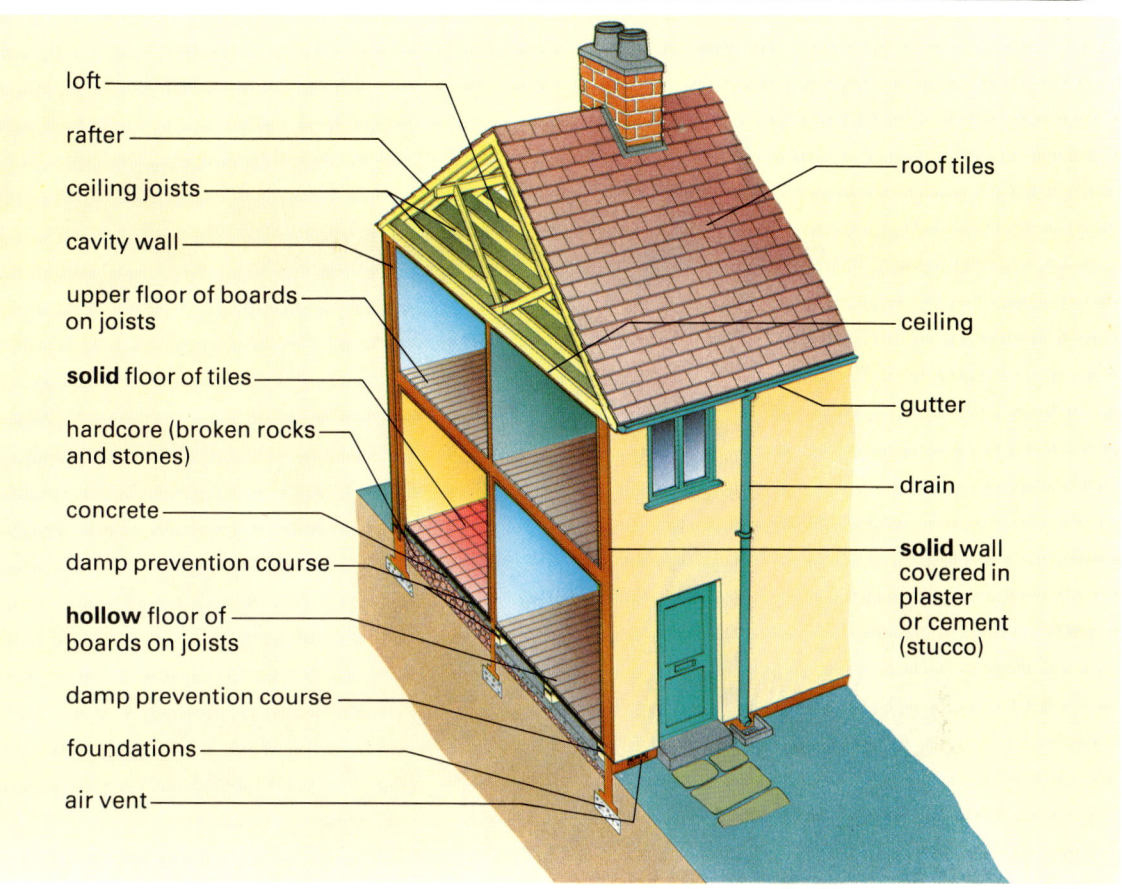

Fig. 96.3 The parts of a house.

Walls

There are two main types of outside wall in houses, **solid** and **cavity**. Solid walls are good **insulators,** stopping heat loss in cold weather and over-heating in warm weather. Solid walls also keep out the rain. To do these two jobs they must be more than 35 cm thick. The cavity wall was developed around 1918 (Fig. 96.3). It is made from two layers of bricks five centimetres apart. The layers are held together by metal wall ties. This space breaks the path through which moisture can travel. This means the 'inside' wall of bricks is always dry. The air space is also a good insulator.

Water can travel up bricks and other materials that are in contact with damp ground. A **damp prevention course** (**DPC**) is laid between bricks and timbers 15 cm above ground level. In modern buildings the DPC is polythene sheeting (Fig. 96.3).

Floors

Thick beams of wood or **joists** are fixed into the walls. Floor-boards are then nailed across these to make safe floors.

Roof

A roof has to keep out rain and perhaps snow as well. A leaky roof can cause a lot of damage. Water must flow off a roof, so it is sloped; even a flat roof has a slight slope or **pitch**. The roof is supported by strong joists and is covered with roof **tiles**. A pitched roof has a large air space, the **loft**, under it. This is an insulator and often contains the water tanks.

Rainwater flowing from a roof must not run down the walls. **Gutters** catch the water which is led away through drain-pipes.

177

15 Homes

97 Building and health

The dangers of damp

Without a damp prevention course and cavity walls, water may soak through building materials. This will make the building damp, uncomfortable and possibly dangerous. When houses are damp, microbes start to feed on the materials making them rot.

If wood gets damp and is not open to the air, a fungus may start to grow in the wood. This causes the wood to crumble. The fungus is **dry rot** which is hard to treat. If wood gets soaked, it may be damaged by **wet rot** (Fig. 97.1). The damaged parts must be removed and replaced. Rotten wood is very weak. This could lead to the collapse of floors and ceilings. If the walls of a house become damp, the wallpaper and plaster may fall off.

Damp walls can be treated to prevent further damage. Drainage pipes can be drilled into the wall at a low level so that rising water flows out. Or a rubbery, waterproof liquid can be squirted into the brickwork and allowed to set. This then stops water rising.

Fig. 97.1 Wet rot in a window frame.

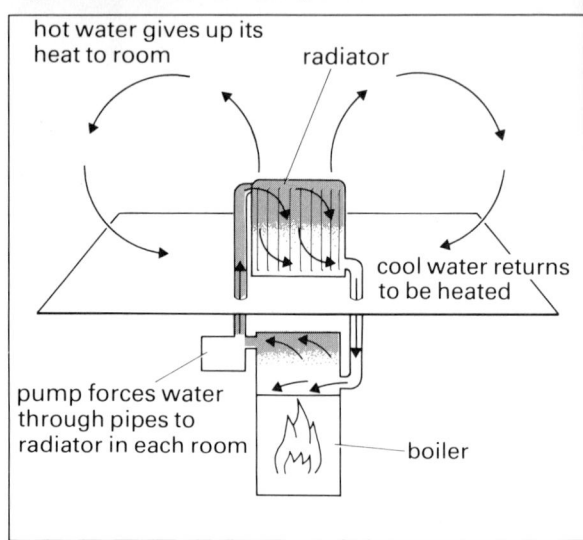

Fig. 97.2 How a central heating system works.

Heating

In cold weather a good heating system is needed to keep people warm. The right room temperature depends on how the room is used. Living rooms should be about 20–22 °C. Bedrooms should be a few degrees cooler.

Ways of heating

Fires of wood and coal were burnt in fireplaces until recently. These produce smoke. Now coal fires in rooms must use solid, **smokeless** fuels like **anthracite**. These **open fires** are not only dirty, they are a source of accidents and should be protected by fire-guards.

Gas fires are clean. When gas burns it produces some **water vapour**. This means the air is not dried.

Electric fires are very clean. A **radiant** heater uses electricity to make wire glow red hot. A shiny surface behind the glowing wire 'throws' heat out into the room. A **convector** heater warms air and helps move it round the room. Electric heating dries the air. Dry air may make people cough. This can be prevented by leaving a dish of water in the room. The water **evaporates** and moistens the air.

Central heating uses gas, oil or solid fuel to heat water in a boiler. The hot water flows through pipes to **radiators** in each room (Fig. 97.2). The radiators 'throw out' heat and warm the air flowing past them.

The fuel we use depends partly on the cost. Electricity is expensive as other fuels are used to produce it. Underground supplies of gas, oil and coal are running out. This will make all fuels more expensive in the future. New ways of heating homes will have to be found.

15 Homes

Heat insulation

Heating a house costs a lot of money. The heat will not be lost if the house is properly **insulated**. The air spaces in the loft and cavity walls help stop heat loss. Even so, in cold weather much of the heat can be lost (Fig. 97.3). Blocking the gap under a door with a **draught-excluder** will help. Other methods of insulating a house are shown in Fig. 97.4.

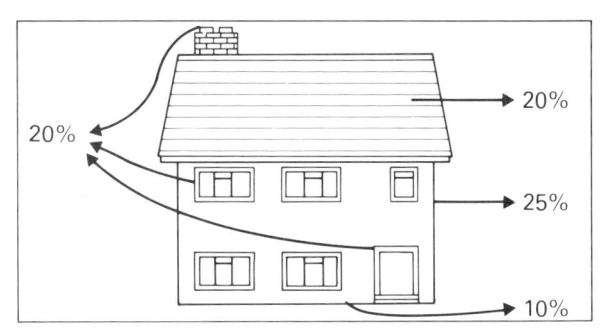

Fig. 97.3 The amount of heat lost from different parts of a house.

Heat loss from the windows can be reduced by fitting two layers of glass with a small air-gap between the layers. This is **double-glazing**.

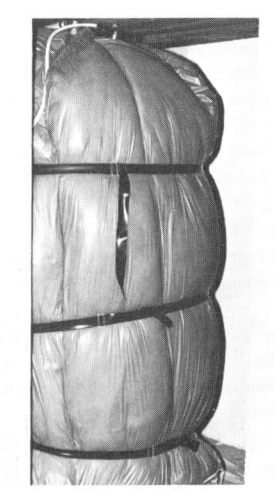

Hot water tanks and pipes can be wrapped to **conserve** (save) heat. This is called **lagging**.

Cavity-wall insulation stops heat escaping through walls. Here foam is being injected into the space between the 2 layers of bricks.

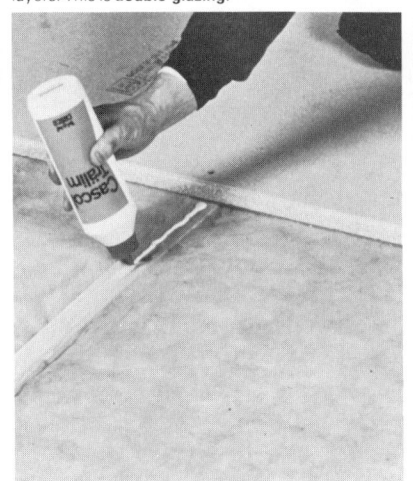

New houses can have **under-floor insulation**. This is a layer of polystyrene foam covered by chipboard.

A carpet with good **underlay** beneath it will also cut down heat loss through the floor.

Different materials can be used to stop heat loss through roofs. Here glass fibre is being laid. Small pieces of polystyrene foam can be used instead.

Fig. 97.4 Ways of insulating houses to cut down heat loss.

15 Homes

Needing fresh air

People in rooms need a steady supply of fresh air. Breathing uses up oxygen from the air and makes the amount of carbon dioxide in the air go up. If the amount of carbon dioxide in a room gets too high, people will start to yawn and feel sleepy. The room will be stuffy. The stale air must be replaced by fresh air. Stale air may also carry fumes like cigarette smoke or cooking smells that can be unpleasant. **Ventilation** means replacing stale air with fresh air. Rooms should be properly ventilated at all times even when people are asleep. A person at rest needs about 480 litres of fresh air every hour. More air must enter a small room containing several people than a large room with the same number.

Ways of ventilating a room

Houses are ventilated by openings in doors, windows and chimneys. Air in a room is heated by the people in it as well as the heating system. Warm, stale air is 'lighter' than cooler fresh air. The warm air rises to the top of the room. It flows out through the upper part of open windows and the top of the door. Cooler air from outside flows in to replace the warm, stale air. Air flows in through the lower parts of the door or windows (Fig. 97.5). Heating systems help **circulate** (move round) the air more quickly. An open fire causes rapid ventilation. The hot air moves up the chimney and so cool air is drawn into the room. In winter this may cause unpleasant, cold **draughts** across the floor. These can be cut down by fitting a draught-excluder on the bottom of the door (Fig. 97.6). **Extractor fans** can be used in rooms where many fumes are produced. An extractor fan in a kitchen will remove cooking smells quickly.

Air-conditioning

Air-conditioning means making an artificial climate inside a room or building. It is used in offices, shops, restaurants, theatres and cinemas. (In some warm countries it is used in people's homes.) Heat from lights, large numbers of people and sunshine through large windows can make the air uncomfortably warm.

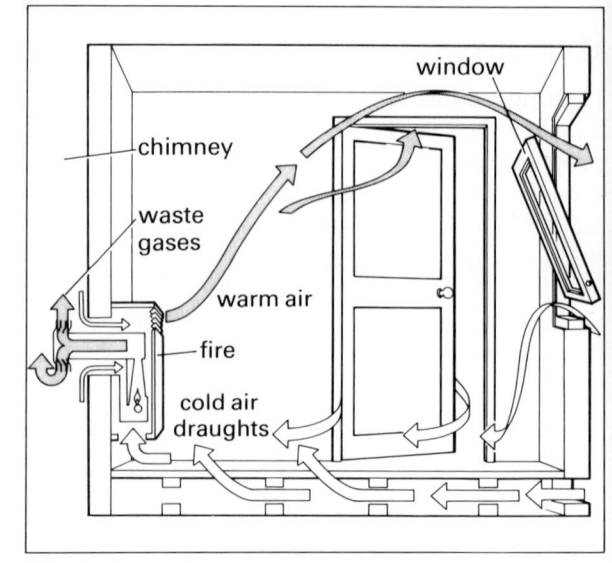

Fig. 97.5 Ventilation in a room with a gas fire.

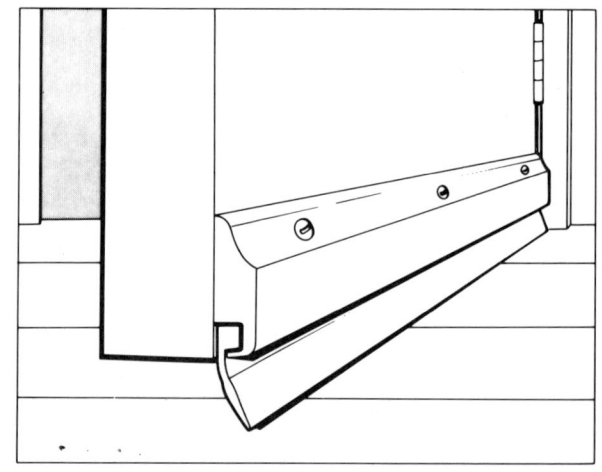

Fig. 97.6 A draught-excluder.

So air-conditioning usually supplies fresh, cool air.

In hospitals, air-conditioning is needed in operating theatres. Here the air must be sterile so patients having operations are less likely to become infected.

Lighting

For our health and comfort, the rooms where we live and work must be properly lit. Enough light is needed to let people see what they are doing and prevent **eye strain**.

15 Homes

Types of lighting

Natural light from the sun is powerful and free. To make the best use of natural light, each room must have windows of a suitable size. Building rules make sure that there is enough window area for the size of the room.

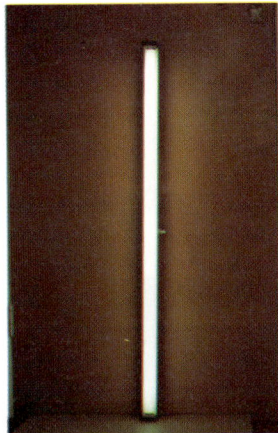

Artificial lighting is needed in dull weather and at night. Today most artificial lighting is provided by electric light bulbs or fluorescent tubes (Fig. 97.7). In towns, artificial lighting is also used to make night driving less dangerous and for advertising (Fig. 97.8). Light shades or a piece of shiny material (**reflector**) placed behind the light source will produce an even light which will spread to the dark corners of a room.

In some parts of the house, special lighting may be needed. Dark places, such as corners on the stairs, and back doors where there are steps, should be lit so people can see where to walk. The bathroom should have a cord switch fitted for safety.

Fig. 97.7 Two types of electric lighting – a filament bulb on the left and a fluorescent tube on the right.

Fig. 97.8 Electric lighting can be used in many ways. This is Piccadilly Circus in London.

Summary: Homes

* Homes give us shelter and comfort.
* They must be safe.
* Homes are built with natural and man-made materials.
* House foundations must be strong.
* Walls and floors must be protected against damp.
* Homes can be heated in several ways.
* Heat is expensive, so homes are insulated to prevent heat loss.
* Fresh air must be circulated so that carbon dioxide is not allowed to build up.
* Houses must be properly lit.

16 Using drugs

98 Drugs

Alcohol, penicillin, tea and diet pills can all be looked on as **drugs**. A drug is anything which affects the way the body works. Scientists look on a drug as a chemical which:
1 people can take to do their body good,
2 can change anyone's state of mind or mood,
3 can sometimes make the taker depend on it to cope with life.

Some drugs are made by plants, whose parts are collected. The chemicals from them are then purified by humans. The resin from poppies can be changed into **morphine**. Other drugs are made in laboratories or chemical factories.

Drugs in the body

There are different ways of getting drugs into the body. The two ways that are used are 'by mouth' and 'by injection' (Fig. 98.1). The time it takes for a drug to work depends on the amount of drug taken and the way it is put into the body. A large amount will produce a quicker and longer lasting effect than a small one. A drug that is injected will show its effect quickly as it is put straight into the blood. One that is swallowed may not produce its effect for half an hour or more as it has to pass through the wall of the gut before getting into the blood.

Most drugs are known as **medicines**. They are **prescribed** or given to us by doctors to cure diseases (Fig. 98.2). Some can be bought from

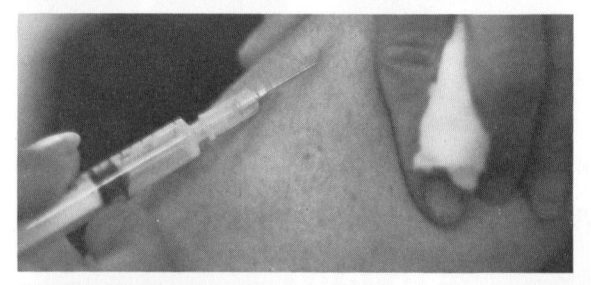

Fig. 98.1 A person receiving an injection of a drug.

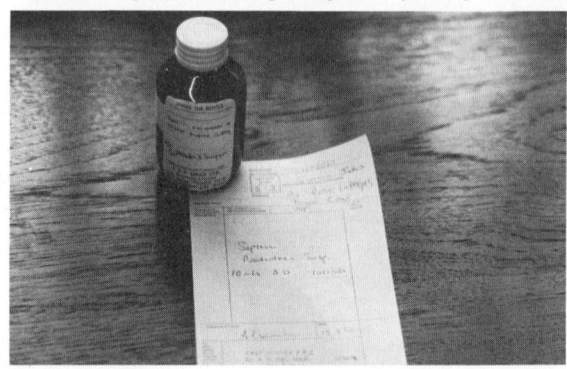

Fig. 98.2 A doctor's prescription and the medicine prescribed. The label on the bottle must show how much and how often the medicine should be taken.

the chemist. For instance, if you have a cold, you may take **aspirin**. This drug lowers fever if the normal dose of two tablets every four hours is taken by an adult. If much more is taken often it may cause bleeding in the stomach. No drug is completely harmless so it is important to take the right dose and follow all instructions carefully. Children usually need much lower doses of drugs than adults.

16 Using drugs

Drug safety

Some drugs that are used by adults are harmful to young children. Today, many drug packets have child-proof tops so that children do not eat tablets or pills accidentally.

The amount of drugs prescribed in one year in England is enormous (Fig. 98.3). Many drugs affect the nervous system. They change a person's mood in some way. Nowadays many people use drugs in ways not intended by doctors. This is **drug abuse**. Some of the drugs which are used incorrectly are shown in Fig. 98.4. The more often a drug is taken, the more the body gets used to it. So, the next time the drug is 'needed', the more someone will have to take to produce the same effect. The body is becoming **tolerant** to the drug. Many people come to rely on drugs to get through their daily lives. They come to depend on the drug and are said to be **addicted**. It is then extremely hard for them to stop taking the drug. As more and more of the drug is taken, the addict's body and way of life are seriously harmed.

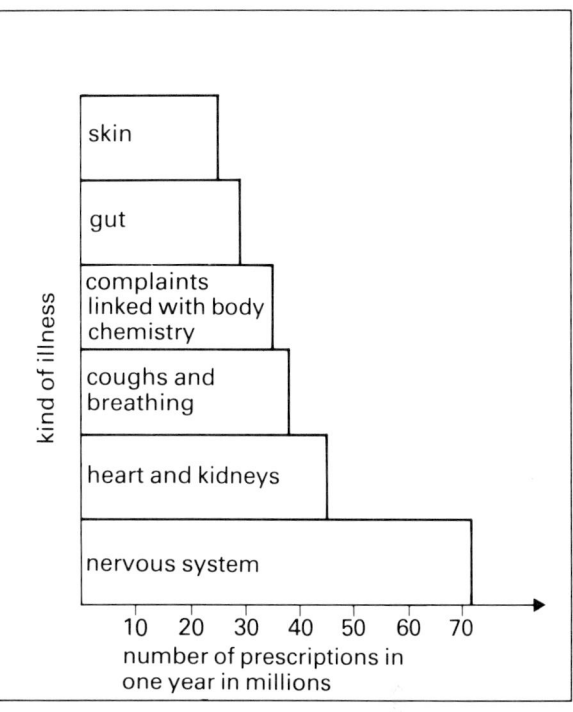

Fig. 98.3 The number of prescriptions given for some diseases during one year.

Drug groups	Other names	Appearance of drug	How it is usually taken	Effect on the body
Opiates opium		reddish gum (resin)	smoked	**narcotic** – they kill pain; also called **analgesics**
morphine	M	white powder	dissolved in water and injected	
heroin	H, horse	white powder or tablets	dissolved in water and injected	
Cocaine	C, coke, snow, Charlie	white powder	sniffed	
Cannabis marijuana	pot, weed, grass	dried leaves and flowers of cannabis plant	smoked	gives a feeling of happiness
hashish	pot, hash	sticky lumps of gum from cannabis plant	smoked or eaten	
Amphetamines benzedrine dexedrine methedrine many others	benny dex meths, speed uppers, minstrels, black bombers	pills of different shapes, sizes and colour	swallowed	'pep' pills – they relieve depression
Barbiturates librium valium phenobarbitone	purple hearts, French blues, sleepers goofballs, downers	pills of different sizes, shapes and colour	swallowed, sometimes dissolved in water and injected	sedatives – sleeping pills, they also relieve depression
LSD	acid, purple haze	colourless liquid or powder	injected or swallowed	**hallucinogen** – affects the mind

Fig. 98.4 Some drugs and their effects on the body.

16 Using drugs

99 Smoking and drinking

There are many drugs which some people take every day. **Caffeine** in coffee and alcohol in drinks are examples. In small doses they may be harmless but large doses over a long period of time can be dangerous. Smoking **cigarettes** can affect health.

Cause of death	Number of times a smoker is more likely to die of the disease than a non-smoker
lung cancer	×11
bronchitis and emphysema	×6
cancer of the voice box	×5
disease of heart arteries	×1·5

Fig. 99.1 Smoking and the risk of death.

Cigarettes

Cigarettes are made from dried, shredded leaves of the tobacco plant. The habit of inhaling tobacco smoke for pleasure started hundreds of years ago, probably in South America. The smoke contains dozens of chemicals. The main drug in cigarette smoke is **nicotine**. It is likely to be addictive making it hard for a smoker to give up the habit. Nicotine may stop the cleaning cells of the breathing tubes from working. Nicotine also enters the blood through the lungs and affects the nervous system. The **tar** in smoke collects deep in the lungs staining them brown. Tar irritates and damages the breathing tubes. It may lead to serious illnesses. **Carbon monoxide** in the smoke joins on to haemoglobin in the red blood cells. It stops them from carrying oxygen. So a smoker may have to breathe faster and this may strain the heart.

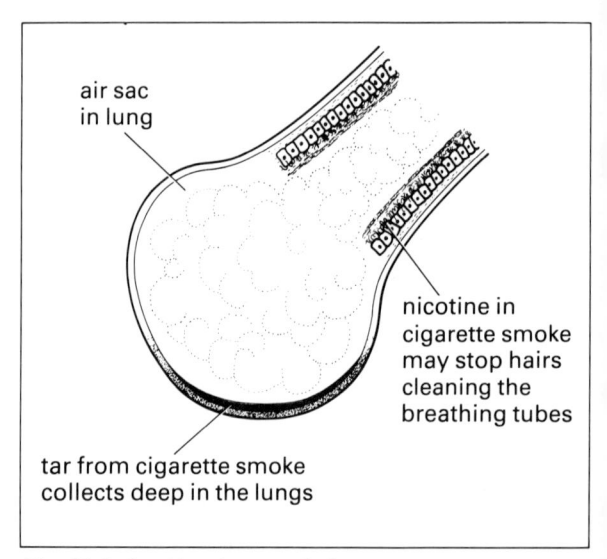

Fig. 99.2 Smoking damages the lungs.

Illnesses linked to smoking

Smokers may get short of breath easily. They are more likely to have gum disease than non-smokers. Many very serious illnesses are known to be linked to smoking. There is definite evidence that people who smoke die, on average, at younger ages than non-smokers. For instance a man of 25 who smokes 40 cigarettes a day can expect to live 8·3 years less than a 25-year old who does not (Fig. 99.1).

Bronchitis

When dust or smoke particles enter the breathing passages, they are trapped in mucus. The dirty mucus is swept towards the mouth for swallowing. If the tiny hairs stop working, maybe because they are numbed by nicotine, the mucus may build up. A person coughs to remove it. As more mucus collects, the person will have to cough more violently and the tubes may become 'inflamed'. This is **bronchitis**. The coughing can strain the heart (Fig. 99.2).

16 Using drugs

Emphysema

Smoking damages the delicate air sacs in the lungs. They work less well and so the person must breathe faster and will cough. Sometimes the air sacs burst. This means there will be less surface area in the lungs for gas exchange. This illness is **emphysema**.

Lung cancer

Lung cancer, like other cancers, starts with a single cell. Just why a cell becomes cancerous is not known. It is known that some of the chemicals in smoke do cause it. The single cell multiplies until it forms a lump called a cancer **tumour**. This affects the way the lung works. Cells may break off and spread the cancer to other parts of the body.

Alcohol

People first learnt how to make alcoholic drinks thousands of years ago. The type of alcohol in wine, beer and spirits is **ethanol**. It is a drug which is absorbed through the stomach. Alcohol can affect the nervous system. Small quantities work as a **stimulant** but larger amounts are a **sedative**. Alcohol changes a person's view of the world (Fig. 99.3); distances are judged wrongly; reactions are slowed; walking and standing become difficult; eventually the person falls asleep. As with many drugs, people can become dependent on alcohol. These people are called **alcoholics**. An alcoholic may suffer from deficiency diseases. The alcohol can be used as a food in the body but does not provide vitamins and minerals. The liver is seriously affected by large amounts of alcohol. This is **cirrhosis** of the liver. The behaviour of an alcoholic damages their own life and those of others, particularly their family (Fig. 99.4).

Fig. 99.3 A person under the influence of alcohol has slower reactions than normal. He is a danger to himself and others especially near traffic.

Fig. 99.4 An alcoholic.

Summary: Using drugs

* Drugs are chemicals that change the way the body works.
* Drugs are put into the body by swallowing them or by injection.
* Most drugs are prescribed by doctors.
* Dose instructions must be followed as all drugs involve a risk.
* The body can become tolerant to some drugs so that large doses are needed to produce the same effect.
* Some people become addicted to drugs.
* Cigarette smoke contains the drug nicotine.
* Coffee contains the drug caffeine.
* Alcoholic drinks, like whisky, wine and beer, contain the drug ethanol.

17 Pollution

100 Air pollution

Damaging our surroundings

Primitive man, living in small groups, did little damage to his surroundings. Sewage decayed naturally and only small amounts of smoke were made. When the population grew men started to live in towns and cities. In Britain the industrial revolution started around 1750. Machines were invented to produce goods more quickly. Engines were developed to drive the machines. Factories were built to house the growing industries. Man-made chemicals were used more and more. Today most countries have industrialised regions. Factories and towns produce large amounts of waste. When natural processes cannot deal with the wastes, the surroundings will be damaged. This is **pollution**.

Fig. 100.1 A British industrial town in the eighteenth century.

Burning fossil fuels

Today the burning of **fossil fuels** (coal, oil and natural gas) is the greatest cause of air pollution. Burning coal produces particles of many different sizes. Large particles make up dust and the smaller ones make smoke. The dust made our towns filthy and dark (Figs 100.1 and 100.2). The dust harmed vegetation that it settled on. The smoke irritated people's eyes and breathing tubes.

A Clean Air Act was passed in Britain in 1956. The use of coal for heating our homes was banned in areas known as **smokeless zones**. The amount of smoke in the air has dropped. Even so, burning smokeless coal, gas or oil does release dangerous chemicals into the air. Factories are particularly likely to cause **air pollution**.

Fig. 100.2 Many important buildings are now being cleaned to remove years of dirt.

17 Pollution

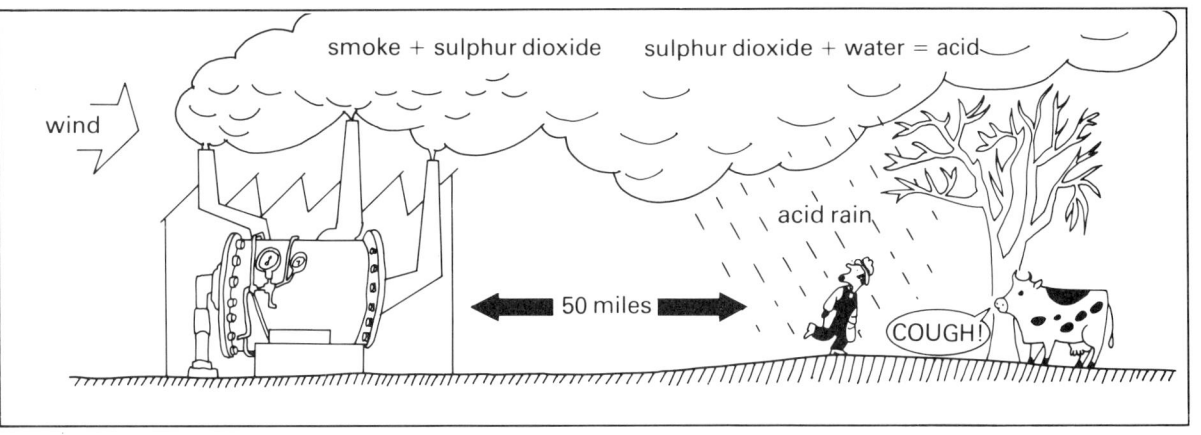

Fig. 100.3 Sulphur dioxide can be carried a long way by wind and rain.

Sulphur dioxide

Burning fuels produces **sulphur dioxide**. This gas dissolves in rainwater and may be carried away from the place it was made (Fig. 100.3). Experiments have shown that in very small amounts, it does not harm plants. Larger amounts will slow plant growth (Fig. 100.4). Some plants are easily damaged by sulphur dioxide; they are **susceptible**. These can be used to **indicate** or show if air is polluted. The best known indicators are **lichens** (Fig. 100.5).

Sulphur dioxide is an **acidic** gas. When the gas is breathed in, it may cause a runny nose. The breathing tubes and air sacs in the lungs are damaged by the acid. This makes lung diseases more likely.

Sulphur dioxide also damages building materials. Rainwater containing sulphur dioxide will gradually dissolve some types of bricks, rocks and metals used in buildings.

Carbon monoxide

Fuels also produce **carbon monoxide** gas when they burn. This gas combines with haemoglobin in the human red blood cells. The cells no longer carry oxygen and must be replaced by new cells. If there is a lot of carbon monoxide in the air people have to breathe faster to get enough oxygen.

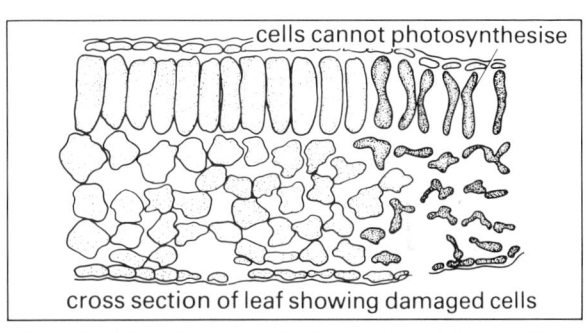

Fig. 100.4 How leaves may be damaged by sulphur dioxide.

Fig. 100.5 A lichen growing on tree bark.

Other industrial pollutants

Some industries produce other dangerous chemicals that pollute the air. These **pollutants** include coal dust down a coal mine. Miners are likely to suffer from a lung disease called **pneumoconiosis**, unless they wear masks. Dust from asbestos causes **asbestosis**. Workers in an asbestos factory must wear masks and the air leaving through its chimneys must be filtered.

17 Pollution

101 Cars and air pollution

Petrol and diesel engines are blamed for much air pollution. Lorries are often seen belching smoke from their exhausts. These fumes contain **carbon monoxide**, **oxides of nitrogen**, **ozone**, unburned **hydrocarbons** and **lead**. The level of carbon monoxide in busy streets has caused much concern. In Tokyo, Japanese policemen are issued with oxygen masks on traffic duty (Fig. 101.1).

Fig. 101.1 Japanese police wearing oxygen masks when working near cars.

Lead

Tetraethyl lead is added to petrol so that car engines will run smoothly. The lead is passed out of the engine in the exhaust. Vegetation growing near roads may contain so much lead that it cannot be eaten by animals or humans. There is great concern for the health of children who live near motorways. Their blood has been found to have high levels of lead and this may interfere with the development of their brains. Other less dangerous chemicals can be added to petrol. Unfortunately it means using specially altered car engines. Lead-free petrol is on sale in the United Kingdom but it is more expensive (Fig. 101.2).

Fig. 101.2 This car has an engine designed to run on unleaded petrol.

Smog

The oxides of nitrogen may cause damage in special circumstances. Sometimes air pollutants are not spread through the air but are trapped near the ground. In bright sunshine, the oxides are changed into chemicals which will damage crops and irritate human eyes. These **photochemical smogs** occur wherever there is bright sunlight, exhaust fumes and temperature changes in the atmosphere. They are common in California (Fig. 101.3).

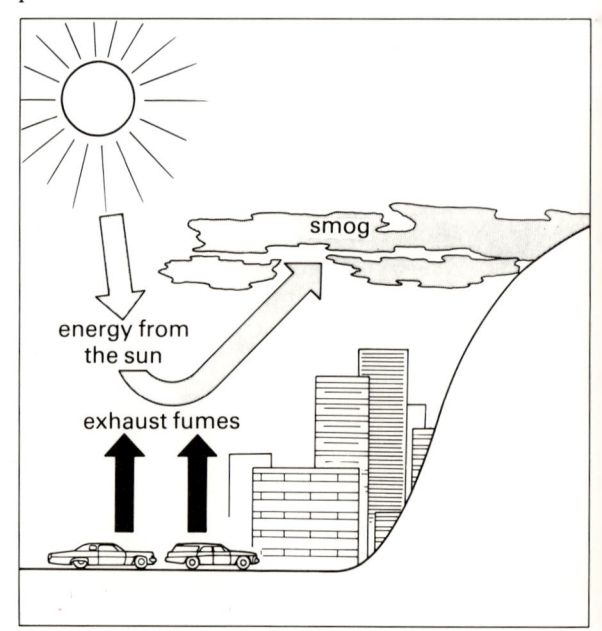

Fig. 101.3 How photochemical smog is produced.

17 Pollution

102 Noise

Noise is unwanted or unpleasant sound. Year by year the noise level in towns and cities goes up. Much noise is produced by road traffic and planes. Factories may be extremely noisy.

People who work in factories may have to listen to noise for more than 8 hours each day. Jobs which need a lot of concentration and thought are most affected by noise. Some tests have been carried out on workers in postal sorting rooms. When the noise was increased, the amount of work done dropped. The workers made four times as many mistakes when it was noisy compared to when it was quiet. Many factories try to make their workers wear **ear protection** (see page 86, Fig. 45.1).

Measuring noise

Noise is measured in units called **decibels** (**dB**). In some cities there are **sound meters** that measure traffic noise (Fig. 102.2). The meters are used near airports to check on the noise made by aircraft as they take off and land. To cut out some of the noise of aircraft and traffic, houses or rooms can be **sound-proofed** (Fig. 102.3).

Fig. 102.2 A sound meter.

Fig. 102.3 A sound-proof room in which car noise levels are being tested.

Fig. 102.1 The noise levels at a pop concert are often high enough to cause damage to the nerve cells in the inner ear.

17 Pollution

103 Water pollution

Healthy water

Rainwater is not pure. It contains dissolved **carbon dioxide** from the air. The streams and lakes in mountains are clear. As the water flows, it picks up substances from the soil and rocks. The water in lowland areas contains enough dissolved nutrients. It provides a healthy and balanced place for plants and animals to live.

Upsetting the balance

Many farm animals are kept in sheds. They make a lot of waste; in one day a cow produces as much waste as ten men. There may not be enough land on which to spread the manure, so the waste goes into the river.

Farmers use **fertilisers** to make their crops grow better. Most fertilisers contain **nitrogen**. Some of this fertiliser may drain into rivers and streams (Fig. 103.1). The level of nitrogen in the water goes up. Plants will grow better but their growth will upset the balance. The community of plants and animals will be damaged. The water is polluted by these waste chemicals.

Water containing a lot of nitrogen could be used in water supplies and be drunk by humans. This does little damage to adults, but it could damage the haemoglobin in the blood of babies.

A lot of waste is pumped into rivers from towns and factories. Some animals and plants survive in polluted water; many do not. The animals present can indicate if water is polluted (Fig. 103.2).

Oxygen in water

Oxygen in the water is needed to break down the waste. If a lot of waste is present a great deal of oxygen is used up in its decay. Less oxygen will be available for the animals and plants. A healthy river should not use up more than half of its oxygen to break down waste. The **Biological Oxygen Demand** (**B.O.D.**) is a way of measuring the level of water pollution.

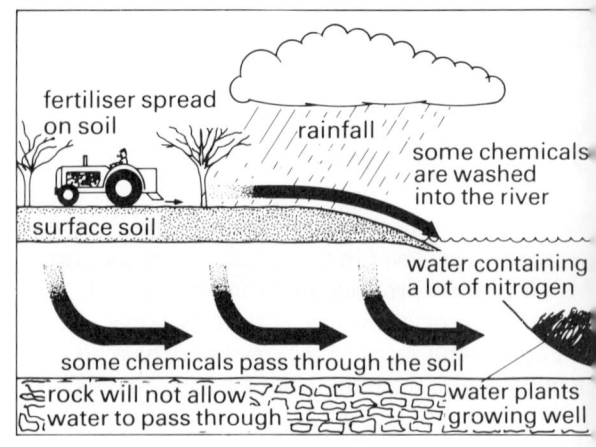

Fig. 103.1 Fertilisers and other chemicals are washed into rivers by rainwater.

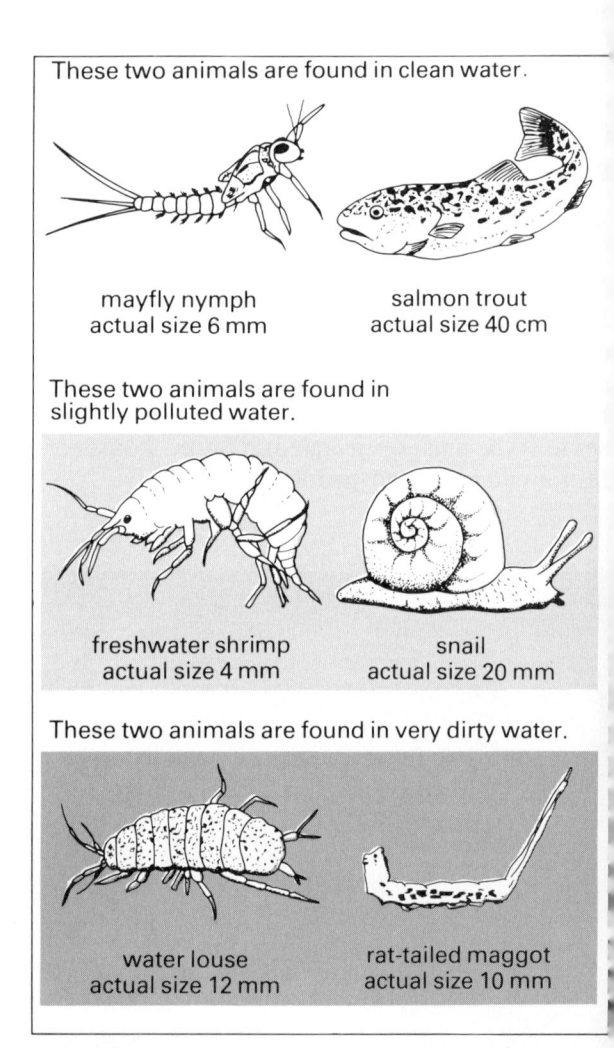

Fig. 103.2 These are indicator animals in fresh water. The presence of these animals indicates if water is clean or polluted.

17 Pollution

Heat can pollute water

If the temperature of water goes up, the amount of oxygen dissolved in the water will go down (Fig. 103.3). There will be less oxygen available for animals and plants. Fish cannot control their body temperature. They seek water at a temperature that suits them. Most fish seek cool water. They cannot survive in water above 30 °C.

Many factories and industrial processes use water is taken in at 18 °C and is pumped out at can be hot. Cooling towers of power stations use thousands of litres of water a day (Fig. 103.4). Measurements at one power station showed that water is taken in at 18 °C and is pumped out at 27 °C. Heat pollution in some rivers in America has prevented salmon and trout from living in them.

At 5°C, 1 litre of water contains 9 cm^3 oxygen.
At 20°C, 1 litre of water contains 6 cm^3 oxygen.

Fig. 103.3 The temperature of water affects how much oxygen it contains.

Fig. 103.4 Cooling towers at a power station.

Checking for pollution

Since 1974, ten **Regional Water Authorities** have been responsible for supplying clean water in Britain. They have made great progress by checking water samples regularly and controlling the dumping of waste in rivers and lakes (Fig. 103.5). For instance, in 1957 there were no fish in the River Thames because of pollution. Now the water is much cleaner and even salmon have been caught.

Oil pollution

Oil floats on water. The presence of oil in water is most obvious in the seas and oceans of the world. When oil tankers are wrecked, or if dirty oil is pumped out of a ship's engines, oil **slicks** are formed (Fig. 103.6). The oil can damage birds, other animals and plants in the sea. It also spoils beaches. **Detergents** may be used to break up oil slicks. But detergents, and the **phosphates** they contain, can also damage marine life.

Fig. 103.5 Scientists collecting river water to check for the level of pollution.

Fig. 103.6 This sea bird (a guillemot) cannot be saved even if someone cleans its feathers. The bird's gut has been damaged by swallowing oil while preening its feathers.

17 Pollution

104 Pest control

We use poisons to destroy pests on our crops. **Herbicides** are used to kill weeds; **fungicides** destroy fungi and **insecticides** kill insect pests. Spraying gardens or fields with these chemicals kills the pest. However the **pesticide** may fall on to other animals and plants and on to the soil.

DDT and food chains

DDT insecticide was developed in the 1930s. It was sprayed in buildings and on people to control fleas, lice and mosquitoes. These animals are parasites on humans. DDT was sprayed on crops to rid them of pests. DDT does not break down into other chemicals very quickly; it remains harmful for a long time. It has got into the soil and rivers. The chemical passed into plants. These plants were eaten by animals and so the chemical entered and stayed in their bodies. As more **contaminated** plants are eaten, the amount of DDT builds up in the animal's body. In this way the DDT passes along a food chain (Fig. 104.1). If DDT builds up in the bodies of humans and other animals, it can slowly poison them. Other pesticides, such as **dieldrin**, involve similar dangers. In Britain there is a **Pesticide Safety Precautions Scheme**. This means manufacturers have agreed not to sell any new pesticide until the Government has given permission.

Biological pest control

Now greater use is being made of **biological** methods of pest control. These use animals, plants, bacteria or viruses to kill pests. In America apple growers needed a way to get rid of a mite that damaged their apples. They introduced an insect, the **ladybird**, to the orchards. These beetles feed on the mites and so the pest was reduced in numbers (Fig. 104.2). Rabbits were a pest in Britain. Farmers killed them off by introducing the disease **myxomatosis**. Foxes and owls eat rabbits and so ran short of food. Foxes started raiding chicken farms instead!

Both chemical and biological methods of pest control have disadvantages. Whenever man upsets the balance of nature, there can be unexpected effects on the surroundings and other living organisms.

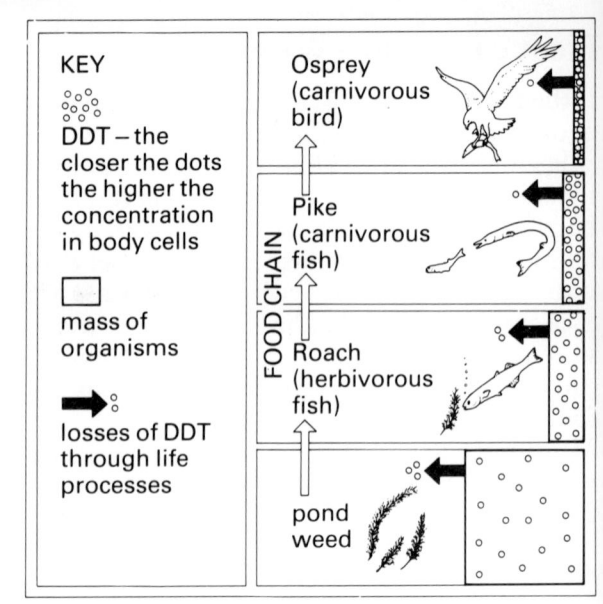

Fig. 104.1 How DDT builds up in animals' bodies as it passes along a food chain.

Fig. 104.2 A ladybird on an apple. These beetles eat the mite that damages apple crops.

17 Pollution

105 Radiation

Since the discovery of **X-rays** in 1895, man has begun to pollute the environment with more and more **radiation**. Energy in the form of rays is called radiation. It is invisible. X-rays are used to treat and diagnose disease. Some of the first people to operate X-ray machines developed skin cancer or blood diseases.

Nuclear power

The splitting of the atom led to the development of nuclear power stations (Fig. 105.1). There are strict safety precautions at these places. However, a massive explosion at Chernobyl nuclear power station in Russia in 1986 caused a leak of radiation. This formed a cloud which meant that some radiation fall-out travelled as far as Scotland and Wales. Power stations produce waste that gives off radiation. It is **radio-active**. Some is dumped at sea in concrete and lead containers, but the disposal of this waste can be a problem.

Damage by radiation

Background radiation is with us all the time. It comes from the Earth's materials, the sun and outer space. It is at a very low level. Very low doses of radiation do not damage adults. High doses cause different types of cancer and sometimes death. However a low dose may damage a baby growing inside its mother's womb – so pregnant women should not be X-rayed. High doses can cause **mutations** (see page 117). The radiation damages chromosomes and may cause unusual growth and development in future generations. This has been seen in Japan where two nuclear bombs were dropped in 1945 (Fig. 105.2).

Summary: Pollution

* Pollution occurs when human activities damage the surroundings.

Fig. 105.1 A nuclear power station.

Fig. 105.2 The explosion caused by a nuclear bomb.

* Air is polluted when fuels are burned.
* Air pollutants include smoke, carbon monoxide and sulphur dioxide.
* Petrol is burned in car engines. Exhaust fumes contain lead and oxides of nitrogen.
* Noise is unwanted sound. Too much noise affects our concentration.
* River water is polluted by animal and factory wastes.
* Water used by factories heats up the rivers on its return.
* Fertilisers spread on farm land may drain into rivers.
* Oil pollution occurs in sea water.
* Crop pests can be controlled by chemicals.
* The use of chemicals can upset the balance of nature.
* More use is being made of biological pest control.
* Radiation can pollute our environment and is dangerous as it is invisible and has long term effects.

18 First aid

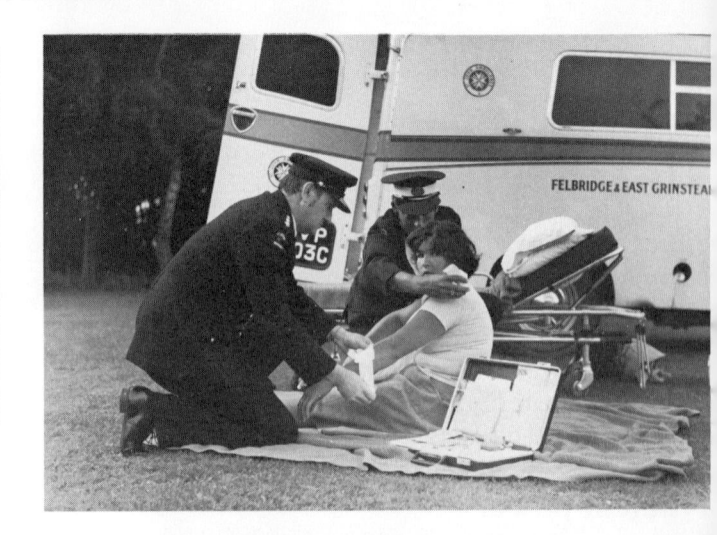

106 Accidents

Every year many people suffer from some sort of accident. We may hurt or **injure** our bodies. Most accidents are not serious; they cause bumps and bruises, small cuts or slight burns. Some accidents are more serious and may even lead to death. Accidents are more likely to happen in some places than others. In Britain during 1977, there were about 850 deaths and 500 000 injuries from accidents in industry and farming. During the same year, road accidents caused 6600 deaths and 341 000 injuries. Accidents in the home caused about 6200 deaths and over one million injuries! These figures show that most accidents happen in the home. Young children and old people are the most likely to suffer (Fig. 106.2).

Fig. 106.1 A car accident.

The home is where most accidents happen. The table shows the causes of death in home accidents in 1976.

Cause of death	Age group in years:					Total	Percentage of total
	0–4	5–14	15–44	45–64	65+		
Falls	40	15	103	332	3406	3896	**61**
Poisoning	17	14	276	230	173	710	**11**
Burns and scalds	83	49	86	141	460	819	**13**
Suffocation and choking	171	26	123	98	118	536	**8**
Other causes	61	18	84	84	199	446	**7**
Total	372	122	672	885	4356	6407	**100**
Percentage of total	**6**	**2**	**10**	**14**	**68**	**100**	

Fig. 106.2 Accidents in the home that led to deaths in Britain during 1976.

18 First aid

Preventing accidents

It is very important to know how to prevent accidents. There are many simple **safety precautions** that can be taken. These are important when young children and old people are in your home.

Falls

Stairs should be well lit and not too steep. Carpets and rugs should lie flat and be fixed to the floor.

Poisoning

Many common chemicals are poisonous if swallowed. Cleaning liquids, pesticides, petrol, paraffin and all medicines should be clearly labelled. They should be kept out of children's reach. Many plants such as wild berries and toadstools contain poisons and should not be eaten.

Burns

Guards must be used round open fires. Electrical wiring must be checked for safety. Children must not be able to reach hot pans on a cooker, hot electric irons or matches. Fireworks should be handled carefully by adults. Even too much sun can burn the skin.

Cuts

All knives and sharp objects must be handled carefully and kept out of children's reach. Broken glass is dangerous so windows and glass doors must be treated with care. Machinery should be fitted with safety guards. Lawn mower blades are sharp and could cause a bad cut.

Suffocation

A person will **suffocate** without air. Plastic bags over the face could kill. Children should not be allowed to play in cupboards or old refrigerators. If trapped inside they might suffocate.

Road accidents

Pedestrians should cross roads carefully and wear something light at night. All vehicles should be in good working order. People must never drive while under the influence of drugs such as ethanol in alcoholic drinks.

First aid

If an accident does happen it is useful to know how to help. The aid that is given is **first aid**.

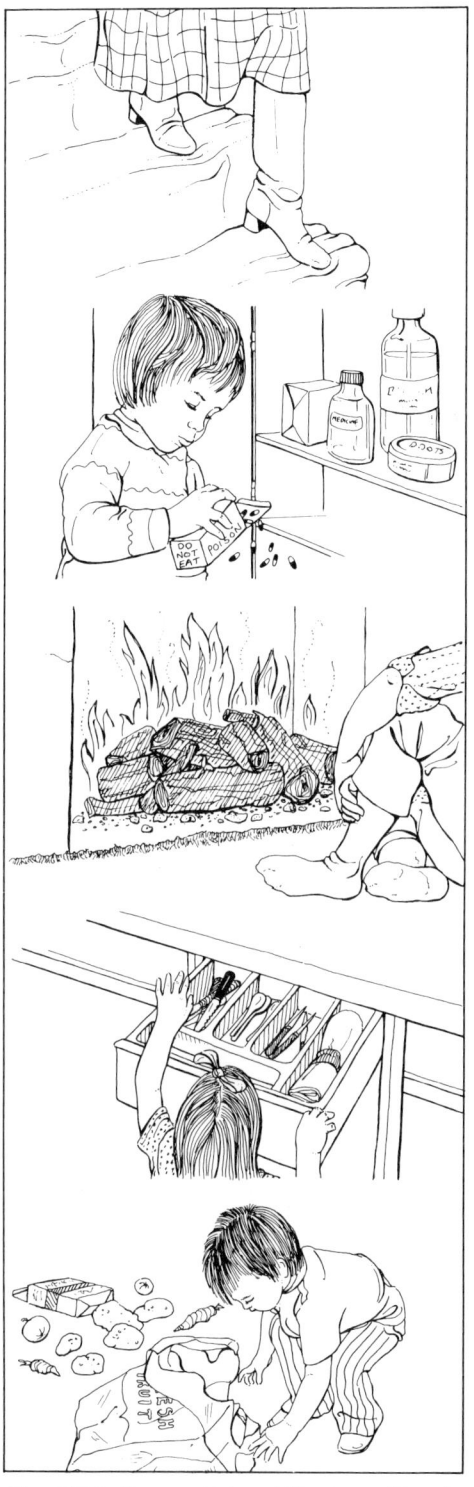

Fig. 106.3 Scenes which could lead to accidents in the home.

18 First aid

107 Helping others to breathe

Some accidents cause a person to stop breathing. This is called **asphyxia**. It may happen when someone drowns, has an electric shock or suffocates. It is important to get oxygen into the casualty's blood. More than four minutes without oxygen could cause serious brain damage. Ways of starting the breathing again are called **artificial resuscitation**. Two methods are shown.

The Holger-Nielson method

This method of resuscitation is suitable for a casualty whose face is injured. By moving the arms in the correct way, air is drawn into and forced out of the lungs. This method can be practised on someone who is breathing normally, **except for step C. You must not press down hard.**

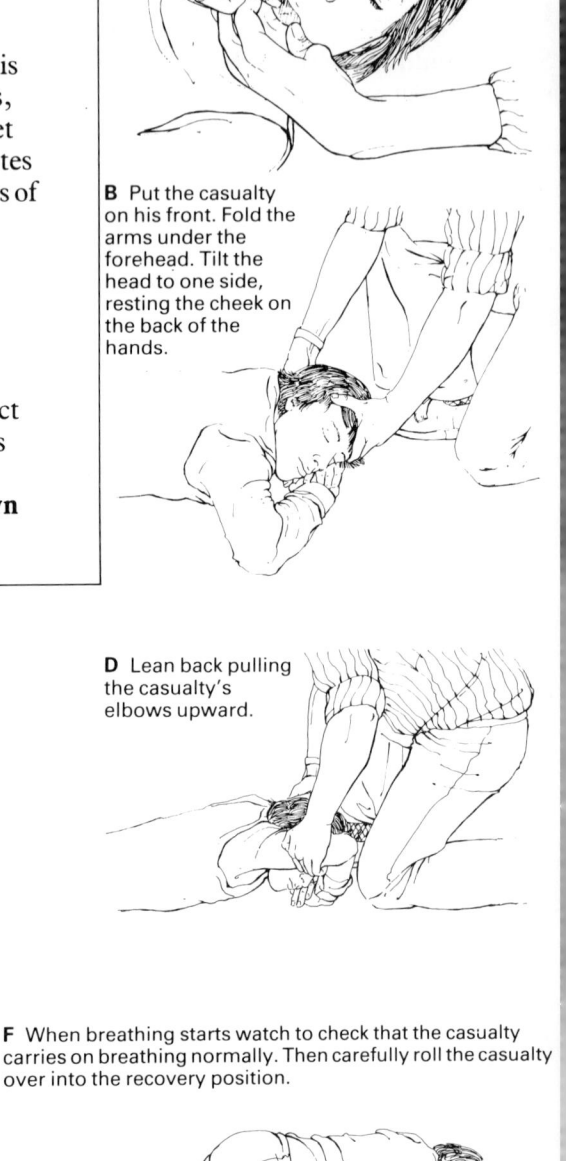

A Check the mouth for blockages. Take out false teeth etc. Loosen clothing.

B Put the casualty on his front. Fold the arms under the forehead. Tilt the head to one side, resting the cheek on the back of the hands.

C Kneel at the casualty's head. Put your palms on the shoulder blades. Rock forward so your weight pushes down on the chest.

D Lean back pulling the casualty's elbows upward.

E Lower the elbows and repeat steps G and H every 4 to 5 seconds.

F When breathing starts watch to check that the casualty carries on breathing normally. Then carefully roll the casualty over into the recovery position.

Fig. 107.1 The Holger-Nielson method of artificial resuscitation.

18 First aid

Mouth-to-mouth resuscitation

This method can be used if the face is not injured. Breathed out air is blown into the casualty's mouth or nose. The air contains oxygen. If you blow into the mouth, the casualty's nose must be held closed (pinched). If you blow into the nose, the casualty's mouth must be closed. In both ways it is important to tilt the head well back (Fig. 107.2) so that the tongue does not flop down over the casualty's windpipe.

This method can only be practised on a model. **It is very dangerous to try it on a person who is breathing normally.**

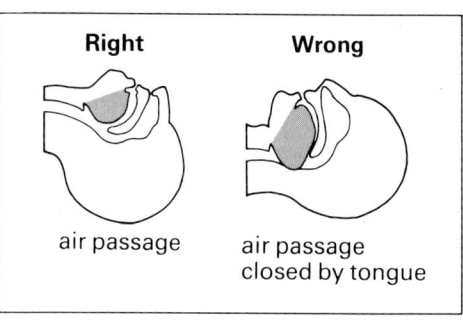

Fig. 107.2 Tilting the head correctly is important in mouth-to-mouth resuscitation.

A Check the mouth for blockages. Take out false teeth etc. Loosen clothing.

B Grip the lower jaw and forehead. Push the head backwards. Pinch the nostrils.

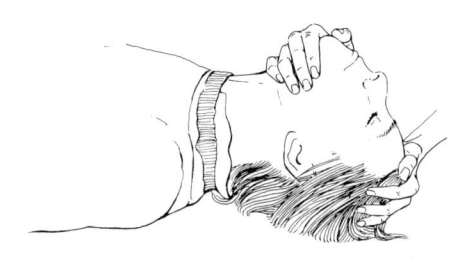

C Take a deep breath. Put your lips round the casualty's mouth and blow. The casualty's chest should rise.

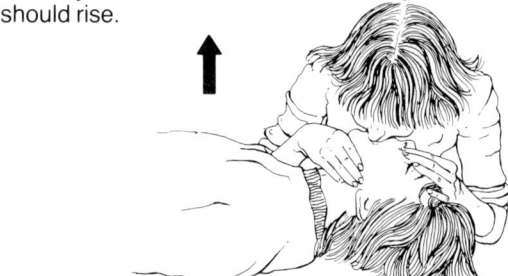

D Stop blowing. Watch for the casualty's chest to fall. Repeat the blowing at your normal rate of breathing.

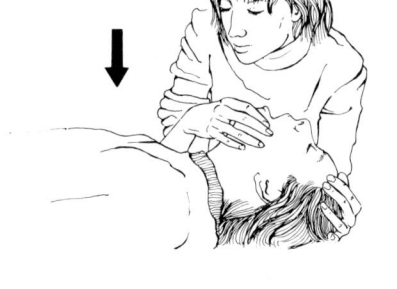

E When breathing has started, watch to check that breathing has become normal.

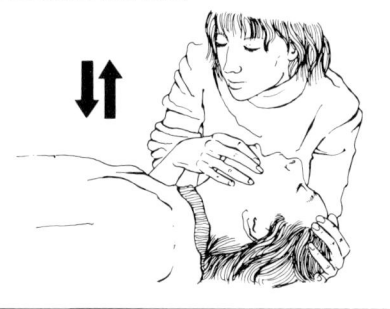

F Then carefully roll the casualty over into the recovery position.

Fig. 107.3 The mouth-to-mouth method of artificial resuscitation.

18 First aid

108 Bleeding

Minor cuts

Small cuts are not dangerous. If the skin is broken, microbes can enter, so small cuts can lead to infection. A minor cut should be washed thoroughly in clear, cold water. If the cut is dirty a mild **antiseptic** like iodine solution can be used. This should be dabbed on with **sterile** (absolutely clean) cotton wool. The bleeding normally stops quite quickly. A smooth pad covered with a sticking plaster or light bandage can be fixed over the wound. These coverings must be sterile.

Nose bleeds usually stop quickly if correctly treated (Fig. 108.1). A heavy nose bleed can make the **casualty** feel **faint**. This may be due to **shock** caused by the accident or due to blood loss. The person should be allowed to rest.

Serious bleeding

Losing a lot of blood can be very dangerous. If a person has a deep wound it should be treated as shown in Fig. 108.2. It is important to get trained medical help quickly. In this country an ambulance should be called by telephoning 999.

Fig. 108.1 Treating a nose bleed.

A person with severe bleeding will be treated in hospital. The sides of the cut will be held or **stitched** together. A **blood transfusion** may be given if much blood has been lost. Anyone with a serious injury should *never* be given anything to eat or drink (except when severely burnt, see page 199). When they arrive at the hospital, a casualty may be given an **anaesthetic**. This is a drug to make them unconscious during an operation. If someone has food or liquid in the stomach they may vomit during the operation. They could choke on the vomit.

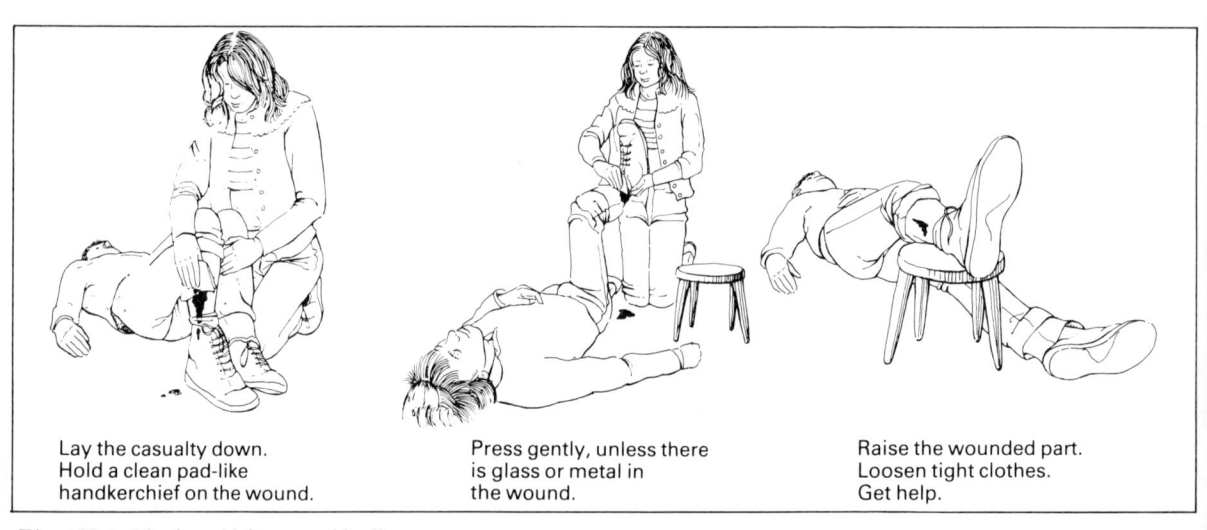

Lay the casualty down. Hold a clean pad-like handkerchief on the wound.

Press gently, unless there is glass or metal in the wound.

Raise the wounded part. Loosen tight clothes. Get help.

Fig. 108.2 The first aid for severe bleeding.

18 First aid

109 Burns

Types of burns

The skin is sensitive to heat and too much heat can damage the skin. **Burns** are caused by **dry heat** from fire, hot objects, the sun, electricity and lightning. Some chemicals can burn the skin; they are **corrosive**. Burns can also be caused by **friction** as happens to your palms when you slide down a rope quickly. **Scalds** are caused by **moist heat** such as boiling water, steam, hot oil or tar.

Effects of burns

Burns and scalds cause the skin to go red and swell. **Blisters** may form. These are 'pools' of tissue fluid under the skin. Burns are painful and the casualty may suffer from shock. Burns on young children are particularly serious.

Treating burns

The burnt area must be held under cold water for at least ten minutes. The water could be in a bowl or running from a tap. The water removes heat from the burn and prevents more damage. The burn should be covered lightly with a sterile, smooth cloth to prevent infection, especially if the skin is broken (Fig. 109.1).

If a person is seriously burnt, send for help quickly. The burnt part should be held under water. Tight clothing and jewellery must be removed quickly before swelling starts. Lay the

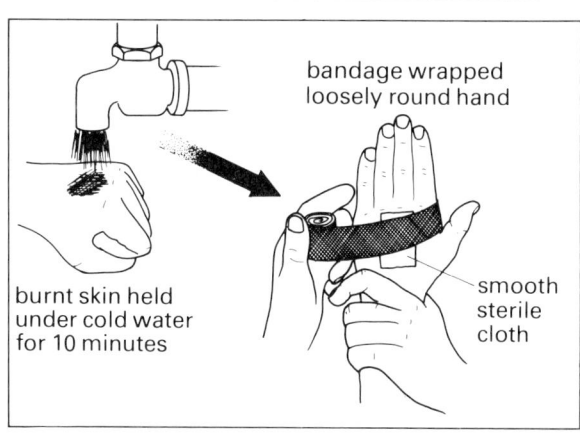

Fig. 109.1 Treating a minor burn.

Fig. 109.2 If you see someone with burning hair or clothes, act quickly to put out the flames. This is done by stopping air getting to the burning item: water, a thick coat, blanket or rug can be used. Take care not to burn yourself.

casualty down and cover the burns with sterile cloths. Do not allow the casualty to move. Give small, frequent drinks of cold water. This is necessary as tissue fluid escapes quickly from burnt, broken skin.

It is important to **reassure** anyone who has had an accident. The first aider must keep calm and tell the casualty that help is coming and that he or she will recover.

Summary: First aid

* Most accidents take place in the home.
* Many accidents can be avoided or prevented.
* First aid is the first help that is given to anyone injured in an accident.
* Expert help can be obtained by dialling 999 on a telephone.
* People suffering from asphyxia can be helped by artificial resuscitation.
* A cut or wound could open the way for pathogens to enter the body.
* All cuts should be cleaned and covered with sterile dressings.
* Too much heat can damage the skin. Burns are caused by dry heat, scalds by wet heat.
* Special procedures must be followed if someone has a serious cut, burn or scald.

19 Health in the community

110 The health service

There are many people who can help us when we are ill. There are many others who check our health to prevent disease. If discovered at an early stage, diseases can be treated before they cause damage to the body. These people work for the **Health Service**. Most health services in this country are controlled by the **National Health Service** (**NHS**). Others are run by **Local Authorities**. The main types of services available are shown in Fig. 110.1.

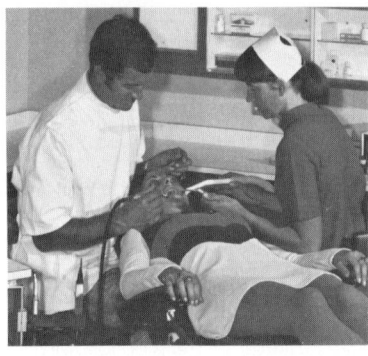

Fig. 110.1 The health services available in Britain.

19 Health in the community

General practitioner

Everyone should be signed on the list of a **general practitioner** (**G.P.**). This is the 'family doctor'. The doctor runs a **surgery** either on his own or with a group of doctors (Fig. 110.2). When a person feels unwell a visit to the family doctor is the first step. Usually the doctor can treat the patient. This may mean giving or **prescribing** certain drugs. For more serious diseases, the doctor will send the patient elsewhere. This is called **referring** the patient. Usually arrangements will be made for the patient to see a **specialist** doctor at a hospital.

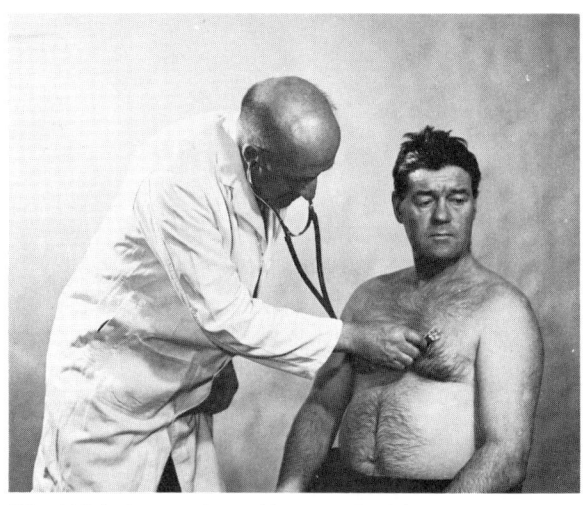

Fig. 110.2 A general practitioner can be visited at certain times. Often an appointment is necessary.

Hospitals

A general hospital is divided into many departments (Fig. 110.3). Each department deals with one type of medical problem. For instance, the **paediatric** department deals with diseases of children; the **surgical** department performs operations; the **medical** department treats people by using drugs; the **accident and emergency** department treats people who need immediate attention. Each department has one or more **wards**. These are large rooms containing beds for the patients. Each department has a team of trained doctors and nurses. Hospitals often have **out-patients clinics**. These are for people who need treatment occasionally. This could be massage and exercise (**physiotherapy**).

Fig. 110.3 Hospitals have many departments.

Preventative medicine

Some health services try to prevent ill health or discover diseases early. For instance, immunising young children against diseases may prevent them catching diseases such as polio. When a large number of people are given a short medical examination, they are **screened** and checked for disease. An example is the checking of school children at various ages. **Preventative medicine** like this should mean that in the future fewer people become seriously ill.

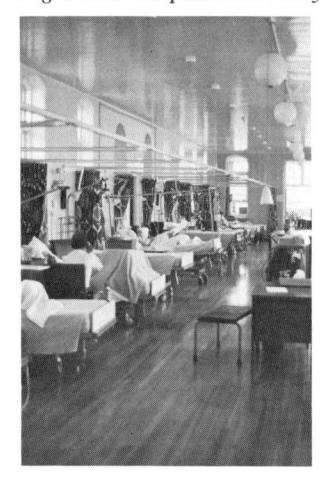

Fig. 110.4 A typical hospital ward.

19 Health in the community

111 Healthy adults

Many diseases of adults can be successfully treated if their symptoms are discovered early. For instance regular tests of blood pressure may show up a heart problem.

Mass radiography

This service X-rays a person's chest. The centre may be at a hospital or in a **mobile unit** – a lorry fitted with an X-ray machine. The X-ray will show up early stages of **tuberculosis** or lung cancer before someone feels ill. The disease can be treated. As it has been caught in its early stages, treatment may be successful.

Fig. 111.1 A mobile X-ray unit.

Cancer in women

Cancer in a woman may start in a breast. A woman can be taught how to examine her breasts for unusual lumps. (These may *not* be cancer.) The **family planning clinic** or her family doctor can show her how to check if a lump is there. She can have an **infra-red scan** of the breasts; areas where there is cancer have a slightly higher temperature than the rest of the body. The scan will show these (Fig. 111.2). Cancer may also start in a woman's **cervix**. This is the narrow opening into the womb. A **cervical smear** is a way of testing the health of the cervix. It is lightly scraped and the cells collected are examined under a microscope. Any unhealthy cells will be spotted and the woman can be treated. A smear should be carried out on women over 35 years old every two years. The smear can be carried out by the family doctor or by a doctor at the family planning clinic (Fig. 111.3).

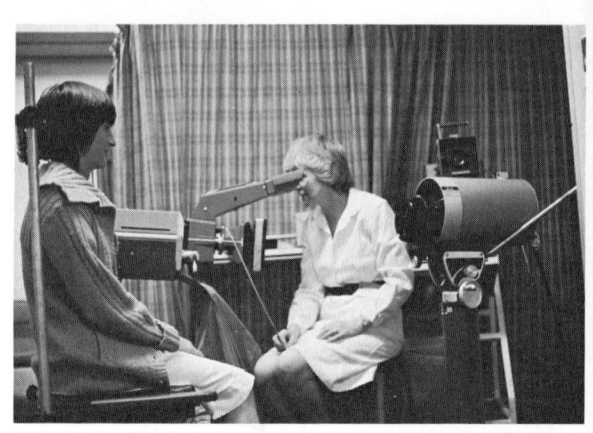

Fig. 111.2 The infra-red scanning apparatus used to check for breast cancer, patients do not wear clothing during the scan.

Health visitors

Health visitors check on the health of people living at home. Old people, or those who have just returned from hospital, need help. The visitor can arrange for **home helps** to come and do domestic work. **Home nursing** can be arranged in some cases. **Social workers** can help with housing and money problems.

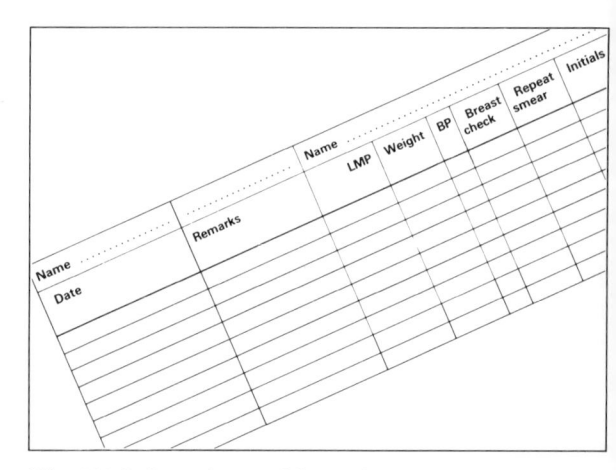

Fig. 111.3 Part of a record from a family planning clinic. It shows the regular tests that are carried out. 'LMP' means the date of the last menstrual period and 'BP' means blood pressure.

19 Health in the community

Old people

Old people, especially those living alone, may have many problems. Stiffening joints often make it hard for them to do simple things like climbing the stairs (Fig. 111.4). They may need the help of the health services. Loneliness can be a great problem for the elderly. Clubs run by volunteers can help those who have no family to care for them. Sometimes it is necessary to move a person into an **old people's home** (Fig. 111.5). These provide a place to live, company and trained staff. If an old person is very ill they are usually treated in the **geriatric** ward of a hospital.

Mental health

Special health services are available for people suffering from **mental diseases**. These diseases affect the way a person feels, thinks or behaves. Some patients may have to go to a **psychiatric** hospital; others can attend out-patient clinics or **day centres** instead.

Mental diseases are becoming more common. Some people cannot cope with the stresses and strains of living in our society. When under pressure or extremely lonely, a person may develop a **neurosis**. The neuroses include **anxiety**, **depression** and **phobias**. At times we all get worried or depressed and many of us have slight phobias, such as a fear of spiders or high places. If these feelings stop a person living normally, specialised treatment is needed. Most neuroses are easily cured.

The **psychoses** are more serious. They include **schizophrenia** and **manic depression**. Both of these lead to strange ways of thinking which affect behaviour. The causes of these illnesses are not fully known and treatment may take a long time. Even so they are sometimes cured completely or brought under control.

Fig. 111.4 Some old people need help with everyday chores.

Fig. 111.5 Part of the lounge in an old people's home.

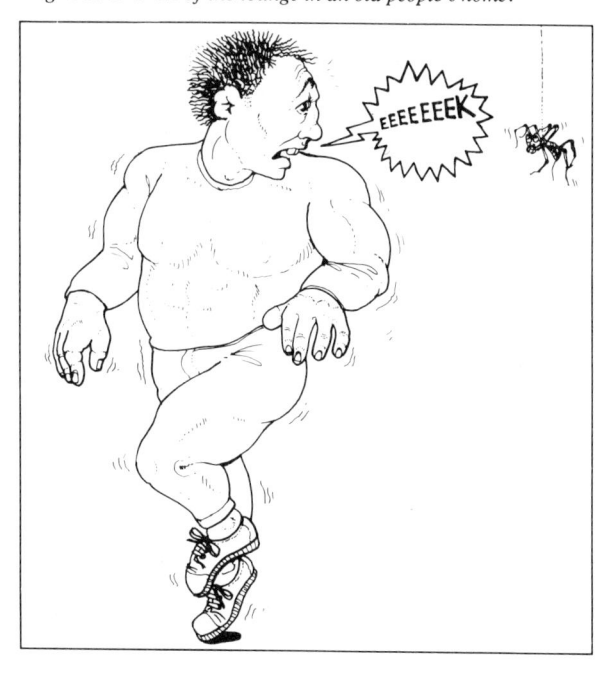

Fig. 111.6 We all have worries and fears. When these seriously affect daily life they are mental illnesses.

19 Health in the community

112 Healthy children

If children grow up healthily, they are likely to be healthy adults. There are various clinics and other services that check children's development. Regular **medical examinations** help find any problems so that treatment can be started before the growing baby is damaged.

Infant

Ante-natal clinics check on the health of children before birth (see page 99). **Post-natal clinics** deal with children's health during the first year of life (see page 101). **Child welfare clinics** then take over. During the first five years of life children are at risk. They are more likely to die from infectious diseases. To prevent this, parents are encouraged by the clinics to have their children **immunised** (Fig. 112.1). Immunity to diseases such as polio, smallpox and diphtheria should be given when a child is very young. Also many tests are performed to check that children are growing and developing normally. These include measuring height, weight, eyesight and hearing. Parents can discuss the problems linked with the care of their children.

School children

The **School Medical Service** carries on the work of child welfare clinics. Medically trained people visit schools. They make quick examinations of large numbers of children. These happen often for children between the ages of five and eleven years. A record of each child's health is kept. Eyesight, hearing and posture are tested (Fig. 112.2). A child's cleanliness and hygiene are also checked. The hair and skin are examined for nits and lice. There are also regular dental inspections to check the health of the teeth. If any problem is found the parents and family doctor or dentist are informed. As children get older further immunisations may be given. For instance, at the age of 14, all school children are given a **B.C.G. test**. This shows if they need to

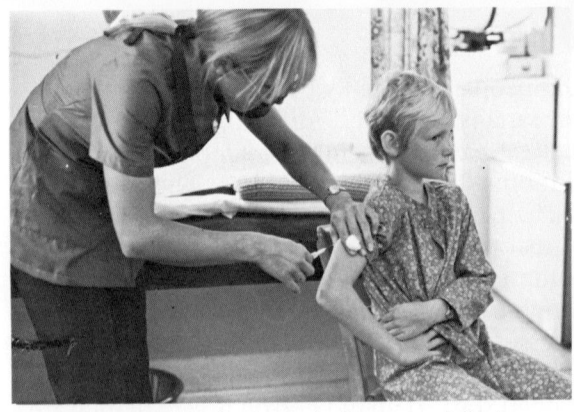

Fig. 112.1 A child being immunised to prevent infection.

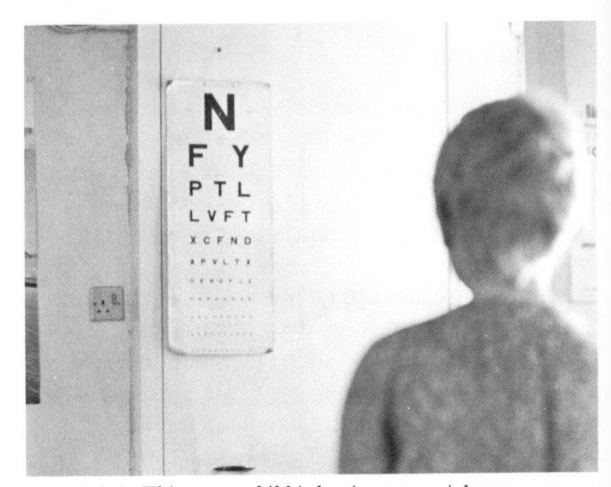

Fig. 112.2 This young child is having an eyesight test.

Fig. 112.3 Physical education helps keep school children healthy.

be immunised against tuberculosis (T.B.). The **vaccination** is given if necessary. The school teachers will know if any child has learning or behaviour difficulties. A **child guidance clinic** may then be asked to give special help. The parents must give their permission for this step.

19 Health in the community

113 Community services

Many other services are organised by various authorities and voluntary groups. They work to make the environment healthy and safe and to help people in distress. These can all be called **community services**.

Public services

It is easier for people to stay healthy if their surroundings and food are safe and hygienic. Local Authorities collect rubbish and dispose of it (see page 175). They also control the removal and treatment of sewage (see page 172). They operate road cleaning and maintenance services. This makes sure litter is removed and that roads are safe for traffic (Fig. 113.1). **Health** and **safety inspectors** are employed to check the levels of hygiene and safety in buildings. They visit shops, offices, restaurants, factories, food markets and schools. If they find poor sanitation, unhygienic food or dangerous machinery, they can force people to make the necessary changes (Fig. 113.2). Pest control experts are also employed to keep down the numbers of mice, rats and insect pests. Local Authorities also control most of the education services in an area. Regional Water Authorities make sure clean water is supplied to all buildings (see page 170).

Emergency services

Dealing with accidents, fires and crimes needs specially trained people. The Local Authorities provide these emergency services. They include the **ambulance service**, the **fire brigade** and the **police force**. They can be called by dialling 999 on a telephone (Fig. 113.3).

Voluntary help organisations

Many people have **volunteered** to help people in distress. There are many groups. The Salvation Army is an organisation that helps many people in distress. They do a lot to help alcoholics and the homeless. The Samaritans run a 24-hour phone service. Anyone with problems such as depression or anxiety can phone for advice or reassurance. **Self-help groups** are becoming more common. People with similar problems, such as alcoholism, meet to discuss their problems and try to help each other.

Fig. 113.1 A road-cleaning lorry.

Fig. 113.2 An inspector checking the condition of meat.

Fig. 113.3 Fireman working to put out a blaze.

19 Health in the community

114 International health

Each country has its own health service. The highly-developed countries tend to have better medical care than the poorer ones. People throughout the world are trying to get all health services up to a high standard.

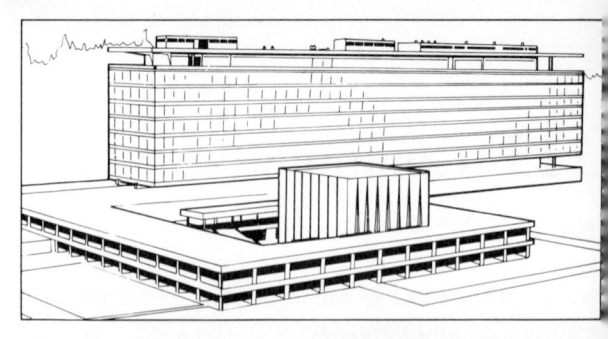

Fig. 114.1 The headquarters of the World Health Organisation in Geneva, Switzerland.

World Health Organisation

The **World Health Organisation (W.H.O.)** tries to improve the health of people in all countries (Fig. 114.1). Their medical experts and advisers work in many ways. They keep detailed records of dangerous diseases that break out in various countries. They have completely wiped out smallpox (except for accidents with the virus in laboratories). They keep figures about the health and **Life expectancy** of people in different countries (Fig. 114.2). They provide advice about how to improve sanitation, housing and medical services. In the poorer countries they may provide money to improve medical care. The organisation also helps train medical staff. The World Health Organisation was set up in 1948. Its headquarters are in Geneva, Switzerland.

Many other organisations help increase the welfare of people all over the world. The **United Nations Organisation** plays a leading part. There is also the **Food and Agricultural Organisation (F.A.O.)**, the **International Red Cross** and **OXFAM**. Some of these are important when there has been a disaster – such as famine or war (Fig. 114.3).

Fig. 114.2 Experts studying a world map which shows where help is needed.

Fig. 114.3 Red Cross ambulances and supplies being loaded to help the Ethiopia famine in 1978.

Summary: Health in the community

* The Health Service is made up of many branches that work to prevent and cure disease.
* Cases of disease in anyone are first seen by general practitioners (G.P.).
* General hospitals treat people sent to them by the doctor.
* Checks are made on children at special clinics and by the School Medical Service.
* The dentists work with people with tooth problems. There are dentists in the School Medical Services.
* Checks are made on adult health when screening is done.
* Home visitors check on people who have to stay at home.
* Public services control hygiene in the community.
* Emergency services deal with accidents.
* Voluntary organisations help people in distress.
* The World Health Organisation is concerned with health of people in all countries.

Learning your Human Biology

You cannot learn your work properly unless you **understand** it. After you have been taught a topic in class, read the pages in the textbook again after the lesson. If you do not understand the work, ask your teacher to go through it with you.

When you understand your work **learn and revise** it. Read through a whole section and end with the summary. As you read the summary, try to remember the details that go with each of the main points. Read the section and summary again.

When you have learned your work, **test** yourself. Use the word tests that match each section. If you cannot match any statement with any word, read the whole section again. When you are sure you understand and know the work, try some of the examination-type questions.

Getting ready for an **examination**. If you have understood, learned and revised your work during your course you will not have much 'swotting' to do. Before the examination, find out from your teacher:
(a) the date and time of the examination;
(b) the number of papers you have to take;
(c) the number or kind of questions on the papers.

Try to look at some examination papers that have been done before. Find out:
(a) the instructions you are given;
(b) the materials you need (like pencils, rulers);
(c) how much time you should spend on each question.

On the night before the examination, try to get some sleep!

Questions

The questions are in section order.
There are two kinds of question used.
1 **Word-test questions**
In these there is a list of words in alphabetical order. There are ten sentences. You have to match each word with one sentence. In this way you will learn and revise technical words.
2 **Examination-type questions**
Examinations contain many kinds of question.

There are **multiple-choice** or **objective** questions. Here you pick the **one** letter for the right answer to the question from **five**.

There are **short-answer** questions. Here you have to look at a diagram, table or graph and answer questions about it. The answers are usually just one short sentence.

There are **essay** questions. You have to write about a page on the topic in the question. Your sentences must be short and to the point. Do not put in lots of extra detail (this is waffle).

There are **diagram** questions. These are very hard. You have to draw a diagram to show something – for instance, a section through skin. Always draw large diagrams in pencil. Do the lines faint at first – go over them in thicker lines when you are sure the drawing is right. Do not copy the diagram from the book. Try to build up the drawing from your understanding of the topic.

1 The human body (pages 1–7)

Word test

cytoplasm	epithelium	membrane
microscope	mitochondria	nucleus
organs	organelles	section
smear		

1 Cells in a thin layer covering or lining parts of the body.
2 Jelly-like material making up the main part of a cell.
3 On the outside of a cell.
4 Carry out processes that release energy inside a cell.
5 A piece of apparatus used for magnifying parts on a slide.
6 Made up from cells and tissues.
7 A thin slice through a tube and put on a slide.
8 A preparation made from a liquid like blood.
9 Tiny parts inside a cell.
10 Controls the activities of a cell.

Questions

1 A micrometre is
A 1 millimetre   B $\frac{1}{10}$ millimetre   C $\frac{1}{100}$ millimetre
D $\frac{1}{1000}$ millimetre   E $\frac{1}{10\,000}$ millimetre

2 A microscope fitted with a ×5 eyepiece and a ×20 objective lens, will magnify an object
  A ×5   B ×20   C ×25   D ×100   E ×520

3 Which of the following is not a tissue?
A bone   B nerve   C cartilage   D stomach
E epithelium

4 Why are cells stained before being looked at under a microscope?

2 Nutrition (pages 8–15)

Word test

amino acids   fat   food
drugs   kwashiorkor   malnourishment
protein   starch   thyroid
water

1. Nutrient group that contains nitrogen. *Protein*
2. All foods contain this nutrient. *Water*
3. Molecules made from chains of sugar molecules. *Starch*
4. What happens if you have too much or too little food. *Mal.*
5. Olive oil and suet contain a lot of this nutrient. *Fat*
6. The gland that makes use of iodine. *Thyroid*
7. Chemicals that affect the nervous system. *Drugs*
8. Provides the body with energy, materials and chemicals. *Food*
9. Caused if the diet of a child is lacking in protein and energy foods. *Kwashiorkor*
10. The small molecules that build up protein. *Amino acids*

Questions

1. The table shows the protein, fat and energy content of four foods and one drink. The foods include tomato, cheese and butter.

Foodstuff	Total weight in grams (g)	kJ energy released per 10 g food	g protein per 10 g food	g fat per 10 g food
1	80	100	0·8	0·1
2	50	150	2·5	3·5
3	10	350	0·0	8·5
4	90	6	0·1	0·0
drink	300	0	0·0	0·0

  (a) Which foodstuff is the tomato?
    A 1 B 2 C 3 D 4 E none of these
  (b) Which foodstuff is the cheese?
    A 1 B 2 C 3 D 4 E none of these
  (c) Which foodstuff is the butter?
    A 1 B 2 C 3 D 4 E none of these
  (d) The drink in the table is
    A tea with milk
    B coffee with milk
    C coffee with milk and sugar
    D black coffee
    E tea with milk and sugar

2. The lack of which vitamin from the diet is linked with scurvy?
A vitamin A   B vitamin B
C vitamin C   D vitamin D
E vitamin E

3. Describe how James Lind discovered that fresh fruit could stop sailors getting scurvy.

3 Food and the future (pages 16–23)

Word test

carbohydrates   cereals   chlorophyll
fertilisers   irrigation   leaves
nitrates   pesticides   paraffin
photosynthesis

1. The process of food-making by green plants in light. *Ph*
2. Compounds taken up by plants from the soil and used to make protein. *Nitrates*
3. The green substance in plants that traps light energy. *Chl*
4. Chemicals added to soil to get better yields from crops. *Fe*
5. Crops named after the Greek goddess of the harvest. *Ce*
6. The green parts of plants where most food-making takes place. *Leaves*
7. Improving soil by increasing the supply of water. *Irri*
8. Used in industry to make new foods. *Paraffin*
9. Chemicals used to kill animals that destroy crops. *Pesti*
10. A nutrient stored by green plants like the potato. *Carboh*

Questions

1. Which of the following is not food from a plant?
A tomato   B potato   C rice   D egg   E apple

2. Which of the following gases is used by a green plant during photosynthesis?
A oxygen   B nitrogen   C carbon dioxide
D sulphur dioxide   E hydrogen

3. Explain how wheat is processed to make breakfast food.

4. What is a food chain? Trace back the food chains from these human foods.
(a) spaghetti   (b) eggs   (c) milk   (d) cheese
(e) pig's liver

4 Energy release (pages 24–31)

Word test

alveoli   breathing   bronchi
diaphragm   kilojoules   nitrogen
oxygen   respiration   trachea
voice-box

1. It contains the vocal cords.
2. The gas present in largest amounts in air.
3. The two tubes which branch from the windpipe.
4. The sheet of muscle and fibre which separates the chest cavity from the abdomen.
5. It lies on top of the gullet in the neck.
6. As you climb a mountain, the amount of this gas in air gets less.
7. Units to measure energy.
8. The release of energy from food.
9. Getting air into and out of the lungs.
10. Found in the lungs at the tips of the finest breathing tubes.

Questions

1. During breathing in, which of the following does not take place?
   A movement of the diaphragm down
   B contraction of intercostal muscles
   C movement of the rib cage down
   D increase in volume of thoracic cavity
   E the liver is pushed outwards

2. A human trachea is lined with cilia which beat
   A downwards carrying moisture to the lungs
   B in all directions spreading moisture in the trachea
   C upwards moving foreign material towards the mouth
   D downwards carrying saliva to the stomach
   E only when smoke is breathed in

Questions 3 to 6 are about the diagram.

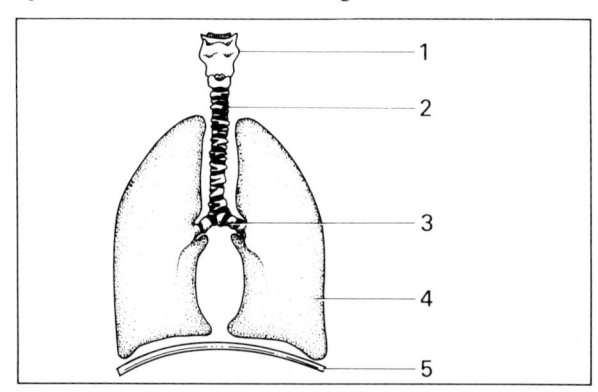

3. The part labelled 1 is the
   A throat   B gullet   C voice-box   D bronchus
   E oesophagus

4. The part labelled 4 is the
   A pleural membrane   B rib   C lung
   D intercostal muscle
   E diaphragm

5. The part where you would find air-sacs is labelled
   A 1   B 2   C 3   D 4   E 5

6. The part where half hoops of cartilage are found is labelled
   A 1   B 2   C 3   D 4   E 5

7. Draw a large diagram of the human chest. Label intercostal muscle, rib, diaphragm, lung, pleural membrane, trachea, bronchus.

8. We measure energy in kilojoules (kJ). Different people need different amounts of energy each day.

Type of person	kJ needed each day
baby	4000
boy aged 12 years	12000
man (light work)	11000
woman (light work)	9000
man (heavy work)	15000

(a) Why does a teenager need more energy than an adult?
(b) Why does a male bank clerk need more energy than a female doing the same job?
(c) If the man doing heavy work does not eat enough food to give him 15 000 kJ each day, what might happen to him?
(d) If we take in more energy (food) than we need, what will happen to our bodies?

5 Digestion (pages 32–43)

Word test

acid   amino acids   amylase
duodenum   epiglottis   gastric
lymph   peristalsis   protease
villi

1. It stops food from getting into the windpipe.
2. Enzyme that works on starch substrate.
3. Movement that pushes materials down a tube.
4. Bile duct and pancreatic duct open into this tube.
5. Finger-like processes in the small intestine.
6. Glands in the stomach.
7. Made when proteins are digested.
8. Fatty acids pass into this transport system.
9. Enzymes that work on protein substrate.
10. This destroys bacteria that reach the stomach.

Questions

1. This is a drawing of a tooth from the lower jaw cut in half.

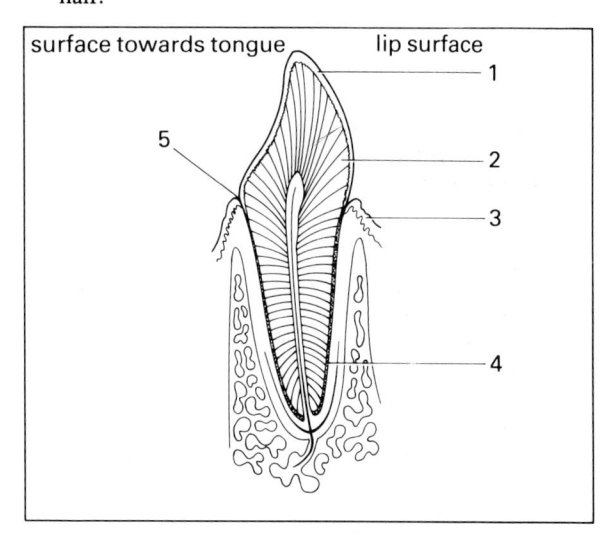

(a) The tooth in the drawing is
   A an incisor   B a canine   C a premolar
   D a molar   E a wisdom tooth
(b) Most bacteria would be found at
   A 1   B 2   C 3   D 4   E 5

209

2 Which of the following is not a feature of enzymes?
   A Their names usually end in -ase.
   B They have a certain shape.
   C They speed up chemical reactions.
   D They work better as the temperature gets higher.
   E They are made by living cells.

3 Give one way in which the shape of the human incisors make them suited to the job they do:

4 Describe how tooth decay takes place.

5 What is digestion? Explain what happens to protein as it passes from the mouth to the large intestine.

6 Transport in the body (pages 44–55)

Word test

arteries   bicuspid   capillary
coronary   lymph   pace-maker
plasma   semi-lunar   tricuspid
veins

1 Blood vessel whose wall is one cell thick.
2 Blood vessels that take blood from the heart to the body.
3 These long blood vessels contain valves.
4 The blood vessels that supply the heart muscle with blood.
5 Valve between right atrium and right ventricle.
6 The liquid part of the blood.
7 Valve found in the aorta at the place where it leaves the heart.
8 It makes the heart beat regularly.
9 Valve between left atrium and left ventricle.
10 These vessels drain away the tissue fluid.

Questions

1 When blood flows through the heart, it follows which one of the following paths?
   A pulmonary artery – right atrium – right ventricle – vena cava – lungs
   B pulmonary artery – right atrium – left atrium – vena cava – lungs
   C vena cava – right atrium – right ventricle – pulmonary artery – lung
   D vena cava – right atrium – left atrium – pulmonary artery – lungs
   E vena cava – right atrium – left atrium – pulmonary vein – lungs

2 Which of the following statements about red blood cells is true?
   A They are irregularly shaped.
   B They have a nucleus.
   C They destroy bacteria.
   D They can squeeze through capillary walls.
   E They carry oxygen.

3 Which of the following statements about a vein is not true?
   A They always return blood towards the heart.
   B Long veins contain valves.
   C Blood flow in veins is steady.
   D The vein wall is very thick and made of muscle and elastic.
   E In most veins blood is dull red.

4 What is the difference between each of the following pairs?
   (a) heart atrium and heart ventricle
   (b) pulse and blood pressure
   (c) lymph and tissue fluid
   (d) lymph and plasma

5 What can anyone do to cut down the chance of having a heart attack?

7 Keeping the steady state (pages 56–71)

Word test

diffusion   excretion   hepatic
hypothermia   nephron   renal
shivers   sweat   urea
urethra

1 The body does this to lose heat.
2 The getting rid of chemical waste from the body.
3 The tiny tubes that make up the kidney.
4 A condition caused by a fall in body temperature.
5 Produced in the liver when amino acids are broken down.
6 Movement of molecules in air or liquid.
7 The artery which goes to the kidney.
8 The artery that goes to the liver.
9 The body does this to produce heat.
10 The tube that goes from the bladder to the outside of the body.

Questions

1 Which of the following is not in the urine of a healthy person?
   A water   B urea   C ammonia   D glucose   E salt

2 The number of ureters in the human body is
   A one   B two   C four   D several hundred
   E several thousand

3 The diagram shows two solutions separated by a selectively permeable membrane.

In the experiment, osmosis is the name given to the movement of
A water from R to S
B water from S to R
C sugar from R to S
D sugar from S to R
E sugar and water from R to S

4 The diagram shows a section through skin.

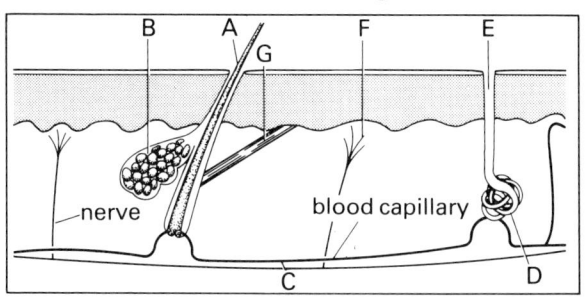

(a) Describe how parts C, D and E work together to regulate body temperature.
(b) Which labelled parts of the diagram would you not find in a section of skin on the palm of the hand?
(c) What is the function of the part labelled B?

5 Describe how you would use a clinical thermometer to take someone's temperature.

2 Insulin is secreted by
A the salivary glands   B the liver   C the gut
D the islets in the pancreas   E the adrenal gland

3 Hormones are carried around the body by
A blood   B lymph   C nerve cells   D nerves
E blood vessels

4 When sound enters the ear, which of the following pathways does it follow?
A oval window – stirrup – anvil – ear drum
B anvil – stirrup – oval window – ear drum
C stirrup – anvil – oval window – ear drum
D ear drum – stirrup – anvil – oval window
E stirrup – oval window – anvil – ear drum

5 The pituitary gland is often described as the master gland or the most important gland in the body. Give one reason for the description.

6 Adrenalin is a hormone that prepares the body for flight or fight. Give three effects of the hormone on the body.

7 The diagram is a simple one of an endocrine gland.

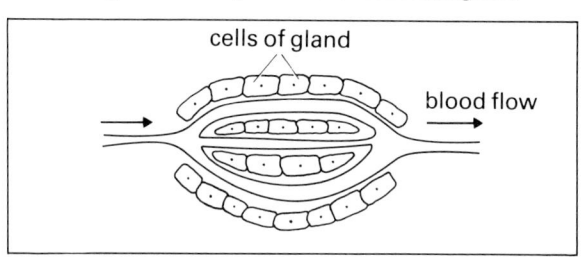

(a) Copy the diagram and label the artery and the vein.
(b) On your diagram draw and label an arrow to show the path the secretion from the cells would follow.
(c) Give 2 ways in which a salivary gland differs in structure from this gland.

8 Coordination (pages 72–93)

Word test

adrenalin	conditioning	conscious
effector	motor	puberty
reflex	sensory	stimulus
synapse		

1 A change inside or outside the body.
2 The nerve cell that carries instructions out to muscles or glands.
3 An action in which the response to a stimulus is always the same.
4 The time when menstruation starts in girls.
5 A part of the body which makes a response.
6 The hormone that works on the heart and cells of the liver.
7 The gap between nerve cells.
8 An action that can be controlled.
9 The nerve cell that takes information into the brain or spinal cord.
10 An action that is used in learning.

Questions

1 The pituitary gland is found
A in the neck   B at the base of the brain
C in the mouth   D beneath the stomach
E near the kidneys

9 Reproduction (pages 94–105)

Word test

amnion	fertilisation	fraternal
identical	implantation	intercourse
ovary	placenta	testis
uterus		

1 The male sex organ that produces sperm.
2 Where the baby grows inside the mother.
3 The sac of fluid around the baby that protects it from knocks.
4 The female sex organ that releases eggs.
5 When sperm are passed into the body of a woman.
6 Twins formed from one egg.
7 When the nucleus of an egg and sperm fuse.
8 Twins formed from two eggs.
9 An organ that develops from the tissues of baby and mother.
10 When the dividing egg sinks into the womb wall.

Questions

1 The diagram shows a developing human embryo.

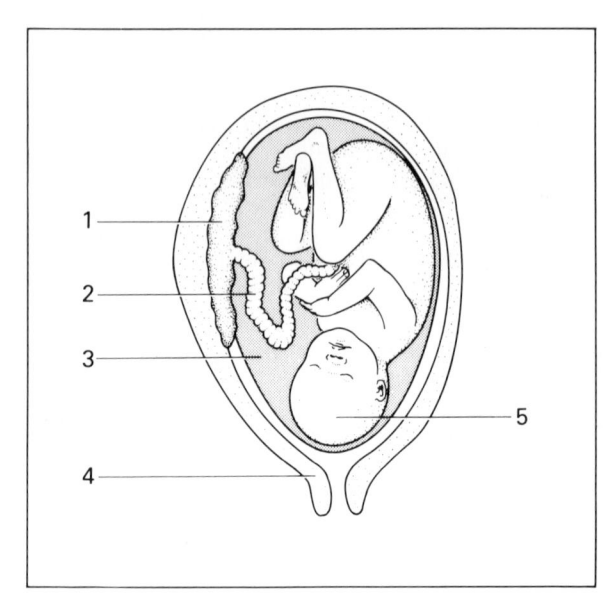

(a) Which of the parts labelled does not contain blood vessels?
A 1 B 2 C 3 D 4 E 5
(b) Which of the parts labelled will not be passed out of the mother before, during or after the birth?
A 1 B 2 C 3 D 4 E 5
(c) Which of the parts labelled is where food and oxygen are exchanged for wastes?
A 1 B 2 C 3 D 4 E 5

2 Why should a pregnant woman visit an ante-natal clinic?

3 What is labour?

10 Inheritance (pages 106–117)

Word test

chromosomes   diploid   haemophilia
haploid   heterozygote   homozygote
meiosis   mitosis   mutation
phenotype

1 The type of cell division that makes the sex cells.
2 The type of nucleus in a sex cell.
3 Threads inside a nucleus.
4 The physical appearance of an organism.
5 An organism with the same genes on each member of a pair of chromosomes.
6 The sex-linked disease that stops blood clotting properly.
7 The type of cell division that takes place in growth.
8 The type of nucleus formed after fertilisation.
9 An organism with different genes on each member of a pair of chromosomes.
10 The sudden appearance of a new characteristic.

Questions

1 The number of chromosomes in a sperm nucleus is
A 23 B 23 pairs C 46 pairs D 46 E 44

2 The sex chromosomes in the body cells of a normal human female are
A X B XX C XY D YY E Y

3 The genetic make-up of an individual is described as its
A genes B genotype C phenotype D nucleus E chromosomes

4 The genotypes in the offspring of this cross
    Bb   ×   BB
heterozygous   homozygous
will be
A all homozygote B all heterozygote
C half homozygote half heterozygote
D ¾ homozygote ¼ heterozygote
E ¾ heterozygote ¼ homozygote

5 What is meant by each of the following?
(a) gamete (b) gonad (c) zygote (d) fertilisation (e) nucleus

6 Brittle bones is an inherited condition in man. In the family trees shown here, shaded symbols represent individuals with brittle bones, and white symbols represent individuals with normal bones.

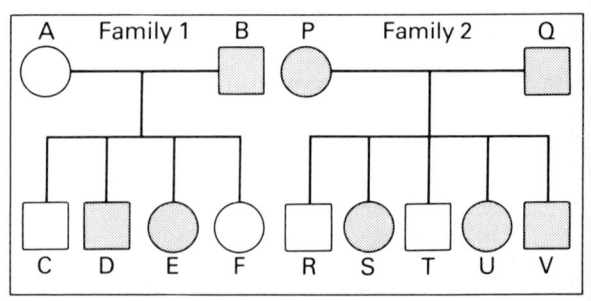

(a) List all the individuals who are
(i) female (ii) male.
(b) List all the individuals with
(i) normal bones (ii) brittle bones.
(c) Is the mother in family 1 a person with normal or brittle bones?
(d) How many children does the mother in family 2 have?
(e) How many sons in family 2 have
(i) brittle bones (ii) normal bones?
(f) How many daughters in family 1 have
(i) brittle bones (ii) normal bones?
(g) Which of the characteristics, brittle bones or normal bones, is controlled by a dominant gene? Give a reason for your answer.
(h) Suppose F and R marry and have a child. Is it likely that this child will have brittle bones?

11 Support and movement (pages 118–135)

Word test

biceps   bone   cartilage
centrum   extensor   fracture
joule   ligament   marrow
tendon

1. Tissue that contains calcium and phosphate.
2. The flat supporting part of each vertebra.
3. Part of a long bone that makes blood cells.
4. Tissue that joins bone to bone.
5. A muscle that straightens a joint.
6. A break in a bone.
7. Flexible support material in the ear flaps and nose.
8. The muscle that is antagonistic to the triceps.
9. A unit of work.
10. Tissue that joins muscle to bone.

Questions

1. Which of the following bones is found in the human leg?
   A humerus   B radius   C femur   D ulna   E scapula

2. A pivot joint is found
   A at the knee
   B at the hip
   C between the skull and the backbone
   D between the bones of the backbone
   E at the ankle

3. A girl lifts 300 N through a vertical height of 2 metres. How much work has she done?
   A 150 J   B 300 J   C 300 N   D 600 N   E 600 J

4. What are the functions of the skeleton?

5. The diagram represents a human skeleton?

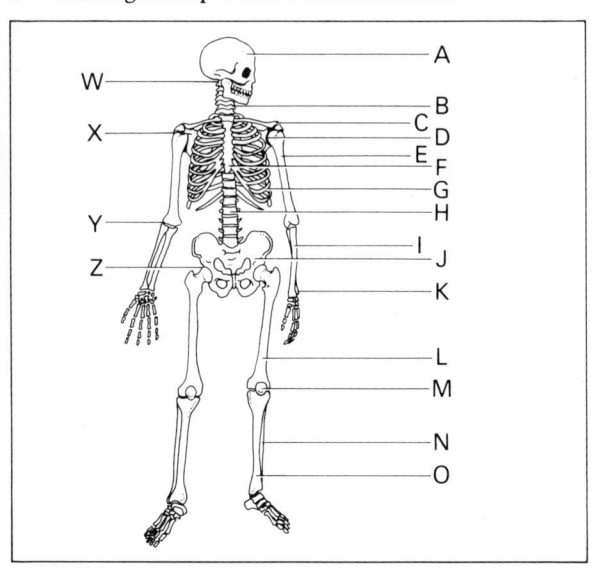

   (a) What are the names of the bones A to O?
   (b) What type of joint is found at W, X, Y, Z?

12 Disease and its causes (pages 136–151)

Word test

bacteria   contagious   pathogens
Plasmodium   *Schistosoma* symptom
toxins   vectors   venereal
viruses

1. Microbes that cause disease.
2. Animals that spread disease.
3. Diseases that are spread by touch.
4. The parasite that causes malaria.
5. Diseases that are spread by love-making.
6. A parasite worm that spends part of its life cycle in a snail.
7. They can only be seen with an electron microscope.
8. They are round, rod or spiral shaped.
9. Poisons made by bacteria.
10. The sign of a disease.

Questions

1. Which of the following is not an infectious disease?
   A influenza   B mumps   C diabetes   D measles
   E polio

2. The disease athlete's foot is caused by
   A a virus   B a bacterium   C a fungus
   D a protozoan
   E a flea

3. Which of the following does not feed on human blood?
   A female mosquito   B louse   C flea   D tsetse fly
   E tapeworm

4. Which of the following diseases is not spread by water?
   A cholera   B typhoid   C dysentery   D bilharzia
   E smallpox

5. What are Robert Koch's rules?
6. What is a parasite?

13 Using and fighting microbes (pages 152–165)

Word test

acid   alcohol   antibiotics
antibody   antigen   antiseptic
autoclave disinfectant immunity
sebum

1. A chemical which stops the growth of microbes.
2. Protein on the surface of red blood cell membrane.
3. A chemical which kills microbes.
4. Apparatus used to sterilise instruments in a hospital.
5. Protein in plasma that helps protect the body.
6. Diluted disinfectant.
7. Made by yeast cells when they respire anaerobically.

8 Antiseptic fluid made by glands in the skin.
9 Liquid in the stomach which kills microbes.
10 When the body is protected against disease.

Questions

1 Which of the following people discovered how to protect the body by immunisation?
  A Koch   B Pasteur   C Jenner   D Bowman
  E Spallanzani

2 Which of the following blood groups is known as the universal donor?
  A A   B B   C AB   D O   E Rhesus

3 How do humans make use of microbes?

4 Explain how a boy and girl must care for their bodies to keep them healthy.

14 Clean food and water (pages 166–175)

Word test

additives	analyst	canning
drains	methane	pickling
preservatives	rising main	sewage
smoking		

1 Waste water.
2 The gas given off when sewage sludge is broken down.
3 A way of preserving wet foods.
4 Pipes that carry waste water away from homes.
5 Chemicals put into foods to help them stay fresh.
6 An old-fashioned way of preserving fish, like kippers.
7 Chemicals put into foods to improve their flavour or colour.
8 A public official that checks on the chemicals added to food.
9 A way of preserving in vinegar.
10 The main pipe that brings cold water into a house.

Questions

1 Chlorine is a gas added to water at a waterworks to
  A colour the water   B clean the water
  C make the water taste better   D to kill microbes
  E to stop tooth decay

2 Which of the following is not true about pasteurised milk?
  A Pasteurisation is a way of preserving milk.
  B Pasteurised milk never goes sour.
  C Pasteurised milk contains some live bacteria.
  D During pasteurisation, milk is heated and then cooled quickly.
  E Pasteurised milk tastes like untreated milk.

3 What is the water cycle?

4 What is recycling? Why should materials like paper be recycled?

15 Homes (pages 176–181)

Word test

carbon dioxide	cavity	construction
evaporate	foundations	inert
joists	mortar	ventilation
wall		

1 Another word for building.
2 A material which holds bricks together in a wall.
3 These support the weight of a building.
4 Most heat is lost from this part of a house.
5 Replacing stale air with fresh air.
6 Light bulbs contain this kind of gas.
7 A build-up of this gas in air makes people sleepy.
8 The space between bricks in a house wall.
9 Beams of wood to which floor boards are nailed.
10 When liquid water changes to vapour.

Questions

1 Which of the following is not true about bricks?
  A Bricks are made from clay.
  B Bricks were first made about 6000 years ago.
  C A damp prevention course is put between bricks in walls.
  D Mortar is used to hold bricks together in a wall.
  E All brick walls are solid.

2 Which of the following is not used in home insulation?
  A draught excluder   B double glazing
  C cavity walls   D glass-fibre strips in a rod
  E radiators

3 What is the difference between each of the following?
  (a) a radiant heater and a convector heater
  (b) central heating and air conditioning
  (c) mortar and concrete

4 What are the advantages and disadvantages of large windows?

16 Using drugs (pages 182–185)

Word test

aspirin	barbiturates	caffeine
cirrhosis	ethanol	injection
morphine	nicotine	tar
prescription		

1 A drug used to lower temperature of someone who has a cold.
2 A drug in coffee.
3 A drug which numbs the cleaning hairs of the breathing tubes.
4 The group of drugs that are 'sleeping pills'.
5 The resin from poppies can be changed into this drug.
6 The alcohol of wine and beer.

7   Damage to liver caused by drinking too much alcohol.
8   The chemical in cigarette smoke that stains the lungs.
9   One way of getting drugs into the body.
10 A doctor's instructions to a chemist.

Questions

1   Which one of the following illnesses is not linked with cigarette smoking?
    A emphysema   B bronchitis   C lung cancer
    D tuberculosis   E heart attack

2   Which of the following is not true of a drug?
    A it may change anyone's mood
    B it may help someone cope with life
    C they may be prescribed by a doctor
    D they may be bought over a chemist's counter
    E some drugs are completely harmless

3   What is the difference between the following pairs?
    (a) stimulant and sedative
    (b) bronchitis and emphysema
    (c) drug tolerance and drug abuse

4   What effect does alcohol have on the body?

17 Pollution (pages 186–193)

Word test

detergents   fossil   herbicides
indicators   insecticide   lead
lichen   myxomatosis   nitrogen
phosphate

1   Chemicals used to kill fleas, lice and mosquitoes.
2   A disease used to kill off rabbits.
3   Chemicals used to kill weeds.
4   Chemicals used to break up oil slicks.
5   Most fertilisers contain this substance.
6   Detergents contain these substances.
7   Animals or plants that show if water or air is polluted.
8   The word that describes coal, oil and natural gas fuels.
9   These plants are susceptible to air pollution.
10 This metal is added to petrol.

Questions

1   The gas that can combine with haemoglobin in red blood cells to stop them carrying oxygen is
    A carbon dioxide   B carbon monoxide
    C sulphur dioxide   D nitrous oxide   E nitrogen

2   The lung disease from which coal miners may suffer is
    A tuberculosis   B pneumonia   C pneumoconiosus
    D asbestosis   E lung cancer

3   Which of the following is not true of a healthy river?
    A It contains living animals and plants.
    B It contains dissolved gases.
    C It will contain no waste.
    D It will contain bacteria.
    E It will contain dissolved nutrients.

4   Explain what is meant by the following.
    (a) smokeless zone
    (b) photochemical smog
    (c) sound-proofing
    (d) fertilisers
    (e) radiation

18 First aid (pages 196–199)

Word test

anaesthetic   blister   burn
corrosive   first aid   iodine
scald   sterile   suffocate
transfusion

1   Caused by moist heat.
2   A pool of tissue fluid beneath the skin.
3   Caused by dry heat.
4   A drug that makes someone unconscious.
5   The name of an absolutely clean wound dressing.
6   This is given if a person has lost a lot of blood.
7   This will happen if a person cannot breathe.
8   A mild antiseptic.
9   Chemicals that burn the skin.
10 Help given to someone immediately after an accident.

Questions

1   Which of the following would you not do if you found someone with a badly bleeding leg?
    A Lay the casualty down.
    B Put ointment on the wound.
    C Raise the wounded part.
    D Press gently on wound if no glass or metal present.
    E Loosen tight clothing.

2   You find someone who has had an electric shock. She is lying on the floor of the laboratory and she is unconscious. The first thing you should do is:
    A Check that she is still breathing.
    B Look to see if she is bleeding and bandage the wound.
    C Check that her heart is still beating.
    D Pull the person away from the electric wire or appliance.
    E Switch off the electricity.

3   What dangers are linked with the following?
    (a) badly lit stairs
    (b) factory machinery
    (c) pans of hot water on a cooker
    (d) plastic bags
    (e) wild berries
    (f) cleaning fluids

4   How would you treat a nose bleed?

Index

bold figures – major reference
italic – reference to illustration

abdomen 14, 32
absorption 40, **41**, *41*
accidents **194–195**, 200
accommodation (of eye) 81
adrenal gland 90
adrenalin 90
afterbirth 100, *100*
ageing 135
air 16, 21, *23*, 24, *24*, 25, *26*, 27, *27*, 28, *28*, 29, 31, 44, 63, 84, 154, 168, 178, 180, 196
   conditioning 180
   pollution 186–188
   sac 25, *25*, 27, 29, *29*, 44, 48, 185, 187
   tube *24*, 25, 27, 159
alcohol (ethanol) 8, 99, 153, 182, 185
alcoholism 205
alimentary canal 32
alveolus *see* air sac
amino acid 9, *9*, 20, 36, 40, 41, 42, 57, 69
ammonia *23*, 67
amnion 98, *98*
amniotic fluid 97, 98, 117
amylase 36, 37, *37*, 38, 39
anaemia *11*, 54, 99, 146
animals 1, 8, 18, 19, 20, 22, 137, 150, *158*, 174
ante-natal care 99, *99*, 204
antibiotics 155
antibodies 101, 160, *160*, 161, *161*, 163, 164, 165
antigens 160, *160*, 161, *161*, 163, 164
antiseptic 154, 198
antitoxins 160
anus 32, *32*, 40, 95, 156
aorta 46, 49, *52*
artery 47, 48, 49, 50, 51, 56
   coronary 46, *46*, 54
   hepatic 56
   hepatic portal 56
   pulmonary *46*, 48
   renal 67
artificial resuscitation **196–197**
astigmatism 82
atrium (of heart) 47, 48, 49, 50, 55
axon (of nerve) 74

baby 34, 69, 94, **97–103**, 107, 114, 117, 121, *162*, 165, 190, 193
backbone 7, 27, 76, *95*, **120**, *120*, 132
bacteria 35, *35*, 39, 45, 97, 139, *139*, **142–143**, *142*, *143*, 144, 148, 151, 152, 153, 154, 158, 159, 160, 166, 167, 174, 175, 192
BCG test 204
behaviour **78–79**
bends 31
bile 39, 43, 57
   duct *39*

salts 43
biological oxygen demand (BOD) 190
birth 99, 100, *100*, 102, 121, 134
   control 22, *and see* contraception
   multiple 102
   rate 103
bladder 7, 66, 67, 69, *69*, 95
bleeding 12, *13*, 144, 151, 182, 198
blood 3, 7, 11, *11*, 25, *25*, 29, 31, 32, **44–45**, 46, 47, 50, 51, 54, 56, 57, 67, 71, *71*, 89, 90, 91, 93, 95, 96, 97, 99, 133, 141, 143, 144, 146, 150, 159, 182, 184, 188, 190, 193
   cells 29, 44, 45, *45*, 53, 54, 57, 64, 71, 119, 122, 144, 159, 161, *161*, 164, 184, 187
   clotting 45, 116, 129, 158, **159**
   deoxygenated 48, 53
   groups **163–165**
   immunity **160–165**
   loss 163, 198
   oxygenated 49, 53
   pressure 50, 51, 54, 202
   proteins 44, 54
   smear 4, *44*, *164*
   stream 35
   transfusion **163–165**, 198
   vessels 25, 29, *29*, 31, 33, 42, *45*, 46, **47–48**, 50, *50*, *52*, 53, 54, 60, 68, 71, 73, 97, 124, 130, 131, 146, 159, 160
body (human) **1–7**,
bolus 38, *38*
bone 6, 33, 45, 51, 46, 84, 97, 118, *118*, 120, 121, 122, *122*, 123, 125, 126, 128, 129, 130, 132, 133
   broken 128–129
   marrow 45, *119*, 122, *129*, 159
brachydactyly 113, *113*
brain 7, 31, 54, 73, 74, *74*, **76–77**, *76*, *77*, 80, 81, 85, 87, 88, 90, *119*, 120, 133, 149, 196
breast 92, *94*
   cancer 202
   feeding 101, *101*
breathing 7, *17*, **24–27**, *25*, *26*, 28, 29, 31, 38, 48, 63, 66, 76, 100, 120, 130, 141, 151, 158, 159, 180, 183, 184, 187, 196, 197
breeding 110, 111
bronchiole 25, *25*, 27
bronchus 25, *25*, 27
bruise 57, 194
buildings 178, 181, 187
burn/burnt/burning 28, *28*, 29, 30, 194, 195, **199**

calcium 11, 15, 35, 118, 121, 169
Candida 145
capillaries 41, **50**, 53, 62, 97, 160, 164
carbohydrates 9, **10**, 11,. 14, 15, 16, *16*, 18, 30, 32 *and see* starch, sugars
carbon dioxide 16, *16*, 17, 18, 20, 28, *28*, 29, *29*, 31, 45, 48, 49, 50, 69, 97, *97*, 153, 180, 190
carbon monoxide 184, 187, 188
cardiac muscle 46, *46*

cars 188, 194
cartilage 27, 118, 121, *121*, 123, 132
cattle 20, 22, 160
cells 3, **4–5**, 29, 30, 36, *36*, 49, 64–65, 130–131, 140–141, 142–143
   blood 45
   division **108–109**
   organelles 5, 7, 29
   sensory 72, 87, 88
   skin 60, 158, 160
cellulose 10, 40
central heating 178
cereals 9, **19**, *19*, 22
cervical smear 202
cervix 94, 96, 98, *100*, 202
characteristics (genetic) 106, 107, 110, 112, 114, 116
chemicals 18, 19, 21, 22, 23, 28, 29, 30, 33, 36, 40, 41, 44, 45, 50, 53, 56, 64, 72, 87, 97, 99, 117, 136, 152, 153, 154, 155, 167, 168, 173, 182, 184, 185, 186, 188, 192, 195, 199
chest (thorax) 24, *24*, 26, *26*, 46, 53, *119*
chlorophyll 16, 23, 145
chlorine 171
chromosomes 107, *107*, 108, *108*, 109, 110, 113, 114, 115, 116, *116*, 117, 193
chyme 39
cigarettes 99, 180, 184
cilia 27, 159
circulatory system 3, *52*, **53**
climate 59, 62
clothes 63, 170
clouds 170
coal 28, *28*, 178, 180, 187
cochlea (of ear) 84, *84*
cold 63, 135, 151, 180
colon 40
colour-blindness 115
community services 205
conception 96, 104
connective tissues 6, 74, 118, 122
constipation 40, 143
contraception 22, *22*, 103, **104–105**
cooking 166, 170, 171, 180
coordination **72–93**
copper 169
copulation 96
cornea (of eye) 82
coronary thrombosis 54
coughing 151, 184
cowpox 162
cranium *119*, 120, *120*
crops 19, 20, *20*, 21, 22, 23, 190, 192
cytoplasm 5, *96*

deafness 86
death 118, 184, 193, 194
   rate 103, 137
decibels 86, 189
defaecation 40, 156
dehydration 40, 167, 168
depression 183, 203
diabetes 91
diaphragm 25, 26, *26*, 27, *27*, 31, 32
diarrhoea *13*, 40, 143, 144, 151

diastole 48, 49
diet 8, *12*, 14, 18, 54, *69*, 103, 136, 156, 182
diffusion 65, 97
digestion **32–43**, 57, 69, 101, 159
digestive juices 36, *36*, 72, 73, 91, 159
   system 3, *32*
dirt 27, *27*, 75, 77, 78, 156, 159, 172, 186
diseases 12, 22, 45, 54, 59, 103, 116, **136–151**, 166, 170, 174, 176, 184, 187, 193, 200, 201, 202, 203, 204, 206
   deficiency 11, 13, 185
   mental 203
   plant 21, *21*, 22
   sexually transmitted 148–149
disinfectant 154
dogs 78, 79, 150
Down's syndrome (mongolism) 116
drinking 184
drugs 8, 19, 23, 75, 153, **182–185**
duodenum *32*, 39, *39*, 43
dust 27, 31, 137, 159, 184, 186

ears 72, **84–86**, 118, 119, 156, 189
effector 72, 73, *73*, 75
eggs 9, 92, 93, 94, 95, *95*, 96, *96*, 97, *97*, 102, 104, 107, 108, 109, 110, 113, 114, 116, 146 (of worms), 150 (of lice), 166 (of chickens), 174 (of flies)
   follicle 193
   implantation 97
ejaculation (of semen) 96, 104
electricity 178
electro-cardiogram (ECG) 55
electroencephalogram (EEG) 133
elements 11
embryo 97, *97*, 102
endocrine glands 76, 89, 90, 91
energy 1, 8, 10, 11, 14, 15, 16, 20, *20*, 23, 32, 42, 58, 59, 91, 124, 130, 131, 153, 193
   light 16, 18, 23, 28
   heat *28*
   release **24–31**
   sound 84
   stored 18, 28, 30, 60
engine 28, *28*, 186, 188
Entamoeba 144, *144*, 151
enzymes 36, *36*, 37, *37*, 38, 39, 40, 59, 145
epidermis 60, 88
epiglottis 38, *38*
epithelium 6
erection 92, 96
excretion 7, 7, **67**, 67, 69
exercise 30, 101, **130–131**, *130*, *131*
exocrine glands 89
eye 63, 66, 72, 75, 77, 78, **80–83**, *81*, 151, 156, 180, 186, 188
   faults 82–83
eyeball 81, 83, 133, 141
eyelid *11*, 60, 63, 75, 80, *80*, 116
eyesight 77, 82, 83, 135, 204

faces 63, *63*, 196
factories 186, 187, 189, 190, 191
faeces 40, 66, 137, 146, 150, *174*
faint 191

family planning clinic 202
famine *14*, 103, 206
farming **19**, 20, *20*, 21, 23, 190, 192, 194
fats 9, **10**, 11, 14, 15, 16, 23, 30, 32, *36*, 39, 43, 54, 60, 74, 91, 101, *101*
fatty acids *36*, 40, 41, 42, 43
feet 60, *119*, 121, 157
fertilisation 94, 96, 100, 104, 107, 109, *109*, 110
fertilisers 21, *21*, 23, 190
fertility (of soil) 21
   drugs 102
fever 59, 143, 144, 146, 151, 160, 182
fibre 19, 23, 40, 118, 122, 124
   elastic 50
   nerve 6, 74
fibrin 54
fibrinogen 45
fires 178, 180, 199
first aid **194–199**
fish 1, 8, 9, 146, 168, 172, 191
fitness **130–131**, 132
flatworms 146, 151
flea 150, *150*, 151, 192
Fleming, Alexander 154, *154*
flower 17, 110
fluoride 35, 171
fluorine 11
foetus 97, 98
food **8, 16-23**
   chains 18, *18*, 23, 192
   clean **166–175**
   poisoning 150, 158, 166
   preserved 167–169
   processed 169
   supply 20, 22, 23, 59
   web 18, *18*, 23
foreskin (of penis) *95*, 157
fracture 128–129, *129*
freckles 112
fruit 12, *16*, 17
fuels 28, *28*, 175, 178, 187
   fossil 186
   of body 10, 30, 59
   smokeless 178
fungi 139, **145**, *145*, 151, 152, 153, 155, 158, 167, 178, 192
fungicides 192
fur 1, 63

gall bladder *32*, 39, *39*, 57
gametes 94, 95, *94*, 95, 96, 107, 108, 112
gases 17, 28, 25, 178, 186, 29, *29*
gastric juice 39, 43
genes 102, **107**, 109, 110, 111, 112, 113, 114, 115, 116, 117
genetic counselling 117
genotype 112, 113
gestation period 98
gingivitis 35
glands 36, *36*, 43, 60, 73, 74, 75, 76, 80, 89, 90, 92, 101, 141, 151, 159
glucose **10**, 11, 13, 42, 45, 57, *57*, 66, 68, 91, 97,
glycerol *36*, 40, 41, 42, 43
gonads 92

groin 145, 151
grow 1, 14, 15, 16, 154
growing up/old **134–135**, *134*, *135*, 204
growth 8, 9, 11, 14, 30, 57, 98, 99, 121, 155, *174*
   hormone 133
   plant 187
   rate of 134
gullet *32*, 38, *38*, 43
gums 12, *13*, 35, 184
gut 32, 37, 38, *38*, 40, *40*, 41, 44, 73, 118, 124, 141, 143, 144, 146, 150, 151, 182, *183*

haemoglobin 45, 53, 57, 184, 187, 190
haemophilia 54, 115, 116
hair 1, 11, 62, 63, 145, 150, 156, 174
   follicles 88, 158, 204
   roots
hands 60, 72, 77, 137, 156, *170*
head 85, *100*, 120, 134
health 156, 158, 178, 188, 190
   in the community 200–206
   international 206
   service 200–201
hearing 77, 79, 84, 135, 204
heart 3, *25*, 31, 42, **46–49**, *46*, *47*, *48*, *49*, 50, 51, 53, 54, *54*, 55, 76, *116*, *119*, 124, 130, 131, 149, *183*, 184, 202
   attack 54
   beat 46, 50, 55, 73, 90, 124, 131
   –lung machine 55
   muscle 44, *46*, 73, 55, 124
heat 20, 37, 57, 59, 63, 160, 167, 175, 177, 180, 191, 199
heating *178*, 180
herbicides 192
heterozygous 113
hip girdle 7, *119*, *123*
   joint *123*
homeostasis 66
homes **176–181**
hormones 45, 89, **90**, 91, 92, 93, 97, 101, 104, 133
housefly 1, 150, *150*, 174
houses 103, 171, 176, *177*, 179, *179*, 180, 189, 206
hyphae (of fungi) 145, *145*
hypothermia 63, 135
hygiene 156, 204

ileum *32*, 40, *40*, 41, 42, 43
immunity 45, **160–165**, 204
immunisation 162, 204
incubation period 140, 141
industrial revolution 186
industry 186, 187, 191, 194
infection 100, 150, 160, 162, 170, 198, 204
inflammation 160
inheritance **106–117**
injuries 193, 194, 198
insecticides 192
insects 150
insulators 10, 179, *179*
insulin 91
intercostal muscles 25, 26, *26*, 27

217

intestine 3, 53, 57, 124
  large *32*, 40, 43
  small *32*, 39
intestinal juice 40, 43
iodine 11, *11*, 154, 198
iris (of eye) 80
iron 11, *11*, 15, 54, 99, 169
irrigation 22, *22*, 146
islets of Langerhans 91

Jenner, Edward 162
joints 14, *14*, 121, **122–123**, *123*, 125, 126, 149, 203

kidney 7, 7, 10, 42, 53, 57, **67–71**, *67*, *68*, *69*, *70*, *70*, 71, *71*, 69, 70, *70*, 116, 183
kilojoules 14, 30
kitchens 163, 166, 180
knee 75, *122*, 123
Koch, Robert 130
kwashiorkor 14, *14*

labour 100
lactation 101
lacteal 41
lactic acid 30, *30*, 131
larynx *see* voice box
lavatory (toilet) 156, 172, *172*
lead 188
leaves 16, 17, *17*, *21*, 174, 187
lens (of eye) 81, 82, 83
lice 150, *150*, 192, 204
lifting *131*, 132
ligament 46, 122, *122*
light 20, 63, 72, 80, 81
lighting 181
limbs 73, 122, 128
lipase *36*, 39, 43
Lister, Joseph 154, *154*
liver, 10, *32*, 39, 41, *42*, 43, 45, 53, **56–57**, *56*, 67, 70, 90, 118, 144, 185
lungs 7, *25*, 25, 27, 29, *29*, 30, 31, 45, 46, 47, 48, 49, 50, 69, *119*, 151, 184, *184*, 185, 187, 196
lymph 41, 42, *42*, **53,** *53*, 53
  node 42, 53, 159
  vessel 41, 53

machines 21, 22, 23, 186
male 92, *95*, 114
malnourishment 14, 15, 16
mammary gland *see* breast
meat 8, 9, 19, 20, *20*, 23, 167, 168
medicine 103, 153, 182, 195, 201
meiosis **108,** *108*
melanin 63
membrane 5, 45, 64, 65, *64*, *65*, 65, 71, 76, 96
Mendel, Gregor 110–111
menopause 95
menstrual cycle *93*, *95*
menstruation *see* periods
mental health *13*, 203
microbes 136, 138, 139, 143, 144, 148, 149, 150, **152–165,** 166, 167, 170, 171, 172, 174, 178, 198

micrscope, electron 5, 140
  light 4, 44, 68, 107, 138, 139, 202
milk 1, 8, 9, 35, 101, 153, 168
minerals 9, 11,. 13, 15, *23*, 32, 42, 45, 185
mitosis **109,** *109*
molecules 10, *10*, 32, 36, 40, 41, 64, 65
mongolism (Down's syndrome) 116
mosquitoes 144, 150, 151, 192
month 3, 24, 27, *27*, 32, *32*, 33, 35, 38, *38*, 43, 66, 78, 87, 137, 145, 146, 151, *158*, 159, 162, 182, 184, 197
movement **118–135**
mucus 27, *27*, 38, 43, 156, 159, 184
muscle 10, 11, 20, 26, 30, 38, 45, 49, 50, 51, 53, 62, 69, *72*, 73, 74, *75*, *76*, 80, 81, 87, 90, 91, 99, 100, 118, 119, **124–127,** *124*, *125*, 125, 126, 130, 131, 132, 133, 162
  cells 3
  tissue 6
mutation 116, 117, 193

nails 11, 156, 157
nephron 68, *68*, 69, 70
nerve cells (neurons) 3, 11, **74,** *74*, 75, *75*, 76, 77, 80, 81, 84, 90, 135
  endings 33, 35, *35*, 60, *72*
  impulse 74, 75, 76, 77, 81, 84, 85, 87, 88, 124
  tissue 3, 6
nervous system 7, 8, 73, **74–75,** 90, 124, 183
neurons *see* nerve cells
nipple 92, *94*, *101*
nitrogen 16, 28, *28*, 31, 42, 69, 188, 190
nose 42, 27, *27*, 63, 66, *72*, 74, 87, 120, 137, 151, 156, 158, 159, 187, 197
  bleed 198, *198*
nuclear power 193, *193*
nucleus 5, 45, 94, 96, 107, 109, 114
nutrients 8, 14, 15, 32, 36, 39, 40, 41, 42, 57, 99, *145*, 169, 174, *174*, 190
nutrition **8–15**

oesophagus *32*, 38, *38*
oestrogen 92, 93, 95, 97
offspring 1, 110, 111, 136
optic nerve 81
organ 7
osmosis 65
ossicles (or ear) 84
ovaries 92, 93, 94, *94*, 95, *95*, 96, *96*, 97, *97*, 102, 104, 108, *108*
oviduct *94*, *95*, 96, 104, *104*
ovulation 93, 96, 97, 104, *104*
ovule 110
oxygen 7, 16, *17*, **24,** 27, 28, 29, *29*, 30, 31, 33, 44, 45, 48, 49, 50, 53, 54, 97, *97*, 99, 100, 124, 130, 131, 153, 167, 180, 184, 187, 188, 190, 191, 196, 197
ozone 188

pace-maker 55
pain 33, 54, 60, *72*, 76, **88,** 128, 148, 151, 183
pancreas *32*, 39, 43, 91

pancreatic juice 39, *39*, 43
paralysis 141, 151
parasites 136. 137, 144, 145, 145, 150, 192
Pasteur, Louis 138, *139*, 139, 162
pathogen 136, 137, 150, 162, 170
Pavlov 78
pelvis *94*, *95*, 100
penicillin 154, 182
penis 92, *95*, 96, *96*, 104, 105, 148, 149, 157
pepsin 39, 43
periods (menstruation) **93,** 97, 104, 157
peristalsis 38, *38*, 40, 69
pest damage 21, 174, 176
  control 192
pesticides 21, 23, 192, 195
phagocytes 159, 160
pharynx *38*
phenotype 112
phosphate 191
phosphorus 11, 35
photosynthesis 16, 17, *17*, 18, 20, 23, 145
pill (contraceptive) 104, 105
pituitary gland *76*, 90, 92, 93
placenta 97, *97*, *98*, 102, 165
plants 16, 149
plaque (on teeth) 35, *35*, 156
plasma 29, *29*, 41, 44, **45,** 53, *53*, 64, 71, 159, *162*, 166
Plasmodium 144, *144*, 150
platelets **45**
pleural cavity *25*
  membrane *25*, 26, *26*, 27, *27*
poison(ing) 69, 142, 144, 154, 160, 161, 169, 192, 195
pollen 110
pollution **186–193**
population 20, 22, 23, **103,** 186
post-natal care **101,** 186
posture 132, 204
pregnancy 93, 97, 98, 99, *99*, 100, 102, 104, 105, 132, 151, 165, 193
pressure point (pulse) 51, *51*
progesterone 92, 93, 95, 97
proprioceptors 87
protease 36, *36*, 39, 43
protein *9*, 9, 11, 14, 15, 16, 20, 23, 30, 32, 36, *36*, 37, 39, 43, 44, 45, 57, 60, 69, *69*, 71, 91, 159, 160, 161, 162
protozoa 139, **144,** *144*, 150, 151
puberty 92, *92*, 95, 134
pulse 50, **51**
pupil (of eye) 80, 81
pus 35, 148, 151, 160

quarantine 143

rabies 150
radiation 117, **193**
radiography, mass 204
rainfall 22, 170, *170*, 177, 187
  water 174, *174*, 187, 190
rats 150, *150*, 151
receptors (in skin) 72
rectum (bowel) *32*, 40, 58, 95
reflex action **75,** *75*, 77, *77*, 78, 80
rennin 39, 43

repair (of body) 1, 8, 9, 14, 15, 32, 57, 69, 133, 154
reproduction **94–105,** 142 (bacteria)
reservoir 22, 171
respiration **24,** 29, 29, 30, 31, 42, 59, 131
　aerobic 29, 32
　anaerobic 30, 31, 153
response 72, 73, 75, 77, 79
retina (of eye) 81, *81*, 83
rhythm method (contraception) 104, 195
riboflavin 13
rib 7, *25*, 26, *26*, 27, *27*, *119*
　cage 26, 27, 31, 46, 67
rice 9, 10, **19,** *19*
rivers 21, 171, 172, *172*, 175, 190, 191
rocks *174*, 176, 187
roundworm 146
roughage 10, 40
rubbish 170, 174, 175, *175*

saliva 38, 43, 73, 78, *158*
salivary glands 38, *38*, 43, 73, 141
sanitation 103, 206
scalp 62, 76, 145, 151
Schistosoma 146, *147*, 151, 158
scrotum 95
scurvy 12, *12*, 13
sebaceous glands/sebum (in skin) 60, 158
secretions 73, 80
seeds 17, 19
semen 96
semi-circular canals 85
seminal fluid 96
seminal vesicle 95
sense organ 60, **72–73,** *72*, *73*, 75, 76, 84, 88, 119, 120
sensation 77, 87
senses 87
septic 154, 160
serum 45
sewage/sewers 153, 172, *172*, *173*, 186, 205
sex cells 91, 92, 94, 104, 107, 109, 110
　chromosomes 114, *114*
　glands 90
　hormones 92, 91, 95, 97
　inheritance of *114*
　linked characters 114, 115
　organs 92, 94, 104, 117, 148, 151
sexual intercourse 96, 104, 105
shivering *59*, 62
shock 63
sickness 143, 151
skeleton 7, 67, 118, 119, *119*, 121, 122
skin 10, 11, *13*, *14*, 59, **60–61,** *60*, *61*, 62, 63, 66, 72, *74*, 75, 88, 116, 121, 131, 136, 141, 143, 144, 145, 146, 151, 158, 159, 160, *183*, 198, 199
skull 7, 76, *76*, 84, *119*, 120, *120*
sleep 59, **133,** *133*
　REM 133
slipped disc 132

smoking 168, 184
soil 16, 21, 22, 144, 146, 153, 170, 174, *174*, 190, 192
sound 72, 78, 84, 86, *119*, 189
space 31, 130
speech 27, 31, 77
sperm 92, 94, *94*, 95, *95*, 96, 102, 104, 105, 107, 108, 109, 113, 114, 116
　duct 95, 104, *104*
sphygmomanometer 51, *51*
spinal cord 7, 73, 74, 75, *75*, 76, 76, 141
spine 120, 132 *and see* backbone
spleen 53
starch **10,** *10*, 16, 23, 30, 36, *36*, 37, *37*, 43
starvation 14, *14*
steady state **56–71**
sterile 148, 180, 198
sterilise 101, 154
sterilisation 104, *104*, 105
stimulus (of nerve) 72, 73, 75, 77, 78, 79, 88
stomach 3, 27, *32*, *39*, 39, 43, 72, 73, 158, 159, 182
sugars **10,** *10*, 16, 23, 29, 30, *36*, 37, 38, 40, 41, 43, 65, 71, 91, 99, 153
sulphonamides 154
sulphur dioxide 187, *187*
sun 18, 63, 181
　light 13, *16*, 60, 63, 180, 188
sweat/sweating *59*, **62,** 63, 66, 131
　glands 60, 62, *62*
synapse 75, 76
systole 48, 49

tapeworms 146, *147*
taste 87
tears 66, 75, 80, *80*
teeth *13*, **33–35,** 35, 156, 170, 171, 204
temperature 1, 33, 37, 57, 58, *58*, 59, 60, 62, 63, 66, 72, 88, 93, 136, 144, 151, 160, 167, 178, 188, 191, 202
tendons 6, 26, 87, 122, *122*, *125*
testes 92, 95, *95*
testosterone 92, 95
thirst 66, 143, 151
thorax *see* chest
throat 27, 159
thyroid gland 11, 90
tissue 3, **6,** 7, 29, 64, 68, 89, *95*, 122, 124
　fluid **53,** *53*, 64, 199
toilet *see* lavatory
tongue *25*, 27, 38, *38*, 58, 72, 87, 197
Toprina 23
touch 60, *72*, 88, 96
toxin 142, 144, 160, 166
trachea *see* windpipe
transport (in body) **44–55**
tsetse fly 150
tumours 185

umbilical cord 97, *97*, 98, 100
uranium 153

urea 42, 53, 57, 67, 69, *71*
ureter 7, *7*, 67, *67*, 69, *69*, 95
urethra 7, *7*, 67, 69, 69
urine 42, 66, **67,** 68, *68*, 69, 91, 136, 137, 148, 151
uterus (womb) 92, 93, 95, *95*, 96, *96*, 97, *97*, *98*, 100, 101, 104, 121, 134

vaccination 162, 204
vagina 96, *96*, 104, 105, 145, 151
valves (of heart) 47, 48, 51
　of veins 50, *50*
variation 106
vectors (of disease) 150, *158*, 176
vegetation 186, 188
veins 46, *46*, 49, 50, 51, 53
　coronary 46, *46*, 54
　hepatic 56
　hepatic portal 41, 56, 57
　pulmonary *46*, 49
　renal 67
　varicose 54
vena cava 46, 48, *52*, 56
ventricle (of heart) 47, 48, 49, 50, 51
vertebral column *see* backbone
vertebrae *119*, 120, *120*, 133
villi 40, *40*, 41, *41*
viruses 139, **140–141,** *140*, *141*, 150, 151, 158, *158*, 160, 161, *162*, 192
vitamins 9, 12, 13, 14, 15, 18, 32, 42, 45, 60, 121, 169
vocal cord 27, *27*
voice 92
　box (larynx) 27, *27*, *38*

waste 1, 43, 56, 67, 69, 71, *97*, 100, 151, 152, 153, 172, 174, 186, 190, 193
　chemicals 7, 45, 53, 69, 97, 190
water 8, 9, *11*, 11, 14, 15, 16, *16*, 18, 20, 21, 22, *22*, 23, 24, 29, 31, 40, 43, 59, 64, 65, 66, *66*, 67, 69, 71, 137, 144, 151, 152, 170
　balance **66**
　clean **166–175,** 177, 178
　cycle 170
　pollutants 190–191, 199
　vapour 28, *28*, 31, 170, 178, 187
　works 170
　systems 170, 177
weather 178, 179, 181
wheat 9, **19,** *19*, 20, *21*
windpipe (trachea) 7, *25*, 25, 27, *27*, *32*, 38, *38*, 197
worms **146–147**
wounds 12, 154, *158*, 159, 160, 163, 198

X-rays 24, 34, 99, 117, *121*, 129, 193, 202

yeast cells 23, 153

Acknowledgements

The publishers wish to thank the following for kind permission to reproduce photographs:
Keystone Press Agency, Figs 1.1, 7.1, 7.2, 101.1, 105.2; Jeol Ltd, Fig. 3.4; R. Hutchings photo collection, Figs 3.6, 3.7, 21.6, 24.3, 34.4, 67.1, 67.3, 67.7; Unicef Photos, p.8; Charing Cross Hospital, Department of Medical Illustration, Figs 6.8, 14.2, 70.5; Kings College Hospital, Department of Medical Photography, Figs 6.9, 6.11, 6.13, 7.3, 19.5, 29.3, 29.4, 32.2, 37.1, 37.4, 50.1, 62.1, 63.4, 70.4, 77.6, 85.1; C.J. Webb photo collection, Figs 6.12, 77.4, 78.4, 78.5, 78.6, 78.7, 79.1, 79.4, 81.1, 81.3; St Marys Hospital, Department of Medical Photography, Figs 6.14, 30.5, 63.1, 63.2, 76.4, 80.3, 80.4, 82.3, 82.5, 82.4, 85.6, 87.3, 88.1; International Harvester Ltd, p.16, Fig. 12.3; Mirco Decet, Figs 8.3, 16.2, 24.1, 25.6, 32.1, 33.4, 43.4, 54.1, 57.1, 57.2, 61.3, 68.6, 71.5, 73.2, 80.1, 83.2, 83.4, 84.1, 84.2, 85.3, 91.1, 91.3, 91.4, 92.2, 92.3, 94.1, 94.4, 95.4, 96.2, 97.7, 98.1, 98.2, 99.4, 100.2, 102.2, 110.1, 110.3, 110.4, 111.1, 111.2, 111.4, 111.5, 112.1, 112.2, 112.3, 113.1, 113.2 and pp.72, 94, 118, 136, 152, 176, 182; Rothamsted Experimental Station, Figs 12.1, 12.2; Oxfam, Visual Aids Department, Fig 13.1; USDA, Soil Conservation Service, Fig 13.2; COPR, Fig 13.3; Ministry of Agriculture Fisheries and Food, Fig13.4; Eric Blackadder, Loughborough University, Fig 17.2; Orbis photo collection, Figs 17.4, 48.1, 113.3; Dr Chernin photo collection, Figs 24.2, 77.2; Medi-cine Limited/ICI Pharmaceuticals Division Ltd, Fig 29.1; ROSPA, Fig 38.1; Radio Times Hulton Picture Library, Figs 41.1, 63.3, 76.1, 85.2, 85.5, 100.1; David Clulow, London, Fig 43.3; Aston Martin Ltd, Fig 45.1; Granada TV, p.106; Zeiss Ltd, Fig 58.3; SATRA, Fig 66.3; RAF, Brize Norton, Fig 70.1; Institute of Orthopaedics, Medical Photographic Department, Fig 70.7; Foto-call, Fig 71.5; WHO photo, Fig 77.5; St Batholomews Hospital, Department of Medical Illustrations, Fig 77.7; Vickers, Photographic and Audio-visual Department, Fig 78.8; Rentokil Ltd, Figs 83.1, 83.3, 97.1; Tetley Walker Ltd, Fig 84.4; Danish Food Centre, Fig 84.5; National Blood Transfusion Service, Fig 89.1; ICI Plastics Division, Fig 97.4C; Dennis Mansell photo collection, Fig 97.4D; Uniroyal Ltd, Fig 97.4F; Photoflex, Fig 97.4A; Peter Wakely, Nature Conservancy Council, Taunton, Fig 100.5; Shell Petroleum Ltd, Fig 101.2; Ford Motor Company, Fig 102.3; Central Electricity Generating Board, Figs 103.4, 105.1; Thames Water Authority, Fig 103.5; Evening Argus, Brighton, Fig 103.6; Commissioner of Police of the Metropolis, Fig 106.1; Barnabys Studios Ltd, Fig 110.2; British Red Cross Society, Figs 114.2, 114.3.

The publishers regret that they have been unable to trace the copyright for some photographs.

The publishers are grateful to the Family Planning Association for permission to use details of their case card in Fig 111.3.